ESSAYS ON CHURCH, STATE, AND POLITICS

NATURAL LAW AND
ENLIGHTENMENT CLASSICS

Knud Haakonssen
General Editor

Christian Thomasius

NATURAL LAW AND
ENLIGHTENMENT CLASSICS

Essays on Church, State, and Politics

Christian Thomasius

Edited, Translated, and with an Introduction
by Ian Hunter, Thomas Ahnert,
and Frank Grunert

LIBERTY FUND
Indianapolis

This book is published by Liberty Fund, Inc., a foundation established to encourage study of the ideal of a society of free and responsible individuals.

𒀀𒈪𒄀

The cuneiform inscription that serves as our logo and as the design motif for our endpapers is the earliest-known written appearance of the word "freedom" (*amagi*), or "liberty." It is taken from a clay document written about 2300 B.C. in the Sumerian city-state of Lagash.

11   10   09   08   07   C   5   4   3   2   1
11   10   09   08   07   P   5   4   3   2   1

Frontispiece: Portrait of Christian Thomasius by Johann Christian Heinrich Sporleder (1754), oil. Reproduced courtesy of Bildarchiv der Zentralen Kustodie der Martin-Luther-Universität Halle-Wittenberg.

Library of Congress Cataloging-in-Publication Data
Thomasius, Christian, 1655–1728.
[Selections. English. 2007]
Essays on church, state, and politics/
Christian Thomasius;
edited, translated, and with an introduction
by Ian Hunter, Thomas Ahnert, and Frank Grunert.
p. cm.—(Natural law and enlightenment classics)
Includes index.
ISBN-13: 978-0-86597-498-2 (hardcover: alk. paper.)
ISBN-13: 978-0-86597-499-9 (pbk.: alk. paper)
1. Church and state.   2. Christianity and politics.
I. Hunter, Ian, 1949–   II. Ahnert, Thomas.
III. Grunert, Frank.   IV. Title.
BV630.3.T46   2007
322′.1—dc22   2006037493

LIBERTY FUND, INC.
8335 Allison Pointe Trail, Suite 300
Indianapolis, Indiana 46250-1684

CONTENTS

INTRODUCTION

Christian Thomasius's principal contributions to the public life of early
modern Protestant Germany were made in his roles as a political jurist
and engaged commentator on religious and political affairs, although he
was also a noted educational reformer and moral philosopher. Thomasius was born into a family of Lutheran jurists and academics in Leipzig,
in the German territorial state of Saxony, on January 1, 1655.[1] His father,
Jacob (1622–84), was a philosophy professor at the University of Leipzig,
where Christian enrolled in 1669 and graduated with a master's degree
in 1672. That year also saw the publication of Samuel Pufendorf's mon-
umental and controversial antischolastic reconstruction of natural law,
the *De jure naturae et gentium.* Written by someone who had grown up
in the shadow of the Thirty Years' War, and dedicated to providing a
purely secular foundation for ethics and politics—in the cultivation of
sociability rather than the pursuit of holiness—the *De jure* had a profound effect on all those Protestant intellectuals for whom peace was
more important than purity. Thomasius would later recall that it was
Pufendorf's "incomparable" work, together with his father's lectures on

---

1. There is as yet no full-scale scholarly biography of Thomasius. For a helpful
English overview of his life and work, see Knud Haakonssen, "Christian Thomasius,"
in *The Routledge Encyclopedia of Philosophy,* ed. E. Craig (London: Routledge, 1997),
376b–80b, and, for a discussion of his key doctrines, Ian Hunter, *Rival Enlighten-
ments: Civil and Metaphysical Philosophy in Early Modern Germany* (Cambridge:
Cambridge University Press, 2001), 197–273. See also T. Ahnert, Religion and the
Origins of the German Enlightenment: *Faith and the Reform of Learning in the
Thought of Christian Thomasius* (Rochester, New York: University of Rochester
Press, 2006). The pathbreaking German study is that of Werner Schneiders, *Natur-
recht und Liebesethik. Zur Geschichte der praktischen Philosophie im Hinblick auf Chris-*

Grotius, that determined him to study jurisprudence, seeking there an understanding of natural law unavailable to him in the philosophy faculty, with its scholastic mixing of philosophy and theology.[2] Already chafing against the Lutheran scholasticism of his native Leipzig, in 1674, at age nineteen, Thomasius moved to the University of Frankfurt/Oder in order to undertake a doctorate in law. He completed this in 1679, the year before he was married to Auguste Christine Heyland (1655–1739).

In relocating to Frankfurt, Thomasius was not just moving from philosophy to jurisprudence; he was also moving to a different country, electoral Brandenburg, where the Calvinist commitments of the ruling dynasty imbued the university with a religious and political complexion quite different from Leipzig's orthodox Lutheranism. Like other proponents of the north German "second Reformation," Brandenburg's rulers had sought to combine religious reform with state-building.[3] In doing so, they used a moderate form of Calvinism—one that required inward piety and stripped the churches of ritual and pictures while downplaying the harsh doctrine of predestination—as a means of creating a more disciplined population. This reform process was, however, only partially successful in the case of Brandenburg, owing to the entrenched resistance of the Lutheran clergy, supported by a nobility who

---

tian Thomasius (Hildesheim: Georg Olms, 1971). Schneiders treats Thomasius as a moral philosopher rather than as a political jurist. A more recent overview in German is Helmut Holzhey and Simone Zurbuchen, "Christian Thomasius," in *Grundriss der Geschichte der Philosophie. Die Philosophie des 17. Jahrhunderts,* Band 4: *Das heilige Römische Reich deutscher Nation, Nord- und Ostmitteleuropa,* ed. H. Holzhey and W. Schmidt-Biggemann (Basle: Schwabe, 2001), 1165–1202, which also treats Thomasius primarily as a moral philosopher. Important biographical accounts are contained in Max Fleischmann, ed., *Christian Thomasius: Leben und Lebenswerk* (Halle: Niemeyer, 1931; repr. Aalen, 1979); and an annotated bibliography of Thomasius's writings is provided in Rolf Lieberwirth, *Christian Thomasius: Sein wissenschaftliches Lebenswerk* (Weimar: Böhlau, 1955).

2. Christian Thomasius, *Institutiones jurisprudentiae divinae* (Leipzig: Weidmann, 1688).

3. Heinz Schilling, "The Second Reformation—Problems and Issues," in *Religion, Political Culture and the Emergence of Early Modern Society: Essays in German and Dutch History,* ed. H. Schilling (Leiden: E. J. Brill, 1992), 247–301.

regarded the independence of the Lutheran church as guaranteed under imperial law.[4]

Thomasius responded positively to both sides of this reforming absolutism: to its encouragement of a nondoctrinal inward Protestantism and to its insistence on the absolute sovereignty of the territorial prince as the key to achieving religious peace and social reform. On the one hand, he developed an "Epicurean" form of Protestant Christianity.[5] This was a style of piety that was skeptical of the "visible" church with its creeds, sacraments, and rituals; mute regarding the afterlife; and focused on the achievement of inner peace through a calming of the passions and desires.[6] On the other hand, Thomasius endorsed Pufendorf's secularized political absolutism. In making social peace the goal of politics and the source of its norms, Pufendorf had sought to exclude the church from the political arena, giving the civil sovereign the exclusive right to issue the laws and exercise the power required to achieve this goal, but only this goal.

While powerful, the link between these two dimensions of Thomasius's thought was forged through volatile historical circumstance rather than settled philosophical reflection. This helps to account for significant fluctuations in his opinions, particularly over the question of whether the state should be wholly secular or whether it should be used to enforce a nonsacramental, inward, Epicurean style of Christianity. More generally, Thomasius had no interest in building a philosophical system; his concern was with the problem posed by the existence of metaphysics itself, as the university discipline responsible for the corrupting mixture of philosophy and theology. The circumstantial coherence of the two

4. Bodo Nischan, *Prince, People, and Confession: The Second Reformation in Brandenburg* (Philadelphia: University of Pennsylvania Press, 1994).

5. See, in particular, Horst Dreitzel, "Christliche Aufklärung durch fürstlichen Absolutismus. Thomasius und die Destruktion des frühneuzeitlichen Konfessionsstaates," in *Christian Thomasius (1655–1728). Neue Forschungen im Kontext der Frühaufklärung,* ed. F. Vollhardt (Tübingen: Max Niemeyer, 1997), 17–50.

6. Thomas Ahnert, "The Prince and the Church in the Thought of Christian Thomasius," in *Natural Law and Civil Sovereignty: Moral Right and State Authority in Early Modern Political Thought,* ed. I. Hunter and D. Saunders (Basingstoke: Palgrave, 2002), 91–105; Dorothee Kimmich, "Lob der 'ruhigen Belusting': Zu Thomasius' kritischer Epikur-Rezeption," in Vollhardt, ed., *Christian Thomasius,* 379–94.

sides of Thomasius's thought was quite unmistakable, however, when it came to that which Thomasius opposed: namely, a church that proclaimed the necessity of certain creeds and sacraments for salvation, and one that used the apparatus of the state to enforce its doctrines by threat of civil punishments. This was the state of affairs that Thomasius called "papalist" and, despite the title, identified not just with Counter-Reformation Catholicism but with the Lutheran confessional state—Saxony in particular—whose intellectual delegitimation would be his life's work.[7]

On his return to Leipzig in 1679, Thomasius practiced law for a short time and then offered private lectures at the university. Initially he avoided controversy, perhaps in deference to his father. A few years after his father's death in 1684, however, Thomasius launched a series of disputations, lectures, and publications that amounted to a frontal attack on Leipzig's reigning Lutheran Scholasticism. His objective was to undermine the mix of Aristotelian philosophy and Lutheran theology that dominated the philosophy and theology faculties, and to replace this with an array of modern subjects—politics, history, economics, public law—within an overarching normative framework provided by Pufendorfian natural law.[8] In his *Introductio ad philosophiam aulicam* (Introduction to court philosophy) of 1688, Thomasius provided a historical genealogy of the reigning metaphysical scholastic philosophy, which he characterized as a species of "sectarian philosophy." Drawing on earlier antischolastic histories, including one by his father, Thomasius described metaphysics as emerging from the corruption of Christ's original teachings through Greek philosophy, introduced by the Platonizing church fathers. Further, he held this hybrid of philosophy and theology responsible for turning Christianity into a body of doctrine and for the introduction of highly intellectualized creeds through which the clergy baffled and exploited the laity.[9] In place of this sectarian philosophy,

7. See, above all, Dreitzel, "Christliche Aufklärung."

8. For a characteristic program statement from 1689, see Christian Thomasius, "Wie ein junger Mensch zu informieren sei," in *Kleine Teutsche Schriften* (Halle: 1701), 233–70 (repr. Hildesheim: Georg Olms, 1994).

9. Christian Thomasius, *Introductio ad philosophiam aulicam* (Leipzig, 1688) (repr. Hildesheim: Georg Olms, 1994).

Thomasius argued for an "eclectic" style of philosophizing. Here scholars would avoid mixing theology and philosophy, faith and reason, and would demonstrate their independence from the ruling Aristotelianism by selecting from all available philosophies in accordance with their own judgment.[10]

Thomasius kept up the pressure in his *Institutiones jurisprudentiae divinae* (Institutes of divine jurisprudence).[11] Published in the same year as the *Court Philosophy,* the *Institutes* rejected the views of Thomasius's theological colleagues, many of whom defended the linkage of Christian doctrine and civil law by positing a metaphysical continuity between divine and human reason. In keeping with his drive to separate faith and reason, Thomasius denied this continuity, arguing that the damage done to man's faculties at the Fall meant that he could not hope to derive the norms of natural law by exercising a reason similar to that informing divine law. Man's access to natural law derives instead from a decidedly nontranscendent source, namely "sound reason," understood as a faculty for deducing rules of conduct from the purely worldly imperative of sociability, an argument that parallels Grotius's construction of natural law. This natural law may be supplemented with "divine positive" or biblical law, but only if the latter is treated as commands addressed to man's corrupt will rather than his transcendent reason, and only if it is interpreted by jurists interested in social peace rather than theologians pursuing absolute truth. The linkage that remains between Christian doctrine and civil law in Thomasius's early work is thus radically transformed and attenuated, as responsibility for it has been shifted from theologians claiming to grasp divine reason to jurists aiming no higher than civil peace.

Despite making significant changes to his natural law doctrine—which resulted in him deriving its norms solely from the need for inner calm and outer security, and discarding divine positive law altogether—Thomasius would remain within the broad intellectual framework he developed during the 1680s. We can see this from the first essay of our

10. Ulrich Johannes Schneider, "Eclecticism Rediscovered," *Journal of the History of Ideas* 59 (1998): 173–82.

11. See note 2, above.

anthology, "On the History of Natural Law Until Grotius," published
as the foreword to the first German translation of Grotius's *Law of War
and Peace* in 1707. Here we find a mature restatement of Thomasius's
comprehensive rejection of the scholastic tradition. Once again he attacks its illicit mixing of philosophy and theology, criticizes the clerical
misuse of Aristotelian and Platonic metaphysics, and praises the enlight-
ened secularization of ethics and politics. This had been proclaimed by
Grotius and massively consolidated by Pufendorf in a new postscholastic
tradition of thought, to which Hobbes and Bayle had made contributions, as had Thomasius himself.

Thomasius's antischolastic writings of the 1680s, many of which were
thinly disguised attacks on theological colleagues, had already provoked
counterattacks from the Leipzig theology professoriate—Valentin Al-
berti, Augustin Pfeiffer, and Johann Benedict Carpzov in particular—
and had led to complaints against Thomasius at the Saxon court and the
Lutheran Superior Consistory in Dresden.[12] But the text that made it
impossible for him to remain in Saxony and that pointed forward to the
next phase of his life and work was the *Fürstlicher Personen Heirat* (The
marriage of royal persons) of 1689. In this work Thomasius intervened
directly in a volatile religious and political issue, the marriage of one of
the Saxon elector's Lutheran nephews to one of the Brandenburg elector's Calvinist sisters. Against the Saxon interest but in keeping with
Brandenburg religious policy, Thomasius argued that the difference between the confessions was of no interest to God and that the marriage
was justified by the *Staatskirchenrecht* (constitutional church law) enunciated by the Treaty of Westphalia, which accorded Calvinists the same
civil rights as Lutherans.[13] Before the year was out, Thomasius had been

---

12. Rolf Lieberwirth, "Christian Thomasius' Leipziger Streitigkeiten," *Wissen-
schaftliche Zeitschrift der Martin-Luther-Universität Halle-Wittenberg (Gesellschafts-
und sprachwissenschaftliche Reihe)* 3 (1953): 155–59. See also Frank Grunert, "Zur auf-
geklärten Kritik am theokratischen Absolutismus. Der Streit zwischen Hector
Gottfried Masius und Christian Thomasius über Ursprung und Begründung der
summa potestas," in Vollhardt, ed., *Christian Thomasius,* 51–78.

13. Christian Thomasius, "Fürstlichen Personen Heirat," in *Auserlesene deutsche
Schriften, Zweiter Teil,* ed. (Leipzig, 1714), 1–102 (repr. Hildesheim: Georg Olms,
1994).

prohibited from lecturing and publishing by the Saxon court, making continued residency in his homeland impossible, and had decamped to Halle in neighboring Brandenburg, where he was instrumental in setting up a new university. The groundwork for this move had been laid by Pufendorf himself, who was ending a stellar career by moving to the Brandenburg court, and by Johann Rhetius, who had been one of Thomasius's law professors at Frankfurt/Oder and was now a member of the Berlin privy council.

The core of the many lectures, disputations, books, and essays that Thomasius produced over the next decade, and from which the remaining chapters in this anthology are taken, is *Staatskirchenrecht*. This term can be translated as "constitutional church law," although not without a degree of anachronism. It refers to the regulation of the churches through the public law of the Holy Roman Empire of the German nation, particularly that enunciated at the two great religious peace treaties, Augsburg in 1555 and Westphalia in 1648. *Staatskirchenrecht* was less a consolidated discipline than a fluid and rapidly evolving mix of jurisprudence and politics that joined the law faculty to the princely court. Through it the princes overseeing Protestant jurisdictions transformed the legal regulation of their churches in the wake of the Treaty of Westphalia and in accordance with its complex rules for recognizing the entitlements of diverse religious communities within a system of state-controlled toleration.[14] For Thomasius, it provided the field on which he would do battle with the juristic and theological representatives of the early modern confessional state.

Thomasius's campaign was part of a much broader struggle. On one side of this battle were those for whom the consolidation of territorial sovereignty required the exclusion of the churches from the exercise of civil power. On the other side were the clerical estates whose imperial rights had permitted the exercise of such power, through the threat of

14. Martin Heckel, "Zur Entwicklung des deutschen Staatskirchenrechts von der Reformation bis zur Schwelle der Weimarer Verfassung," in Martin Heckel, *Gesammelte Schriften: Staat, Kirche, Recht, Geschichte,* ed. K. Schlaich (Tübingen: J. C. B. Mohr, 1989), 366–401.

excommunication or, more fatally, the laws covering blasphemy, heresy, and witchcraft. Yet the intensity of Thomasius's attack on the armory of the confessional state also had a personal dimension, fueled by outrage at his treatment by the Leipzig theologians and finding expression in his recognizably modern propensity to make his own story symbolic of the larger struggle: "I could well have something to say to all the estates, because things are amiss in all of them, but I have been charged by God to speak the truth above all to the clergy. And I am already so far committed to this, which I do not from any hatred, that I cannot turn back."[15]

One of the most powerful weapons in Thomasius's intellectual armory was the category of *adiaphora,* or "indifferent things" (*Mitteldinge* in German). This term refers to all matters that are neither commanded nor forbidden by God and are thus irrelevant to the question of salvation. As we learn in the second of our selections, "The Right of Protestant Princes Regarding Indifferent Matters or *Adiaphora,*" things declared to be *adiaphora* could either be left to the individual's conscience or else be treated as superstitions to be reformed by the prince, to the extent that this could be done without disrupting public peace. In fact, according to Thomasius's antidoctrinal, Epicurean style of Protestantism, the number of divine commandments relevant to salvation could be reduced to just three: to love God, to love one's neighbor, and to have contempt for oneself (as a creature of passions always prone to disorder). As a result, all the things that the competing confessions declared to be essential, and over which so much blood had been spilled—all of the church liturgies and sacraments, the vehement doctrinal disputes over the Trinity, the nature of Christ's presence in the Eucharist, the relation between Christ's "two natures and one person," and so on—could be declared to be matters of moral indifference, turning them into matters of "Christian freedom" or else of political regulation. Displaying the contextual coherence between this anticredal inward religion and a Pufendorfian political absolutism, Thomasius proceeds to argue that

---

15. Christian Thomasius, *Dreyfache Rettung des Rechts Evangelischer Fürsten in Kirchen-Sachen* (Frankfurt am Main, 1701), 58.

the civil sovereign has an unfettered right to regulate all such religious matters, to the degree that this is compatible with social peace.

The *adiaphora* disputation thus shows Thomasius dividing the fields of religion and politics in a way that both removed salvation from the domain of church ritual and removed political authority from the domain of salvation. This left individuals privately free to pursue salvation as they saw fit, and it left the public churches with the status of voluntary associations under state supervision. The third selection, "On the Power of Secular Government to Command Its Subjects to Attend Church Diligently," sheds light on what this changed division of the field could lead to in practice. Here we have the case of a Lutheran nobleman seeking leave not to attend church services in his local village, on the grounds that his villagers and their pastor were Calvinist and because true religion has no need of public services, which the nobleman could as well perform in the privacy of his own house. Somewhat unexpectedly, and against the advice of his own faculty, Thomasius advises that the nobleman should be denied his estate right and be required to attend his local church, on the grounds that the differences between Lutheran and Calvinist forms of worship are not morally significant and that the nobleman's insistence on his right thus smacks of fanaticism. As far as Thomasius is concerned, the nobleman's appeal to the indifferent character of external services, as a reason for not attending them, is trumped by the right of the secular authorities to compel him to do so, lest his nonattendance lead to hatred and unrest.

Despite his antischolasticism and anticlericalism, and regardless of his modern standing as a founding father of the early Enlightenment, Thomasius was neither a rationalist nor a liberal, at least not in the Lockean or Kantian sense of those elastic terms. In approaching the fourth and fifth selections—Thomasius's celebrated attacks on heresy and witchcraft prosecutions—we must thus observe that his prime concern here was not to defend individual freedom and rights but to dismantle what he regarded as the illicit exercise of clerical power in the juridical and political domain. In the dialogue "Is Heresy a Punishable Crime?" Thomasius does indeed make use of an argument also used by Locke, that, as a matter of the understanding, erroneous or heretical opinions cannot be subject to coercive authority. Yet the main line of Thomasius's discourse heads in a direction quite different from Locke's, for he argues that religion is not a matter of doctrinal knowledge or understanding at all. The canon law definition of heresy, as an error in the doctrinal articles of faith, is thus a product of the church's fabrication of obligatory creeds and their use by the clergy to coerce the laity by denouncing dissenters as heretics. Heretics must therefore be tolerated not on the Lockean ground that the state cannot tell which of the "visible" churches might be the true one, but on the quite different ground that none of them can be, as their articles of faith are morally indifferent. This means that while all religions, dissenting and dominant, are to be tolerated—because opinions about the Trinity (for example) have no necessary impact on social peace—religious freedom is not a natural right, and toleration will be politically circumscribed by the state's policing of the threshold between private opinions and public disturbance.

Similarly, it was not as a natural rights theorist that Thomasius attacked the laws pertaining to witchcraft and sorcery, but as a jurisconsult intent on tearing the levers of civil power from the hands of the clergy. Witchcraft had been tied to heresy during the late Middle Ages by Catholic theologians and canon lawyers waging war against the great heretical movements of the time. In doing so, they had downplayed the actual harms supposedly caused by sorcery and focused instead on its status as a secret diabolical religion—devil worship—characterized by the cursing of God and the diabolical pact, and consecrated through intercourse with the devil. This was the form in which the crime of sorcery had passed into the criminal codes of such early modern Protestant states as Saxony.[16] It is thus significant that in his disputation "On the Crime of Sorcery," Thomasius does not begin from the Enlightenment premise that belief in the devil is an absurd superstition. Rather, he begins from the accepted belief that the devil does indeed exist but then insists that the devil's mode of existence is purely spiritual, incapable of corporeal

16. Winfried Trusen, "Rechtliche Grundlagen der Hexenprozesse und ihrer Beendigung," in *Das Ende der Hexenverfolgung,* ed. S. Lorenz and D. R. Bauer (Stuttgart: Franz Steiner, 1995), 203–26.

embodiment or effects. This enables him to undermine the specifically legal bases of the crime of sorcery—the diabolical pact and intercourse with the devil—and thereby to invalidate the church's claim to civil jurisdiction in this area. As in the case of heresy, any actual harms alleged to arise from sorcery are divorced from their supposed spiritual causes, being treated instead as ordinary crimes against civil peace at the disposal of the civil sovereign.

The central themes and arguments of Thomasius's discourses on church, state, and politics are conveniently summarized in the propositions of our final selection, "On the Right of a Christian Prince in Religious Matters." Published in 1724, just four years before Thomasius's death, this text originated in lectures first given in 1695, at the height of his concern with these issues. Here he again returns to the central theme of the *adiaphora*, arguing that saving faith is not to be found in the laws and ceremonies introduced into Christianity from Judaism, or in the "pagan" metaphysical doctrines elaborated in the creeds of the church fathers. Rather, it is to be found in the simple trust in God's will and in the teachings of Christ, as these can be known by anyone who reads the Bible. On the one hand, this means that all attempts by the clergy to prescribe religious worship for the laity—all creeds, liturgies, sacraments, religious oaths, and religious laws—are an illicit infringement of Christian freedom and a fundamental misunderstanding of the status of the church, which is that of a voluntary association of teachers and learners. On the other hand, because he rules over all things capable of affecting the security of the commonwealth, the prince must also have the right to supervise religious matters when these fall within the domain of the morally indifferent—and whether they do is itself a matter for the prince to decide.

Thomasius's prince must thus walk a fine line between respecting religious freedom and tolerating religious diversity, and repressing ostensibly religious conduct that gives rise to civil tumult, particularly conduct leading to religious intolerance, hatred, and violence. Thomasius finds a basis for this difficult set of judgments neither in a unified reason through which citizens might agree to respect each other's freedom of action nor in a single moral law commanding them to treat each other as morally autonomous. Rather, he finds it in a conception of diversified moral "offices" or personae, which he drew from Pufendorf's *De habitu religionis christianae ad vitam civilem* (On the nature of the Christian religion in relation to civil life) of 1687.[17] According to this conception, in order to live in the postconfessional society whose intellectual architecture Thomasius was outlining, it is necessary for individuals to separate their personae as Christians and as citizens. As Christians their duty is to acknowledge their own miserable moral condition and seek salvation through simple inward faith; as citizens it is to obey the sovereign's laws while accepting all men (including heretics and atheists) as fellow citizens. Similarly, in order to rule such a society, the prince must separate his duties as Christian, as man, and as prince. As a Christian he must seek salvation like everyone else; as a man he must do the duties prescribed by natural law. As a prince, however, he has the special duty of preserving external peace by means of sovereign coercive power, which can be wielded properly only when restricted to this specific secular end, with the prince setting aside his Christian persona in order to put an end to the state's clerical capture.

It is easy to misunderstand Thomasius, or to fail to arrive at a proper estimation of his historical significance, particularly if we approach him from the perspective of modern moral and political philosophy; that is, if we consider his discourses on church, state, and politics as early attempts to defend a social order based on the free rational judgments of consenting subjects. For Thomasius, the freedom of citizens comes not from their reason as such but from their capacity to be left alone in matters having no impact on social peace. The greatest threat to their freedom arises not from the state as such but from its clerical domination, which leads to the misuse of civil power for religious purposes and gives rise to mutually hostile confessional communities. Under such circumstances, it is vain to imagine social peace being reached through free agreement of communities. The state itself must assume responsibility for this goal, which it can do only if it withdraws from the religious

17. Samuel Pufendorf, *Of the Nature and Qualification of Religion in Reference to Civil Society*, ed. S. Zurbuchen (Indianapolis, Ind.: Liberty Fund, 2002).

commitments of the communities it must govern. This was the architecture for a pluralized religious society governed by a secularized state to which Thomasius dedicated his enormous energy and talent, leaving us these discourses as vivid testimony to the birth pangs of a cultural and political order indispensable to modern civility but increasingly removed from modern intelligibility.

Ian Hunter
Thomas Ahnert
Frank Grunert

A NOTE ON THE TEXTS AND
THE TRANSLATIONS

Three of our six texts—"On the History of Natural Law Until Grotius," "On the Power of Secular Government to Command Its Subjects to Attend Church Diligently," and "On the Right of a Christian Prince in Religious Matters"—were originally published as essays in German. The remaining three—"The Right of Protestant Princes Regarding Indifferent Matters or *Adiaphora*," "Is Heresy a Punishable Crime?" and "On the Crime of Sorcery"—were university disputations first published in Latin and then translated into German under Thomasius's supervision and published under his signature. (Publication details are provided in the notes to individual works.) The latter three texts pose two difficulties. The first is that of authorship, as these were first presented as disputations by Thomasius's doctoral students as part of their graduation requirements, with Thomasius taking the role of *praeses*, or supervisor. This problem is less severe than it first appears, however, as in early modern universities it was normal for students to simply rehearse their supervisor's ideas in dissertations that the supervisor might well have written himself. Thus, there was nothing unusual in Thomasius later collecting these disputations for publication under his own signature. The second difficulty is that of establishing an authoritative text for English translation when there are two versions—one in Latin, the other in German—both apparently authorized by Thomasius yet differing in certain regards. In addressing this problem we have not attempted to present a variorum edition, cross-tabulating all of the differences between the Latin and German versions. Rather, we have drawn on both versions in order to produce an English text accessible to the general reader, aiming to present Thomasius's substantive arguments as clearly as possible while recording major differences between the Latin and German texts in our notes. Additionally, in response to Thomasius's often abbreviated and occasionally cryptic way of referencing his sources, we have added a bibliographic list of works cited by Thomasius, wherever possible citing the editions that he used. Thomasius's own footnotes are indicated by alphabetic letters; those of the editors by numbers. Editorial interpolations within Thomasius's notes are signified by the use of square brackets.

ACKNOWLEDGMENTS

During the course of this work we have incurred various debts of gratitude, both jointly and individually. We are grateful to Knud Haakonssen for welcoming this work into his series and for his helpful advice along the way. Several colleagues are to be thanked for reading various essays in draft form and offering helpful comments, including Andreas Goessner, Michael Lattke, David Saunders, and Michael Seidler. Ian Hunter's participation was made possible through the award of an Australian Professorial Fellowship and with the assistance of the Centre for the History of European Discourses at the University of Queensland. Thomas Ahnert would like to thank the Institute for Advanced Studies in the Humanities at the University of Edinburgh, where he has held a research fellowship during the preparation of the text. Frank Grunert is grateful to Holger Nath for his assistance in translating essays 1 and 5.

ESSAYS ON CHURCH, STATE, AND POLITICS

On the History of Natural Law
Until Grotius

1. All men by nature are in the same miserable shape.[1] All demand to   **Common human misery**
live long and happily, that is, cheerfully, well-off, and honored. In spite
of this, every thought and desire they have had since their youth leads
them to do things that make their lives unhappy, wretched, or both.
Thus, the natural end of life is cut short. Man becomes the agent of his
own misfortune.

2. Few recognize this misery. Even fewer use their knowledge of this   **General means against it**
misery to seek the reasonable means of saving themselves from it. Fewest
of all, however, when investigating these means, take the necessary care
or muster up the strength to grasp these means. Everywhere it is not the
Creator but man himself who is thus to blame, despite the fact that God
has bestowed upon him and presented him with partly natural, partly
supernatural teachings, means, and powers. It lies thus in man's obstinacy and negligence if he neither recognizes nor utilizes such teachings
and means, nor wants to accept those offered, but rejects them willfully
and pushes them away with his feet, so to speak.

---

1. This essay on the history of natural law was published as the foreword to the
first German translation of Grotius's *De jure belli ac pacis* (The right of war and
peace), which appeared under the title *Drei Bücher vom Recht des Krieges und des Frie-
dens* in 1707. For a modern edition, see *The Rights of War and Peace*, 3 vols., edited
by Richard Tuck (Indianapolis, Ind.: Liberty Fund, 2005).

Careful use of
the natural
and super-
natural lights,
so that they
will not be
confused

3. This misfortune can be ascribed, among other causes, to the fact that man confuses the natural and supernatural lights, reason and divine revelation, thereby bringing disorder to all knowledge. As a result, man regards true teachings as errors and passes off errors for truths. He attempts to assert them by force. In doing so, he misses the right path and, while intending to help, seduces others, plunging them and himself into misery. Thus sincere lovers of truth have always recognized that the light of reason and divine revelation, as well as nature and grace, should be clearly distinguished. Recently, not only in France but also in Germany, learned men have published treatises about this, some scholarly, others polemical.[2]

Simple differ-
ence between
natural and
supernatural
lights

4. Truth is simple. There is thus no great need to rack one's brains or for quarreling if one seeks truth in the simplest way. The light of reason and of divine revelation are expressed by intellect, nature, and grace, but also by the will. Often, both are generally understood in such a way that the light of reason is needed for the natural powers and grace for supernatural knowledge. In this broad sense, we are able to grasp the difference between natural and supernatural lights most clearly in the following way: the natural light comprehends the miserable condition of mankind in this temporal life by means of sound reason, without any particular divine revelation. Especially, though, it requires each person to concern himself first with his own misery. The natural light thus shows man the means and ways by which he can get out of this misery using his natural powers and without any special supernatural grace, so that he can place himself in a happy state as far as temporal life is concerned. The supernatural or immediate divine light, however, is concerned with the eternal happiness which man lost by his Fall. Thus it

2. Here Thomasius is referring to such late-seventeenth-century works as Samuel Pufendorf, *De officio hominis et civis* (1673), translated as *The Whole Duty of Man, According to the Law of Nature,* edited and with an introduction by Ian Hunter and David Saunders (Indianapolis, Ind.: Liberty Fund, 2003), 16–26; Pierre Bayle, *Various Thoughts on the Occasion of a Comet,* trans. R. C. Bartlett (New York: SUNY Press, 2000); Pierre Bayle, *Dictionnaire historique et critique (An Historical and Critical Dictionary)* (Rotterdam, 1697).

first teaches the condition of man after his loss of innocence and how he ended up in temporal and eternal misery through his Fall. It shows how after this temporal life there will be a different life and a resurrection of the dead. It also shows what difference there is between the state of the eternally blissful or chosen and the state of the hapless or damned. It shows the means determined by God for attaining eternal bliss and avoiding eternal damnation. It also teaches whence come the supernatural powers needed to apply these means, and how man must behave in regard to them. All of this goes beyond the boundaries of the natural light, since reason by itself knows nothing about the state of innocence, nor about the Fall, nor about the immortality of souls, nor about eternal life or the eternal torments of hell, nor about Christ and his merits or the belief in Christ as the only means of grasping these merits. Neither, by themselves, are the powers of the will capable of obtaining this eternal bliss. With regard to his reason, man thus needs a special divine revelation, while with regard to his will he needs supernatural divine assistance. At the same time, this shows the simple but clear difference between theology and philosophy or between theology and the other three faculties. theology has to do with the light of grace; jurisprudence, medicine, and philosophy have to do with the natural light and should teach accordingly.

5. Considering how simple is the difference of this double light, and how easily it can be understood by even the least educated, it is all the more astonishing that it is neglected, or even contested and challenged by the most educated. This comes about because people readily know what to say in general about these two lights and their boundaries. When it comes to an exact investigation of this, however, then no one can give a clear explanation to those eager to learn. Much controversy then arises from ignorance of the boundaries of the two lights. One party accuses the other of turning naturally good or evil things into supernatural, divine or diabolical effects. The other party, however, tries to pass off divine and diabolical matters for natural ones, which were caused by human powers or malice. Others seek to abandon the difference entirely and want to accept only the natural light and natural powers. They want

Errors of the scholars who depart from this simple conception

to abolish all supernatural matters. Still others recognize only the supernatural light as the true light. They reject the natural light and sound reason, as well as the natural powers of the human will, even in temporal matters, or else pass them off as something diabolical.

Two main causes for these errors

6. The causes that have led scholars into these errors and quarrels are numerous and varied. I consider the following two to be the most important ones: (1) either through their comparison of the two lights they wished to examine the matter all too exactly; or (2) in investigating the difference between the two lights, they made no use of a formal method.

The unreasonable view, as if these two lights were opposed to each other

7. According to our simple teaching on the difference between the two, it can easily be understood that temporal happiness and eternal happiness do not oppose each other, that they are rather similar in many respects, and that their difference primarily depends on the degree of perfection and on the degree of duration or immutability. So the two forms of happiness differ in several ways, similar to the differences between the two lights given to man by God, but they never oppose each other and nor can they. There is rather perfect harmony between them. The understanding in fact knows nothing about these supernatural matters, but after Holy Scripture has revealed them finds nothing in these revelations that would contradict sound reason. Rather, through revelation, reason recognizes the wisdom, justice, and omnipotence of God all the more clearly. The light of nature provides reason with various arguments— for example, the doctrine of God's trinity, the doctrine of the immortality of the soul, of the resurrection of the flesh—to show at least that there is nothing counternatural in these and similar supernatural mysteries. Man also needs the natural light for interpreting the Bible, in the sense that God and the men driven by God have written the Holy Scriptures for reasonable people and not for irrational beasts. The rules of reasonable explanation should thus be applied to the interpretation of the Holy Scriptures. One should refrain from all unreasonable interpretation, which would result in something contradictory, impossible, and obviously foolish. Even though the supernatural light should have precedence over the natural light, on account of the eternal happiness to

which it leads man, the natural light should never be tossed away, but must always be maintained. Otherwise no subordination between the two would be possible. For instance, a subordination does exist between two straight parallel lines, but there is no opposition. If one took away the lower line, one could not talk about subordination and parallelism. Since it is certain that as divine gifts the supernatural and the natural lights will never be opposed to each other, so the controversies which have arisen among scholars—when they rack their brains over whether the natural light should be preferred to the supernatural one—are completely in vain and unnecessary. This question presupposes an unreasonable condition, as if the two lights contradict each other. Thus, on the one hand, they must err who place the natural light above the Scriptures in such a way that they will not believe anything which cannot be proven by rational natural arguments. On the other hand, of course, they also grossly err who impute an irrational interpretation to Holy Scripture, cutting short those who reasonably point this out, and even persecuting them under the vain pretext that the natural light is inferior to the supernatural. This concerns those who are wont to say that reason needs to be captured by faith.

8. First, there is a practical rule in the standard teaching method: when investigating the differences or boundaries between different things, one should begin with the easiest and most familiar. But the natural light deals with the things that are easiest and most familiar to man. On this basis, the supernatural light gives rise to faith, not to a science in the human understanding. In supernatural matters the human understanding gropes in the dark, even after divine revelation, recognizing everything only as in a mirror. Therefore, both the rules of good teaching as well as the designation of supernatural things require that one begins first with natural things and learns to understand their limits before trying to understand supernatural things. Of course, it would be unreasonable for someone to label as supernatural that which others can explain as natural, by means of causes that are reasonable and even open to the senses of commonsense people. But how few there are who apply this method, beginning with the natural light and philosophy and then

Negligence in investigating natural matters and in beginning with the most difficult supernatural ones

leading their audience to the boundaries where the teaching of super-natural matters begins. It is quite true that most teachers of the super-natural light have themselves studied little or nothing of the natural sciences. (The natural sciences also include moral philosophy and all sciences that deal with human conduct or with the difference between good and evil). As a result, these scholars, whose irrational teachings regarding supernatural things arise from their ignorance of natural things, pass them off as articles of faith, and attempt to uphold them with cunning and force.

Common corruption of the moral sciences among the pagans

9. Once someone who has searched honestly for the truth carefully recalls these cardinal errors, it will not be difficult for him to recognize whence so many common mistakes in moral philosophy and natural law emerged and how they could have lasted such a long time. With regard to the pagans, a scholarly man of letters recently noted and proved thoroughly that the pagan priests concerned themselves little about these sciences, so necessary for the human race.[3] Rather, on account of their reputation and other interests, they vigorously persecuted those philosophers who did concern themselves with these things. Until Socrates, the philosophers either completely neglected moral philosophy or focused only on the study of nature.[4] When they did deal with moral philosophy in their works they did not derive it in an appropriate way—from their own reasonable observation of the human soul and the natural powers—but grounded it instead in common palpable errors. In knowledge of good and evil, it is true that the understanding is clouded by the desires of the will. As long as he is in this state, where the natural

3. Perhaps a reference to Pierre Bayle, who comments on this in his *Dictionnaire historique et critique* (*An Historical and Critical Dictionary*).

4. During the seventeenth and eighteenth centuries, Socrates (ca. 470–399 B.C.) was esteemed as a nonspeculative philosopher dealing in a practical way with the moral question of how to live one's life. This is the way he is seen in François Charpentier's *Vie de Socrate* (The life of Socrates), published in his *Les Choses memorables de Socrate* (Memorable things from Socrates) (Paris, 1650). Thomasius translated Charpentier's book in 1693, with a second edition of this translation appearing in 1720.

light turns into a will-o'-the-wisp, man must nonetheless strive for correct use of the natural light, for the improvement of the understanding, and the correct arrangement of knowledge. Daily experience shows, however, that this is not enough for obtaining true wisdom, but that one should also be concerned with the peculiar inclinations and desires of the human will. For every day one sees in oneself and in others that man fails to do things recognized as good by his own reason, and that he does other things which his understanding regards as evil. In treating an ulcer caused by impure blood, a decent doctor will first attempt to use a plaster, but he will not therefore refrain from cleansing the impurities of the blood with the help of internal medications.[5] Nonetheless, the pagan philosophers, even the wisest of all, Socrates, taught that to attain a virtuous life it was enough for the human understanding to be instructed in the difference between good and evil. Plato, a student of Socrates, departed from the laudable but simple teachings of his master, introducing in their place a supersubtle way of disputing over useless things. Overall, not only were his teachings grounded in the need all men have to secure an inner approval, but many ostensibly uncontroversial and credible things were derived from the fraudulent revelations of supposedly divine pagan oracles.[6] Many of Plato's listeners thus took it into their heads to doubt everything and to treat as the only certainty that everything is uncertain and dubious. At first glance, the Stoics possess many wonderful teachings regarding virtue and the difference between good and evil. Nevertheless, the abovementioned general error [regarding the sufficiency of mere moral knowledge] causes them to say extremely overblown things about the character of their sages and extremely detrimental things about the shortcomings of divine goodness and wisdom; yet they typically foolishly insist that their virtuous sage

---

5. In other words, even if he corrects the understanding, a moral philosopher must still treat the underlying cause of moral pathologies, in the impure condition of the will.

6. See, for example, Plato's dialogue *Socrates' Defence* (*Apology*), where the character of Socrates speaks of his *daemon,* a divine inner voice that prevents him from doing anything unjust.

cannot be found anywhere in the world and is a mere chimera.[7] If one were to talk impartially about this issue, then Epicurus—so hated and so often slandered by the Stoics and Platonists—in fact has many good things to say in his teachings regarding the character of a wise man. But how can one find something healthy in the moral philosophy of a person who introduced such dangerous teachings about the nature of God and of divine Providence, about the origin of the world, about matter and the corporeality of the human soul?[8] For his part, Aristotle reworked and changed much in the moral philosophy and teachings of his master, Plato, without, however, improving moral philosophy.[9] Even the most modest of Aristotle's current followers admit that he neither introduced nor sufficiently explained the doctrine of the means by which a virtuous life is to be attained through rational advice and laws. Afterward, all these errors in moral philosophy passed from the Greeks to the Romans and then from both to the Jews. Among the latter, the sects of the Pharisees, Sadducees, and Essenes[10] spread these errors in such a way that during the time of Christ blatant errors were in full swing among the Greeks, the Romans, and Jews—and, yes, throughout the entire world.

The short duration of the Christian-apostolic teachings

10. In fact, one would have hoped that through the teachings of Christ and the apostles the proper use of natural light would rise again, even though Christ and his disciples primarily dealt with the supernatural light and its proper use. It is not our opinion that Christ and his disciples

7. The Stoic school was founded by Zeno in Athens in 300 B.C. Here Thomasius is somewhat uncharitably alluding to the fact that Zeno and his followers did not claim to be sages, owing to their inability to attain the state of complete inner equanimity or absence of passion.

8. These remarks capture something of Thomasius's ambivalent attitude toward Epicurus (341–271 B.C.), whose moral focus on earthly happiness he applauded but whose materialistic and nonprovidential cosmology remained a scandal for most seventeenth-century philosophers and theologians.

9. Despite his continuing preeminence in early modern academic philosophy, Aristotle (384–322 B.C.) was regarded skeptically by Thomasius. In particular, Thomasius regarded Aristotle's ethics as overly intellectualist and incapable of actually teaching people how to become virtuous and live a good life.

10. Rival Jewish sects that were founded respectively in 200 and 150 B.C.

ever intended to write a philosophical system, neither with regard to nature nor to ethics. But it is certain that, except for the Holy Scriptures, no other philosopher rejected so clearly the basic errors of pagan philosophy, in particular the confusion of the will and the understanding and the foolish improvement of the understanding alone. Nor did any so clearly advise mankind on the proper use of the natural light in improving the will, or delineate the three main vices of lust, ambition, and avarice. Despite all of this, soon after the death of Christ and even during the lifetime of the apostles, the old errors and confusions about the natural and supernatural light reemerged. After the death of the apostles, it is apparent from church history that these errors again captivated the minds of all so-called Christians, although a few were worried about the reason for this sudden change. This is not the place to investigate this matter in detail, although it will serve our purposes if we discuss it briefly.

11. The wisdom of the natural as well as the supernatural light is simple. Most errors come from hairsplitting scholars. As long as the teaching of Christ remained in the simple hearts of fishermen and unlettered people, it remained good and pure. But this teaching was not to the liking of the pagan-educated Pharisees until, with his resurrection, Christ finally converted the Pharisee Paul through an extraordinary miracle.[11] Paul then had to endure persecutions both by the Pharisees and the Sadducees, but also by the Stoics and Epicureans when, following his [apostolic] appointment, he strove to spread the simple teachings of Christ among the pagans as well—teachings that were to the learned Jews an irritation and to the Greeks stupidity. Since among the Jews there were many of a Pharisaical disposition, and among the pagans many scholars, in particular Stoics and Platonists, who professed Christianity, they falsified the pure teachings with their pagan principles. They began anew to hone the understanding solely by hairsplitting and useless questions, which provided the occasion for the Jewish and pagan scholars to begin to quarrel. The bitterness arising from this discord, which had broken

Old pagan errors were soon reintroduced by scholars up to the time of Constantine

---

11. For the conversion of Paul, see Acts of the Apostles IX, 1ff.; XXII, 6ff., and XXVI, 12ff.

out during the lifetime of Paul at the Council of Jerusalem, became ever more widespread after his death.[12] As long as the Jews constituted the strongest party, they suppressed the pagans, so that the first heresies were mostly hairsplitting questions arising from the Jewish Kabbalah.[13] But after those who had formerly been pagans became the strongest party, it was their turn, and they made those of a Jewish persuasion pay for the earlier persecution. The latter is easily traced during the time of Constantine the Great.[14]

From the time of Constantine onward, through Plato's teachings the natural light is elevated too high

12. Together with the history of the controversies and heresies, the pamphlets of the most famous teachers published during that time reveal the condition of the learned world under the rule of the so-called Christians and show that it did not improve for several centuries, but in fact worsened. The use of the natural light was cultivated to excess. These teachers sought to use it to scrutinize the most incomprehensible secret of the divine being, not happy with the fact that Christ and his apostles presented the secret of the divine will by means of a doctrine simple enough to be also understood by the unlettered. They employed useless Platonic philosophy, initially under the pretext that through this they could better combat the pagan Platonic philosophers, who had chiefly persecuted and defamed the Christians. But they soon fell all too much in love with Platonic philosophy, wanting to use its false light to give the divine light a greater clarity. When honest souls complained that in this way the light of divine revelation was obscured, they were called heretics and the Platonist esoterica were forced upon them as articles of faith. Thus the true old apostolic Christianity, while not in fact exterminated,

12. The Council in Jerusalem took place in A.D. 48. The reason for the meeting between the apostles of the original parish in Jerusalem and the emissaries of the parish in Antioch (Paul and Barnabas) was a conflict between the pagan (Greek) Christians and the Jewish Christians of the original parish.

13. Jewish esoteric mysticism, which appeared in the thirteenth century in the north of Spain and the south of France. Thomasius's claim that the heresies of apostolic times first arose from disputes over the Kabbalah is thus anachronistic.

14. Constantine the Great was Roman emperor from 306 to 337. He promoted the Christian religion in his empire and prepared the political conditions for its development into a state church.

was suppressed, and Platonist Christianity generally gained the upper hand. Were anyone to doubt this he should carefully read what the great Augustine—who is usually known as the greatest of all the so-called Fathers of the Church—wrote in his books on the *City of God* praising and glorifying Plato.[15] One should also read the glosses on Augustine written by Ludovicus Vives [Juan Luis Vives] and Leonardus Coquaeus.[16]

13. Soon the proper use of the natural light was abandoned in all three main areas of sound philosophy, namely, logic [*Vernunftlehre*], natural philosophy, and moral philosophy. By the time of Constantine the Great the learned pagans had already introduced into Christianity a verbose and pleasant-sounding, yet also a sophistic, pompous, quarrelsome, impassioned way of teaching. Rather than striving to purge the lies of pagan philosophy from the truth of Christian teachings in an honest, gentle, clear, and simple way—thereby tangibly shaming and removing pagan errors—all kinds of pagan and fraudulent paths were followed. Soon the pagans were attributed false opinions that had never entered their heads, followed by the wrathful and vehement refutation of these chimeras. In the place of reasonable refutation, a rhetoric of exclamations, questions, objections, or learned invective was employed, which did not advance the matter. Soon doubt was no longer answered at all. The presentation of doubt initiated not an answer but long-winded exaggerations, to prove good sound Christian teachings with inadequate reasons. In this way the upright minds among the pagans were only made more puzzled, suspicious, or bitter. I remember that when he was a professor in Leipzig my blessed father explained to his audience in public

In other domains the proper use of natural light is completely neglected, partially in logic

15. Augustine of Hippo (354–430), who began his intellectual life as a Neoplatonist, was converted to Christianity but then used Neoplatonic philosophy to elaborate Christian doctrine, particularly in his seminal *The City of God against the Pagans* (Cambridge: Cambridge University Press, 1998).

16. Thomasius seems to refer to the following text: *S. Aurelii Augustini Hipp. Episcop. de civitate Dei libri XXII . . . cum commentariis novis & perpetuis R.P.F. Leonardi Coquaei . . . et Joanni Ludovici Vivis* (St. Aurelius Augustine, bishop of Hippo. On the city of God book XXII with new and complete commentaries by Leonardus Coquaeus and Juan Luis Vives) (Paris, 1651).

lectures several of Lactantius's disputations with the pagans,[17] applying
the rules of sound logic, and thereby frequently pointing out these
above-mentioned flaws. The thoughts he dictated at that time are in my
house among his manuscripts. Lactantius had been the teacher of Constantine, and his good and honest intentions radiate from his writings.
It was not his fault that he was led into making such a mistake, but that
of the miserable state of logic prevailing among the pagans and Christians. Since this happened to this famous church teacher, it can easily be
inferred that in subsequent times things did not get better but worse, as
the more scholarship declined, the more quarrels, controversies, and passions increased, day by day. Also relevant here is the question of how the
Holy Scriptures of the Old and New Testaments should be understood
according to the rules of a reasonable interpretation. Through the al-
legories of the evangelists and apostles against the Jews, it became normal
to reject the sensible and literal understanding of the Bible as carnal, and
to make the interpretation of Christianity taken from Stoic and Platonic
philosophy into its foundation. Many famous theologians—among
them Luther and Chytraeus,[18] and also Catholic writers—have complained about this way of reading found in the works of Philo, Ambrose,
and Origen.[19] For a better understanding, all truth-loving people should
refer to the work of Samuel Werenfels: *De logomachiis eruditorum.*[20]

17. Jacob Thomasius, *Analysin Dispp. Lactantii adversos Ethnicos* (Analysis of Lactantius's disputations against the pagans). Christian Thomasius's father, Jacob Thomasius (1622–84), taught ethics, logic, and rhetoric at the University of Leipzig where
he was also rector of the Thomasschule. He is regarded as an important pioneering
historian of philosophy. Lucius Caelius Lactantius lived from ca. 250 to ca. 335. His
Divinae Institutiones (Divine institutions), written between 304 and 313, marks the
first attempt to develop a system of the Christian doctrine.

18. David Chytraeus (1531–1600), a Lutheran theologian who taught theology,
philosophy, and history at the University of Rostock, played an important role in
the internal organization of the Lutheran church.

19. Philo, a Jewish philosopher who lived between ca. 20 or 15 B.C. and A.D. 42 in
Alexandria, and Origen (ca. 185–253/54), one of the most influential fathers of the
church, were famous for their allegorical interpretations of Holy Scripture. See Origen, *Peri archon sive de principiis libri 4* (Peri archon or four books on principles),
where he developed his doctrine of the threefold meaning of Scripture.

20. Samuel Werenfels (1657–1740) was professor for theology at the University of

14. What should one say about natural philosophy? One can find little that is sound about it in the most famous church teachers. It cannot be denied that they contested with laudable intent the central error of pagan natural philosophy, regarding the eternity of the world and its two coeternal origins, God and prime matter; nor that they were committed to combating this error by laying the basis of Mosaic natural philosophy in the creation of invisible and visible things. It would take us too far afield to examine whether this was done with sufficient prudence and in an honest way, or whether many and diverse Platonist fictions were often mixed in. It is enough to say that in the doctrine of the condition, difference, and nature of the invisible and visible creatures, we find little that is well grounded and properly purged of the old corrupt Jewish and Platonic philosophy. Rather, pagan and Jewish superstitions lurk behind everything. It was not enough that Christians were presented with errors contrary to sound reason and the common sense of reasonable men. These errors had to be forced on people as necessary articles of faith, through heretic-mongering and the coercion of conscience. Those who objected had their mouths shut by force, because it could not be done via reason. For an explanation of this, one should check what Servatius Gallaeus and Johannes Blaucanus have written about the roundness of the earth and the existence of the antipodes, in their commentaries on Lactantius or Juan Luis Vives or Leonardus Coquaeus or Augustine's *The City of God.*[21] In his book III, Aventin thus mentions how in the

The correct use of natural light in natural philosophy

Basel. His *Dissertationes VII. de Logomachiis eruditorum* (Seven dissertations on the nonsense of learned men) was first published in 1688, later editions in 1692 and 1742.

21. Servatius Gallaeus (1627–1709) was a Dutch philologist who published *Lucii Caecilii Lactantii Firmiani opera, quae extant cum selectis variorum commentariis* (Genuine works of Lucius Caelius Lactantius, presented with selected diverse commentaries) (Leiden, 1660). Lactantius defended the idea of a flat earth, and Gallaeus republished his works in order to attack the new heliocentric astronomy of Kepler and Galileo. "Johannes Blaucanus" was probably Josephus Blancanus, the author of *Sphaera mvndi sev Cosmographia demonstratiua, ac facili methodo tradita: in qva totivs mvndi fabrica, vna cvm novis, Tychonis, Kepleri, Galilaei, aliorumque astronomorum adinuentis continetur* (The globe of the world or demonstrative cosmography, related in an easy method, which contains the construction of the whole world according to Tycho, Kepler, Galileo, and the inventions of other astronomers) (Bologna, 1620). Blancanus was a Jesuit at Parma who also opposed the new astronomy. (We are grate-

eighth century the so-called German apostle Boniface branded the good priest Virgilius as a heretic for claiming that the antipodes existed.[22] This seemed to endanger the true teachings of the Lord Christ and the Holy Scriptures. Pope Zachary approved of this unreasonable action by Boniface, and poor Virgilius had to remain a heretic per force. All of this indicates blindness and the confusion of natural light with divine revelation, since in our times even pupils in the lower classes know that Boniface and the pope Zachary committed the greatest injustice against Virgilius in front of God and the entire world.

The use of natural light in moral philosophy

15. If their negligence had arisen from an eager and honest desire to learn more about human nature, one could excuse the fact that the teachers of the church did not care very much about the nature of higher beings and earthly creatures. But their writings indicate the opposite. They do not investigate human nature on the basis of their own judgment. Instead, through the consideration of useless things and the retailing of received opinion they investigate human happiness in accordance with pagan doctrine. In doing so, they completely forget to think for themselves. If these teachers occasionally engage in self-reflection, then it only ends up in Platonist deification and enthusiasm rather than in an assured sensible perception. Thus it is easy to understand the barren appearance of moral philosophy and what was then called natural law. It is not surprising that many Protestants cannot stand it if one says the slightest thing about the teachings of the Fathers of the Church that might di-

ful to Michael Seidler for helping us to avoid the red herring thrown out by Thomasius's misleading reference to "Blaucanus.")

22. Johannes Aventinus (1477–1534) was a Bavarian historian. Thomasius is referring to book III of his *Annalium Boiorum libri VII* (Annals of the Bavarians in seven books), completed in 1521 and published posthumously in 1554. Bonifatius (672/73–754), "the apostle of the Germans," thought that Virgilius's (d. 784) doctrine of the antipodes entailed the existence of another world with a different mankind and without the redemption of Christ. Pope Zachary threatened Virgilius, who was at that time bishop of Salzburg, with excommunication and removal from office. Since the pope died in 752, it seems that the threat was inconsequential. Virgilius in fact remained as bishop until 754 and received the posthumous satisfaction of canonization in 1233.

minish their holiness and reputation in even the slightest way. They immediately erupt into abusive words and brand others as heretics, misuse the Holy Scriptures, and curse all who, from love of truth, warn the inexperienced of errors. They completely extinguish the natural light and prefer to rob themselves and others of one of the most noble gifts—God-given sound reason—rather than give in to inopportune and unreasonable love of those who are weak or easily deceived. As I know full well the abuses and slanders suffered by several learned men who attempted this [warning of the inexperienced], I will not permit myself to elaborate the matter in more detail or to translate into our mother tongue what others have presented. But a desirous reader will know how to find the necessary things without my help. The previous suppression of sound reason has been one of the most secretive stratagems of political papalism, which the reformers of the Protestant church were not immediately able to discern. Neither could the politicians see this for quite some time, as they were not instructed in a true and reasonable politics at the universities, looking only for theological errors in papalism but not for the most cunning political statecraft. But fortunately day is breaking. No struggling and unruliness will hinder the breakthrough of truth. Thanks to divine Providence, a hundred years ago a famous reformer, the theologian Abraham Scultetus, wrote a book on the *Core of the Theology of the Church-Fathers*.[23] Here, besides their good but generally morose and long-winded teachings, he also uncovered their errors. This book is written in a such way that even politicians, who otherwise do not have time to read the Fathers of the Church, can observe the miserable condition of these times as if in a mirror. After the mystery-mongering had been exposed, even reasonable Catholic writers realized that it was futile to avoid these things, for example, the famous Frenchman Du Pin in his *Library of the Ecclesiastic Teachers*.[24] The numerous

---

23. Abraham Scultetus (1566–1624) was a Calvinist theologian whose *Medulla theologiae patrum* (Kernel of the theology of the fathers of the church) appeared for the first time in 1598.

24. Louis Ellies Du Pin was a Catholic theologian and philosopher who taught at the Collège Royal in Paris. His *Nouvelle Bibliothèque des auteurs ecclésiastiques* (New

writings cleared a path that can no longer be hidden. Now the truth can no longer be concealed. Unfortunately one may not mention the astute, but much-loathed Pierre Bayle who has also dealt with these matters very effectively.[25] To those who have neither the time nor opportunity to consult the above-mentioned authors, I recommend the very learned preface of Monsieur Barbeyrac to his French translation of Pufendorf's book.[26] He took laudable pains to compile everything he could find from the above-mentioned writers—a task which cannot be praised highly enough by politicians and jurists. Evidently he proved that there were many among the Fathers of the Church—Athenagoras, Clement of Alexandria, Tertulian, Origen, Cyprian, Lactantius, Basil, Gregory Nazianzus, Ambrose, Chrysostom, Hieronymous, Augustine, Leo, Gregory the Great—who understood little or nothing of moral philosophy. In fact, in the course of interpreting Holy Scripture or on other occasions, they spread among their listeners sundry damaging and erroneous teachings, which were contrary to the bright light of the Gospel and to the natural law.

Two of the most prominent types of Christian

16. In order to better understand the political secrets of the papacy we recommend the study of church history and its commentaries to all lovers of the truth. This will permit Protestants to better protect themselves

---

library of ecclesiastical authors) was published between 1686 and 1714, during which time sixty-one volumes appeared.

25. Pierre Bayle (1647–1706), one of the most famous partisans of religious liberty and freedom of conscience. His *Dictionnaire historique et critique* (1697) teaches the fundamental contradiction between sound reason and religious belief.

26. *Le droit de la nature & des gens, ou systeme general des principes les plus importans de la morale, de la jurisprudence & et de la politique. Traduit de latin de feu monsieur le baron de Pufendorf, avec des notes du traducteur & une preface, qui sert d'introduction a tout l'ouvrage* (The law of nature and nations, or general system of the most important principles of ethics, jurisprudence, and politics. Translated from the Latin of the late Baron Pufendorf, with the translator's notes and a preface serving as an introduction to the whole work) (Amsterdam, 1706). Later editions: 1712, 1713, 1732, 1734. Jean Barbeyrac's translation of Pufendorf's *De jure naturae et gentium,* first published in 1672, was very influential for the development of natural jurisprudence across the whole of learned Europe.

against such secrets and to grasp more clearly the occasions on which the natural light—in particular moral philosophy, state-theory, and natural law—became increasingly corrupted. Among the large number of church teachers, who are known in part through their writings and in part through their actions, there have always been two types. The first kind saw the path to eternal bliss in rarefied concepts of the secrets of the divine nature. In accordance with the idea that the improvement of the will follows automatically from the improvement of the understanding, one need no longer strive for a Christian, God-pleasing life because, proverbially, God will care for all. With regard to living, they fooled their audience into believing that God is a pious, kindly father, who is not too particular with his dear children who call themselves Christians, but gently tolerates their corrupt flesh and blood as a human weakness. This is why Jesus was sent to earth, to deliver these dear children from the yoke of Mosaic law. With regard to his divine nature, however, and its eternal emanations and effects—which concern the operation of salvation through Christ—God is a strict and fervent God. He wants all Christians to be of one opinion in accordance with a particular formula. These formulas, though, were prepared by the highest teachers following the custom of decision-making in the Imperial Diet, through majority vote. But those not satisfied with these formulas who wish to alter even the tiniest detail, regardless of whether they trust in God and fervently attempt to live in accordance with his son, Christ's, commandments, not only be punished by God with the eternal torment of hell, without mercy or forgiveness as the worst of malefactors, but the secular authorities should also reinforce the holy bishops in such cases. The thorities should let themselves be guided by the bishops as the spiritual leaders and fathers, and they should persecute such people as the most harmful misbegotten monsters with fire and sword, gallows and wheel.

The second group, however, had a completely different viewpoint. [They argued that] such a way of dealing with God and Christ utterly contradicts not only the truth of the Old Testament but also that of the New and the teachings of Christ. Christ did not abolish the Ten Commandments, but commanded his disciples to follow the Commandment

teaching: theorthodox and the esoteric, and their opposition to each other

of Love, which includes all the others. He gave them emphatic advice
that in this they should follow his model and example. Neither in the
teachings of Christ nor in those of the apostles does one find much in
the way of theological formulas. These arose a few hundred years later,
when the passion and honesty of the first love had become rather luke-
warm and dull. [According to this second group], the Lord Christ would
not examine what people believed about the mysteries of God's nature.
Instead, given that he had himself purged the mystery of God's will from
the corrupt statutes of the Pharisees and had impressed [this] on his disciples, so he would much rather inquire into the works of love that he
had commanded and would separate those who practiced these as sheep
from goats, regardless of whether they could rehearse correct views about
God, or prophesies, or miracles. Thus, they argued, it is not necessary
to concern oneself with the improvement of the understanding, but one
should much rather strive to improve the will. In accordance with the
freedom bestowed by God, one must seriously and willfully and with
true zeal attack the thing itself. One must renounce and rid oneself of
the three vicious main desires: lust of the eye, lust of the flesh, and the
haughty life. One must oppose and subdue those evil desires with vows
of spiritual poverty, chastity, and of humble obedience. One must for-
tify the spirit by crucifying the flesh with all its lusts and desires, carefully arranging one's life according to certain beautiful rules of living,
carefully crafted by experienced minds. In addition, the inexperienced
should choose a certain person from the skilled and experienced who
would be charged with the direction of their conscience, and whose
teaching and good advice they should obey with all simplicity, even
when the advice sounds strange. All evil comes from Satan or from the
corrupted reason, whose sly advances are no better avoided than by
repudiating blind reason and making it a captive of faith. To summarize, we will call the first approach the dogmatic, which is the one
most influential in orthodoxy and which is much given to heretic-
mongering. But the other approach, which aims at the purification of
the heart, while insisting on the secret and concealed exegesis of the
Scriptures, we will call the esoteric or mystical approach.

17. The two groups were bitterly opposed and persecuted each other wherever they could. When they were persecuted, each complained about the other and claimed that it is unjust to coerce someone simply because of differing opinions. But whenever the secular authorities were on their side and they were too powerful for the other party, both groups defended the view that it is just to persecute others with such coercion of conscience and to force the others to side with them. (This is confirmed by the example of the Donatists[27] in church history and by two well-known letters by St. Augustine.) The main difference lies only in the fact that the orthodox were lucky in having the secular authorities on their side more often than the esoterics. The doctrines of the orthodox were more to the taste of the court than the doctrines of the esoterics, who were far too strict and melancholic or, in a word, too monkish for courtly life. Both groups praised kings who were often not praiseworthy according to the natural light, but would be blessed if they did everything their spiritual advisers wanted. They bestowed golden words and great titles on kings; such epithets, for example, as the Great, the Pious, the Holy (although one knows why so many kings have received the epithet of the Great, fewer though the epithet of the Pious, and even fewer the epithet of the Holy). If kings or secular authorities failed to live exactly in accordance with their principles, or failed to approve sight-unseen everything that they did and said, then both groups in turn cursed and damned the kings and the authorities, even if they were not impious; but they only did this when they had the power to wreak their revenge. In this way the two groups obtained power and dominion over the powerful and the secular authorities, and turned them into vassals. The two groups of teachers are thus the most preeminent pillars of papalism. Each has accused the other of seducing innocent people and of

Differences and similarities between the two groups

---

27. The Donatists, followers of Bishop Donatus of Carthage, were a religious group whose doctrines caused a schism in the African church in the fourth century. They controversially denied the possibility of valid baptism outside the visible institutional church. Augustine's theology played a leading role in resolving this conflict.

defending false teachings maliciously and contrary to their better conscience; and yet amongst both bunches there were malicious, cunning
people. Both groups have tried to control the minds and the will of the
people, the orthodox under the pretense of orthodoxy and the esoterics
under the pretext of spiritual direction. In each bunch there were also
good, honest, simple people whom the cunning led up the garden path
and who, in their simplicity, believed that they were serving God if they
spread in any way possible the doctrines previously instilled in them.
The orthodox invoked the tradition of the church, yet did not want to
get a name for teaching against the Scriptures. The esoterics argued that
their teachings were based on the Holy Scriptures and claimed that they
were much closer to the church's way of life. Both interpreted the Scriptures by way of their doctrines rather than orientating their doctrines to
the Scriptures. Both elevated the powers of the human soul much too
high: the orthodox elevated the understanding, the esoterics the freedom
of the will. Both thus abused the natural light. The orthodox did so by
overstepping the boundaries of reason, using its powers to fathom matters that God did not deem necessary to reveal, and thereby egregiously
neglecting the will and its improvement. The esoterics, on the other
hand, made the powers of the will greater than they are, and belittled
the light of reason too much. Both scolded the pagans and pagan philosophy, and yet both originated in pagan wisdom and its students. The
orthodox originated in rarefied Platonic disputations about the divine
being, while the esoterics originated from the Platonic doctrines on the
goal of true wisdom, namely, union with God through the path of purification and illumination. Thus everything led either to vain specula-
tion or to enthusiasm, and simple, active Christianity was forgotten.

Both parties impressed on the laity that it is more blessed to give than
to receive, only for them this meant that it is more blessed to receive than
to give. Both sought to substantiate the claims of their teachings with
pious deceptions, the fabrication of many evidently false stories, and
with false miracles. Both began on opposing paths, but they ended up
in the same place. The orthodox had tasted too much of the sweetness
of worldly honor and splendor, wealth too, so that initially they laughed

at the shy and melancholic esoterics. But later on, when they saw that this had accomplished as little as their persecutions, and that the esoterics were followed by ordinary people, the orthodox came closer to their teachings and accepted their three vows: poverty, chastity, and obedience. They also prescribed certain maxims for their disciples and afterward called them Canons or Regulars, that is, those who live according to a rule of life. In the long run, however, the disciplined life did not suit them, and they began to take the tender souls into consideration and to absolve them, so that the Canons were divided into the Regulars and the Irregulars. Of course, none among the laymen were allowed to laugh or to carp at these contradictory things. The esoterics, on the other hand, at first taught that one should separate oneself from the world and choose the life of a hermit or monk, living alone outside the cities. First they gathered in monasteries, then they moved to the cities, and soon they involved themselves in all kinds of secular affairs. Both groups had finally found the secret of obtaining objectionable things through objectionable means: all lusts through the vow of chastity, all treasures through the vow of poverty, and through the vow of obedience to enjoy, arrogate, and possess all power and honor in the world. Both groups thus became central supports of papalism, with the only difference being that the pope freed the esoterics from the supervision of the orthodox and adopted them as if they were his bodyguards, in order to ensure his safety against the power and reputation of the orthodox. However, he did not entirely suppress the orthodox, so that the esoterics in turn could not get beyond his control. Who could finally explain the similarities of these two objectionable doctrines! These brief remarks may suffice for our orientation. Those who want to know more should read the learned book about the origin and development of monasticism by Rudolf Hospinianus, so important for church history.[28] There they will find enough

---

28. See Rudolf Hospinianus (1547–1626), *De origine et progressu monachatus ac ordinum monasticorum, equitumque militarium omnium, libri VI* (Six books on the origin and the progress of monks and monastic orders, and on all military knights) (Zurich, 1588).

material to continue these comparisons. It should be added that both parties robbed their audience of their God-given proper use of reason: the orthodox by tying reason to their formulas, the esoterics by binding it to inner inspirations. In this way were spread abroad the two worst prejudices of human reasoning: in the former case, human authority, and in the latter, untimely haste.

General igno-
rance and slav-
ery among
Christians,
which origi-
nated through
the suppres-
sion of com-
mon sense and
of the cer-
tainty of sen-
sibility

18. Under these circumstances a coarse ignorance and lack of learning rose among those who called themselves Christians. This ignorance was so bombastic and presumptuous that it could not tolerate even the slightest indication that someone knew something about the proper use of the natural and supernatural lights or the investigation of truth, especially in the theory of human conduct or the doctrine of good and evil. Since Constantine's time all of Christendom has been divided into clergy [*Geistliche*] and laity [*Weltliche*], albeit on the basis of a clear misuse of the Holy Scriptures. According to the Holy Scriptures both teachers and listeners have spiritual [*geistliche*] dispositions, that is, live in this world but not in the foolish way of most people in the world. Yet the teachers alone arrogated the title of the spiritual and labeled the listeners with the scornful title of the laity or profane. Apparently the latter, from the king down to the lowest beggar, are so inept that in their conduct, as well as in their understanding and their will, they are capable of nothing reasonable or pleasing to God, when they want to use their understanding by themselves or read the Holy Scriptures for themselves. If the goal of the laity is to be blessed or to lead a happy life in this world, they would have to believe and to do what the clergy or clerisy prescribed and prompted them to believe and do. For this reason they were excluded from that in which the supernatural light is found: the Holy Scriptures and their use. As for the natural light, they were told that the truths discovered through this would be harmful even in this life, unless they were previously examined and approved by the clergy who alone possess supernatural light. Now it can be understood why we said above that the suppression of the natural light was one of the central pillars of papalism. Once the laity were convinced that they should do and believe everything that the clergy had ordered, and imagined that their temporal

and eternal happiness depended on this conviction, then it is easy to see that they fell into blind obedience, and thus willingly entered into the greatest slavery. As soon as the clerisy had achieved this, it needed no great deliberation or study to bring the laity under their yoke. The clerics increasingly fell ever more deeply into ignorance, to such an extent that they could hardly read and write Latin, let alone engage in useful arts and sciences. If one or other of the laity wanted to use the light of his mind or of the Holy Scriptures to oppose this ignorance and lust for power, he could not do so for fear of his property and his honor or even of being executed as the worst of villains. This became even more pressing after the clergy began to destroy emperors, kings, and princes by excommunication, deposing them from office, and other similar political acts, all because the rulers wanted to use their reason and did not want to be made fools anymore. Most of the laity did not even think about using their sound reason during their military or court service, or in the course of their daily work and agricultural labor. This is partially due to the fact that by nature people live in unreason and foolishness, and it is rare that someone finds the path toward wisdom on his own, if the example and deeds of others do not guide him. This was absent at that time because of the corrupted condition of the clergy. Sound reason was also lacking because the clergy was bent on supporting the desires of the most powerful, the richest, and the most cunning, turning a blind eye toward them no matter what they did. The main thing was that they worshipped the clergy, that they bequeathed them charitable goods, monasteries, hospitals, poorhouses, orphanages, and generous endowments; and that they helped to denounce, drive away, persecute, and even burn the other party that opposed the clergy. The clergy went so far as to deprive the laity of the common certainty of their external senses. If someone induced me so far as to not believe what my senses see, hear, and so on, and if that someone talked me into believing the opposite, then he could make me jump into water or fire at his pleasure. Or he would make me do the most dangerous and adverse things by fooling me into believing that they were the most reasonable, graceful, and useful. If the clergy had not enchanted the senses of the laity in this way, how could they make them believe in the most elevated and most foolish superstitions and idolatry; for example, that real bread—that can be seen by the eyes of all men and which all hands can touch, all noses smell, all tongues taste—is not real bread, but has been changed into someone else's body. John,[29] who proved the honesty of his teaching to his listeners by nothing more powerfully convincing than simply preaching what his eyes had seen, his hands had touched, and his ears had heard, stands in stark contrast to that which the clergy will have us believe; namely, that the only certain thing is that of which my eyes see nothing, my hands cannot touch, but rather in which they feel everywhere the opposite.

Miserable condition of the higher and lower schools. Origin of the four faculties

19. One would not be astonished about all of this if one took a look at the appearance and condition of schools in Christendom during those times. Here is a brief sketch of the state of affairs. After the western empire had been destroyed by several German and Scythian peoples and the oriental empire by the Saracens, public schools were devastated. From the sixth century onward in the western empire they suffered ruin in Italy, France, England, Spain, and Africa; and from the seventh century also in the oriental empire, in Asia, Greece, Egypt, and so on. It is true that in the fifth century St. Benedict had established in Italy many new cloisters and monasteries as well as the rules of life belonging to them, and that he had arranged for schools in them.[30] But these were not public schools, being dedicated solely to monks. So, after the decline of public schools, only monks were regarded as learned people, until King Alfred reestablished public schools at Oxford in England and Charlemagne at Paris in France, after which more and more public schools began to appear.[31] But there is a story behind this: the teachers for the

29. See 1 John 1:1.

30. St. Benedict established twelve monasteries, each containing twelve monks, not far from Subiaco in Italy. In 530 he founded the monastery of Montecassino, where he wrote his influential *Rule of St. Benedict*.

31. After his successful campaigns against the Normans and the Vikings, King Alfred (849–99) promoted public culture and education. He also supported the school of Oxford, which was a precursor of the later university. He followed the example of Charlemagne (768–814), who prescribed that in every cathedral town a school should be established. One of these schools later became the Sorbonne in Paris.

public schools were taken from the monasteries. At that time the greatest ignorance reigned in the monasteries, and anyone who knew something about philosophy, natural philosophy, and mathematics was regarded as a sorcerer. Nobody then knew anything about today's four faculties; that is, the faculties of theology, medicine, law, and philosophy. In the lower and, as we say today, common schools the divisions of rhetoric or today's Donat were taught.[32] In the higher and upper schools there was instruction in the so-called seven liberal arts: grammar, dialectic, rhetoric, and the four mathematical sciences: arithmetic, geometry, astronomy, and music. For the most part they stayed with the first three, and one struggled with them for most of one's life, more than was actually necessary. A more precise investigation of the mathematical sciences was mostly absent, since it was inconvenient for the clergy and monks to train laymen in sciences which do not particularly respect any person's authority, possessing instead confirmation through the senses or reason. These so-called liberal arts were already being taught in the schools of St. Augustine, who had a particular liking for Plato. At that time [during the period of monastic education] nothing was known about metaphysics or ethics. When Aristotle, who had been ignored for a long time, was taken up again by the Saracens and translated into Arabic and then brought to Spain by them, several French professors also acquired a taste for him.[33] These professors also tried to introduce Aristotle into the schools of Paris. But this proved very difficult since, through a decision of the Council of Paris, the older professors forced the pope to ban Aristotle's books together with several works by his first devotees, Peter

32. Thomasius is referring to the divisions or parts of a discourse in classical rhetoric (exordium, propositio, narratio, tractatio, peroratio). In ca. 350 the Roman grammarian Aelius Donatus wrote two Latin grammars that were frequently used during the Middle Ages. For this reason elementary Latin grammar was often called the "Donat."

33. The works of Aristotle were translated into Arabic by Al-Farabi (ca. 950) and later commented on by the Persian physician and philosopher Avicenna (i.e., Ibn Sina, 980–1037), whose works were influential in Islamic-dominated Spain. Because of his influence the works of Aristotle were translated into Latin in Toledo. Another Spanish Islamic scholar, Averroës (i.e., Mohammed ibn Ruschd, 1126–98), played a central role in introducing Aristotle's works into Christian Europe.

Abelard and Peter Lombard.[34] Abelard and Lombard were considered
to be dangerous and suspicious types. In particular St. Bernard helped
to make Abelard into a heretic.[35] When the pope and the clergy realized,
however, that Aristotle's metaphysics, physics, and ethics did not damage their dignity—since Aristotelian philosophy contains little or nothing about the true use of natural light and seemed rather to increase
clerical authority—then the first harsh decrees were very soon changed.
In fact, to the degree that it was separated from the liberal arts, *Real-
philosophie*—or physics, metaphysics, and ethics—was taught publicly
in accordance with the Aristotelian teachings.[36] Theology faculties, in
particular the still well-known Sorbonne, were first founded under the
Capetian dynasty.[37] Afterward the faculties of law were created, first
dealing with imperial and shortly afterward with canon law, until finally
the faculty of medicine was founded, which emerged from the monasteries where it had been hidden for several hundred years. For those who
want to know more, it would do no harm if they carefully read the wonderful dissertation on academic antiquities by the blessed Conring, my
father's *Meditationes de philosopho Artista* (which have been included in
the sixth volume of the Halle *Observationes selectas*), and the treatise on
the choice and order of study by the learned Frenchman Claude Fleury.[38]

34. Peter Abelard (1079–1142) was one of the most famous and independent philosophers of early Scholasticism. In his *Theologia* he tries to harmonize faith and
reason, and he argues against the claim that salvation can be obtained only through
the church's articles of faith. Peter Lombard (1095/1100–1160) taught at the cathedral
school in Paris, becoming a bishop 1159. His compilation *Sententiae in IV libri distinctae* (Four books of sentences) was the most influential medieval textbook for studies in theology.

35. Bernard of Clairvaux (1090–1153) participated in the condemnation of Abelard. Bernard argued that Abelard's theology led to God being dominated by reason.
See Thomasius's remarks on this in paragraph 25 below.

36. That is, philosophy dealing with real things as opposed to the arts of grammar,
rhetoric, and dialectic.

37. Founded by Hugh Capet, who became king of France in 987, the Capetian
dynasty lasted until 1328. The college of Sorbonne was established in the 1250s.

38. Thomasius is referring to *De Antiquitatibus Academicis Dissertationes* (Academic dissertations on antiquity) (Helmstedt, 1651) by the influential political jurist
Hermann Conring (1606–81); to his own father, Jacob Thomasius's, *Meditationes de
philosopho Artista* (Thoughts on the philosopher's art), also in *Observationes Selectae*

The various documents and diplomas by Johannes Launoius[39] are no less helpful. One may also find many useful, pertinent things in Johannes Filesaco, in that he wrote a treatise on the origin of the statutes of the theological faculty in Paris.[40] In any case, one finds a lot about these issues in the notes of my blessed father.

20. The monks who were supposed to teach the youth at the universities were ignoramuses. They were incapable of using their own basic reason. These people, who were supposed to set the minds of others into motion, had to be given certain books as crutches so that their own intellects could be trained. But a secret state-interest was also involved; for if it had been left to the teachers to use their own solid reason on the issues of concern to them, then they would have soon discovered the secret of clericalist and papalist power and its idolatrous standing, and they would have imparted this realization to the laity. Clerical prudence thus required that the teachers be bound to certain books, for if these books were themselves mired in the prejudice of human authority, this prejudice could be more virulently spread to the audience, as the foundation of papalism. The philosophers had so far only taught the seven liberal arts according to Augustine or Cassiodor.[41] Now they also began to explicate Aristotle's books on metaphysics, physics, and ethics. Soon it appeared that Aristotle's *Organon,* as well as the discourses of the philosophy professors were given to the teachers. But since Aristotle had not written anything about mathematics, mathematical studies became increasingly neglected. The theologians took up Peter Lombard's *Sen-*

The useless ethics of Aristotelian philosophy and of the schoolmen in the faculty of philosophy

---

ad rem litterariam spectantes, tomus VI (Select observations on considered literary matters, vol. 6) (Halle, 1706); and to Claude Fleury's *Traité du Choix & de la Methode des Etudes* (Treatise on the choice and method of studies) (Brussels, 1687).

39. See Jean de Launois, *Academia Parisiensis illustrata* (The academies of Paris illustrated) (Paris, 1682ff.).

40. See Jean Filesac, *Statutorum sacrae facultatis theologiae parisiensis origo prisca* (The ancient source of the statutes of the holy theology faculty of Paris) (Paris, 1620).

41. The seven liberal arts are grammar, rhetoric, dialectic, arithmetic, geometry, music, and astronomy. Cassiodor (ca. 477–ca. 565/70), statesman and theologian in the service of the Ostrogoth monarchy, wrote an influential textbook, *De artibus ac disciplines liberalium litterarum* (On the arts and disciplines of liberal letters).

tences,[42] the lawyers the two juristic *corpora* [imperial and canon],[43] and the physicians Galen.[44] Thus each faculty was given as it were its own space in which to exercise its understanding, across whose borders, though, nobody could step (like slaves chained to the galleys).

Let us now see how things stood with moral philosophy and natural law at the universities, and let us begin with the philosophers at that time. Aristotle's *Nichomachean Ethics* and his *Magna Moralia* are not absurd. However, they are filled with unnecessary subtleties and a useless wordiness in the Aristotelian way. Epictetus's small compendium[45] thus contains more about relations and realities than Aristotle's long-winded works. Aristotle, like all pagan philosophers, believed in the principle that correcting the understanding was sufficient for improving the will. In fact he does teach about virtues; yet regarding what they actually consist in, and how true virtues can be distinguished from pseudovirtues, he says little or nothing. Moreover, he says little or nothing about the means of becoming virtuous. It is a fact that he did not write any books on the prudence required to give counsel or on the laws of nature. Theology thus soon usurped ethics, leaving the philosophers with nothing to work with. It is certain that ethics was so poorly taught by the first philosophers at the universities established by the pope that it could not attract anybody. The profession of the politician [*Politiker*] did not develop until much later. Mr. Pufendorf has remarked in his treatise on papal monarchy that it was one of the secrets of the papalist state to refrain from teaching politics at the universities, or else to do so only

42. Peter Lombard, *Sententiae in IV libri distinctae,* see note 34.

43. Thomasius refers to the Roman *Corpus iuris civilis* (Body of civil law), codified in 533 and 534 by the Roman emperor Justinian, and the laws of the Roman Catholic Church, the *Corpus iuris canonici* (Body of canon law).

44. Galen was the most important physician during Roman antiquity. In his numerous books he made a synthesis of the different medical doctrines and constructed a uniform system of medicine that remained influential until the seventeenth century.

45. Epictetus was a Stoic philosopher who lived between 55 and 135. The "small compendium" is his *Encheiridion,* which contains his main doctrines as compiled by his student Arrian.

according to the interests of the clergy.[46] That is why even the term *politics* has become tarnished and suspect. We will talk more about this elsewhere, since politics and natural law and also moral philosophy—which are remarkably different from each other—are frequently confused.

21. The *Corpus juris* received by the lawyers contains a lot of fine things about the natural law, but it was of little use to law professors at law schools.[47] First of all, Roman jurists had touched on natural law only slightly, in their occasional discussions of the law of nature and nations. The *Corpus juris* thus did not contain satisfactory advice on how to distinguish between natural law and specifically Roman law. The lawyers themselves disagreed about this, and the *Corpus juris* was thus patched together from conflicting opinions, regardless of differences in levels of learning among the jurists. Even if not all of the jurists who compiled the *Pandects* were deeply learned, still, most of them were, and they were quite familiar with natural law.[48] The jurists who lived during the time of the Roman emperors, however, and whose laws are included in the codes, were no longer as learned as their predecessors, since at this time the era of the uneducated had already begun in the Roman Empire. Under these circumstances it is not surprising that the *Corpus juris* itself contains teachings which confuse the general law of nations with the Roman law. This occurs, for example, in the chapters on paternal authority, on the authority of masters over their servants, on the ways of acquiring property according to law of nations, on imprisonment, and on the right [of exiles or refugees] to return. I have already shown in a separate treatise that the good lawyers—who had advised

The miserable condition of natural law among the jurists

---

46. See Samuel Pufendorf, *Basilii Hyperetae Historische und politische Beschreibung der geistlichen Monarchie des Stuhls zu Rom* (Basilius Hypereta's historical and political description of the clerical monarchy in Rome), published for the first time in 1679; a Latin version appeared in 1688. In 1714 Thomasius published a new edition accompanied by his commentary.

47. That is, the *Corpus juris civilis,* the body of Roman law, also known as Justinian law or civil law, which provided the legal framework for the Holy Roman Empire during the Middle Ages and was also adapted for a similar use by the early modern territorial states of continental Europe.

48. The *Pandects* are the second part of the *Corpus juris civilis.*

Diocletian[49] to reverse contracts of sale if someone was injured by more than half—understood neither moral philosophy nor the law or nature, and still less the nature of buying and selling. Nor did they understand that this law of Diocletian's was unjust and had not found practical application, indeed, could not find practical application. But let the *Corpus juris* be as it may, the professors of the newly established faculty of law were supposed to explain it, and they were such people who had a lot of perseverance and diligence and had even memorized the *Corpus juris* by heart. But this did not help the cause. They lacked the basic means for interpreting the *Corpus juris,* namely philosophy,[50] and through it ethics and politics, as well as knowledge of Roman history. The smartest and the most notable among them wrote plenty of commentaries on the *Corpus juris,* and these glosses soon attained the same standing as the laws themselves. We can find signs everywhere, though, that ethics and natural law were not the forte of these good people, not through any fault of theirs but because of the circumstances of their period. Even though many followed who wanted to combine Roman history and other congenial studies with jurisprudence, nevertheless, they became for the most part addicted to grammatical disputations or got stuck within the limits of Roman law and only very rarely engaged with natural law and the law of nations. Both classes[51] maintained the general view that disputes between crowned heads like kings and princes could and should be solved according to the *Corpus juris.* Thus, they tried to act accordingly whenever there was an opportunity, as was the case with the Spaniards Didacus Covarrubias and Ferdinand Vasquius or, among the Frenchmen, François Hotman and Jean Bodin.[52] Concerning this

49. Diocletian (243–313) was Roman emperor from 284 to 305.

50. Here Thomasius is using philosophy in the broad sense, to refer to the disciplines of the philosophy or arts faculty, as the rest of the sentence makes clear.

51. That is, both the strict glossators and also the jurists who had taken an interest in Roman history.

52. Didacus Covarruvias (1512–77) and Fernando Vazquez de Menchaca (1512–69) were exponents of Spanish "Second Scholasticism," whose jurisprudence influenced the development of early modern natural law thought. François Hotman (1524–90) was professor of Roman law at the universities of Strasbourg, Valence, Bourges, and Genf. Nevertheless he criticized the Roman law in his *Anti-Tribonianus* and argued

matter there might be more to say about the canon lawyers, since the pope had given the *Corpus juris canonici,* as it is known, to the canonists with the aim of them further undermining the legists, who were beginning everywhere to defend the rights of secular authority against the tyranny of the clerics. The *Corpus juris canonici* considers natural law as little as the imperial *Corpus juris [civilis]* considers divine laws. But the *Corpus juris canonici* contains more and it is arranged in a such way that a credulous person would swear that everything was only of a divine and suprarational character. However, anyone who scrutinizes the secrets of the papalist clergy will quickly see that canon law aims only at subverting all principles of sound reason concerning the true difference between good and evil, as well as the fundamental principles of government and secular authority. Under the guise of zeal for the glory of God and with much chatter, clerical power attempts to arrogate these principles to itself. It is much to be wished that Protestant lawyers would show in even more detail the politically erroneous state-secrets of papalist law. I am certain that not a single title can be found in either Gratian's *Decretum* or in the *Decretals*[53] to which such political maxims of the clergy have not been added.

22. The faculty of theology seems to have originated in the following way: The school in Paris was unhappy with Peter Abelard and Peter Lombard, because they began to teach Aristotle instead of Augustine. But it happened soon afterward that Peter Lombard, who had been the teacher of the prince, became bishop of Paris. As such, he used his authority to give great weight to Aristotelian teachings, obtaining permission from the kings of France to establish a separate faculty of theology at the university. Instead of explaining the Holy Scriptures, the professors of theology then explained Peter Lombard's *Sentences.* This work

Similar condition of the university theologians who at the same time continued the old sect of the orthodox

for national law codifications. Jean Bodin (1529/30–1596), in his *Six livres de la République* (Six books of the republic), developed a modern concept of sovereignty that was based on the Roman law's idea of "imperium."

53. Gratian's *Decretum* refers to the collection of church laws compiled by the twelfth-century canonist Gratian that eventually formed the first part of the *Corpus juris canonici*. The *Decretals* refer to the papal decrees that were added subsequently.

consisted of four books. In the first he dealt with the unity of God and with the Holy Trinity. In the second he dealt with creation, with angels and humans, and with God's grace; in the third with the incarnation of Christ, with virtues and vices; and in the fourth with the sacraments, death, the Day of Judgment, eternal life, and the torments of hell. It is likely that in these books Lombard tried to unite the teachings of Augustine with those of Aristotle. The entire work contains a mishmash of theology and philosophy. The Holy Scriptures are explained with the principles of pagan philosophy, while in moral philosophy and natural law the old ignorance is perpetuated. Lombard's book represented the basis for the faculty of theology, and the professors of theology competed in writing glosses on it, just as the lawyers did with their *Corpus juris.* William of Auxerre, Albertus Magnus, Thomas Aquinas, Bonaventura, William Durandus, John Duns Scotus, Ockham, Estius, and many others teach about Lombard in their commentaries.[54] Since they were not of the same opinion in their explanations and since each one of them wanted to be right, various sects consequently came into being among these orthodox Scholastics, such as the Albertists, the Thomists, the Scotists, and the Ockhamists, among which the reputation of Thomas Aquinas prevailed over all others. The latter had not only written a commentary on Lombard, but had also composed a new system of theology. Many thus forgot Lombard in order to write about Thomas's commentary, including Thomas de Vio Cajetan, Bartholomew Medina, Gabriel Vasquez, and Francisco Suárez.[55] One should not expect anything rea-

54. These philosophers and theologians are leading representatives of high and late Scholasticism: William of Auxerre (early thirteenth century), Albert the Great (1206–80), Thomas Aquinas (1224/25–1274), Giovanni Fidanza Bonaventure (1221–74), Gulielmus (William) Durandus (the Elder, ca. 1237–96), John Duns Scotus (1265/66?–1308), William of Ockham (1290/1300?–1349), Willem Hessels van Estius (1542–1613).

55. Thomas Aquinas (1224–74) wrote his commentary on the *Sentences* of Peter Lombard around 1254–56 and his *Summa theologiae* between 1266 and 1273. The latter aimed to synthesize Augustine's Platonic theology with Aristotelian philosophy. During the sixteenth century Aquinas's *Summa* replaced Lombard's *Sentences* as the central text for theological training in universities, and commentaries on Aquinas were central to the Spanish "Second Scholasticism," which emerged at this time. Cajetan (1469–1534) and Medina (1527–81) were Dominicans, Vasquez (1549/51–1604) and Suárez (1548–1617) Jesuits.

sonable from any of them, since everything issues in subtleties, authority, and dogmatism. Even teachings belonging to moral philosophy and natural law began to be appropriated by the theology faculty, under various titles. These included such titles as the *Summulas* of Sylvester Prierias, *Relectiones morales* by Francisco de Vitoria, the *Resolutiones morales* by Antonius Diana, the *Theologiam moralem* of Antonius de Escobar, *Casus conscientiae* by Bartholomew Medina, the same by Johannes Azorius, books called *de justitia & jure* by Dominic de Soto, Ludovicus Molina, Leonard Lessius, and others.[56] The Jesuits in particular aimed to teach the most damaging and most dangerous moral principles drawn from many periods. They continue to do so today, for example, Gabriel Vasquez, Francisco Suárez, Johannes Azorius, Ludovicus Molina, Leonard Lessius, Antonius de Escobar, all of whom were Jesuits.[57] In addition to that which has been briefly sketched here, one can read a learned book by Adam Tribbechov, written in Latin in Giessen in 1665, dealing with the Scholastics and the way they ruined the sciences of divine and human things.[58] In it he diligently compiled everything concerning this matter, and this book deserves to be published anew. Rudolf Hospinianus has

---

56. Sylvester Prierias (1456–1523) was a Dominican inquisitor in Lombardy, a witch-hunter, and one of Luther's early opponents. Antonino Diana (1586–1663) belonged to the Theatine order and was a noted casuist. The Spanish Jesuit Antonio Escobar y Mendoza (1589–1669) was also a casuist and moral theologian. Azorius or Juan Azor (1535–1603) also belonged to the Spanish Jesuits and was an influential moral theologian. Francisco de Vitoria (1492–1546) was a Spanish Dominican theologian instrumental in the form of Thomist natural law and political theology known as the School of Salamanca. Bartholomew Medina (1527–81) and Dominico de Soto (1494–1560)—both Dominicans—were active in the Salmanca school, as was the Jesuit Ludovicus Molina (1535–1600), while Leonard Lessius (1554–1623) was a Jesuit in the low countries.

57. Founded in 1534 by Ignatius Loyola, the Society of Jesus spearheaded the Catholic church's attempt to turn back the Protestant Reformation. The Jesuit order sought to tighten Catholic doctrine and enforce theological discipline within the church, becoming the dominant force in Catholic universities across Europe and playing a leading role in Second Scholasticism.

58. See Adam Tribbechov (1641–87), *De doctoribus scholasticis et corrupta per eos divinarum humanarumque rerum scientiae* (On the scholastic doctors and their corruption of the divine and human sciences) (Giessen, 1665).

also written much concerning the origin and advance of Jesuits in his books.[59]

Scholars who had discovered this miserable condition even before the Reformation

23. In all times one finds various men who contradicted the confusion and blindness propagated by the orthodox Scholastics. But the strongest party eventually suppressed and persecuted them as heretics in the time-honored way, so that little testimony concerning them has reached us. With regard to their works, several were published right before and around the time of the Reformation. In his chronicle Aventin complained much about the corruption of true scholarship brought by scholastic theology.[60] Similarly, in several books on the causes of the corruption of the disciplines, Juan Luis Vives dealt with this theme in the most varied parts of philosophy.[61] The aim of Cornelius Agrippa's book on the vanity of the sciences is specifically to show this vanity of the sciences as they were then undertaken by the professors in the universities.[62] Johannes Reuchlin lanced this boil very artfully in his *Epistolis obscurorum virorum,* after the orthodox had earlier irritated him sufficiently and attempted to label him a heretic.[63] However, no one damaged the Scholastics more severely than Erasmus of Rotterdam. Erasmus not only revealed the errors of scholastic theology and philosophy in his writings,

---

59. See, for example, Rudolf Hospinianus, *Historia iesuitica, Hoc est, De origine, regulis constitutionibus, privilegiis, incrementis, progressu et propagatione ordinis Iesuitarum* (History of the Jesuits, that is, on the origin, rules, constitutions, privileges, growth, progress, and propagation of the Jesuit order) (Zurich, 1619).

60. See note 22 in this chapter.

61. Born in Spain and teaching in England and the Netherlands, Juan Luis Vives (1492–1540) was a well-known humanist and philosopher. For examples of the works to which Thomasius refers, see his *De disciplines Libri XII* (Twelve books on the disciplines) (Bruges, 1531); *De initiis, sectis et laudibus philosophiae* (On the beginnings, sects, and merits of philosophy) (Leuven, 1518); and *Introductio ad veram sapientiam* (Introduction to true wisdom) (Bruges, 1524).

62. Heinrich Cornelius Agrippa von Nettesheim (1486–1535), *De incertitudine et vanitate omnium Scientiarum et artium et de excellentia verbi Dei* (On the uncertainty and vanity of all sciences and arts and on the excellence of the word of God) (1530).

63. Johannes Reuchlin (1455–1522) was one of the most important humanists in Germany. The *Epistolae obscurorum virorum* (Letters of obscure men) (Hagenau, 1515/16) were written by supporters of Reuchlin and contained a satirical attack on scholastic method.

but also painted a vivid portrait, in sharp and biting tones, of the malice, foolishness, and ignorance of the monks and professors, partly in his *Colloquies* and partly in his book called the *Praise of Folly*.[64] The blessed chancellor Esaias von Pufendorf often took these two books by Erasmus on his trips as a diversion.[65] When I saw the *Colloquies* on his desk while I was traveling through Leipzig twenty years ago, I asked him what he was doing with it. He told me that even the cleverest would find instruction in this book by Erasmus and in the other one, the *Morias Enkomion*. Since that time I found this to be true through frequent reading, and I offer this good advice to all those striving to recognize the masked papalism of our times in places where one would least expect to find it.

24. But we should not forget the esoterics or mystics. We have already seen that their teachings contradicted those of the orthodox, but that they fell into the same abuse as the orthodox and became a pillar of papalism. In his *Schediasmata historico*—which I republished several years ago under the title *Origines historiae philosophicae et ecclesiasticae*—my blessed father has compiled many remarkable things regarding the origin and progress of mystic theology.[66] Reflective people who want to read about this will find this little treatise very helpful indeed. Briefly, the state of affairs is as follows: It is known that the Jews had a secret doctrine called Kabbalah, which they claim God had given to Moses alongside the commandments. Moses had passed on this *Doctrina cabbalistica* through oral revelation to Joshua or to the seventy-two elders,

On the origin of esoteric theology

---

64. Erasmus of Rotterdam (1469–1536), theologian and leading humanist. The two works mentioned here are: *Morias Enkomion sive Laus Stultitiae* (Basel, 1511) and *Familiarum colloquiorum formulae* (Basel, 1518). In English: *Desiderius Erasmus, Praise of Folly*, translated with an introduction and notes by B. Radice (London: Folio Society, 1974); and *Desiderius Erasmus, Colloquies*, translated and annotated by C. R. Thompson. *Collected Works of Erasmus*, vol. 40 (Toronto: University of Toronto Press, 1997).

65. Esaias von Pufendorf (1628–89), secretary of state in Sweden, brother of Samuel Pufendorf.

66. Jacob Thomasius, *Origines Historiae philosophicae et ecclesiasticae* (Origins of philosophical and ecclesiastic history) (Leipzig, 1665).

and they passed it on to others in the same way.[67] There is no doubt that many of the learned Jews who converted to Christianity were fond of this kabbalistic doctrine and that it was probably the initial foundation for the esoteric theology. But it is equally certain that pagan philosophers like Plato and the Stoics contributed their share. Even during the times of the apostles, Simon Magus introduced an abominable heresy into Christianity.[68] As the basis of his sect he took Zoroaster's teachings of the two gods, a good and an evil one,[69] and from the common pagan philosophy he took two eternal principles, God and prime matter, on which he later framed a wicked and dissolute life. The heretics who descended from Simon spread under various names in the first and second centuries. Following his doctrines and his way of life, they called themselves the "spiritually discerning" (Gnostics) and the "perfect ones," despising all those who did not side with them. Since at that time the teachers of the Christian church had to engage with these people, they allowed that true Christians should also be perfectly spiritually gifted with knowledge of holy things, although they showed Christians a quite different way of attaining this knowledge, perfection, and spirituality. Clement of Alexandria developed this, writing a book about it and striving for it in all his writings.[70] Yet the dear man was unfortunate in that he could write neither clearly nor properly. Mixing everything together in a disorderly way, he earnestly strove to render his writings unintelligible, so that only the "perfect ones" could understand these secret things. This otherwise famous teacher of the church fell much in love with pagan, Stoic, and Platonic philosophy and grafted parts of it onto

67. Joshua, Moses's successor, led the Israelites over the Jordan River. The seventy-two elders were representatives of the Israelites and are mentioned several times in the Book of Exodus.

68. Simon the Magician was the leader of the Gnostics and in the view of the Fathers of the Church the author of all heresies. See, for example, Acts of the Apostles 8:9–24.

69. Zoroaster, who lived in Persia around 600 B.C., founded a religion based on the dualism between good and evil.

70. Titus Flavius Clemens, called Clement of Alexandria, lived at the beginning of the third century. Thomasius seems to be referring to Clement's *Stromateis* (Miscellanies).

apostolic Christian doctrine wherever possible. He transferred entire Stoic paradoxes to Christian doctrine. He borrowed from Plato the doctrine of the emanation of the human soul from the divine being, together with the doctrine of the four degrees of virtue (namely, that through certain virtues man would turn from beast to human, through others from human to angel, then from angel to god, and finally from a god to the highest god). He also copied the (later so-called) threefold way of mystical theology, which the falsely named Dionysius the Areopagite presented at great length.[71] A lot of the Jewish Kabbalah was also mixed into these Platonist fictions, as is clear if we compare Dionysius's teachings on the classes of angels with those of the Jewish Kabbalists. During the lifetime of Clement of Alexandria, at the end of the second century, this esoteric doctrine with its suppression of sound reason had already progressed so far that by the fourth century it had given rise to a particular kind of heretic, the Messalians.[72] They did no work of any kind apart from begging or, as we would say today, they went with pious souls from one prayer meeting or spiritual exercise to the next, thereafter boasting of secret revelations. That is why they were also called enthusiasts. Monasticism contributed much to this. In fact, in the fifth century this esoteric monastic doctrine, that man can live in this world free of all passions, finally gave birth to Pelagianism.[73]

25. As we have already explained above, the esoterics and the orthodox cultivated opposing doctrines, but they united in order to support the power of the clergy and the papacy. There was a similar situation when Aristotle's teachings were used as the foundation of theology and phi-

The state of esoteric theology among schoolmen

71. The name Dionysius the Areopagite is a pseudonym used by an unknown author of Neoplatonic texts written at the beginning of the sixth century. The real Dionysius the Areopagite, who is mentioned in Acts of the Apostles 17:34, was a member of the *areopag* (court of justice in Athens) and was converted by Paul.

72. The Messalians were an ascetic movement that arose in Mesopotamia around 360. Its followers wanted to expel the inner demon by permanent prayer as a way of reaching the Holy Ghost.

73. Pelagianism denies original sin and emphasizes humanity's freedom of will and moral abilities, thereby downplaying Augustinianism's insistence on the necessity of divine grace for salvation. The term goes back to Pelagius, a British theologian who lived and taught in Rome until ca. 410 when he went to North Africa, following the fall of Rome. His teachings were condemned at the Council of Carthage in 418.

losophy in the universities. Initially, there could not have been much unity between the orthodox Scholastics and the esoterics, because Aristotle and Plato were not bosom friends. The orthodox Scholastics tried to elevate their Aristotle and to push Plato aside, but the latter returned as the foundation of the esoteric theology. It is known from church history that the monk Bernard of Clairvaux, ranked by scholars of mysticism as a leading figure, vehemently persecuted the first orthodox Scholastic, Peter Abelard, simply on account of his Aristotelianism, even labeling him a heretic.[74] Of course, nothing good came out of these two teachers and their followers. Nonetheless, the two varieties agreed in this: just as the orthodox began to turn dogmatic theology into an art form or into certain systems or compendia of maxims, so too Richard of St. Victor began at the same time to turn esoteric theology into a system.[75] This happened in the twelfth century. Soon thereafter John Scotus Eruigena translated the work of Dionysius on the lordship of the clergy into Latin and promoted Dionysius's mystical doctrines.[76] At the beginning of the thirteenth century, these doctrines gave rise to the heresy of Almaric, whose teachings nearly resemble those of today's Spinozism.[77] The two great minds among the orthodox Scholastics, Albertus Magnus[78] and Thomas Aquinas, flourished during the thirteenth century. They began to unify the otherwise opposing lines of thought by commenting on Lombard's *Sentences* while also writing numerous mystical

74. Bernard of Clairvaux (1090–1153). For Abelard, see note 34 in this chapter.

75. Richard of St. Victor (d. 1173) became prior at the abbey of St. Victor in Paris in 1160. As a student of Hugh of St. Victor he argued for an encyclopedic concept of science, which led to a theology based on Scripture.

76. Johannes Scotus Eriugena (ca. 810–77) taught liberal arts at the palace school of Charles II in Paris. Apart from his Latin translation of the works of Dionysius the Areopagite (see note 71 in this chapter), he also translated Greek authors (e.g., Gregory of Nyssa). He saw the unity of true religion and true philosophy in their common origin in God.

77. Almaricus of Bena (d. 1206) taught liberal arts in Paris. His central aim was to synthesize the cosmological and historical revelation of God with the help of the dialectical argument that God is everywhere and God causes everything. These arguments indeed have a certain similarity to the pantheism of Baruch de Spinoza (1632–77) and the Spinozists.

78. Albert the Great maintained the compatibility of Christian belief and Aristotelian philosophy.

books. They confirmed once again that the two ways of writing and teaching agreed in robbing men of their sound reason and therefore of their freedom, and forced their souls, bodies, and conscience under the yoke of tyranny.

26. One might have thought that in addition to other good works, the reformers Luther and Zwingli[79] together with other instruments of God, would have introduced the difference and the proper use of the natural and supernatural light into both the church pulpit and the university podium. In their writings and books against the papacy, one finds many fine sentences dedicated to this end. Thus they readily rebuke Aristotelian philosophy, vividly portraying its uselessness, which leads only to strife. In their conflict with the papal doctrine of transubstantiation they show that the natural light cannot be completely set aside in theological questions, and that the words of the Holy Scriptures cannot be explained in an unreasonable way. However, the transformation of such deeply rooted errors can be achieved neither by the work of a single person nor in a single lifetime. The unfortunate quarrel that arose and then escalated between the two reformers was thus one of the major reasons why this very necessary investigation made no progress. This quarrel was over the article of faith dealing with the Eucharist and the central question of the use of natural light in explaining the Holy Scriptures. Through this dispute the two doctrines of the orthodox Scholastics and the esoteric theologians made their way back into the two Protestant communities. Scholastic doctrine recommended itself under a similar pretext to that by which Platonist doctrine was adopted by the Christians after Christ's ascent; namely, that by using such doctrine one could more readily do battle with the papalist theologians—who fought with the sword of Scholasticism—and thereby counter the charge of ignorance in theological matters. For many centuries after Christ's birth orthodox and then scholastic teaching had thus equipped theologians with spiritual weapons needed to keep the wolves away from the sheepfold of the

The reasons why the often-discussed misery could not be eliminated during and after the Reformation. Revival of the orthodox doctrine

---

79. Ulrich Zwingli (1484–1531) was a leader of the Swiss Reformation who had begun as a follower of Erasmus but was radicalized under the influence of Luther.

Christian churches, by means of Platonic, and then Aristotelian arts of disputation. It was thought that if the denunciation of heretics did not proceed apace, then the professors would have nothing to dispute about at the universities. Polemical theology would thus fall by the wayside, and the cost of maintaining theology professors would be in vain. This restless and fractious theology served to perpetuate the quarrel between the papalist and the Protestant theologians, as well as preventing peace between the two Protestant churches. Yes, if they had nothing better to do, these theologians fought amongst themselves and denounced each other as heretics year after year, as church history attests with innumerable examples throughout the centuries and, especially, in each decade following the Reformation.

Revival of esoteric theology 27. Nonetheless, esoteric theology also spread among the Protestants. Many causes contributed to this fact. First of all, the blessed Luther had the *German Theology*, a mystical booklet, republished and provided a preface for it.[80] Luther's entire doctrine and his life show that he was not a mystical theologian. Vexation with the scholastic teaching, with whose intrigues and tricks he was familiar from the monastery, led him to do this [publication]. He also found that the mystical writings pressed for a holy Christian life and that the sharpening of the understanding for its own sake was not prized by them, as it had been in scholastic doctrine. Many Christian theologians felt sorrow in their hearts that Protestant Christianity should be continuously kept in discord through the theological quarrels. They witnessed the oafish and dissolute character of the university students, especially the students of theology, and saw that if such dissolute people were appointed to churches and schools, an unchristian dissolute life would spread through all ranks of Protestant Christians. They believed that it would be better if they taught a peaceful

---

80. See Martin Luther, *Eyn deutsch Theologia. Das ist eyn edles Buchleyn von rechtem verstand, was Adam und Christus sey, und wie Adam yn uns sterben, und Christus ersteen sall* (A German theology. That is a noble booklet showing rightly what Adam and Christ are, and how Adam should die and Christ be resurrected in us) (Wittenberg, 1518).

theology instead of theological polemics, because Christ was called the Prince of Peace and had left peace and love as a sign to his disciples and students. But they could not readily speak of all this, owing to the power and standing of scholastic doctrine. Johannes Valentin Andreae was a clever and thoughtful theologian who wrote at the beginning of the seventeenth century, and his writings can be recommended to all impartial lovers of the truth.[81] In various ways—sometimes in short conversations, sometimes in instructive and pregnant fables and poems, and also in other ways—Andreae vividly portrayed the misery and the general corruption of Christendom, especially with regard to the universities, providing advice on how to remedy this ill. It is highly regrettable that this learned and Christian man fell into the hands of the mystical theology of those ignorant times, for he fared like all mystics. In their discovery of general corruption and misery, and in their exposure of the folly of scholastic teaching, they are incomparable, they are great and to be praised for upholding a virtuous Christian life. When it comes to how this is to be implemented, however, their counsels are inadequate. The writings of the good Andreae, especially those dealing with the creation of a Christian republic, show that this was also the case with him.

28. So, at the beginning of the seventeenth century, moral philosophy, ethics, natural law, and the like were in a pitiful and terminal condition, among both Catholics and Protestants. In their books called *On Justice and Right* (or whatever other titles they used), the Catholic schoolmen taught everything needed to buttress the standing of the pope and the clergy and to keep the secular authorities and other laity under their thumb. When it suited their purposes, they mixed natural and international law, Mosaic, Judaic, Greek, Roman, imperial, and papal laws, copying happily from each other. They drove kings into illegitimate wars

Summary condition of moral philosophy and the natural law at the beginning of the seventeenth century

81. Johann Valentin Andreae (1586–1654) was a Lutheran theologian who criticized the science of his times in his writings on the Rosicrucians. In his *Rei publicae christianopolitanae descriptio* (Description of the republic Christianopolis) (1619) he presented a utopian image of a Christian community whose devotion to science and erudition precluded social and theological conflict.

under the pretense of spreading the name of Christ and bringing the infidels under the yoke of the Christian religion. Drawing on the works of Aristotle and their own books, they knew how to present such wars as lawful and laudable. Everything the laity did out of obedience to the clergy was supposed to be good and right, even deserving of heaven. The things that the laity did according to their sound reason, however, or according to the clear words of the Holy Scriptures, were supposed to be evil, unjust, and deserving of hellfire, if this was not in accord with the purposes of the Scholastics. The Jesuit Mariana even defended the notion that kings who followed the wrong religion could be murdered.[82] The jurists supported the Scholastics, partly for fear of being branded heretics if they failed to do so, and partly because the Scholastics frequently cited and praised imperial law in their treatises. But this also happened because when they dealt with justice and injustice, the jurists were accustomed to deriving everything from imperial and canon law, as if the two *corpora* provided the core of natural law and the law of nations, from which conflicts between great rulers had to be settled. Never less than astute, the Jesuits supported both sides of the theological divide. Some of them spread the doctrines of the Scholastics, while others sought to unify esoteric theology with scholastic. Not only the founder of the society, Ignatius Loyola,[83] known for his esoterica, but also Francisco Suárez[84] at the beginning of the seventeenth century and soon thereafter Maximilian Sandaeus[85] began to present mystical theology using scholastic method. As a result of the fact that the *Augsburg Confession*[86] is oriented around a theological system and not around

82. In his *De rege et regis institutione* (On the king and the institution of the king) (1599), Juan de Mariana S.J. (1536–1624) developed a theory of tyrannicide by purporting to distinguish tyrants from kings.

83. See note 57 in this chapter.

84. Francisco Suárez S.J. (1548–1617) was one of the most important exponents of Spanish Second Scholasticism, writing influential treatises on metaphysics and natural law.

85. Maximilian Sandaeus S.J. (1578–1656) was famous for his *Theologica mystica* (1627).

86. The *Augsburg Confession* is the declaration of the Lutheran articles of faith. It was written by Philipp Melanchthon and presented to Emperor Charles V in January 1530.

moral philosophy, natural law, or the *Corpus juris,* Protestant theologians, jurists, and philosophers (the ones concerned with the difference between good and evil, justice and injustice) allowed themselves to follow Catholic writers on these questions without any embarrassment. In their disputations, treatises, compendia, and systems, the Protestant philosophers thus copied the Catholic authors to their heart's content, depending on whether they felt drawn toward theology or to scholastic philosophy, toward the mystics or toward the imperial or canon laws. Thus it happened in Protestant universities that ethics and jurisprudence were thrown together from many, sometimes opposed writers, without a proper basis. In questions of law and of conscience, many words and opinions from various authorities were compiled, but with precious little grounding or understanding. If a mystic had dealt with the topic, then reason was cast away and faith installed in its place, or whatever the spirit had just delivered to this kind of esoteric teacher.

29. Who could imagine that this general corruption among Christians, Protestant and Catholic — that this confusion, abuse, and suppression of the light of nature so deeply rooted for thousands of years — could be purged and rectified? But nothing is impossible for Providence. It does everything in its time, and when error rose highest, the breakthrough of truth was nearest. Specious nonsense came from the teachers of the pulpit and the podium. All three faculties—theology, jurisprudence, and philosophy—were taken in by the glitter. But divine wisdom stirred a man who taught neither from the pulpit nor the podium, who was no professor of theology or law or philosophy, but who was a profound theologian, an excellent jurist, and a solid philosopher. The evil had been spread abroad by scholastic orthodoxy and esoteric theology, so he who would begin to root out this evil could be neither scholastic nor mystic. However, he had to understand the Scholastics and grasp the inadequacy of their doctrine. (No one can understand the mystics because they strive to write in an incomprehensible way and want to eradicate reason completely.) He had to have experienced the persecution of the Scholastics and also had to be urged by other scholars, who were not Scholastics, to undertake this endeavor. He had to deal carefully with the moral philosophy of the Scholastics, in order to avoid exciting

Divine Providence uses Hugo Grotius as its instrument to bring natural law into the light

their wrath too strongly against the reasonable moral philosophy that he was developing. On the other hand, he did not have to fear their hatred too much because he could expect protection from elsewhere. This was the incomparable Hugo Grotius who can never be praised enough.[87] Everything we have said so far is true of him. One could expand at length on this portrayal if the pen were not already exhausted and drawing near to the conclusion. To put it briefly, he was already more learned in his youth than many professors will ever become. Early on he was appointed to important political offices in his homeland. His misfortune or, rather, his fortune caused him to side with the weakest party during the emerging internal unrest in his country. For this reason he was condemned to lifelong imprisonment. Through the loyalty of his wife he was liberated in a wondrous way.[88] France offered him refuge, and the famous parliamentary adviser Peiresc encouraged him to purge the vain glitter from the truth in moral philosophy, and to compose a law of nations in accordance with the true natural light.[89] This Grotius did. In order to show that conflicts among princes, which commonly give rise to wars, should not be decided by Justinian or canon law, but by the natural law alone, he entitled his book *On the Right of War and Peace*.[90] He proceeded very

87. Hugo Grotius (1583–1645) was a Dutch humanist scholar active in philology, history, jurisprudence, and theology, and the author of a natural-law theory based on human sociality. He was also a poet and a politician. As a syndic of Rotterdam, he was a member of the Dutch Estates and closely allied with Jan van Oldenbarnevelt, the de facto prime minister of the Dutch Republic. When van Oldenbarnevelt fell, Grotius's support of liberal Calvinist religion and politics led to his jailing by the strict Calvinist political faction. After escaping, he lived in exile in Paris, becoming a Swedish ambassador to the French court in 1634. In 1644 he was recalled by the Swedish queen. He died the following year on his way from Sweden to Holland after a shipwreck on the Baltic Sea.

88. With the help of his wife, Grotius escaped, hidden in a chest of books.

89. Nicolas-Claude Fabri de Peiresc (1580–1637) was one of the great humanist scholars of the time and the center of an international network of correspondence.

90. The full Latin title is *De iure belli ac pacis libri tres in quibus Jus naturae et Gentium, item Juris Publici praecipua explicantur*. The book was first published in 1625 and became the most important early modern text on law in general and natural law in particular. "Iure" in the title is translated either as "law" or as "right," according to one's interpretation of Grotius's theory.

cautiously, however, and even if he sought to isolate and to separate those laws that the Scholastics had previously confused—the divine law, the universal, the Mosaic, and all human laws—he did not want to fall out with them completely and immediately. Therefore he praised them in his preface and tried to unite their obscure and partially false principles of natural law with Cicero's viewpoint.[91] He thus avoided being attacked as viciously as others later would be when they dropped the mask and openly impugned the scholastic obsessions. In a word, Grotius was the tool which God's wisdom used to lift the natural light's long-standing confusion with the supernatural light and to provide it with a new beginning. I say beginning, for just as God does not suddenly change night to day, so it is with errors and truth. Dawn glows before the day breaks, and between the break of day and the brightness of noon there is also a great difference. However, the glory belongs to Grotius, who broke the ban first and who showed others the way to separate truth from errors.

30. In rendering this wonderful book of Grotius's in the German language, the translator has thus performed a truly useful service.[92] Until now, even in Protestant universities the common error persisted that learned works could not be presented in the German language. We did not notice that this error originates in the secret political machinations of the pope. Were it to become the fashion to teach wisdom at the universities in the mother tongue, then the Scholastics might lose their authority. Is there anything that habit cannot contribute to the prejudice of human authority? Even if those in authority at the universities quarrel over the most trivial things, the poor students imagine them to be the most secret treasures of wisdom, just because they are in Latin and the unlettered cannot understand the substance. If one presented these mag-

Particular benefit of the German translation of Grotius

---

91. Marcus Tullius Cicero's (106–43 B.C.) book *De officiis* (On duties) was an important source for Grotius and generally played an influential role as a mediator between the natural law of antiquity and modern natural law.

92. The translator of *De iure belli ac pacis* was Philipp Balthasar Sinold von Schütz (1657–1742), a well-known journalist and Pietist poet. The translation was published in 1707, when Sinold von Schütz was a tutor at the court of the Duchess of Sachsen-Merseburg.

nificent things in the German language, and if reasonable soldiers, coun-
trymen, noblemen, merchants, and artisans, even reasonable peasants,
heard these things and wanted to know what their children are studying
at such great expense, then they would cross themselves more often and
show even more hostility toward the scholars than, unfortunately, is already happening in many places. Thank goodness that God has already
begun to remedy this error. For about twenty years many noble minds
have been endeavoring to publish in German numerous useful works of
true wisdom, especially political, moral, and historical writings. On account of his great diligence and his unpedantic scholarship, as well as
his rare judgment, the translator has become known through many
pleasing and useful works. Lovers of wisdom are now very much in-
debted to him for translating Grotius into German. What Grotius has
written is so reasonable and well expressed that it is a pure pleasure to
read, but he has often lacked impartial readers. The minds of most educated people, afflicted by the jaundice of the Scholastics, receive many
good and sound teachings of Grotius as if they were bad and dangerous.
These teachings would be better judged if they were read by those who
had not studied but were gifted by God with a sound understanding—
and there are as many of these among all estates as there are among the
Latinate—because the prejudices of the Scholastics do not blind them
to the simple truth.

End of this   31. If I wanted to continue this nascent German history of natural law,
preface   then I should report on the following things: the life of Grotius and his
writings; the fate of this book; on the many remarks that various kinds
of people made about it; on Selden and Thomas Hobbes who soon
thereafter produced similar works; and on those who lent a hand to defend Hobbes.[93] I would have to report on the blessed Baron Pufendorf

93. John Selden (1554–1654) was an English jurist and politician whose theory of
natural law is developed in his *De jure naturali & gentium juxta disciplinam Hebrae-
orum, Libri VII* (Seven books on the law of nature and nations according to the
teachings of the Hebrews) (London, 1640). In the early modern period, Thomas
Hobbes (1588–1679) was commonly seen as a natural-law thinker. He had a significant

and his opponents,[94] when he attacked the irrational opinions of the scholastics, and also on the continuation of the scholastic moral philosophy after Grotius and how shamefully the Jesuits abused it. It would also be necessary to record the similar continuation of mystical doctrine after Grotius, which now acts insolently, gouging out its eyes in order to see better, and believing—just like little children who cover their eyes with their hands—that everyone else is blind and incapable of seeing their folly just because they cannot. I would have to report on how today this mystical doctrine shamelessly reviles and vilifies the doctrine of natural law as a hopeless and dangerous doctrine. Further, I would have to write about common revealed divine law, about the occasion and the manner in which I myself attempted to bring this into order, and about the grumbling and hostility this provoked. This would then mean discussing why I abandoned this doctrine that I had first elaborated, why many did not understand this and wanted to quarrel with me, and why I have written so little that is positive about mystical doctrine when I had earlier praised and honored it in my writings.[95] All of this would be dealt with if I wanted to continue the history of the natural law that I have begun. However, this is not my endeavor, as I was asked to write a preface to the present translation of Grotius. The issues mentioned above may suffice or are, perhaps, too much, because I had planned to frame everything that has been said more briefly. Hopefully everyone knows that I have more in store than I have written, and that I presented

---

influence on continental, including German, political theory and natural jurisprudence, not least through Samuel Pufendorf's critical reception of his work.

94. Pufendorf was vehemently attacked by Protestant theologians and jurists seeking to defend a Christian version of natural law against what they took to be Pufendorf's profane Hobbesian version.

95. Thomasius wrote two quite different books on natural law: first the *Institutiones iurisprudentiae divinae* (Institutes of divine jurisprudence) (1688), which seeks to harmonize biblical law and Pufendorf's natural law; then the *Fundamenta iuris naturae et gentium* (Foundations of the law of nature and nations) (1705), in which biblical law is dropped in favor of a naturalistic theory. Between these works Thomasius was temporarily open to the influence of mysticism and asserted that human morality is completely dependent upon the grace of God. Later he changed his mind and developed a theory of natural law based on the passions and the primacy of the will over reason.

as much as possible as briefly as possible. The matter is so rich, though, that the preface grew longer than I had intended. In any case, I held this to be an indispensable treatment of the history of natural law, which has so far been studied only superficially by myself and others. If one takes a closer look, however, as we have done here, then new light is shed on many otherwise obscure things, not only on church history but also the development of the history of natural law, and one sees everything with other eyes.

The Right of Protestant Princes Regarding Indifferent Matters or *Adiaphora*

SEPTEMBER 13, 1695[1]

Ecclesiastical Ordinances for the Duchy
of Magdeburg, by the Elector of Brandenburg

Title 1, §1

As often as there is occasion to do so, and on the basis of God's word
and these Ordinances, ministers shall instruct their congregations that
external ecclesiastical ceremonies and practices in themselves are not divine worship, nor an essential part of it, but that they are there only so

---

1. The date is that of the public defense of the dissertation by Thomasius's student
Enno Rudolph Brenneisen from Esen in the principality of East Frisia, which had
close diplomatic and military ties to Brandenburg. Brenneisen later became chancellor of East Frisia and in 1720 published a historical work on *Ostfriesische Geschichte
und Landesverfassung* (East Frisian history and territorial constitution), which was
intended as a defense of the East Frisian prince's rights against his territorial estates.
The *adiaphora* dissertation was written under Thomasius's direction, if not by himself, and conforms to Thomasius's views, as is shown by his comments at the end of
the dissertation. The Latin text of 1695 includes several third-person references to
Thomasius as supervisor of the dissertation (*praeses*). The German translation published in his *Auserlesene und in Deutsch noch nie gedruckte Schriften* (Selected writings,
which have never before been printed in German) (Halle, 1705) replaced one of these
in §4 of chapter 1 with a first-person reference, implying that Thomasius considered
himself to be the author.

that divine worship is conducted at an appropriate time and at an established place in an orderly and honorable fashion.

Augsburg Confession, Article 7

The true unity of the church does not require there to be a general uniformity of those ceremonies which have been introduced by man.

Augsburg Confession, Article 15

Of the ecclesiastical ordinances introduced by man, those should be taught to be observed which can be followed without sin, and which serve to preserve peace and good order in the church. But it is necessary to emphasize that consciences should not be burdened with these, as if they were necessary for salvation.

Augsburg Confession, Article 16

It is a Christian duty to obey the magistrate and his orders whenever this is possible without sin.

CHAPTER I

On the Foundations of the Right of the Protestant Prince Concerning Indifferent Matters or Church Ceremonies

Contents

§1.   According to natural religion all external worship of God is an indifferent matter [*adiaphoron*].[2] Why did the pagans place so much

---

2. *Adiaphora* is the plural of the Greek *adiaphoron,* meaning "indifferent," for which early modern German used the term *Mitteldingen* (lit., middle or in-between things). The ancient Stoics had used *adiaphora* to refer to things they wished to treat as morally neutral, things neither good nor bad by nature. In early modern Europe, Protestant theologians used the term to refer to things that were neither forbidden

emphasis on external worship and consider philosophers who derided their stupidity or hypocrisy as atheists? The sanctification of one particular day out of seven is not determined by natural law.

§2. In the revealed religion of the Old Testament external worship was not an indifferent matter. But in the New Testament Christ introduced a simple form of worship, consisting of very few ceremonies.

§3. On what occasion were ceremonies introduced into Christianity after the times of the apostles, especially in the age of the emperor Constantine?[3] The reformers of papalism took a variety of different approaches, also with respect to ceremonies. The state of the controversy is set out.

§4. Our subject pertains to jurists. Cases of conscience also pertain to jurists. The abuse of the term "conscience." Jurists cannot be kept away from the Bible.

§5. Indifferent matters are taken either in a strict sense or a broad sense. The former are the subject here, and are defined. Title X of the *Formula of Concord* is noted.[4]

§6. In deriving the right of the prince in religious matters, hasty appeals are made to the examples of the Israelite kings, even though our kings hold greater power than the Israelite kings.

§7. Even hastier appeals are made to the examples of Constantine, Theodosius,[5] etc., even though the Code of Justinian shows how badly the law concerning religious affairs in this period was infected by the

---

nor required by Scripture, and to "external" elements of Christian worship and sacraments, which they held to be irrelevant to individual salvation. For Thomasius's understanding of the term, see his comments in §5.

3. Contrary to more traditional orthodox Lutherans, who considered Constantine the Great to be the exemplary godly prince, Thomasius argues that his rule caused the corruption of Christianity by turning it into a state religion.

4. The *Formula of Concord* (1577) was a theological codification of Lutheranism, intended to define its differences to Calvinism and to provide Lutheran princes with an instrument for the reform of their churches.

5. Roman emperor from A.D. 379 to 395, Theodosius the Great declared Christianity the state religion of the Roman Empire in A.D. 380.

principles of Anti-Christ. Nor is this catchphrase of any relevance here: *Cuius regio, illius est religio.*[6]

§8.   With regard to the prince's right in religious affairs, Christ established nothing new in his law. It is clear from the purpose of commonwealths that the prince has the power to coerce those who disturb the external peace under the pretext of religion; further, that the general supervision of all his citizens' actions in both secular and religious affairs pertains to him, and that all actions of his citizens, which are within their power, are subject to his management. The common distinction between internal and external matters of religion is obscure and subject to sophistic arguments. The prince cannot compel Jews to attend Christian churches.

§9.   Therefore actions concerning indifferent matters are also subject to his will, because these are nowhere excepted. The consensus of Brunnemann and Conring.

§10. This right pertains to a prince whatever religion he adheres to, even to the estates of the empire on the basis of territorial overlordship [*superioritas*][7]—and thus prior to the Peace of Westphalia—without contradicting the Concordats of Germany in article 16 of the Electoral Capitulation of Charles V.[8]

---

6. Literally, "whose country it is, his religion it is." This stated the right of the territorial prince to impose his confession on the lands under his jurisdiction. It was a principle associated with the Augsburg Peace of Religion of 1555 in particular, though the phrase itself did not appear in the text of the treaty. Although it was conceived as a temporary measure, until religious differences had been resolved by a general council, it gave Lutheranism a degree of legal security within the Holy Roman Empire and helped to justify the right of Lutheran princes to bring the Reformation to their territories.

7. This is distinct from modern sovereignty, in that *superioritas territorialis* is based on the accumulation of regalian rights by a territorial prince, rather than being derived from an abstract notion of state power. For Thomasius's views on the compatibility of territorial *superioritas* with the "sovereignty" (in the early modern sense) of the Holy Roman Emperor, see his disputation *De iniusta oppositione jurium majestaticorum superioritatis territorialis et reservatorum imperatorum* (On the unjustified opposition of the rights of majesty in territorial overlordship to the rights of the emperors) (Halle, 1696).

8. In return for their vote, the seven electoral princes in the empire required certain

§11. Paragraphs 48 and 50 of article 5 of the Westphalian peace are explained. The peace treaty permits a doctrinal interpretation.[9] A Catholic prince can forbid his Lutheran subjects singing: "and restrain the pope from his murderous deeds."

§12. The prince can also change indifferent matters even if they have been decided in general church councils. The fourth law in the title on the Holy Trinity in the Code [of Justinian] seems to be a product of Anti-Christ. Not all the canons concerning indifferent matters in the books of the apostles are now observed.

§13. The arguments of those who deny princes the right over indifferent matters.

§14. We reply to these: first (1) concerning the supposed violation of Christian liberty. Meisner's doctrine is confuted by reference to Meisner himself.

§15. (2) Princes who exercise this right do not control consciences. Control of consciences is exercised by persecuting dissenters and by forced reformation.

§16. (3) The fact that the church consists of three orders presents no obstacle [to this right]. It is an error to search for aristocratic forms of government in the church.

§17. (4) It is inappropriate to refer to the examples of the kings and judges of Israel.

§1. Man acquires knowledge of his duty, and of the honest actions he must perform in this life and the despicable ones from which he must

---

concessions, the so-called Electoral Capitulations, from the candidate for the title of Holy Roman Emperor.

9. That is, as the contemporary German translation explains, "an interpretation following the rules of sound reason," which is permitted to any jurist. It is opposed to the "authentic interpretation" (*interpretatio authentica*), which is the preserve of the legislator; see Johann Friedrich von Rhez, *Institutiones Juris Publici Romani-Germanici* (Institutes of Romano-Germanic public law) (Frankfurt an der Oder, 1687), bk. I, title I, §80.

abstain, from two sources: the light of reason and the light of revelation. Religion is thus also twofold, one part being natural and the other revealed. It is not our intention to list everything which can be put forward about the differences between these two forms of religion, mainly because we do not want to encroach on the territory of venerable theology. On this occasion it may suffice for us to consider how these two differ from each other *with respect to indifferent matters,* as this question pertains to a proper investigation of their origin. Here I believe it is not controversial to say that *natural religion* orders man to worship and revere God as the supreme legislator and express his will in our actions insofar as we are able to understand it with our reason, to further sociality with the greatest assiduity, and to cultivate peace and tranquillity in our relations with other humans. *Does this natural religion require humans to perform some kind of external worship consisting in ceremonies?* This is doubtful, and we know that this has recently been discussed in writing. We believe it does not, even though this may appear dubious to many or even blasphemy to certain sophists and hypocrites. For whether we look toward God or man, we will find nothing from which it can be firmly concluded that God requires this kind of worship from us; for he is the most perspicacious scrutinizer of hearts, and he has no need of external ceremonies for us to declare our will to him; and that which pleases him most in man's worship lies entirely open to his gaze. Therefore our reason cannot but conclude that there is nothing in the nature of God that commands us to worship him in an external way. If our reason turns to human nature, it cannot see the necessity for such worship there either. For it does not see any necessary connection between life in society and the external worship of God, as human society does not suffer if we fail to perform the latter. It might be in the interests of sociality that I declare my inner reverence for the Deity before others as, so to speak, the foundation of all obligation, so that they may not consider me an atheist and shun me. Yet even here I can sufficiently indicate my inner worship by other means and by more reliable signs, that is, by observing the law of nature and performing the duties I owe to other men. Compared to this, religious ceremonies are merely fallible signs, as even a hypocrite and a fellow devoted to all vices can perform such ceremonies. And this I believe—just to mention it in passing—could have been the reason why the pagans themselves, who being without grace were very prone to hypocrisy, put so much emphasis on this external worship, and were little concerned with internal worship. It is not surprising that those philosophers who recognized the vanity of this custom were immediately declared to be atheists in those societies. This is no different from our society where, if someone wants to worship God in true humility and self-abnegation, and does not cling to outward ritual in the manner of the vulgar populace, he is as good as publicly denounced as a Quaker if not a scandalous heretic.[10] Therefore I cannot help but conclude that *all external worship in natural religion is an indifferent matter.*[11] Even if I know very well that most doctors assert the sanctification of one particular day among seven to be founded in natural law, *see Major in the disputation on the Sabbath, Thesis 35; Dannhauer, in the Collegium Decalogicum on precept 3; Osiander on the Sabbath, thesis 22, cited by the illustrious and great pro-rector Mr. Stryk in his comments on Brunnemann, Jus Ecclesiasticum, book 2, chapter 1, membrum 1, §8.*[12] We will not spend time disproving their opinion, because they presuppose a hypothesis that we have already refuted.

§2. Indeed, the condition of humanity is such that it cannot achieve the more sublime end for which it is destined by God by means of the wor-

10. Here the Latin text refers only to such a person being declared "an enthusiast if not something worse," which is a pointer to the more emphatic character of the German version. In the seventeenth century, many people regarded the Society of Friends, dubbed Quakers by their enemies, as religious fanatics driven by inner revelations.

11. This is an important difference between Thomasius and his friend Samuel Pufendorf, who believed natural religion required a certain measure of external worship.

12. These works are Johann Tobias Major's *Disputatio Theologica de Sabbato* (Theological disputation on the Sabbath) (Jena, 1647), Johann Conrad Dannhauer's *Collegium Decalogicum* (Course on the Decalogue) (Strasbourg, 1638), Johann Adam Osiander's *Dissertationes de Sabbatho* (Dissertations on the Sabbath) (Tübingen, 1672), and Samuel Stryk's edition of Brunnemann's *Jus Ecclesiasticum* (Ecclesiastical law) (Frankfurt an der Oder, 1681).

ship suggested by natural reason alone; for man can by his natural powers attain to some recognition of his weaknesses and miseries, but cannot find out the remedy for these and reach the door of salvation without the particular assistance of divine grace. God thus *wished to open a special path to men* by which he was to be reconciled with them, and by which he wanted to be revered by them. And biblical history teaches us that *this worship had from the creation of the world certain external elements mixed with it.* For without doubt it was *at the suggestion of the Deity himself* that *the sacrificial slaughter of animals was introduced* from the very first ages of the world, as a symbol for the Messiah, who would atone for the Fall of humanity. Otherwise, if we abstract from divine revelation and examine the matter according to the principles of reason, it is incomprehensible why the destruction of a creature should please God, as *Pufendorf* rightly reasons in his *On the Relationship of Religion to the Commonwealth* §8.[13] But it is still dubious whether God immediately introduced *other external ceremonies.* For I know that *concerning the Sabbath* the theologians themselves are not in complete agreement, and that some decree that it was the *Mosaic Laws* which declared the seventh day to be holy before all others, but that *previously* the patriarchs and others performed the same worship of God *on all days.* Their opinion seems quite sensible to me. It is certain that after God linked himself to the *Jewish* people in a *peculiar covenant*—subjecting them to his own law after they had been liberated from the Egyptian servitude—*he formed a particular religion for them with peculiar laws and countless ceremonial commandments.* This was to last until the advent of the Messiah, and was in a certain sense a prefiguration of the future kingdom of Christ. But after *our Savior* had been sent in the fullness of time into this world, he introduced what was plainly *another* and *different religion* as far as external rites were concerned, namely, one which almost completely conformed to natural religion in terms of its external ceremonies.

13. Pufendorf, *De habitu religionis Christianae ad vitam civilem* (Bremen, 1687). For a modern edition of the 1698 translation of this work, see S. Pufendorf, *On the Nature and Qualification of Religion in Reference to Civil Society,* trans. Jodocus Crull, ed. S. Zurbuchen (Indianapolis, Ind.: Liberty Fund, 2002).

The pomp of sacrifices and other rituals was abolished, *and all external ceremonies, with the exception of those which Christ specifically imposed on his disciples—for example, baptism, the Eucharist, etc.—became indifferent matters.* The Christian religion would thus appear to be content with an internal worship, that is, with the true humility of a self-abnegating mind, which devotes itself entirely to God. And, through the grace of the Holy Spirit, the disciples of Christ and the apostles devoted themselves to this practical religion with all their powers, in order to take part in the kingdom of Christ, which consists in justice, peace, and joy.

§3. But the Christian religion did not remain for long in this state of simplicity, far removed from all external pomp. After various sorts of people had converted to Christianity—especially the *Jews* and *Greeks* with whom the apostles frequently came into contact[14]—they directed all their efforts toward *introducing those ceremonies to which they had been accustomed into this new religion of theirs,* and toward making it more splendid, so to speak. There is a famous example of this in the Acts of the Apostles, chapter XV, where it is said that Christians, newly converted from *Judaism,* wanted to force *circumcision* onto the other Christians, claiming it was a necessary part of faith. This was until Paul and Barnabas called a gathering of each and every Christian in Jerusalem and in this uniquely holy council taught that Christians could leave aside this ritual as something superfluous. They pointed out that, even though the pagans had not been circumcised, the Holy Spirit had been communicated to them through the preaching of the word of God, if they listened to it with pious and ardent desire. Nevertheless, in order that the Jews be satisfied in some respect, and admit all the more willingly the company of the faithful among the Gentiles, or rather, in order that the new Christians be separated from the Gentiles by some external mark, they believed that they should abstain from anything concerning idols, from unchastity,[15] from what is strangled, and from

14. The clause "with whom the apostles frequently came into contact" is missing from the German text.

15. The phrase "from unchastity" is missing from the German text.

blood.[16] *But the further the times of Christ and the apostles receded, the more that simplicity was left behind, and the more did Christians want to dress up their religion in rituals and external ceremonies,* especially after the Roman emperors had given it their support. For at the time of *Constantine the Great* Christian affairs underwent an enormous change. Until then the church had been oppressed and subject to harsh persecutions, notwithstanding which extremely bitter disputes, envy, and rivalry between priests arose among Christians themselves, even in the second and third centuries; scandalous schisms were born from this, for which see the *Gotha Ecclesiastical History, book 2, chapter 3, section 2;* and *Huber's Civil History, part 2, book 2, section 4, chapter 5, §2.*[17] At the time of Constantine the Great, however, this storm of pagan persecution ceased, and those evils, which spread among those who live in the supreme abundance and superfluity of all things—that is, ambition, avarice, and, developing from this, hatred and persecution of dissenters—immediately infected the Christians too, especially the bishops and the clerics, who most enjoyed the favor of Constantine the Great. For this reason just as the vices of the court crept into the church—rather than Christian simplicity and piety being communicated to the court of the emperor—so it is not surprising that *Christian religion also* changed its character, *and went over to external ceremonies and was absorbed by these,* always with the exception of a kernel of pious believers, who remained concealed. It is appropriate to refer here to the words of Huber's *Civil History part 2, book 3, section 1, §7. When true devotion,* he says, *which is an act of the mind renouncing itself and devoting itself to God in Christ, fell into disuse, together with the internal worship of God in Spirit and in truth, efforts were made to keep the populace occupied in superstitious awe, which they called*

16. This is a reference to Acts 21:25.

17. This is the *Compendium Historiae Ecclesiasticae . . . in usum Gymnasii Gothani . . . deductum* (Handbook of ecclesiastical history, for the use of the Gymnasium in Gotha) (Gotha, 1660). Book III, chapter III, section II is on the history of the church in the third century and up to the times of Constantine the Great. The work by Ulrich Huber is his *Institutiones Historiae Civilis* (Institutes of civil history) (Franeker, 1692).

devotion,[18] *with the help of rituals and ceremonies, taken largely from Judaism and paganism. The veneration of the cross is part of this, as are the kissing of other reliquaries, the pilgrimages to the sepulcher of the Lord, the placing of images in churches, and other examples of physical worship of this kind, which later on degenerated into hideous idolatry.* That this opinion of Huber's is not a figment of the imagination, we can learn simply from *Eusebius,* who, with enormous diligence, gathered everything that could serve to extol *Constantine,* and nevertheless measured his [i.e., Constantine's] piety entirely in terms of his *generosity toward clerics, the construction of churches,* and other such deeds that are no indication of true piety at all. So, considering that the piety of the emperor consisted in *external matters* of this kind, it is not surprising that the populace followed the example of the monarch, and was completely beholden to *external ceremonies.* Even Calixt acknowledges this in his *Dissertation on Baptism, §145,*[19] alleging that *Augustine* already complained about the number of ceremonies in his time, saying, *that Christians were now more oppressed by man-made institutes than the Jewish people had been by the burdens of the ceremonial law. Calixt even adds his own opinion that the more piety decreased, the more rituals, ceremonies, and solemnities increased, and an effort was made to captivate the vulgar populace by the splendid pomp that bewitched their eyes.* Whatever is to be said about the age of Constantine, however, it is clear that the matter *finally* came to this: that the true worship of God was in most cases extinguished from the minds of men, *everything was filled with all kinds of superstitious ceremonies,* until in the last [i.e., the sixteenth] century the matter had clearly become ripe for a Reformation. Once the corruption of the Catholic Church, which had been increasing over many centuries, had become obvious to people—above all as a result of the manifest unrighteousness of the popes

---

18. The clause "which they called devotion": this is missing from the German translation.

19. Georg Calixt (1586–1656) was a Lutheran theology professor at the University of Helmstedt. His preparedness to compromise on doctrinal strictness in seeking peace with other confessions led his orthodox colleagues to denounce him as a "syncretist." The work referred to is a Helmstedt University disputation *De Baptismo* (On baptism) of 1611 that had been written under Calixt's supervision.

and other clergymen—*Luther and the other reformers* toiled to liberate the church from this stain and restore it to its pristine vigor, even though they chose different ways of doing so. *Luther* and his followers retained some apparatus of *external ritual,* in order, as Monzambano argues in *chapter 8, §7* to *divert the minds of the simple people, whose powers of comprehension usually were not up to the bare meditation of piety.*[20] *Zwingli* and others, however, threw out the rites of the Catholics completely, because they were redolent of superstition, and purged their external ceremony of all outward pomp. The result of this was discord among the reformers, though occasion for this was also provided by differences in their ways of speaking about the articles of faith. This was no inconsiderable obstacle to their enterprise and was very shameful. Protestants were divided into two factions whose hostility toward each other was no less than their hostility toward the papalists. *It is therefore appropriate to discuss the prince's right to abrogate these ceremonies and to introduce new ones.* But in order that I do not seem to be interfering in someone else's affairs, we must first see *whether the matter pertains to Jurisprudence or to Theology?*

§4. First the common persuasion of the Doctors seems to present a formidable obstacle to our design. On this basis they commonly imagine that the *cases* which they call *cases of conscience* belong *to Theology* in such a way that if jurists claim to decide such cases for themselves then they trespass on another profession.[21] This argument has typically en-

---

20. Severinus de Monzambano (pseudonym for Samuel Pufendorf), *De statu imperii Germanici* (On the state of the German empire) (Geneva [in fact, The Hague], 1667). In this work Pufendorf criticizes the attempts by political philosophers to fit the imperial constitution into the Aristotelian classificatory scheme, consisting of monarchy, aristocracy, and democracy. For a modern edition of the 1696 translation by Edmund Bohun, see S. Pufendorf, *The Present State of the German Empire,* ed. M. Seidler (Indianapolis, Ind.: Liberty Fund, 2007).

21. In the Latin text Thomasius uses the Greek expression *metábasis eis allò génos* (literally "stepping over into another kind"). This was a term used in Logic to describe the failure to adhere to the subject of an argument. In this case it stands for the mixture of secular and theological knowledge. The term derives from Aristotle, *De Caelo* (On the heavens) I, 268 b.

joyed such authority that jurisconsults on the whole have abstained from such cases, in order not to seem to be causing tumults, leaving them to the theologians. More than all others, however, Havemann urges this argument in his *Treatise on the Rights of Bishops, title XIII.*[22] Here he puts forward his opinion that on this basis the more complex cases concerning matrimony must not be decided by jurists at all, speaking thus: *Who thus would be so utterly obtuse as to keep the ministers of the church away from divine matters and cases of conscience? For they are solemnly entrusted by God with the interpretation of Scripture and the instruction of consciences with the word of God.* Given that many of the cases discussed in this dissertation are commonly considered to be cases of conscience, it would appear that this argument should rightly deter us from our project, forcing us to leave it to those who want to preside over such. Here I should like to oppose this objection by pointing out that *conscience* is nothing other than *the judgment of the intellect on human actions insofar as it is imbued with the knowledge of laws,* and thus the conscience can have a role in directing human actions only insofar as it is imbued with the knowledge of laws. For to attribute to *conscience* some sort of peculiar force of directing actions in any other sense, would be nothing other than *to attribute to random fantasies of men the force of laws* and to introduce utter confusion into human affairs, as the blessed Mr. Pufendorf reasons correctly in his *On the Law of Nature and Nations, book I, chapter 3, §4.*[23] From this it will readily be apparent that just as it would be an injury for anyone to want to exclude theologians from the determination of cases of conscience, so those people who want to leave every decision of cases of conscience to the theologians are very injurious toward jurists. For which faculty the case pertains to depends on the circumstances of the fact. If one must decide on the basis of principles of theology, which *concern eternal salvation,* then the case pertains to theology; if the decision must be based on those laws which concern *man's temporal wel-*

22. M. Havemann, *Dissertatio Theologico-Politica De Jure Episcopali* (Theological-political dissertation on episcopal law) (Hamburg, 1646).

23. Samuel Pufendorf, *De jure naturae et gentium* (On the law of nature and nations) (Lund, 1672).

fare, it pertains to jurisprudence. As we will derive the principles of our dissertation from the law of nature and the human laws based on these, and these undoubtedly belong to the jurists, so our intention thus cannot be presented as a fault. In addition we agree with the opinion of the blessed Mr. Pufendorf. He says *in the book cited above that we must confess that the common meaning of the word* conscience *was introduced first by the Scholastics, but in recent centuries the so-called cases of conscience were invented by cunning priests who wanted to influence the minds of humans according to their own whim.* Our adversaries, however, insist firmly that *the definition of indifferent matters* must be sought from *theology textbooks,* and that theologians, the true interpreters of Scripture, thus know exactly *what indifferent matters are.* Thus, for jurists to discuss this matter is as unsuitable *as if a baker judged a leather hide, a cobbler judged bread, an ironsmith judged a precious stone and a diamond, a tailor judged ambergris,*[24] which is a comparison Havemann pursues at some length in the work cited above, but which is one worthy of pity rather than refutation. Concerning this argument over the definition, we concede that this has to be sought *from Holy Scripture,* but we deny that it is possible to conclude from this that jurists cannot act in this matter. Who would deny that jurists can intervene in cases of *incest, sodomy, simony,* and other religious offenses, which are committed not contrary to natural law, but contrary either to universal divine positive law, or to Christianity? Jurisconsults also deal with *heretics,* and yet the definition of heresy is to be sought from Holy Scripture. (For I believe that the definition of a heretic, which exists in the *second law, §1* of the title *On Heretics* in the *Code,* cannot be acceptable to Protestants.)[25] It would be papist to want to exclude jurists from Holy Scripture. Theologians use Sacred Scripture and jurists use it, but for different ends: the former do so in order to dispose the minds of men to *eternal* salvation, the latter in order to lead them to *temporal* well-being. For the faculties of theology and law must not be distinguished by their books,[26] but by their ends. I therefore can-

---

24. The German has "a tailor judged musk and civet."
25. This is in book I, V of the *Code of Justinian.*
26. That is, Scripture and works on law.

not accept the fact that several theologians, such as Havemann, want to restrict jurists to Roman law, and if they wish to have an opinion on anything beyond that, immediately accuse them of trespassing on their profession,[27] as if this were a barbaric crime, whereas it is merely a scholastic and pedagogical one. Therefore, and this must be carefully noted, *we draw the object of our dissertation from theology.* We do not, however, borrow *our principles* from theology but from natural law. Just as for example arithmetic does not interfere with theology, even if it applies its own principles to examples from sacred history, so we too will not be committing a sin when we apply natural-law principles of rights in religious affairs to the general subject of indifferent matters. To borrow the principles of demonstration from a different discipline is one thing, it is another to seek from elsewhere the object to which the demonstration is to be applied, as I have observed in my *Divine Jurisprudence book 1, chapter 2, §§17 & 18.*[28] Now that we have removed these obstacles we will tackle the matter itself more directly, and we will do so first by providing a *definition of indifferent matters.*

§5. The term, *adiaphoron* [indifferent matter], however, is used in a twofold sense, one *broad* and one *strict. The former* stands for *all things* that are by nature neither good nor bad, or that have not been determined by divine laws, and over which the prince can dispose as the utility of the commonwealth requires. For matters which have been prohibited or commanded by God, in either natural or positive law, need no particular human determination, except insofar as the prince can add some sort of confirmation to these precepts so that the citizens are all the more bound to their observance. In the *narrower* sense of the word, however, which is the one we are concerned with here, *adiaphora* describes *those rites and ceremonies that are usually practiced in the congregations of Christians for the sake of the outward worship of God, and which are neither commanded*

---

27. The term used is *metábasis eis allò génos* (see note 21 in this chapter).

28. These are Thomasius's *Institutiones Jurisprudentiae Divinae* (Institutes of divine jurisprudence) (Frankfurt and Leipzig, 1688). Thomasius there argues that it is legitimate to apply, for example, principles of arithmetic to sacred history.

nor prohibited by either God or Christ, such as the use of certain vestments, of candles, of exorcism [in baptism], *and so on.* For just as in all forms of jurisprudence some matters are considered indifferent when the laws have not determined anything on them, so too in Christianity and Christian affairs some matters, which neither Christ nor the principles of true Christianity prohibit, are considered to be permitted. [See] *Havemann, On the Rights of Bishops, title XI, §1, Carpzov, Ecclesiastical Jurisprudence, book 2, title 15, numbers 1, 2, 3, 4,*[29] *as well as the Formula of Concord title X.*[30]—If only [the *Formula*] had not made the definition [of indifferent matters] so obscure by adding so many limitations and qualifications. For, from the time of that sacred book until today, the fractious and unruly have always used this title X as justification for resistance to the princes and for establishing the second papacy predicted by Luther. This has especially been the case when the issue concerned the abrogation of certain indifferent ceremonies—which tended, however, to incline people more to superstition—but even more so when Calvinist princes acquired Lutheran subjects.[31] And he would be blind who did not see that this little book [the *Formula of Concord*] was for the most part written with hatred against the Calvinists, who at that time were labeled Phil-

29. Benedict Carpzov, *Jurisprudentia Ecclesiastica seu Consistorialis* (Ecclesiastical or consistorial jurisprudence) (Leipzig, 1673). On the Formula of Concord, see note 4 in this chapter.

30. Title or chapter X of the Formula of Concord deals with *adiaphora*. While agreeing with Thomasius's definition that *adiaphora* are things neither forbidden nor commanded by God, and hence form no essential part of Christian worship, this chapter runs quite contrary to Thomasius's viewpoint. This is especially the case where it denies that Lutherans may compromise on *adiaphora* in order to make peace with rival confessions, and where it denies princes the right to override the church when abrogating indifferent rites and ceremonies.

31. This refers in particular to the situation in the territories of the Elector of Brandenburg, including the duchy of Magdeburg. In spite of the elector's conversion to Calvinism in 1613, the population and nobility of Brandenburg and of the duchy of Magdeburg, acquired after the end of the Thirty Years' War, remained largely Lutheran and, in general, very resistant to the Calvinist elector's attempts to reform their churches.

lipists and given other more hurtful names;[32] and [he would be blind who did not see] that the said *title X* points in this direction, even if the formal controversy pretends otherwise; just as [this hatred] is palpably clear from the *said title X of the abridgement, in the line "In this matter however, all fickleness" etc. and from the extensive explanation of the title X toward the end, in the lines "We reject and condemn their folly" etc.,* and from the arguments that the Wittenberg theologians have drawn from these passages to use against Calvinist magistrates. As this seems to me to contradict the *Augsburg Confession, article 7 "it is not necessary" etc., article 15 "they further tranquility," and article 16 "unless they command to sin" etc.,*[33] I will reserve the other comments which can be put forward here for the disputation itself.[34]

§6. As we have already *briefly considered the general principles governing the prince's right in religious affairs,* now we will show what rights a prince has with regard to *adiaphora* or indifferent matters. In this issue, the more rocks there are on which one might run aground, the more cautiously one must proceed. In particular, we must take care not to veer too far to the right or to the left; that is, one should not foster principles which lead to the introduction of either *Caesaro-Papalism* or *Papalo-*

32. "Phillipists" was the term used for the followers of the Lutheran reformer Phillip Melancthon, who were criticized by the so-called Gnesio-Lutherans for corrupting Luther's teachings. The disputes between these two factions were concentrated in the third quarter of the sixteenth century.

33. Presented to Emperor Charles V in 1530, the Augsburg Confession was the earlier statement of Lutheran articles of faith. The articles to which Thomasius refers assert that Christian unity does not require agreement in ceremonies instituted by men; that the performance of such ceremonies is conditional on their not infringing peace and good order; and that Christians are obliged to obey the civil authorities insofar as this can be done without sinning. His argument is thus that in comparison with the Formula of Concord, the Augsburg Confession gives the prince and secular authorities greater freedom in dealing with religious ceremonies. Thomasius develops this argument further in §3 of his comments addressed to Brenneisen, below, p. 112.

34. That is, for the oral disputation in public. The German translation here simply reads "for another occasion."

Caesarism.[35] Therefore those Doctors, who are always appealing to the
Israelite kings on this matter, or to the examples of the *first Christian
emperors,* seem to me to proceed in an inappropriate manner. This form
of proof seems slippery and dangerous in both cases. For, as far as the
examples from the Old Testament are concerned, it must be noted that
the nature of the *Jewish religion* differed from that of *Christian religion,*
not only in its internal matters [i.e., doctrines], but also in the regulation
of its external affairs. For just as the Jewish religion was coeval with the
state, and the laws concerning religious and civil matters were established
at the same time and written in the same book, so the Jewish religion
was so closely connected to the state that the Jewish religion could not
be preserved without the Jewish state and vice versa. On this account
the Jewish commonwealth was distinguished from all others in that it
was a theocracy, and the Jews could not perform any action relevant to
the supreme secular power without particular advice from God, as he
had reserved to himself the supreme overlordship in that commonwealth—not in the [metaphorical] sense that he is called the King of
Kings or the Lord of all Lords, but in the same sense as our most serene
elector is the duke of this duchy [i.e., Magdeburg]. And God exercised
this overlordship concerning the right to wage war, to build the Temple,
and so on, not only at the time of the Judges, but during that of the
Kings, as is clear from the examples cited from Holy Scripture. Therefore
those people certainly do our princes an injustice, when they compare
their rights with those of the Israelite kings. For our princes possess many
rights not enjoyed by those kings.

§7. Concerning the *examples of Constantine the Great and Theodosius,*
and of the other emperors, there is nothing here on which we could safely
depend. For these emperors, not so much by their own fault as by that

35. Caesaro-papalism was usually understood as the prince's interference in the
internal affairs of the church, although Thomasius was quite skeptical of this understanding, treating it as a device used by the clergy to block the prince's legitimate
right in such matters as the *adiaphora.* Papalo-caesarism refers to the subjection of
church and state to the control of the clergy, which is Thomasius's prime concern.

of the clerics to which they were beholden, *brought about many completely indefensible changes in the right in religious matters.* There is no
need to list examples from ecclesiastical history. *Our Code of Justinian*
itself sufficiently indicates the principles of ecclesiastical law at that time,
to such an extent that *there are but few laws concerning religious matters
where Anti-Christ does not rear his head.* Those who base their argument
on that common slogan *Cuius regio eius religio*[36] make poor provision
for the rights of princes. This slogan seems to have been seized by Protestant princes at the beginning of the Reformation as protection against
the authority of the emperor, who wanted to prevent their Reformation.
They pretended that what they did in the territories under their rule was
no concern of the emperor. But already others have observed that this
axiom *has caused much damage to Protestant religion,* as pro-papal princes
turned it against Protestants and under this pretext subjected them to
harsh persecution. For when at the beginning of the [seventeenth] century the papalists formed the plan to extirpate the Protestants in the
hereditary territories of the emperor,[37] and the name of the *Inquisition*
struck horror into everybody who heard of it, they labeled this persecution a *Reformation.* The Protestants' own term and catchphrase was
thus applied to themselves, and the Catholics drew on the same pretext
that the Protestants had previously used in order to expel Roman Catholics from their territories. I could mention other arguments of this kind
which are commonly used to ground the right in religious affairs.

§8. In order to avoid the two extremes we have noted in §6, we postulate
above all *that there is no sentence in the New Testament specifically directed
at supreme secular rulers by which they are entrusted with a particular office
concerning the church*—in the way that there was a precept for the kings
of Israel *Deuteronomy XVII, verses 18, 19, and 20*[38]—or by which a rule

36. This phrase was used to summarize the central principle of the Augsburg Peace
of Religion (see note 6 in this chapter).

37. That is, the Austrian territories of the Habsburg emperors.

38. Here the king of the Israelites is commanded to observe all statutes and ordinances imposed by God in the preceding passages.

for exercising these rights was prescribed to them. I conclude from this *that all rights of Christian princes—regarded as princes*[39]*—are to be learned from the principles of natural law and the genuine nature of civil sovereignty.* All those matters which have not been regulated, expressed, and determined in Holy Scripture must be derived from sound reason. For one reads nowhere that in teaching the Christian religion to the pagans Christ and the apostles brought about a change in the rights of princes, insofar as they flow from natural law. On the contrary, Christ and the apostles always inculcated obedience toward the magistracy. And thus if a pagan commonwealth adopts Christianity, the constitution of the state concerning the rights of the princes is not changed or abolished, but the supreme power remains in all its parts, and the subjects remain with all their offices and duties. For the change that occurs in citizens through Christian faith, or that should indeed occur in them, does not affect the obligation existing between prince and subjects, but refers only to the internal disposition of the mind; and to this extent the rights of the princes over their subjects remain untouched. This is also quite clear from the fact that Christ and the apostles never founded a separate commonwealth among their followers, or encouraged them to leave the commonwealth in which they had lived until then and found a new one, as Moses had done among the Jews at God's command. Therefore Christ's disciples were not subordinate to him in the way citizens are usually subordinate to their prince, but in the way students are subordinate to their teacher. They did not adopt his form of religion with some specific act of homage, which is what the false disciples of Christ introduced over time, but were drawn to him by love and admiration; *see John chapter VI, 66, 67, 68.* On this basis we must see *what right therefore pertains to the prince in religious matters on the basis of natural law and the genuine nature of sovereign power.* Leaving aside the fundamental laws of individual commonwealths, by which the exercise of territorial sovereignty is limited and confined within certain barriers, this question can be decided best by looking at the *purpose of commonwealths* and the reason

---

39. Here Thomasius is distinguishing the prince fulfilling his duties as a prince, as opposed to his duties as a man or a Christian.

for their foundation. The purpose of commonwealths, however, in this corrupt state is *for subjects to provide themselves with some protection against evils and attacks* with which their more powerful neighbors in the state of nature threaten them. For below God there is no more efficient instrument for coercing the malice of humans and for securing their safety than that ingenious invention whereby many humans by a mutual pact subject the direction of their will and their powers to the will of another, for the common benefit of the whole community of subjects. As a result, *it is undoubtedly true that a prince accrues as much power as is required for obtaining this purpose of the commonwealth, namely, for its internal and external peace.* Therefore it is the prince's duty above all to take care, that *vices* liable to disturb this peace, such as greed, ambition, and lust, do not break forth, and that, if by chance they have erupted to the detriment of the commonwealth, *they are again repressed,* in order that they do not spread any further and the commonwealth suffer more serious damage. True religion, natural as well as revealed, must above all serve man in purging his mind from such vices and rendering himself increasingly prepared for the veneration of God. Nevertheless, the experience of all centuries testifies that *religion has such a perverse effect on many humans, that they use it as a sort of instrument for perpetrating the most awful crimes; and not only for causing unrest in the commonwealth in which they live, but also for threatening, disturbing, and overthrowing neighboring states.* Therefore *the prince is obliged to take care that no damage is inflicted on the commonwealth by the religion of these evildoers.* For, by the very fact that they stir up unrest in the commonwealth, they show sufficiently that they care nothing for true religion nor hold it close to their heart. For the true religion and Christian faith abhors quarrels, discord, and disputes which disturb the external civil peace; and it disposes minds rather toward patiently suffering injuries than toward inflicting them on others. From this it follows that they [i.e., those who stir up unrest] cannot appeal to religion, if the prince wants to punish them for these vices. He namely who sins against religion is unworthy of the privilege of religion. On account of the fact that there is nothing so holy that it cannot be abused and defiled when it is in human hands, there is no doubt that *the general supervision of his subjects' actions, both in secular and religious matters belongs to the prince* and that nobody can complain of an injury because of this. For if they conduct themselves properly they have nothing to fear; but if they perform evil deeds, it is their own fault if the prince coerces them. And do not Germany and almost all the kingdoms of Europe provide sufficient testimony of the harmful effects religious disagreements and upheavals can have? If therefore we deprived the prince of the power to suppress the upheavals stirred up by religion, certainly the entire commonwealth would perish. Thus I believe that they reason truly and properly who state that *all actions of subjects are subordinated to the power of the prince, as long as these actions are subordinate to the free will of the citizens both naturally and morally.* For it would be cruel to command subjects to do something *impossible,* and impious to command them to do something *immoral.* For all such actions by subjects can harm the commonwealth, and the prince can prevent them by adopting preemptive measures, so that he is not forced to look around for a remedy after the damage has been done. And this opinion of ours I believe conforms more closely to right reason and is easier to understand than the opinion of those who distinguish between the *internal and the external aspects of religion,* arguing that the prince may regulate the latter but not the former.[40] There is no doubt that the prince does not have power over internal matters, since these are not subject to the will of humans; yet if one turns to the external matters and this distinction is then applied to a controversial case, then determining which matters are internal and which external frequently gives rise to disagreement. I will illustrate the matter with a case study: some doctors are asked *whether the prince can compel Jews living in his territory to attend Christian services?* Those who affirm this say that it pertains to the external matters, those who deny it count it among the internal. Each side argues for its opinion with probable arguments. Our above rule de-

---

40. The distinction between *interna,* that is, doctrinal beliefs and religious ceremonies, and *externa,* that is, all matters concerning the administration of the church as a human institution, was characteristic of orthodox Lutheranism. Orthodox Lutherans argued that while *interna* were the responsibility of the clergy, *externa* were that of the secular magistrate.

cides unambiguously: because the Jews regard it as unjust and repellent to attend Christian churches and take part in their sacred rites, and because this does not contribute anything to the peace of the commonwealth, it is not admissible to coerce their conscience. And although their conscience is mistaken, this error nevertheless must not be corrected by coercion, but by amicable conversation, pious example, and other remedies, which conform more closely to reason and the precepts of Christ. And this is the way in which similar cases ought to be decided.

§9. If somebody considers all these matters justly, I believe that he will easily grant us that there is no need to rack one's brains in order to prove that *indifferent matters concerning the worship of God are also subject to the direction of the prince.* Here there is no principle on the basis of which Christians could pretend that the prince's power to command ceases in this domain. For supreme civil power extends to *everything which is not determined by divine law,* as Grotius proves at length in his *On the Right in Sacred Affairs, chapter 3.*[41] For just as the prince in public law lays claim to his right over all inhabitants of his territory by virtue of his territorial overlordship [*superioritas territorialis*]—and indeed over all goods located in it, unless it is possible to point out an exception—so no distinction must be made between subjects who are constituted in some position of dignity, be it supreme or minor, or between subjects of the lowest and the highest estate in society. (*See the illustrious von Rhez in his work on Public Law, book 2, title 2, §16, and the illustrious Gentleman from Jena in his dissertation on reason of state 19, conclusion 2.*)[42] As a result,

41. Hugo Grotius, *De Imperio Summarum Potestatum circa Sacra: Commentarius Posthumus* (On the authority of supreme powers in sacred matters: a posthumous commentary) (Paris, 1647). E. J. Brill published a modern scholarly edition in 2001.

42. Johann Friedrich von Rhez, *Institutiones Juris Publici Romani-Germanici* (Institutes of Romano-Germanic public law) (Frankfurt an der Oder, 1687); Gottfried von Jena, *Fragmenta de Ratione Status* (Fragments on reason of state) (s.l., 1667), "Dissertatio Nona decima De Ratione Status" (Nineteenth dissertation on reason of state), conclusion II, p. 291. There von Jena comments that "with respect to their subjection and their status there is no difference between subjects, but, with respect to their lord, to the jurisdiction they are under, and their subjection they are and remain subjects without distinction."

all actions of citizens which are not determined by the word of God, and which are within their free will, can thus be determined by civil laws. In order that our argument may not seem paradoxical to anyone, let us hear Brunnemann, who says in his work *On Ecclesiastical Law book 1, chapter 2, §34: However, as the actions of humans are either commanded or permitted by divine law, the prince can assign time, place, form, and persons to them, insofar as they are not defined either by the nature of the matter or a divine law. Further, in these matters the prince can remove obstacles and sometimes add rewards, and impose punishments for illicit actions. But the prince cannot prohibit those actions which are commanded by God, such as the salutary preaching of the word and the administering of the sacraments. The prince can command, though, that the words concerning baptism and sacred communion are proclaimed with a loud voice in public, and similar things.* Let us also hear Conring in *On the Authority of the Sovereign in Sacred Affairs,*[43] thesis 15, where he says that *it is not forbidden to constitute something concerning these matters, and decency requires that what is prescribed in them may be defined by human laws.* As therefore our indifferent matters are of this kind it follows automatically that they depend on the will of the prince. This Brunnemann expresses more clearly in *§28 of the book quoted above.* He says that *the right in religious matters belongs to the prince, not just in regulating external discipline, but also in regulating ceremonies, and all of this to the extent that is permitted by divine law, the fundamental laws of the provinces, pacts, and agreements.* But how should we contradict those who believe that thereby the political Anti-Christ is introduced as, for example, Havemann complains *in the treatise quoted above?* On this *see Brunnemann op. cit. §34 at the end, add Ziegler in his fifth Dissertation, on the Rights of the Sovereign, §59.*[44] I can easily foresee that this doctrine will not please

43. Hermann Conring, *Exercitatio Politica de Maiestatis Civilis Auctoritate et Officia circa Sacra* (Political treatise on the authority and duty of majesty in sacred matters) (Helmstedt, 1645). The passage referred to is actually thesis 17.

44. Johann Jakob Brunnemann, *De Jure Ecclesiastico Tractatus Posthumus* (Posthumous treatise on ecclesiastical law) (Frankfurt an der Oder, 1681); Caspar Ziegler, *De Juribus Majestatis: Exercitatio V, Quae Est De Jure circa Sacra et Religionem* (On

those who believe that there must be an *aristocratic* government in the church; but I ask those people to suppress their passionate hostility for a bit, until we shall have responded to their doubts in §16. In the meantime they should allow us to move on to other matters.

§10. Those rights we have properly ascribed to the prince flow from the character and nature of supreme government which is itself based on natural law. Thus it also follows automatically that this power *is an entitlement of all princes, without distinction, whichever religion they may adhere to.* For religion, as we have already said above, does not alter the rights of government and does not affect them. For just as the subjects, be they Lutherans, Reformed, or Catholic, are, without damage to their religion, equally subject to their prince, whether he is Lutheran or Reformed so, on the other hand, does the prince have the same rights over his subjects, be they Lutheran, Reformed, or Catholic. For authority and subjection are correlates, and where there is equal subjection, there is also equal authority. I know of course that not so long ago a certain well-known author wanted to prove in a published piece that *Lutheranism was more favorable to princes than Calvinism and all other religions,* and therefore the princes should join the Lutheran side, for the sake of self-interest alone; but I also know that this author has already been refuted by the supervisor of this dissertation [i.e., Thomasius] in his *Monatsgespräche.*[45] And I believe that this method of converting princes cannot recommend itself to other true Christians, as it relies too much on political interest and is contrary to the apostolic manner of conversion. Given that the apostles never used this argument to convert the pagans,

---

the rights of majesty: fifth treatise, which is on the right concerning sacred matters and religion) (Wittenberg, 1660).

45. This is a reference to Gottfried Hector Masius, court preacher to the king of Denmark, with whom Thomasius had been involved in a dispute over the foundation of *maiestas* after the publication of Masius's treatise *Interesse principum circa religionem evangelicam* (Interest of princes concerning evangelical religion) in 1687. Masius had argued that Lutheran religion supported the legitimate rights of rulers, while Calvinism undermined them. Thomasius's critique appeared in his *Monatsgespräche* (Monthly conversations), a review journal published in Halle in 1690.

it would have to be the case that one acted in a different manner in the church already established than in the church still to be established. But let us take a closer look at the *princes of the Holy Roman Empire,* and consider to what extent they also have power over indifferent matters and religious ceremonies. Here, however, we abstract from the *pacts of the princes with their subjects,* which produce a great diversity in the rights of our princes, and we will consider the matter on the basis of the general public law in Germany, which is founded in the Golden Bull,[46] the decisions of the Imperial Diet, the Electoral Capitulations,[47] and the Westphalian peace treaties.[48] According to these principles we cannot but *decide* this question *in the affirmative.* For the right in religious matters is part of supreme authority, and therefore also of *territorial overlordship* [*superioritas territorialis*].[49] For what is called majesty in the case of foreign princes, in that of the estates of the Holy Roman Empire is called *territorial overlordship.* This is a term which so far they have wished to use in the terminology of public law, maybe out of modesty, in order to indicate the feudal nexus through which they are tied to the emperor and the empire. And this feudal relationship certainly diminishes the supreme legal authority of the estates, so that they enjoy less than full sovereignty.[50] But this territorial overlordship was not conceded to the estates in the peace treaties of Westphalia. It belonged to them long before that, and most doctors of public law trace its origin already to the era of the Ottonian emperors,[51] especially as it is entirely plausible that most of the fiefs are conferred from the time of Conrad duke of Fran-

---

46. The Golden Bull (1356) regulated the election of the Holy Roman Emperor by the seven electoral princes.

47. On Electoral Capitulations, see note 8 in this chapter.

48. These are the peace treaties of Münster and Osnabrück, which concluded the Thirty Years' War in 1648 and defined the legal status of Lutherans, Calvinists, and Catholics in the Holy Roman Empire.

49. On *superioritas territorialis,* see note 7 in this chapter.

50. This is the first use of the word *sovereignty* in the disputation, and in the German version it is printed thus—Souverainit*ät*—giving the French word a German ending and indicating Thomasius's grasp at a synonym for his use of such terms as "supreme power," "supreme government," and so on.

51. A.D. 919–1024.

conia, as Mr. Monzambano reasons;[52] therefore also the *right over religious matters belonged to the princes long before the Peace Treaty of Westphalia, even well before the Reformation.* Their superstitious beliefs at that time had deprived them of the exercise of this right, but not of the right itself. Nor did the *Concordats of Germany* bind the princes, because these were brought about by deceit and fear, especially as *even the pope himself frequently violated them.* Further, it is true that the electors *in the Electoral Capitulation of Charles V, article 16* approved these concordats again, because they there wanted to require the emperor to try to persuade the pope to act according to these concordats. And so they *seem to have forgiven the injury inflicted on them by the pope,* and to have obliged themselves by force of the renewed and repeated agreement. Nevertheless, this approval of the concordats did not add any efficacy to them. When a right is renounced erroneously as the result of deceit then this renunciation is null and void, just as when someone owes me money and I renounce the right to sue on the basis of a promised repayment [which is then not forthcoming]. For it is clear from German history how great was the superstition that blinded most of Germany in its perception of the pope. And even though in Saxony the light of the gospel had already begun to shine to some extent (for Charles V was elected in the year 1519, but Luther had begun to argue against Tetzel already in 1517) nevertheless this Reformation had not yet penetrated the minds of the electors. It is thus not surprising that this concession had been inserted into the electoral capitulations of the emperor Charles, which was however omitted subsequently. Without doubt the Protestant electors were the first to urge this, because they had sensed that the Roman pope had so far exercised his rights in Germany by force, secretly and on sufferance, and that it was high time to shake off this yoke. One might wonder *how it came about that the pope exercised a greater tyranny over Germany than over all the other kingdoms of Europe.* However, it can be surmised that an important reason was jurists' success in persuading the emperor and the estates that Germany exercised supreme authority [*summum impe-*

52. Monzambano (Pufendorf), *De statu imperii Germanici,* chap. III, sec. 3 (see note 20 in this chapter).

rium] over the city of Rome and the pope, and that therefore the German emperor enjoyed all the rights that Constantine the Great and the other Roman emperors had held. But this was an excuse which was not founded in any right (for Charlemagne only accepted the right of acting as the advocate [*ius advocatiae*] of Rome) and seemed intolerable to the pope. The pope thus never attacked any other prince more frequently with excommunication, and never irritated anyone with more frequent revolts of priests, than the German emperor. But this just by-the-by.

§11. Let us return to the argument. It is clear that according to the Peace Treaty of Westphalia *article 5, §48* the Roman Catholics and the followers of the *Augsburg Confession* agreed that if, for example, Lutheran subjects in the territory of a Catholic prince had possessed the right to practice their religion in 1624, they should have this right in future without disturbance.[53] But it is doubtful *whether this convention also applies to indifferent matters or church ceremonies* in such a way that a Catholic prince cannot decide something regarding indifferent matters in a Lutheran church, even if these had already been observed in 1624. I will illustrate this with a particular case. In a Lutheran church in 1624 this hymn was commonly sung: "Preserve our faith in your word O Lord, and restrain the pope's and the Turks' murderous ways," etc. The *question is whether the prince can command his subjects to omit the words* "the pope's murderous ways" *and substitute others for them without violating the peace of Osnabrück?*[54] Here at first a scruple must be removed, namely that I am guilty of violating the peace of Osnabrück, as it is expressly stated in *article 5, §50 "Utriusque religionis"* that neither priests in preaching, nor Professors in teaching and disputing may cast doubt on the treaty, so that it might not be permissible for me to raise such a difficult question, which has not been discussed before. But I believe that in the

---

53. Signed in 1648, the Treaty of Westphalia determined that the confessional situation of 1624—the so-called *Normaljahr,* or standard year—should be accepted as status quo. Therefore, even if rulers changed their confession after this date, they could not change the confession of the established church in their territories.

54. One of the Westphalian peace treaties of 1648.

said paragraph [of the peace of Osnabrück] there is nothing preventing us from expressing our opinion on this matter. For it only warns us not to cast *doubt* on the peace by discussing it, or to derive assertions *contrary to the intention of the contracting parties;* but it does not prohibit resolving a doubt by appealing to the mind and intention of the contracting parties and from the context itself. For the argument in *Mevius, part 1, decision 67,*[55] that *the peace treaty does not admit a doctrinal but only an authentic interpretation,*[56] has already been solidly refuted by *the illustrious Mr. Rhez in his work on public law, book I, title 1, §§80, 81, 82.*[57] Here he says that *just as in private law one should not resort to an authentic interpretation unless the mind of the legislator is not apparent from the words or the intention, so this is also the case in public law.* Indeed, if there were no doctrinal interpretation in public law, this part of jurisprudence would not belong to jurists, because the whole office of jurists consists in the application of laws to facts through doctrinal interpretation. Having said this, it is easy to reply to the question [regarding the right of the Catholic prince to change the hymn] in the *affirmative.* For in all forms of law, divine and human, whatever is nowhere prohibited is permitted, and usually something is presumed to be permitted until the contrary is proved. In the *above article* there is nothing that could deprive the prince of this power. A Catholic prince of course is there prohibited from *coercing the conscience* of Lutherans, by decreeing something which is contrary to the *Augsburg Confession.* But the regulation of indifferent matters by the prince does not violate either the freedom of conscience or the *Augsburg Confession.* For things which injure conscience are no longer indifferent matters, with which our hypothesis is concerned. The question, though, whether that expression "restrain the pope's murderous ways" is sung loudly in a public congregation or not, is an indifferent matter; because if somebody refrains from this he does not commit any-

---

55. David Mevius, *Jurisdictio Summi Tribunalis Regii quod est Vismariae* (Jurisdiction of the supreme royal tribunal at Wismar) (Stralsund, 1664), 121–22.

56. On the difference between doctrinal interpretation and authentic interpretation, see note 9 in this chapter.

57. See note 42 in this chapter.

thing contrary to the *Augsburg Confession,* nor does he become a worse Christian because of this. It is not necessary to list further similar questions here, as they should be decided on the basis of the same principle.

§12. It is more contentious, though, *whether a prince has the power to change those church ceremonies, such as the date of Easter, which have been determined by general councils?* We intrepidly *affirm* this to be the case. For the councils that introduced rules on such indifferent matters received their binding force from the will of the prince. Therefore just as the prince can change other ecclesiastic regulations again and abrogate them, so he can do the same with decrees of councils. At present we do not want to discuss how much authority councils have in matters of faith, unless to say in passing that the *fourth Law in the Code in the title "On the Most Exalted Trinity,"* which is about the authority of councils, seems anti-Christian to us.[58] But it cannot be denied that bishops assembled in council do not have the power to compel other citizens to accept their decisions without a decree of the prince. Therefore even if the prince has once approved the decrees of some council concerning indifferent matters, he can nevertheless change his will later. For by this approval the prince has not renounced his right in religious affairs, nor has he transferred it into the hands of the clerics. And so the well-known legal maxim—that nothing is more natural than for something to be dissolved in the same way that it had been bound together—does not stand in our way; since this rule is to be understood of contracts between private persons, not in those matters that pertain to the prince by virtue of his supreme territorial power [*hohe Landes-Herrschaft*]. Furthermore, what is even more surprising, *the canonical standing of that which we read in the books of the apostles was not always acknowledged,* and is not acknowledged today, because these books were believed to contain not so much an exposition of divine law, as a piece of advice appropriate to those times. This was the case when *Paul* warned that *a deaconess should*

---

58. Law 4 in this chapter of Justinian's Code asserts that general councils of the church possessed imperial legitimacy and power. Thomasius rejects this as an instance of the clerical abuse of power.

not be elected who was not yet in her sixtieth year. Justinian on the other hand permitted her to be elected if she was at least in her fortieth year, in *Novels 123, c. 13.*[59] Similarly, although *Paul* enjoined that a bishop should be the *husband of one wife,* it is fashionable among our priests to have *four* or *five wives.*

§13. We have now seen the principles on which the right in indifferent matters is based. But already those who disagree with us attack us in hordes. Leading them are Havemann in *On the Right of Bishops, title XI, §2;*[60] Carpzov, *Consistorial Jurisprudence, book 2, definition 247;*[61] the Wittenberg legal reports *volume 1, part 2, membrum 2, section 1;*[62] Meisner, *Treatise on Indifferent matters, disputation 1, §§33, 34, 35;*[63] Schilter, *Institutes of Canon Law, book 2, title 1, §8.*[64] By virtue of their names and authority alone, these are authors fit to terrify their opponents, and all of them deny that the prince by virtue of his supreme authority can change or abrogate church ceremonies and indifferent matters. What shall we do? We will fight, but equipped with the weapons of reason and Christianity. Therefore let us await the first blow. (1) How, these authors ask, can a power over indifferent matters belong to the prince by virtue

59. See R. Schoell and W. Kroll (eds.), *Corpus Iuris Civilis,* vol. 3 (Berlin, 1954).

60. M. Havemann, *Dissertatio Theologico-Politica De Jure Episcopali* (Theological-political dissertation on episcopal law) (Hamburg, 1646).

61. Carpzov, *Jurisprudentia Ecclesiastica.* See note 29 in this chapter. In the passage referred to, Carpzov comments that "the prince or magistrate must not change or abolish ecclesiastical rituals, without consulting the ministers of the Word and the estates of the church assembled in a synod."

62. These appear to be the *Consilia Theologica Witebergensia* (Wittenberg theological opinions), a collection of writings by Martin Luther, assembled by the Wittenberg theological faculty and printed by Balthasar Christoph Wust the elder in Frankfurt am Main in 1664.

63. Balthasar *Meisner, Collegium Adiaphoristicum, in quo controversiae circa Adiaphora inter nos et Calvinianos agitatae, perspicue tractantur, veritasque orthodoxa defenditur* (A Collegium Adiaphoristicum, in which the controversies between ourselves and the Calvinists concerning *adiaphora* are considered and are discussed clearly, and orthodox truth is defended) (Wittenberg, 1663).

64. Johann Schilter, *Institutiones Juris Canonici Ad Ecclesiae Veteris et Hodiernae Statum Accommodatae* (Institutes of canon law, conformable to the condition of the ancient and present-day church) (Jena, 1681).

of his supreme authority, as *Christian liberty,* which belongs to all Christians, is thereby violated? (2) Is it not impious and anti-Christian [they ask] to hand the *power over consciences* to the prince, because *religion* by its very nature cannot be subject to any human authority? (3) They insist that the church does not consist of the prince alone, but of the three estates, the clerical, the political, and the economic;[65] and so *the right to change indifferent matters is held by the entire church,* not the prince alone, as he is only one member of the church. (4) Finally they appeal to the *examples of the kings of Israel* whom God afflicted with severe punishments because they tried to change something in the church by their own authority; that is, they refer to the examples of Gideon, *Judges chapter 8;* to Saul who offered a blasphemous sacrifice, *1 Samuel 15;* and to Uzziah who approached the altar of the Lord to burn incense without permission, *2 Chronicles 26.*[66] From these they believe it is sufficiently clear that it is against the will of God if Christian princes claim the right in indifferent matters for themselves alone. And thus they say that our princes rightly abstain from its exercise, because this would smack of nothing if not of supreme tyranny, as Meisner puts it in the passage referred to above.

§14. To avoid proceeding in a sophistic fashion, we will examine each objection in turn, determining to what extent it has a solid foundation. But I am not surprised that Havemann dared to write these things, as in the said treatise he was so audacious that he did not hesitate to deprive princes of almost every right in religious affairs, leaving them only the

---

65. This is a reference to traditional Lutheran church law and the *Dreiständelehre,* or the doctrine of the three estates. According to this, the church as a human institution was divided into three orders—the magistrate, the clergy, and the laity—each of which fulfilled specific functions in the regulation of the church's affairs, and among which power was to be shared.

66. Gideon, after defeating the Midianites, made a golden idol out of the spoils. Saul had offered sacrifices to God from the spoils of the war against the Amalekites but did not obey God's command to fight against the Amalekites "until they are consumed" (1 Samuel 15:18). King Uzziah went to the temple to burn incense, although this was the prerogative of the priests, and was afflicted with leprosy as a punishment.

glory of obeying the clergy. In fact he went so far as to declare it impious to leave cases concerning matrimony to the judgment of jurists, or to have them sent to faculties of law *see title XIII, §4.* But let us leave these matters aside and examine the *first* argument opposed to us, which they base on the supposed *violation of Christian liberty.* But I believe that Christian liberty here is only a pretext, and that this argument derives from another source. For it is widely acknowledged among us that the prince has the right to make ecclesiastic and consistorial regulations on matrimonial matters, the incomes of the clergy, visitations, consistories, the administration of alms, and similar (see Brunnemann, *Ecclesiastic Law, book 1, chapter 2, §34;* Schilter, *op. cit., book 1, title 2, §14*).[67] If therefore the prince can exercise these rights without infringing on Christian liberty, why should it be violated by laws concerning other indifferent matters in the church? Unless someone wants to assert that the difference is as follows: indifferent matters (or church ceremonies) are to be observed in *public congregations* of Christians, the other laws *outside of these.* This would be absurd though. For who would imagine that *Christian liberty is restricted to churches and public congregations?* Place certainly cannot make any difference to Christian liberty, but wherever there are Christians, be it in the church or outside, Christian liberty accompanies them. Nor are Christians only Christians when they are in church, but outside of it, when they are occupied with other matters. And if it were the church buildings which brought about Christian liberty, which is what they pretend, the Christian citizen who wants to draw up his last will in a church, for example, would not be required to have seven witnesses.[68] Meisner himself seems to have sensed this because he says in *the above disputation 1, §56,*[69] *that if the church or the secular authorities promulgate legitimate laws on indifferent matters for the sake of the public good, which they by virtue of their office are entrusted with, these laws must*

---

67. Brunnemann, *De Jure Ecclesiastico Tractatus posthumus;* Schilter, *Institutiones Juris Canonici* (as above).

68. These were the usual number of witnesses required for a last will, according to Roman law (see *Code of Justinian,* book VI, title XXIII, "De Testamentis: quemadmodum testamenta ordinantur" [On last wills: how last wills are arranged], 12).

69. Balthasar Meisner, *Collegium Adiaphoristicum.*

be obeyed in every case, also for the sake of conscience. For nobody can know-
ingly and intentionally do what is forbidden by these, or fail to do what is
commanded by them, and still have a clear conscience. Nor do the heads of
the church or the commonwealth thereby assume the right to command con-
sciences; for the internal liberty of conscience is not taken away by such laws,
but the use of the external liberty is limited because of certain circumstances.
But who can reconcile this with the previous utterances by Meisner?

§15. *The second* objection they use to attack our opinion is their belief
that [in regulating indifferent matters] the prince thereby arrogates the
right to command consciences, which seems a rather harsh argument to
me, to put it mildly. We have already explained what conscience is above,
and from this it is quite clear what rule over consciences is, namely: when
a prince or someone else wants to force me to agree with something that
my intellect abhors as false; for example, if a Lutheran prince wanted to
force his Calvinist subjects (or vice versa) to profess the same confession
as his own, and to believe in the same articles of faith as he does. For
the human intellect is privileged by God to such a degree that it is not
beholden to any human authority, in that the recognition of truth is the
child only of those reasons which are suitable for eliciting the assent of
the mind. This is especially so when the mysteries of Christian religion
are concerned, which are above the comprehension of human reason,
and which require a special act of divine grace in order to convince our
mind. But this divine grace is incompatible with coercion. Thus I can
be compelled to utter a sound without meaning, to perform some ges-
ture, or to dissimulate the thoughts of my mind and to speak words
which differ from these thoughts; but I cannot be compelled to believe.
For we must believe with our whole heart *Acts VIII 37.*[70] This divine
grace will be attained, however, when the teacher sincerely and ardently
desires and prays that God communicate the grace of the Holy Spirit to
the listener; also when the listeners themselves are sincere, humble, and
directed toward God, and desire this grace with ardent prayers. Therefore it is impossible that human coercion could produce a realization of

70. This verse is omitted in some versions of the Bible.

divine truth within us, as not even those threatening and quarrelsome scholastic disputations, which seem to compel the thoughts of others, are capable of producing this realization in our mind. *Poiret, On Solid Erudition, part 3, §35.*[71] But if only the orthodox had weighed this carefully from the time of Constantine the Great to the present; then there certainly would not have been so many sad examples of persecutions for the sake of differing articles of faith, about which the *Praeses* has spoken at length *in his public lectures on book 1 of the Code* [of Justinian]. But those who accuse princes of this crime [of coercing conscience], just because they alter indifferent matters, do them an injustice. *Divine law has not set down anything* concerning indifferent matters; nor do these belong to the *concepts in the intellect,* but to the decision of the will, which, in these external indifferent matters, is subject to the authority of the prince. Therefore, just as it cannot be said that the prince exercises authority over consciences if he prescribes to Christian citizens which formulae they must observe in contracts, last wills, and similar cases, so it cannot be said here either. Thus when learned authors *distort the term authority over consciences to such a degree, seeking to cloak their stubborn resistance beneath it, there can be no excuse for such an abuse* [72]

§16. The *third* objection which they formulate, on the nature and character of the church, is no better.[73] We concede that the church *consists of three estates,* although attention could be drawn to several matters here that we deliberately omit. But we deny *that therefore anything can be concluded contrary to our opinion.* The family consists of three forms of

71. Pierre Poiret, *De Eruditione Solida, Superficiaria et Falsa* (On solid, superficial, and false erudition), which was published in an edition by Christian Thomasius in Frankfurt in 1694.

72. A reference to the resistance of the Lutheran estates in the territories of the Elector of Brandenburg to the intervention of the Calvinist elector in their ecclesiastical affairs.

73. In this section Thomasius criticizes two standard doctrines of Lutheran church law, the *Dreiständelehre* (the three estates doctrine) and the *Zweipersonenlehre* (the two-persona doctrine). Each of these teaches that the prince has his rights over the church as a member of it. But Thomasius's argument is that the prince's right in the religious affairs of a church is independent of membership in that church.

society, the conjugal, the paternal, and the domestic; similarly, the commonwealth consists of many families, hamlets, villages, towns, and so on. But who would want to argue from this that the family heads and the prince do not have the right to exercise authority over the family and the commonwealth respectively? The line of argument of the learned doctors, however, is similarly stupid. In any case, I know full well that *what is suited to the commonwealth is not on that account suited to the church,* since the prince is not the head of the church in the same way as he is the head of the commonwealth, as Pufendorf shows in his priceless treatise *On the Relationship of Religion to the Civil State.*[74] But as the regulation of indifferent matters is part of the right over religious affairs undoubtedly possessed by the prince, I believe that with the following argument I have been able to dispel this objection effectively. For the right in religious affairs belongs to the prince as such, not to him as member of the church. For even if a prince were not a member of that church—if, for example, we had a Calvinist prince who was not a member of the Lutheran church—he nevertheless would have this right.[75] This means, incidentally, that the authorities on public law do not seem to speak with sufficient accuracy when they ascribe a twofold persona to the Protestant princes of our empire, the one as *princes,* the other as *bishops.* See our supervisor's *Notes on Monzambano, chapter 5, §12, letter x.*[76] But Carpzov pesters us in *definition 247, number 14*—drawing on Menzer's *Exegesis of the Augsburg Confession, article 16* and Reinking, *On Secular and Ecclesiastical Rule, part 1, chapter 6, number 5*—that the *government of the church* must be neither monarchical, nor democratic, but

---

74. Samuel Pufendorf, *De Habitu Religionis Christianae ad Vitam Civilem;* English trans.: *Of the Nature and Qualification of Religion in Reference to Civil Society* (see note 13 in this chapter).

75. This was the case in the territories of the Elector of Brandenburg.

76. Thomasius's comments on Pufendorf's work on the imperial constitution were published as *Scholia continua in textum Severini de Monzambano de statu Imperii Germanici* (Continual comments on the text of Severinus de Monzambano's work on the state of the German empire) (Halle, 1695).

aristocratic.[77] But I do not want to oppose Carpzov to Carpzov, for since he himself declared above that the ecclesiastic, political, and economic estates within the church need to consent to a change in indifferent matters, he should not have said, on the basis of this hypothesis, that the government of the church is aristocratic. But I will rather quote the words of Pufendorf in *On the Relationship of Religion to the Civil State,* *§32: These are absurd questions, whether the most appropriate constitution of the church is monarchical, aristocratic, or democratic. For these constitutions apply only to the political state, which is a conjunction of many human beings, who adhere to a power which exists for itself and does not depend on any other human authority. But the structure which is found in the church obviously is of a different kind.*[78] However, if someone asked me to what form of government does the right over religious affairs or indifferent matters belong? I reply: if the commonwealth in which the church exists is democratic, then it is democratic, and so on. For this right is part of

77. Thomasius is referring to Benedict Carpzov's *Jurisprudentia Ecclesiastica seu Consistorialis* (see note 61 in this chapter). Carpzov drew on Balthasar Mentzer, *Exegesis Augustanae Confessionis: cujus Articuli XXI breviter & succincte explicantur* (Exegesis of the Augsburg Confession: the twenty-one articles of which are explained briefly and succinctly and illustrated after being subjected to the antithesis of the heterodox) (Giessen, 1613); and Theodor Reinking, *De Regimine Seculari et Ecclesiastico* (On secular and ecclesiastical government) (Giessen, 1619).

78. Only the first sentence of the italicized quotation can be found at this point in Pufendorf's text. The following two sentences are an interpolation. Crull's 1698 English rendering of the original passage is broadly accurate: "Neither is it requisite to be solicitous about any particular or certain Form of Government in the Church, *viz.* whether the same ought to be Monarchical, Aristocratical or Democratical. For, these several forms belonging only to a Civil Government are very preposterously made use of in the behalf of the Church, which is far different from a Temporal State. And as Churches and Commonwealths are erected for different Ends: so the Offices belonging to both are altogether of a different Nature" (Pufendorf, *Of the Nature and Qualification of Religion,* p. 68). It is not possible to say whether Brenneisen or Thomasius—or indeed a third party—is responsible for the unauthorized "statist" interpolation in the quotation. We can say, though, that the interpolated sentences are not present in this passage as it appears in Thomasius's own edition of and commentary on Pufendorf's text, which is faithful to the original. For the relevant passage in Thomasius's edition, see Christian Thomasius, *Vollständige Erläuterung der Kirchenrechts-Gelahrtheit* (Frankfurt and Leipzig, 1740), pt. I, p. 237.

supreme territorial authority, therefore it is exercised in the same way as the other parts of supreme territorial authority.[79]

§17. It is not necessary to reply to the *fourth* objection, because we have already shown, in §6, what is to be thought of such examples of reasoning. Nevertheless, in order that no doubt remains, we will consider this again, especially as both theologians and jurists have so far used this argument in similar cases, though its weakness is palpable. For by the very fact that God had furnished the *Jewish religion* and its external rites, and had commanded their observance, no mortal had the power to alter these or to add anything to them or detract anything from them. As a result, it can rightly be said *that in the Jewish religion there were no indifferent matters,* as everything was to be governed by express order of God. It was thus not permitted to clothe this religion, which God had established, in any other external rites, *not even with the consent of the priests and the other Jews. Christ and the apostles, however, never forbade using other indifferent matters in the practice of Christian veneration.* For if they had done this, not only would our princes have sinned if they wanted to introduce these, but all councils, however many there have been, and bishops assembled in these would have been guilty of a severe crime, like those priests among the Jews who wanted to introduce different rituals. We can thus see how foolish they are who pretend that Christian princes are just as worthy of punishment as the Israelite kings. If such punishment were valid, then it would apply when the prince wanted to arrogate to himself those powers which belong to ordained persons (as it is said): the right to baptize, to administer communion, and the other acts of ministry which belong to the divine ministers, from which the prince is in any case excluded. This is true to such an extent that we declare that secular authority and the priestly office cannot coincide in one person, which is a conclusion the *Praeses* has deduced at

---

79. Following Pufendorf, Thomasius treats sovereignty as neutral with regard to the forms of government—monarchical, aristocratic, democratic—through which it is exercised. As a part of sovereignty, the right to supervise religious affairs is similarly independent of particular constitutional forms of government.

length *in his notes on Monzambano*. In any case, it is not worth the effort to discuss the other objections which exist in the writings of the learned authors, especially in the legal opinions published by the Wittenbergers,[80] for they are of a similar kind. Therefore we shall progress to:

CHAPTER II

On How to Practice the Right over Indifferent Matters, and on Some Special Questions to Be Resolved on the Basis of the First Chapter

Contents

§1. The prince should beware that he does not make use of this right at the wrong moment, in order that the populace does not rebel at the instigation of the clerics. Examples. The *Consilium* of the Wittenbergers is hardly Christian. A response is given to the objection concerning the fear that this is a slippery slope, as Brunnemann argues.

§2. The prince should take care to separate the indifferent matters from those which are not indifferent. The testimonies of Gregory Nazianzus and Grotius on the ease with which true theology can be learned by the prince. Even a pagan can easily learn which matters among Christians are indifferent and which are not.

§3. The prince should seek the council of others and take care that in the promulgation of the law the populace is informed of the right of the prince. The admonition of Seneca: law should command, not argue. The tedious disputations of Justinian. Nevertheless the prince should not follow his councillors blindly. Clergymen who obtrude their advice in such affairs become guilty of striving for secular power.

§4. The prince must take care that scandalous indifferent matters are abrogated.[81] Indifferent matters are twofold, some tantamount to a

---

80. See note 62 in this chapter.

81. The term "scandal" (*scandalum*) describes an offense to fellow believers, which

commanded action, some tantamount to a prohibition. The former are to be introduced, the latter abolished. More effort should be devoted to abrogating than to introducing indifferent matters. A reply is given to the objection that those weak in their faith must not be offended.[82]

§5. The prince should take care that the ministers of the word inform the populace of the nature of indifferent matters. The prince does this by his own right according to Brunnemann, and can enjoin the ministry to treat of piety and moral questions. If the priests pretend to be scandalized, this is an offense [*scandalum*] which is taken by them, and does not stand in the way of the right of the prince. The argument concerning scandal is turned around, and it is shown that because of the scandal of others, one should abstain from indifferent matters that scandalize them. It is godless wisdom to teach that one should dance to give offense to the Calvinists.

§6. From what has been said it is deduced: (1) that a Protestant prince can introduce the Gregorian calendar in his territory. A reply is given to the dissenting opinion of Havemann on the authority of the councils with regard to indifferent matters. The Gregorian calendar does not belong to the matters of Anti-Christ, and so on.

§7. (2) Ecclesiastical music is under the direction of the prince. The complaints of Brunnemann and Duarenus about the abuse of this music. The caution against the Wittenbergers.

§8. (3) It pertains to the prince to set down rules for the vestments of ministers. Those vestments are irrelevant to the splendor of the church. They are mistakenly counted among the sacred matters.

§9. (4) It pertains to the prince to regulate the use of images. The abuse of images among us. It is important that the precept of not venerating images is expressed in our catechism. It smacks of superstition

---

is a violation of Christian charity and causes others to commit a sin. This rested in particular on Matthew 18:6: "[W]hoever causes one of these little ones who believe in me to sin [*scandalizaverit*], it would be better for him to have a great millstone fastened round his neck and to be drowned in the depth of the sea."

    82. That is, scandalized, contrary to Christian charity (see previous note).

if the members of the congregation incline their head in front of the altar. A reply is given to the distinction made by the Leipzig theologians.

§10. (5) Brunnemann and the illustrious Stryk agree that it is justified to abolish Latin hymns. The inappropriate zeal of Meisner is noted.

§11. (6) Exorcism as an indifferent matter is subject to the power of the prince, according to Brunnemann and Stryk. The unrest in Saxony over exorcism. Several cases which are relevant here and which were decided differently by theologians in Dedekennus.

§12. (7) The prince can change practice concerning private confession and the fee for confession [*Beichtpfennig*].[83] Conclusion.

§1. In all matters concerning the rights of princes, the question whether the prince has a right to do something is not the same as that whether this is useful to him, or is a prudent course of action. In the same way, the prince very often has a just cause to wage war because of an injury he has suffered, but the condition of his state and his country do not allow him to do so at the time. It is therefore appropriate that the prince should weigh all circumstances of the fact and his means, to determine whether it is to the advantage of the commonwealth to expose itself to the danger of war, or to suffer the injury for a while and to defer the resolution of the matter to a time when it is more opportune. It is the same with our right in indifferent matters, as Grotius correctly observes in *On the Right in Sacred Affairs, chapter 6, §1*.[84] For it can easily happen that *unrest and sedition* spread in a commonwealth, when the populace, which usually is superstitious, attributes a singular sanctity to external things and indifferent matters, venerates them, and therefore imagines

83. In the 1690s Pietist reformers attempted to change confessional practice in the Lutheran church in Berlin. This was opposed by the Lutheran congregations. The changes involved the abolition of private, auricular confession and of the fee (*Beichtpfennig*) paid to the clergyman taking confession.

84. Hugo Grotius, *De Imperio Summarum Potestatum circa Sacra: Commentarius Posthumus* (On the authority of supreme powers in sacred matters: a posthumous commentary) (Paris, 1647).

that violence is being done to religion itself as a result of their alteration. This is especially likely if they are confirmed in this opinion by the clergy, on whose will and judgment the views of the populace usually depend. We have sufficient evidence from ecclesiastical history of the uproar caused by the *removal of images from the churches* under Emperor Leo Isaurus when, at the instigation of the clergy, the populace proceeded with such lack of restraint that in one place they killed workmen who were removing images of the Savior. As the emperor persevered in his plan, the pope excommunicated him and denied him the Italian tribute payments owed to him, in a rather unapostolic manner, as the Gotha Ecclesiastical History says in *book 2, chapter 3, section 7, §4*.[85] If I am not mistaken, Hospinianus's *Discordant Concord* can be consulted on the *tumults which arose in Marburg for the same reason,*[86] not to say anything of the others, which have been stirred up by the immoderate zeal of the clergy, even the Protestant clergy. The rather untheological theological advice in *Dedekennus, part 2, title 5, On Exorcism*[87]—where the question debated is *what the pastor should do if he is commanded by the prince to omit exorcism when the parents of a child which is to be baptized desire it*— provides sufficient indication of the mind of those consulted. For they do not blush to write that if the prince wants to remove such a refractory priest from his office *then the entire ministry must stand by this priest; and if the prince still insists on the removal of this pastor, the ministry must nevertheless take his side, and without doubt the provincial estates will also*

85. *Compendium Historiae Ecclesiasticae . . . in usum Gymnasii Gothani . . . deductum* (Handbook of ecclesiastical history, for the use of the Gymnasium in Gotha) (Gotha, 1660). This refers to the attempts by the Roman emperor Leo III (ruled A.D. 717–41) to abolish the veneration of saints' images. An edict in A.D. 730 ordered the destruction of these images.

86. Rudolf Hospinianus, *Concordia Discors, Hoc est, De Origine et Progressu Formulae Concordiae Bergensis, Liber Unus* (Discordant Concord, that is, on the origin and progress of the Formula of Concord in Berg) (Zurich, 1607). The relevant passage is in chapter LVII, pp. 486–94, "On the Reformation of the Church in Upper Hessia from the Remnants of Papism."

87. This is probably Georg Dedeken, *Thesauri Consiliorum et Decisionum Volumen Primum, Ecclesiastica Continens* (The treasury of advice and decisions, first volume, containing ecclesiastical matters) (Jena, 1671), though the reference in that case is not quite correct. There is a section on exorcism in part II, section VII.

join them, so that resistance is strengthened in order for it to become unnec-
essary to obey the prince. But I do not see how such advice can be given
by those who profess Christianity, unless somebody wants to declare that
impiety and sedition can coexist with Christianity itself. Those who have
expressed the above opinion should see how to reconcile these. But, they
say, if concessions are made in one point, it must be feared that this is
a slippery slope toward a change of the confession itself along Calvinist
lines. Brunnemann responds piously and with gravity in his *On Eccle-*
siastical Law, book 1, chapter 2, §31. This is worldly prudence. You should
act and obey in all matters that do not violate piety. All other matters are to
be committed to the wisdom of divine providence, and should something be
commanded that cannot be obeyed with a clear conscience, then there will
be the time to follow the apostolic rule: It is appropriate to obey God more
than humans. For it is wholly unworthy of a subject of a prince to say: there
is a snake in the grass, that is, the prince intends something other than what
he says; this comes very close to the crime of violation of majesty. For the
words of the prince must be believed as much as his oath and, until something
has emerged which is contrary to conscience and religious truth, one must
presume all good things of him. In order to avoid this danger, we will say
something about the standard by which this right is judged.

§2. In order for the prince to exercise his right in indifferent matters
correctly he requires above all an *understanding of religious matters so that*
he does not go further under the pretext of indifferent matters than the nature of Christianity permits, and does not interfere in the internal matters of religion, as they are called.[88] No prudent prince can put forward
an opinion in a philosophical debate if he is ignorant of this discipline.
On what grounds then could he decide something concerning indifferent matters if he does not know what an indifferent matter is and which
things are indifferent in theological affairs? But maybe somebody will
object to us that it is morally impossible *for the prince to acquire such a*
comprehensive knowledge of theological matters when he is overwhelmed

88. The German texts adds: "For these matters, as we have said above, are not
subject to his government."

by the burden of other affairs. For, if Mr. Conring in his work *On German Courts*[89] has already noted that the German princes could not learn Roman law, because of the prolixity of this doctrine and the rudimentary nature of education at court (I quote the words of Conring), it is asking far too much to oblige princes to study the venerable subject of theology in depth, and to interfere in the disputes of theologians. I should like to refute this objection with the words of Gregory Nazianzus,[90] which have been cited by Grotius in *the said treatise, chapter 5, §9. Theology and religion,* he said, *are simple and unadorned and consist of divine testimonies without much artifice, which nevertheless some have perversely turned into a most difficult art.* Grotius adds: *For there are other matters, partly metaphysical, partly historical, partly grammatical, which are commonly debated by theologians with great controversy and with much clamor, but with which the mind of the prince need not be burdened, no more than with the subtleties of the law, although the king does need to have a complete knowledge of the first principles of law. For those matters, which, as the apostle says in 1 Timothy 1, give greater occasion for disputes than for edification, which is achieved through faith, he can leave aside with complete safety.* This brilliant man hit the nail on the head, and there is no need for the purposes of our argument to add anything to this. And in this manner I think that Christian affairs are sufficiently protected against the interference of *pagan princes,* to whom we already above granted the right in religious matters. For if the pagan prince observes the method we have just mentioned, there is no danger of the consciences of Christians being coerced, especially if he draws on the advice of Christians and on their instruction. Even should he not want to embrace Christianity, he can nevertheless be taught easily what the Christian religion does and does not consider an indifferent matter. For although a man regenerated by the divine spirit is the most suitable judge of spiritual affairs, and all correct judgment on divine matters by a human relies on

89. Hermann Conring, *De Iudiciis Reipublicae Germanicae* (On the courts of the German commonwealth) (Helmstedt, 1647). The passage referred to is §LIX.

90. Gregory Nazianzus (A.D. 329–90): Greek theologian and defender of Nicene orthodoxy against the Arians.

divine assistance, nevertheless there is no reason why the prince, if he draws on his common sense and natural reason, and frees his mind from prejudice just a bit, should not be able to understand easily what in Christianity is held to be an indifferent matter, and what is considered to be commanded or prohibited.

§3. Therefore it is prudent for the prince not to rely on his own judgment only, *but to consult his ministers and other Christians who excel by their piety and their erudition and are endowed with a temperate mind.* For one person does not see or hear everything. If this is a rule he must observe in profane and purely political matters, how much more in those matters where it is highly dangerous to err? And since the multitude is usually bewitched by religious ceremony, and tends to obey its spiritual guides rather than its princes, it is prudent to take care *that the people are clearly informed in the very promulgation of the law about the right of the ruler and the nature of indifferent matters,* in order that the people are not irritated by a reformation at a later point. Seneca indeed reminds us rightly, when he criticizes the preambles of laws: *Law commands, it does not argue.* But this can be appropriate only in purely secular laws (although our Justinian overwhelmed us with his generosity and prefaced his constitutions with their reasons and causes at great length, sometimes *ad nauseam*); in this matter, however, the abovementioned caution is very useful, *so that the populace does not persuade itself that its religion is threatened with a reformation.* Nevertheless, there is nothing more pernicious than when the prince does everything on the basis of the judgment of others; for it is clear from examples that however much princes are otherwise of an upright and mild disposition, they are led to savagery toward the innocent by people who conceal either a stupid eagerness or inhuman malice behind a mask of holiness. In other words, the prince must indeed consult others, both clergymen and politicians, but *he must not acquiesce only in their judgment.* For it is clear from the above, that the prince is not strictly speaking obliged to follow their advice. Those clerics who believe that their judgments on these matters are to be followed unreservedly, shamelessly render themselves suspect of striving for secular authority, from which Christ's utterance should rightly deter them: "But you do not likewise."[91] The passages which they tend to quote for this purpose from the Old Testament are not relevant here, and have been refuted by Grotius in *the said treatise chapter 6, §7, etc.*

§4. But just as the welfare of his subjects is or certainly should be the supreme law of the prince,[92] so he should take care of the well-being of his subjects in indifferent matters. This he does most effectively *if he abolishes ceremonies which tend and dispose more toward superstition than toward edification,* which the *Formula of Concord* itself does not consider to be properly indifferent matters in *title X,* and which today are widespread in Lutheran churches, as experience testifies and Brunnemann observes in his work on *Ecclesiastic Law, passim.* For even if the so-called indifferent matters lie somewhere between precepts and prohibitions as intermediates, nevertheless this middle position should not be understood as a single point, but with some latitude, so that it is now closer to a prohibition, now closer to a precept, roughly the way the Peripatetics explain the right mean in virtue.[93] For that which is conducive to edification or which serves the purpose of Christian congregations—even if not necessarily, but by accident—is closer to the precepts of Christian religion; what, on the contrary, is an impediment to edification and worship, is closer to being prohibited, and so it is praiseworthy to introduce the former and to abrogate the latter. Here the *illustrious chancellor of Jena comments elegantly in his dissertation on Reason of State, number 19, conclusion 7: Because,* he says, *in matters concerning external discipline and ceremonies God did not want to prescribe to us specifically what we have to do, it is here appropriate to take refuge in the general rules he has given, in order that whatever the necessity of the church requires to be taught for the sake of order and decency, is introduced accordingly. Here it is necessary to be cautious so that superstition, sorcery, empty show, cor-*

91. Luke 22:26.

92. The Latin text here alludes to Cicero's dictum that "salus populi suprema est lex" (the welfare of the people should be the supreme law), in his *De Legibus* (On laws), III.iii.8.

93. See, for example, Aristotle, *Nicomachean Ethics* (London: Oxford University Press, 1925), bk. 2, 2.

ruption of the sacraments, and suspect formulae are not introduced into the church under the cover and pretext of ceremonies.[94] Therefore the prince acts correctly and prudently, if he recalls the saying of Paul *Colossians 2, verses 21, 22, 23, and 1 Timothy 4, verses 3, 4,*[95] and takes care *that Christians are not smothered by the multitude of indifferent matters;* or, if they are already smothered by them, *that he liberates them,* and does not lend the clergy his ears, *who claim that the weaker members of the congregation are scandalized and offended.*[96] For this is a pretext which many have used against the princes to tie their hands, to prevent them from exercising their right in indifferent matters and make them dependent on their judgment. For if we investigate the reasons for this scandal, it is certainly the fault of the clergymen that the people are imbued with such principles as lead them to be scandalized. For if they informed their congregations correctly of the nature of indifferent matters, what obstacle would there be for this scandal to cease? They should urge true piety, and nobody will then be offended. For Brunnemann in the *said treatise book 1, chapter 6, part 1, §4 & following* has noted that in the homilies addressed to the people, the study of piety usually is not inculcated sufficiently, and instead sermons are dressed up in fancy oratory and rhetorical figures. I leave it to others to judge whether perhaps the doctrine of indifferent matters is thus often neglected because it does not seem rewarding to priests to be able to merit the grace of God through purity of mind alone, and a scrupulously honest life.

94. Gottfried von Jena, *Fragmenta de Ratione Status* (s.l., 1667), "Dissertatio Nona decima De Ratione Status." See note 42 in this chapter.

95. In the first of these passages Paul refers to unnecessary human regulations, which "are of no value in checking the indulgence of the flesh" (v. 23). The other, by Timothy, is a reference to prohibitions of marriage and to dietary restrictions, which are irrelevant to piety.

96. "Scandal," which violated Christian charity, was an important argument for retaining indifferent rituals, although they were not considered essential for salvation (see note 85 in this chapter). See, for example, the *Formula Concordiae,* chap. X, "De ceremoniis ecclesiasticis quas vulgo adiaphora seu res medias et indifferentes vocantur" (On the ecclesiastical ceremonies which are vulgarly called adiaphora or middle-things and indifferent matters), in *Libri Symbolici,* ed. Franke.

§5. So it will also be a matter for the prince's prudence *to command the ministers of the word at the right time to inform the people frequently of the nature of indifferent matters.* The most powerful Elector of Brandenburg did this most wisely in *the Church Order of the Duchy of Magdeburg, title 2 at the beginning,* the words of which we have already placed at the beginning of the dissertation. I do not know, though, whether these are observed diligently. However, where this admonition and the doctrine are neglected by clergymen, there I believe that the prince can command not only for the sake of prudence, but *justly,* that this matter is treated more diligently, so that the minds of the rude populace are purged of superstitious principles and are imbued with a concept of true piety and Christianity. There is no reason for them to oppose the prince and claim *that he does not have the right to prescribe what they should preach*—on the ground that sermons pertain to the *internal matters* of Christian religion, so that the prince acts impiously if he claims the right to regulate them. For we have already warned above, that this distinction [between internal and external religious matters] gives rise to disputes, and that all that should be considered is whether something is contrary to divine law and Christianity, or not. But this mandate of the prince is far from being contrary to Christianity, rather, it promotes it. For if the priests do not fulfill their office correctly, and conduct inane *theoretical controversies* rather than teaching the *doctrine of Christian piety and virtues* in their sermons, the prince is able to discipline them and remind them of their duty by virtue of his right in sacred matters. If he could not do this, what use would the right in religious affairs be to him? And if the prince were a mere defender and advocate of the church, the right in religious matters would be nothing but a vain name. For in truth the prince would then depend on the authority and the command of ambitious clergy-men. Thus it is also a pious admonition by Brunnemann *in the said treatise, book 1, chapter 6, part 1, §15,* when he says that: *It belongs to the office of the authorities, when they see the preachers' office being neglected— with vices not being punished, and the true fear of God and good works not being properly encouraged—that they should remind them to properly fulfill their office. It is a most certain sign of pride to refuse to be corrected or ad-monished.* Therefore I certainly declare that the misguided conscience of the populace must be suffered to some extent, but when there are suitable means of removing this error it is better to use these, and if the priests refuse to do so the prince can coerce them. For if they *want to resist a prince who gives just commands,* and do not want to teach their congregations the doctrine of indifferent matters,[97] they provide enough evidence of their evil intentions. For I believe that if this matter were explained solidly in two or three sermons, the populace could easily be brought to change its mind for the better, so that they were not offended by the abrogation of useless ceremonies. If the priests themselves want to pretend that *they are scandalized* and say that they cannot with a clear conscience permit the prince to exercise this right, because this right to decide on indifferent matters does not belong to him, I then ask them to examine the above objections to this opinion, and to refute them; or, if they cannot refute them, to acknowledge their error. For if they do not use any better weapons to support their opinion than the authors quoted above, they have no basis on which to fight. Even if we had to admit that the scandal supposedly suffered by the populace is a fact, this it seems cannot present an obstacle to the prince. For this scandal is only *taken,* not given. Unless I am mistaken, the theologians themselves form the rule of the scandal taken: *what is pious and honest must not and cannot be omitted because of the scandal caused.* To abrogate ceremonies which are redolent of superstition is pious and honest: and good things scandalize nobody, except an evil mind. *See the Catechesis of Dieterich on scandal.*[98] And Paul's saying that *he would never want to eat meat if a weaker brother is scandalized by it* does not present an obstacle either.[99]

97. The passage "and do not want to teach their congregations the doctrine of indifferent matters" is not in the German text.

98. Conrad Dietericus, *Institutiones Catecheticae, depromptae e B. Lutheri Catechesi & variis, recenter etiam B. Dn. Christiani Chemnitii Notis Illustratae. Editio novissima* (Institutes of the Catechism, taken from the blessed Luther's catechism and illustrated with various notes, recently also including those of Mr. Christian Chemnitz. The newest edition) (Frankfurt am Main and Leipzig, 1685), p. 555, where the distinction is drawn between a *scandalum datum* (an offense caused by false doctrine or hostile statement) and a *scandalum acceptum* (an offense caused to impious people and hypocrites by true doctrine or something honest and necessary).

99. 1 Corinthians 8:13.

For our case and his are not comparable. To eat meat is clearly an indifferent matter, but to abrogate superstitious ceremonies is something laudable. Nowhere, however, can one read that Paul ever abstained from something which was good in itself because somebody might take offense at it. But Scripture teaches rather that when the Jews tried to force him to accept circumcision as something necessary, he refused to concede this to them, because he considered it to be something tending toward superstition. *Galatians 2 verse 5.* What obstacle thus is there for the prince to use his right, without paying attention to that offense which has been taken? Just as Paul did not want to gratify the Jews, the prince too is not bound to do this. Therefore it seems to me entirely probable that this pretext of an offense taken has flowed from the same source from which, as we have shown above, the abuse of the term "conscience" stems. For, if *this offense taken* is the real reason for the objection here, why do we not also *abstain from certain ceremonies in our* [Lutheran] *church in order to avoid scandalizing the Calvinists?* For I know several Calvinists who, because of exorcism, always refused to be godfather at the baptism of a Lutheran child. Or why did the Wittenberg theologians in the passage cited above refuse to omit exorcism for the sake of the Lutheran parents who desired it to be omitted?[100] You see therefore the snake hiding in the grass and that there is something else behind this, other than the offense caused to the weaker members. And if they were to argue that the Calvinists are outside the fold of the true church, and no attention needs to be paid to their offense, I would reply that Paul also admonished his listeners not to give offense to the pagans *1 Corinthians 10 verse 32 and 33;* not to mention the other responses, which can be found in the *Praeses' On the Marrige of Lutheran and Calvinist Princely Persons.*[101] Therefore I have reason to suspect that this doctrine smacks

100. Georg Dedeken, *Thesauri Consiliorum et Decisionum Volumen Primum* (see note 87, earlier).

101. Christian Thomasius, *Rechtmaeßige Eroerterung Der Ehe- und Gewissens-Frage Ob zwey Fuerstliche Personen in Roemischen Reich deren eine der Lutherischen die andere der Reformirten Religion zugethan ist einander mit guten Gewissen heyrathen koennen?* (Rightful discussion of the question, which concerns marriage and conscience, whether two princely persons in the Holy Roman Empire, one of whom is Lutheran,

of the philosophy of those people in our church who say they dance out of spite for the Calvinists, which is a disgrace to them and to us.

§6. Let us now move on to specific questions, and show in certain examples how from the foundations which have so far been explained (especially in the first chapter) certain conclusions are to be drawn, which are commonly denied by the theologians of our sect. Let the first example be the *Gregorian Calendar, whether a Protestant prince can accept this in his territory and celebrate church holidays according to it?*[102] On the basis of the above principles, we fearlessly *affirm* this; for whether holidays are celebrated according to the Old Calendar or the New, in either case it is equally Christian. Religion does not suffer; and the prince can do this all the more, when he rules over some territories in which the Gregorian calendar is already in use. The establishment of these holidays is thus a regalian right of the prince. Whether Easter for example is celebrated on this day or that has no effect on the veneration of God. But we are contradicted by Havemann in *the work cited above, chapter XI, §4, where he tries by all means to deprive the political magistrate of this right. The prince, he says, can command that holidays are observed; but which days are holidays, when they are, and for how many days they are celebrated, this the magistrate cannot decide without taking advice from the clergy.* He uses the argument based on the Council of Nicaea[103] and says

---

while the other is Calvinist, can marry with a good conscience?) (Halle, 1689). In this treatise Thomasius defends the marriage of the Lutheran Duke Maurice William of Sachsen-Zeitz with Maria Amalia, the Calvinist daughter of the Elector Frederick William I of Brandenburg, who ruled from 1640 to 1688.

102. The Gregorian Calendar, named after Pope Gregory XIII, who proclaimed it in 1582, and now generally accepted in the Western world, was a modification of the earlier Julian Calendar and was designed to align the celebration of Easter with the time agreed to at the Council of Nicaea in 325. It required the deletion of ten days from the solar calendar. Non-Catholic countries initially refused to adopt what they considered to be a Catholic invention, only gradually doing so during the course of the eighteenth century.

103. The Council of Nicaea (A.D. 325) led to the condemnation of the Arian heresy, whose representatives had argued that God and Christ, his son, were not of the same essence or substance (*homousios*).

that at this council the day for celebrating Easter was discussed and decided upon; but this council, he writes, did not consist of princes and
politicians, but of bishops. However, we have already pointed out above,
that insofar as the councils take decisions on indifferent matters, they
require confirmation by the prince in order to be binding on the other
subjects. For bishops have no right to compel other Christians to agree
with them on these indifferent matters or, if they pretend to do so, they
are interfering in another person's affairs. Then there are many doubts
about the integrity of the Council of Nicaea, because it had distanced
itself to an enormous extent from the manner in which the apostles conducted that holy Council of Jerusalem, so that it is not safe to appeal to
the example of the Council of Nicaea. The laws which even now exist
in the *Code* of Theodosius and of Justinian clearly show which method
these bishops used in spreading the decrees of that council. Havemann
insists *that the New Calendar cannot be forced on any Christian because it
is that of Pope Gregory, but the pope is Anti-Christ, and so if the prince
wants to introduce the Gregorian calendar, he approves that which belongs
to Anti-Christ.* But who would not pity such an argument? In order to
prove his opinion Havemann himself cites the *chapter Licet, X "On feast
days"*[104] from canon law, a book that was completed by Pope Gregory
IX, who was no better than the Gregory who was the author of our
calendar. Therefore in the very work that he uses to accuse the princes
who introduce the Gregorian calendar of anti-Christian tendencies, he
accuses himself of the same crime, and simultaneously all those Protestants who have introduced canon law in church affairs. But where does
the fury of our passions not lead us? Another example is the third argument that he makes against the calendar, *that in the calendar many
impious people are included among the holy.* But this does not even merit
a refutation, and neither does his claim *that according to the Gregorian
calendar Easter is celebrated occasionally together with the Jews, and with
the Quartadeciman heretics.*[105] So what? Is this impious or contrary to

104. See the *Corpus Iuris Canonici,* Decreti Prima Pars, book II, title IX, chap. 3.
105. The Quartodecimans celebrated Easter on the same day as the Jewish Pass-
over, whatever the day of the week, rather than on the following Sunday.

Christianity? The Wittenberg theologians agree with Havemann in *Dedekennus, volume 1, part 6, numbers 1 & 2.* But as they put forward the same arguments, we do not want to spend time refuting them.

§7. Among the indifferent matters in the church we also count the *instrumental music commonly played in church,* and thus we declare that this is subject to regulation by the prince. We would like to quote the words of Brunnemann, so that it becomes clear how just the cause is for the prince to regulate these. Thus he says in *On Ecclesiastic Law, book 1, chapter 6, part 8, §4 that in all churches care must above all be taken that everything occurs for the edification of the church; but whatever does not contribute to the edification of the church, that is inappropriate. So, therefore, music is inappropriate, be it organ music or other instrumental music, if the human voice does not accompany it, so that the congregation knows what is being sung, and can say Amen. What does singing in Latin contribute to stimulating devotion? This music is indeed sweet to the ears, but it does not penetrate the mind. Everywhere one hears Italian concerts, Passemezzae, Villanellae,*[106] *and so on in churches, which please some people, because they delight the ears. But what is Saul doing among the prophets?*[107] He adds in §6: *In the meantime, while the organist plays the organ, and adds variations, the members of the congregation let their eyes stray all over the place, or fall into a sweet dream, and this is the devotion of our age.* So far Brunnemann. The papal jurist Duarenus makes similar comments in *On Ministers of the Sacred Church book 1, chapter 14.*[108] He says that *this sober music, closer to speech than song, causes the meaning of the words to flow more effectively into the minds of the listeners, unlike that contrived and theatrical music, which is frequent in the church at our time.* And shortly after this: *Now-*

106. *Passamezzo* was an Italian dance popular from the mid-sixteenth to the mid-seventeenth century. *Villanella* was a term for popular songs that originated in Naples in the same period.

107. That is, Saul, king of Israel, was not one of the Old Testament prophets, just as Italian music is no part of devotion.

108. Franciscus Duarenus, *De Sacrae Ecclesiae, Ministeriis ac Beneficiis* (On the ministers and benefices of the sacred church) (Paris, 1551). This was republished in several editions in the late seventeenth and early eighteenth centuries.

adays this type of music is approved of everywhere, so that it is considered
excellent and most necessary and is celebrated by all ministries of the church.
In the meantime we do not want to interfere in the controversy, whether
organs and other musical instruments are contrary to Christianity. For
our purpose it is sufficient if we have only established that this music
belongs to the indifferent matters, and that therefore the prince by virtue
of his supreme authority can regulate it. I also believe that nobody will
readily deny that in many churches there is a great abuse of this music,
and that many cantors imagine that they thereby contribute a lot to the
honor of God, even though their mind during the music is far from true
devotion and piety, which are the true sacrifices pleasing to God. All
other things are displeasing, no matter with what enormous effort they
are prepared. And in this manner we can avoid the severe censure of the
Wittenberg theologians in *Dedekennus volume 1, book 2, part 2, section*
6, number 6.

§8. Our judgment is the same on *certain kinds of vestments,* which ministers use, and which his *Magnificenz*[109] Mr. Stryk in his comments on
Brunnemann, ibid. §9 lists among the indifferent matters. If you consider this more closely it will become clear that these matters tend more
toward the abuse than to the proper use of edification. For the usual
argument *that they contribute to the external splendor of the church,* has
little to do with Christianity, which requires the mind to detach itself
from all external splendor and pomp. I will not have erred if I say *that*
this custom was invented by the clergy, in order to acquire authority and
veneration among the laity (I speak in the style of canon law), even though
the papalists tend to provide other reasons for justifying these vestments,
as can be read in Durandus *in his Account of Divine Offices, book 3, chapter*
1, Cardinal Bona, On Liturgical Matters, book 1, chapter 24.[110] I think that

---

109. This is the form of address for Samuel Stryk as pro-rector of the university
in Halle.
110. Gulielmus (William) Durandus, *Rationale Divinorum Officiorum* (Account
of divine offices) (Lyon, 1592); Johannes Bona, *Rerum Liturgicarum Libri Duo* (Two
books on liturgical matters) (Rome, 1671).

it is more suitable and Christian to excite veneration in the minds of others in the manner of the apostles, by other means than vestments. We do indeed read about the apostles' belts and other daily clothes, but not of the peculiar form, shape, material, and color of their clothes, by which they were distinguished from other citizens and Christians. *See Voetius' Politica Ecclesiastica Part I, book 4, treatise 4, chapter 4.*[111] And it is probable that at that time the distinction between clergymen and laymen emerged and that this ritual originated at that time. But it is all the more regrettable *that such clothes are included among the sacred objects* even by Protestant jurists, which certainly smacks of papism or paganism. For what is Saul doing among the prophets?[112] What do vestments have to do with what is sacred? And even though according to canon law and Roman law they are counted among the sacred matters, Protestants nevertheless should in all fairness abstain from this manner of speaking, and not describe any object as sacred which is not acknowledged as such in Holy Scripture. But just as Tribonian[113] inserted much from pagan jurists into his *Digests* that was redolent of paganism, so our jurists after the Reformation retained many papalist principles in church law, so that we have in the midst of Protestantism an ecclesiastical law with papalist tendencies.

§9. By common consensus among us [Lutherans] *images in churches* also belong to the class of indifferent matters, although it cannot be denied that they tend more toward superstition than toward the edification of the populace. We have already pointed out above that the cause of images was defended by the Roman Catholics against the Greek emperors,[114] especially because they regarded it as an extremely useful instrument for inculcating superficial rituals of piety into the rude populace.

---

111. Gisbert Voetius, *Politica Ecclesiastica, Pars Prima, Libri Duo Posteriores* (Ecclesiastical politics, part one, the two latter books) (Amsterdam, 1666).

112. See note 107 in this chapter.

113. Tribonian (ca. 475–545) was the Roman jurist who directed the compilation of the *Corpus Iuris Civilis* at the behest of the emperor Justinian.

114. See note 85 in this chapter.

If only we did not have to utter the same complaint against our own [church]. For daily experience shows that not a few among us Lutherans are too devoted to the veneration of images, and that they are not far removed from papist superstition. Therefore it is to be wished *that this precept not to venerate images were inculcated with greater care and earnestness* than we usually see it done. Then minds would be more detached from these external matters and led toward the internal. And this I think is sufficient for this same precept to be contained in the Lutheran catechism by command of the Protestant prince and for this dispute over the *distinction of the precepts of the Decalogue* to be omitted.[115] For it is not to be imputed to Luther, that he omitted this precept [from the catechism]. Because under the papacy he was accustomed to that order which Lutherans still follow today, and did not immediately see all defects of the papacy, he retained this ritual; even though he elsewhere preached and wrote with great severity against the worship of images. Therefore I do not in any way doubt that the prince can abrogate the custom of many places, *according to which people habitually go up to the altar, bow, and so to speak salute the images set up there.* The distinction, which the Leipzig theologians apply *in Dedekennus, volume 3, page 660,* between *adoration and veneration,* or moral and ceremonial reverence, is too subtle for the crude understanding of the populace. Therefore there is no reason why the priests should resist their abrogation, *such that they are rather obliged to encourage the prince to abolish them for the sake of true piety.*

§10. We have already shown above that instrumental music is something indifferent. We believe the same applies to *Latin hymns,* but they also seem to have more abuse in them than true usefulness. *It is regrettable,* said Brunnemann, *in the said treatise book 1, chapter 6, part 8, §9, that the Latin tongue used in the Roman Catholic Church has been retained in sacred*

---

115. This refers to the distinction between the first and the second tables of the Decalogue, that is, between the laws concerning duties toward God and those concerning duties toward fellow humans.

matters, and Mr. Stryk *in his notes on the said book number 4* added after he had quoted the argument of Mengering for retaining Latin songs: *It would have been better to have designated special times for such Latin songs, at which those who know Latin can attend; for in the assembled congregation itself it is more advisable to take account of the greater part of the people and to adapt the song to their understanding, than to look to the few who understand Latin.* It seems that the illustrious man wanted to respond to those who, when they want to keep these songs among other things, tend to appeal to their usefulness for schoolchildren. They believe that thereby their studies and progress are not only encouraged in school, but also in church, *see Meisner in his Disputation on Indifferent Matters 4, §22.*[116] And it certainly is astonishing, that celebrated men do not hesitate to make use of such pitiful arguments and to justify some inane rituals on that basis. Latin does not, it seems to me, deserve so much esteem that Latin songs should be used in church for the sake of learning the language, when there are far more people attending the service who do not know Latin than people who do. Another time is to be devoted to the study of Latin. Ecclesiastical congregations are instituted in order that the church pray to and praise God with one voice, and therefore it is better for this to be done in a language which is known to all. This accords with the apostle *1 Corinthians 14, verse 11,* where he compares those to barbarians who speak things that are not understood by their audience, or, which is the same thing, sing such things. And so I believe that Meisner did not have sufficient reason for inveighing so vehemently against those who criticize this rite, and for then calling them by the slanderous name of crypto-Calvinists in *the said disputation;* as if they who wanted to abrogate these rituals immediately introduced some sort of Syncretism, and opened not only windows to Calvinism (these are

---

116. Balthasar Meisner, *Collegium Adiaphoristicum, in quo controversiae circa Adiaphora inter nos et Calvinianos agitatae, perspicue tractantur, veritasque orthodoxa defenditur* (A Collegium Adiaphoristicum, in which the controversies between ourselves and the Calvinists concerning *adiaphora* are considered and are discussed clearly, and orthodox truth is defended) (Wittenberg, 1663).

the words of Meisner) but double doors, just because they do not want to accept the orthodoxy of Latin prayers. This and other even harsher opinions, which Meisner holds, reveal a very intemperate zeal, as if orthodoxy were dependent on Latin prayers, and as if everybody had to shun all doctrines of the Reformed as something diabolical, and to try, in whatever way possible, not to appear to agree with them in any respect.

§11. We will also add a few examples, which are commonly applied to the questions of baptism and communion, and we will begin with *exorcism.* If we had not already cleared away all opposition to the foundations of our opinion in *chapter 1,* and had not ascribed this right to the prince on the basis of solid principles, we would rightly abstain from controversy here and leave the matter to others who have greater powers of judgment. But as our fellow believers *number exorcism among the indifferent matters,* they cannot but concede to us that the prince has every right to abolish it, and I do not think that it is necessary for us to list new arguments here. For what is right in the case of one indifferent matter is right in the case of another. There is no reason for a difference here, so that it is regrettable that as a result of the abrogation of exorcism under the *Elector Christian I such great unrest* was stirred up in Saxony by the intemperate passion of clergymen. For when the elector wanted to use his right and abolish exorcism at the request of many Lutheran pastors, he offered the treatise of Pierius, entitled *Reflection on the Abrogation of Exorcism,* to the assembled Lutheran superintendents in Leipzig for them to subscribe to.[117] When they refused to do so, however, the superintendents were nevertheless ordered to inform their congregations correctly about [the nature of] exorcism. They did obey this command; but when Doctors Gundermann and Salmuth on July 14, 1591, together with the assembled pastors discussed the abrogation of

117. Urban Pierius (1546–1616) had defended the Saxon elector's chancellor Nicolaus Crell, who was executed as a crypto-Calvinist in 1601. It has not been possible to find the full reference for Pierius's *Ein Bedencken von Abschaffung des Exorcismi* (A reflection on the abrogation of exorcism), but this author produced a number of treatises directed at traditional Lutheranism.

exorcism in the town of Zeitz, they were forced to withdraw and save themselves by flight because of the unrest, which developed as a result of the abrogation of exorcism. Nevertheless the electoral edict on the abrogation of exorcism went ahead, and it would also have been executed if the premature death of the elector had not prevented it. Then, following his death, the theological inquisitors, who abused the indulgence of the administrator Frederick William, expelled not just many theologians, but also jurists and other politicians from the academies and consistories, and deprived them of their offices and honors, which is discussed in more detail by Hospinianus *in his Discordant Concord, page 260.* And if what Nicolaus Blumius tells in the *Funeral Sermon for the Incarcerated Nicolaus Crell* is true, then the failure to complete the abrogation of exorcism was among the causes why Mr. Crell was executed on October 9, 1601.[118] The historical background and an account of the execution can be found in the small book that the friends and relatives of Crell edited in 1605, which is entitled, *A reply and truthful alternative report to the funeral sermon held by Nicolaus Blume at the funeral of Mr. Crell in Dresden, add the dissertation by Frederich Becmann on Exorcism, thesis 22,*[119] where he says several things about Crell and his trial and adds: *But, in spite of that, Crell, that good man, who was beheaded, lives and will live even now after his death.* We do not make this historical controversy our own, but leave it rather to the judgment of others. It is sufficient for us to know that *exorcism is an indifferent matter,* and that even our [Lu-

---

118. Nicolaus Blume's funeral sermon on Crell, the *Leichpredigt uber den Custo-dierten D. Nicolaum Krell, welcher den 9. Octobris, wegen seiner verbrechung, auff der Römischen Kayserlichen Maiestat Endurtheil, öffentlich zu Dreßden enthauptet worden* (Funeral sermon on the captive Mr. Nicolaus Krell, who was publicly decapitated in Dresden on October 9 for his crime, following the final verdict by the Holy Roman Emperor) was published in numerous locations in 1601 and 1602.

119. *Antwort und warhafftiger Gegenbericht auff die Leichpredigt, welche Nicolais Blum, Pfarherr zu Dona, bey der Begrebnuß Herrn Doctor Nicolai Crellens . . . am 10. Octob. Anno 1601 zu Dreßden sol gethan haben* (Reply and truthful account, opposed to the funeral sermon, which Nicolaus Blum, pastor in Dona, is said to have held at the funeral of Dr. Nicolaus Crell on October 10, 1601, in Dresden) (s.l., 1605). Friedrich Beckmann, *Dissertatio de Exorcismo* (Dissertation on exorcism) (Frankfurt an der Oder, 1689).

therans] concede that it is expressed rather harshly. *Brunnemann, book 1, chapter 6,*[120] *membrum 3 §3.* In addition the honorable pro-rector Samuel Stryk says: *Indeed they sin, who leave nothing concerning this ceremony to the power of the prince.* Thus I conclude, that this minister, who in one and the same church retains exorcism for the sake of the Lutherans, but omits it occasionally according to the mandate of the magistrate, all other things being equal, can be considered a true minister of the church of Christ, contrary to the opinion of *Dedekennus volume 3, section 7, number 3 of the Wittenberg Consilia.* I also conclude that the oath to observe the liturgy, which is taken at the assumption of office, presents no obstacle to doing this with a clear conscience. For an oath is not binding in iniquitous cases. In fact, the constitution of the liturgy depends on the decision of the prince, and therefore when the prince changes it he releases the pastor from the previous oath, just as his subjects are always required to observe more recent laws rather than earlier laws that have been repealed. This does not violate the oath by which they were bound to the earlier laws. It is therefore possible to see from this that some theologians at times abuse moral principles in order to conceal their pride and defend their corrupt hypotheses. This is what those people seem to me to be doing who—Dedekennus *in the book referred to above, section 6, number 1, page 394*—do not want to admit the Calvinists to the role of godfathers in the baptism of a Lutheran infant, under the pretext that this would be contrary to the oath by which ministers are bound to the consistorial regulation.

§12. By consensus of our theologians, one of the indifferent matters *related to communion* is *private confession,* which is common in many Lutheran churches to this day.[121] For nowhere is it either prescribed or prohibited by Christ to confess one's sins in this fashion, and so the definition of indifferent matters is applicable here too. But it will seem harsh to most people to uphold the opinion that this act too is subject

---

120. The German translation refers to chapter 5.
121. See note 83 in this chapter.

to the disposition of the prince. Our above principles confirm this, however, and if the prince observes the procedure explained in chapter 2, the clergy will not be able to complain of a violation of Christian liberty, especially as this rite has already been abolished in many Lutheran churches. An alternative can be introduced for the livelihood of the ministers, instead of the *confessional fee.* Here we should like to add the opinion of the eminent Mr. Stryk *on Brunnemann book 2, chapter 5, §6.* There he says *that it is certainly desirable, that this proof of gratitude is performed somewhere other than where absolution is sought; for it cannot be denied that in the very moment in which the words of absolution are pronounced by the minister of the church, the persons confessing must direct their thoughts to the coin, to have it ready, so that once absolution has been granted they can offer it to him, and so on.* I could quote several examples, if what has been listed until now were not already sufficient to illustrate our principles. So I shall leave it at that. I do not doubt that there will be many to whom our principles will seem impious and contrary to orthodoxy. I myself would agree with them, if by orthodoxy they meant opinions that have been commonly accepted to date, and have been dressed up in the authority of many theologians and jurists, but which do not rest on any true principles. You have seen, dear reader, that we have everywhere fought with reasonable arguments, and have only rarely used the authority of Great Men. When we have done so, it has been in order to demonstrate to those who still adhere too much to the prejudice of authority that our viewpoint is not totally new. Further, that it is compatible with the principles which have already been put forward by others and which have been accepted by almost everyone, and that we have done nothing other than to argue against our adversaries on the basis of what is already accepted. Therefore we hope that those who do not like this will treat us in the same way, and if perhaps we have fallen into a harmful and impious error, will correct this error by peaceful conversation, and will try to return us to a sound opinion by exhorting us and teaching us. Truth indeed tolerates no coercion and allows our minds to entertain it only if it is based on true reasons.

Glory to God Alone

Most dear Mr. Brenneisen

Mr. Thoma-
sius's Reflec-
tions on the
Preceding Dis-
putation by
Mr. Brenne-
isen.[122]
I hereby send you your inaugural disputation on the Right of Protestant
Princes in Indifferent Matters, which you handed to me for comments.
I have read it attentively and congratulate you on an outstanding published example of the progress you have made in the recognition of the
truth and the abolition of prejudices that impede the study of wisdom.
You will notice that I have corrected very little, almost nothing in fact,
even if I might have discussed the question in a slightly different way.
But I believed that it would be better if I drew attention to those things
which I wanted to point out, separately, maybe for use in your future
work, rather than if some sort of incoherent and mismatched mixture
of my thoughts with yours emerged. Indeed, we find nothing to be wanting in the truth of your theses, but we would wish that you had elaborated certain matters in a little more detail, both for your own sake as
for that of the reader. For if you had put forward a common opinion,
or one which lacked so many and weighty adversaries, there would be
nothing left for me to warn you about. For I believe that you have
founded your thesis and derived the conclusions which follow from it
so perspicuously, that I do not know what doubt might cause anybody
to disagree, if he is free from passions and from preconceived opinion.
But the opinion you defend is contrary to common beliefs and is denied
by many men who enjoy great authority, and by many theologians, especially those in Saxony and those who are close to us and not very favorably disposed. They will very probably use this as an opportunity to
tar you and your doctrine with the brush of heterodoxy and impiety.
You must therefore protect yourself in time or, rather, as this written
work has shown that you are already protected and prepared, I should
tell you several things to which I am obliged by our friendship, and because several eyes see more than one. I believe that you will ward off the

122. As already mentioned, it was normal in early modern universities for doctoral
candidates to simply re-present the work of their supervisors in order to graduate.
Thomasius's attribution of authorship to Brenneisen and his corrective comments
are thus part of the graduation ritual and did not prevent him from later publishing
the disputation under his own signature.

blows of your adversaries more successfully when you develop these ideas, which will also dispel the clouds from the mind of any reader who might be prejudiced. The force of authority and of human faith in it is very strong, and it is very much to be feared that many will abuse it and cry out that your entire disputation is contrary to the symbolic books, to the *Augsburg Confession,* and the *Formula of Concord,*[123] and that it breathes contempt of the clergy throughout. I wish you had contradicted these sophistic arguments a little more clearly.

2. Regarding the *Formula of Concord,* while you may well pay very little attention to it, since I hear that in your fatherland[124] this little book has not been received—on which I heartily congratulate both your fatherland and yourself—nevertheless care needs to be taken that in future you show more distinctly, from the genuine principles of politics and jurisprudence, the secret statecraft of some among the Lutheran clergy. For by this it has been brought about that this little book has been foisted on princes and estates as if it were something absolutely necessary for salvation, even if so far it has only been the cause of disruptions of the peace, both in the church and in secular life. You may otherwise be in bad repute among the students in the vicinity, among whom we live and who are being told that the *Formula of Concord* is a Palladium[125] of the Lutheran church (a Palladium, however, in its original meaning is a pagan idol). In order to prove this, however, you will not need a very prolix demonstration. For in his *Discordant Concord* Hospinianus has already proved beyond doubt that the foundations on which Hutter constructed that vast *Book of Harmonious Concord*[126] patently contradict history and

123. The symbolic books contained documents central to Lutheran faith, such as the Augsburg Confession and the Formula of Concord.

124. East Frisia had a Calvinist population and a Lutheran prince, Christian Eberhard (ruled 1690–1708), with strong Pietist tendencies. It is therefore not surprising that the orthodox Formula of Concord was not formally accepted there.

125. The German text adds the explanation "a guardian angel" to the term "Palladium."

126. Leonhard Hutter, *Concordia Concors. De Origine et Progressu Formulae Concordiae Ecclesiarum Confessionis Augustanae* (Harmonious Concord. On the origin and progress of the Formula of Concord in the churches of the Augsburg Confession) (Frankfurt and Leipzig, 1690).

sound reason. I believe it will be possible to reduce this demonstration to a few points, as will be shown at greater length elsewhere, God willing.

3. Concerning the *Augsburg Confession*, however, it must be made evident that your doctrine conforms to it exactly. I see, indeed, that you have proved this already in *thesis 5, chapter 1,* but you did this covertly. Therefore you will not criticize me for drawing on the *Augsburg Confession* to show these arguments more clearly to the reader. Article 7 says *that it is sufficient for the true unity of the church to agree on the teaching of the gospel and the administration of the sacraments, and that it is not necessary for similar human traditions or rites and ceremonies to be established everywhere:* From this you wanted to infer that these indifferent matters do not pertain to the internal power of the church, but to the care of the prince, who directs everything instituted by man in the commonwealth. In *Article 15* it is said *that those ecclesiastical rites are to be preserved which can be preserved without sin and are useful for upholding tranquillity and good order in the church.* However, the prince can promulgate law for preserving tranquillity and order in the entire commonwealth (in which, however, the church is too). The order and tranquillity of the church cannot be exempt from this, nor can the care of this order be transferred to the clergy without an open disruption of unity, which is the soul of the commonwealth, or a diminution of majesty, as is clear from the example of the papal teachings. Finally *Article 16* notes that *Christians necessarily must obey their magistrates and laws, unless these command them to sin.* From this it follows that, as sins are prohibited actions, but indifferent matters are indifferent actions, Christians must obey their magistrate's laws on indifferent matters by virtue of the *Augsburg Confession.* From these arguments, however, it will follow automatically that all Protestant theologians and jurists who defend the opinion that the prince does not have the right to decide on indifferent matters, have diverged from the *Augsburg Confession.*

4. The imputation of *contempt for the clergy* is a common pretext, and almost obsolete as it has been misused repeatedly many times. In the meantime it will do no harm if you show that throughout the entire disputation by the term "clergymen" you do not mean pious theologians and ministers of the divine word, who teach only the gospel and live a

holy life according to it—rather, you revere such ministers as being dear to God, as one should—but those people, who under the pretext of the ministry, theology, and the gospel seek power and the tyranny over consciences, and so on. At this point you will be able to show the origin in canon law of the division of all people into clergy and laity, and that this distinction was unknown in the writings of the New Testament. Further, that the *canon of the Decretum 7, causa 12, quaestio 1*,[127] which has been excerpted from Hieronymus, shows nothing more—even to the point of being obvious—than that miserable papalist doctrine already reigned supreme at that time, and that therefore very little foundation for true doctrine or good morals is to be sought in the consensus of the first five centuries after Christ's birth, or in this particular example.

5. You will also have to take care with *the consensus of certain Lutheran theologians.* Indeed you have acted prudently in founding most of your statements on the well-known testimonies of *a pair of jurisconsults,* who are highly esteemed and have never been suspected of heterodoxy by the Gnesio-Lutherans, that is, a father and his son-in-law.[128] Meanwhile it must not be denied that you would have done better to refer to the supporting statements of certain Lutheran theologians, in order to persuade those whose minds have been bewitched by the authority of your opponents. If you had done this, certainly you would have made those young people hesitate to consider you a heretic or something similar, if they see certain theologians of our sect agree with you without diverging from Lutheranism. And in order that I may provide you with support in this matter, behold the testimony of the Helmstedt theologian Gebhard Theodor Meier *in the book On the Three Initiations of Christians*[129] *§71 at the end, page 74: The ancient practice of rites does not prescribe anything for our times, because the sovereign can at one time introduce, at an-*

---

127. *Corpus Iuris Canonici,* Decreti Secunda Pars, causa XI, quaestio I, c. vii.

128. This presumably refers to Johann Jakob Brunnemann and his son-in-law Samuel Stryk, who edited Brunnemann's *De Jure Ecclesiastico Tractatus.*

129. Gebhard Theodor Meier, *Liber Tria Novellorum Nascentis Ecclesiae Christianorum Initiamenta Baptismum, Catechesin et Manuum Impositionem continens* (Three books of novels of the early church, containing the initiation of Christians in baptism, catechism, and the laying-on of hands) (Helmstedt, 1690).

other, reform or abolish rites, which have not been defined by divine law,
just as it seems appropriate to him for the sake of the church or the com-
monwealth. Here you have in three lines a synopsis of your entire disputation. And there is no reason why you should be worried about the
disagreement and conflicts that took place at the time of our fathers
between the Saxon and the Helmstedt theologians, and scandalized the
entire church. It is already well known that the former have acknowledged the latter to be their brothers, and would not dare to criticize this
testimony as an example of Syncretism.[130]

6. I also approve your demonstration in the first chapter that the question on the right of the prince over indifferent matters *pertains to juris-*
prudence, thereby removing the objection which is all too frequent nowadays: What business is this of yours? It might not be inappropriate on
another occasion to put forward the rule for resolving similar difficulties
in a few words. Indeed, when one wants to know to which discipline a
proposition or question belongs, this must be judged on the basis of the
predicate, not the subject.[131] So the question of the gender of *Deus* belongs to grammar; whether he is a substance belongs to logic; that of
whether God's sanctity is the foundation of natural law belongs to moral
philosophy. So the question whether nobles are immediate estates of the
empire belongs to public law; that of the declension of "nobleman" belongs to grammar, and so on. Therefore the question, whether the regulation of indifferent matters is a regalian right of the sovereign, likewise,
whether it belongs to the estates of the empire, is part of jurisprudence
and of politics, which is the instrument of jurisprudence.

7. You will therefore not go wrong in later editions if you *add* from
the *fundamental laws of the empire,* that is, the Peace of Religion[132] and
the Peace of Westphalia and similar, *arguments* from which it can be
proved superabundantly that the right over indifferent matters pertains

---

130. "Syncretism" implied the sacrifice of doctrinal truth to pragmatic compromise. See note 19 in this chapter.

131. The German text adds the explanation: "That is, one should not examine the
thing which is being discussed, but see what is being predicated of it."

132. That is, the Augsburg Peace of Religion of 1555.

to the estates of the empire, in order that thereby hesitant dissenters may be convinced all the more. I say, *superabundantly.* For it will not be strictly necessary to your aim, since in your disputation you have shown sufficiently, that there is nothing in the laws of the empire which could justifiably be opposed to your argument. If you will carefully read through *articles 5 and 8 of the Peace of Münster,* you will easily find the supporting arguments.

8. You have rejected as obscure the *distinction between internal and external matters,* which has commonly been applied in explaining the right of the prince in religious affairs. You will, however, acquire much merit concerning ecclesiastical jurisprudence if you explain this distinction in a little more detail, according to the opinion of those who use it, so that you show that once the prince has been deprived of this right over indifferent matters he is left with virtually no right in external matters. In this case if you were to examine the characteristics of the right over religious affairs, even in our sect it would be nothing other than a burden, designed to protect ecclesiastics and help them persecute dissenters and strengthen their opinions and doctrines.

9. I also approve your reference in *§2, chapter 2* in support of your opinion to the authority of *Gregory Nazianzus,* so that it becomes apparent to the reader that your doctrine is not new but old. And there are many things in Nazianzus which are not to the taste of the adversaries. Thus the statement by which he denigrated the councils is well known. Some of our Lutherans torture themselves about this, as you will remember I have shown elsewhere, in order that this statement should not harm the pretended authority and integrity of the Nicene Council. So this week, while I was doing something else, I noticed, another elegant passage by him, which might be of use to you in further meditations. This is *in oration 35, 150 "Episcopos" 592.*[133] *We use all perfect numbers: the number one through our belief in the single essence of divinity and the undivided adoration of it, the number three, however, through our belief in*

133. Gregory Nazianzus, *Operum Gregorii Nazianzeni tomi tres* (The works of Gregory Nazianzus, in three volumes) (Basel, 1571).

the hypostases,[134] or the persons, as some would rather have it. They who quarrel about this should stop talking ineptly about it, as if the piety which belonged to our faith consisted in names not in real things. For what do you say, who believe in three hypostases? Do you say thereby that you believe in three divine essences? I have no doubt that you would start a terrible uproar against those who believe this. For you profess the essence of these three to be one and the same. What do you say, you who speak of persons? For you pretend this one thing to be a composite, which has three faces or a wholly human form? That is not true, you will cry. He who thinks so never sees the face of God, whatever it is like. What therefore, to continue asking, will you have of your hypostases, and of your persons? Namely, that the three differ not in their natures but in their properties. Very well, and so forth. You will see whether this passage is of use to you. But this is clear, that Gregory here considers it an indifferent matter if someone denies the term "person," as long as he acknowledges the difference between the different properties and the unity of the essence. But maybe this indifferent matter is not directly relevant to the indifferent matters that you speak about.

10. In the same paragraph you instruct the prince that he himself must learn what indifferent matters are. I should think that the prince will exercise his regalian right with no greater security than when he focuses on those things *that the clergy undoubtedly considers indifferent matters.* So, for example, among us it is generally taught that exorcism, auricular confession, etc. are indifferent matters. On this account, the clergy will then not be able to persuade rational and down-to-earth laymen, with any justification or probable pretext, that the prince encroaches on religious affairs. Nevertheless it should be shown to the less cautious how since the introduction of the *Formula of Concord* they have been deceived by the following doctrine, which is contrary to Scripture, reason, and common sense: *That indifferent matters cease to be indifferent matters*

---

134. The concept of *hypostasis,* which means "foundation" or "essence," was part of the doctrine of the Trinity. The question, whether Christ's *hypostasis* was the same as, or separate from and subordinate to that of God the Father, divided Arian heretics, who denied the divine essence of Christ, from the orthodox church in late antiquity. Arianism was condemned at the Council of Nicaea in A.D. 325 (see note 103 in this chapter).

if a controversy arises over them. Thus Blumius says in the funeral sermon for Mr. Crell, p. 37, *Exorcism is a negligible matter, but for the controversy surrounding it, and in emergency baptisms we leave it aside; but as there is such a controversy about this ceremony we cannot well leave it aside with a good conscience. He who does so is guilty of all sorts of cruelties.* So Mr. Lincker, after quoting others, says *in his dissertation On that which is Just concerning Communion,*[135] *chapter 4 §14, page 43, Indifferent matters do not remain indifferent if they involve scandal, or affect the confession and Christian liberty, but become necessary and have to be observed.* And so frequently is this slogan repeated in the Wittenberg *Consilia* collected by Dedekennus that it seems a true palladium of our opponents. Once this has been taken away they are done for. Therefore the harmfulness of this doctrine must be shown, as well as the fact that it is a genuine invention to conceal unrest in the commonwealth and rebellions which have been stirred up under the pretext of piety. In this respect it is comparable therefore to the doctrine of the papalists on not keeping faith with heretics, or that of the Jesuits on mental reservations.[136] For it is the same as saying we could omit them [the indifferent matters] at will. But as soon as the prince commands their omission, then the people must be persuaded that these are commanded by God, so that they need not obey the prince. Or, to put it briefly: certain indifferent matters are [supposed to be] commanded by God in order that subjects may not obey the sovereign. And yet these people write treatises about how much it is in the interest of princes to defend their doctrines with fire and sword.

11. In order to illustrate what you say more distinctly in *§3, chapter 2,* you could also argue a little more clearly on *Theological Councils,* and the great difference between them and *decisions and sentences* which have the force of a judgment. And this doctrine is required since, by a com-

---

135. Nicolaus Christoph Lynker, *De eo quod circa Sacram Coenam justum est* (On that which is just concerning communion), 2nd ed. (Leipzig, 1690).

136. The German text adds: "When they swear an oath and include an unspoken reservation." The idea of mental reservations was part of casuistry and justified the use of misleading or equivocal expressions.

mon mistake, the *Consilia* of Dedekennus and the Wittenbergers, for example, are very often cited as if they were judgments. There was once a time of jurisprudential barbarism, when in courts the quotations from the gloss enjoyed greater authority than the text of the law itself. Now we have lapsed into theological barbarism, so that in the midst of the light of the gospel, when there is a sermon on the cases of conscience, the *consilia* of Wittenberg, for example, are cited with greater effect than the words of the gospel. It must be shown that the Protestant princes did not want theologians to *decide* controversies, and that they therefore did not want theological faculties to pass *sentences* unless a juristic judgment had been pronounced; and that therefore they added secular advisers to the consistories, and gave them a president who was a secular political figure. It must nevertheless also be shown that especially after the time of the *Formula of Concord* certain clergymen tried to persuade the princes that it was part of their regalian rights to *define through them the articles of faith,* and that this decision would have the force of law even outside the territory. When the princes did not immediately notice the fraud, the clergymen later usurped the power of trying such things independently, and with more than papal authority, to the greatest detriment of Germany. Setting aside numerous other examples, we can take that of the remarkable unrest which had been stirred up when the Elector of Brandenburg, of most glorious memory, forbade the use of invective against other confessions in the pulpit. This is still in everybody's recent memory. In 1655 an *Ordinary gloss on the circular letter of Pope Alexander VII, which he wrote under the pretext of bringing about peace* was published.[137] The letter begins: *We, who look around from the supreme summit of the apostolate at the entire world, that is, the matters entrusted to our care etc.* The author of the gloss could not bear the phrase: *matters entrusted to our care. Indeed,* he says on page 16, *these are entrusted to your care?*

---

137. Anon. [Hermann Conring], *Glossa ordinaria ad litteras circulares Alexandri Papae septimi. Quas praetextu pacis procurandae inter catholicos principes ad patriarchas, archiepiscopos, episcopos, cleros, . . . scripsit* (The ordinary gloss on the circular letter of Pope Alexander VII, which he wrote to patriarchs, archbishops, bishops, and clergymen, under the pretext of bringing about peace among the Catholic princes) (s.l., 1655).

How curious you are in matters which do not pertain to you! But you know, I believe, the saying of Homulus to Augustus: In another man's house one should be blind and mute.[138] *And: stop meddling in those matters, which are none of your business.* These admonishments addressed to the pope and similar opinions could easily be applied to the unrestrained and papalizing efforts of our clergy.

12. While you rightly insist in *§4, chapter 2,* that one should take care rather to *abrogate* ceremonies than to *introduce* them, it would also be necessary to show that the *Formula of Concord,* or certainly those who make use of it, *confuse these two actions* when they discuss the right of the prince in indifferent matters. They often apply arguments from Scripture that could be used to cast doubt on the introduction of ceremonies, to argue against abrogation, although there is an enormous difference between the two. A similar sophism is committed, when dissenters, as is common, put forward the scandal caused to the weaker members, and the saying of Paul, on both of which you comment in §§4 & 5. Paul notably says that he wants to *abstain* from eating meat in order to prevent a weak member from being scandalized; not that he wants to *eat* meat for the sake of another who pretends to be weak. This can be easily applied to the question of who is closer to the Pauline example: someone who, let us say, omits exorcism, in order that a weak person is not scandalized; or someone who retains it, in order that another, who claims to be weak, does not take offense.

13. I believe however that there is no means more suitable to the exercise of the right in indifferent matters than that which was the occasion for your dissertation and which you point out, in *§5 of chapter 2, that the populace be timely informed of the nature of indifferent matters by the ministers of the word.* If only the reality always conformed to the most wise intention of the prince. Maybe it would be appropriate to subject the clergy to visitations, in order that they demonstrate their observance of this law, and to discipline those who are refractory and obstinate by using

138. This is presumably a reference to the comedy *Homulus* by Petrus Dorlandus (Pieter Dorland van Diest, 1454–1507), which was published in translation and with additions in Bremen in 1648.

paternal admonition. In the meantime, they have no reason to complain that you have chosen to discuss this topic in your inaugural disputation. For if they themselves remain silent on this any longer, the stones must cry out in protest.

14. I have nothing to add concerning the *refutation of the argument that one should not scandalize the weak brother.* In any case, they here should follow the example of the Reformed. But note the malice [of our opponents]: in order that the passages of Scripture on avoiding causing offense to one's brethren should not seem to stand in the way of their aims, they persuaded the laity that *the Reformed were not brethren,* a pseudopolitical clerical reason of state you should discuss in more detail on a future occasion. For even if you have already shown its insufficiency in the disputation, and have rightly insisted that even pagans must not be scandalized, yet since this reply could give occasion to further calumnies from our opponents, another reason should be explained a little more clearly (which indeed you tacitly point out by appealing to my piece on the marriage between Lutheran and Reformed princes): namely, that according to the rudiments of Christianity and its first foundations (from the discussion or indeed application of which they cannot keep us without open papal tyranny) the Christian brotherhood among the Protestants of either confession[139] cannot be removed.

15. The arguments with which our opponents *attack the reception of the Gregorian Calendar* (which you discuss in *§6, chapter 2*) are such that we laymen should be ashamed that we have allowed ourselves to be blinded for such a long time by such miserable doctrines. It is a common proverb that not he who demands foolish deeds from another is to be considered a fool, but he who commits them or suffers them. It is therefore time for us to shake off our torpor. What can be more absurd than the argument that this Calendar is a thing of Anti-Christ, because the pope made it? What if the pope had written a grammar, or a work on arithmetic—would that too be a thing of Anti-Christ? What will they do about the indifferent matters that have been retained in our church,

---

139. That is, Calvinist and Lutheran.

of which the popes were the authors? What will happen to Terentius, Martial, and Petronius,[140] who have to a very great extent been introduced into schools by the authority of the clergy, or at least recommended to young people for their elegant Latin and their incisive observations? Why do they not consider those authors to be diabolic, though they would do so with greater justification, as all their pages are filled with devilry? Why do they prostitute the doctrine of the gospel to such an extent that entire congregations of those who want to hear the word of God defend these diabolical pagans, and so act against the evangelical admonishments of pious Christians? But regarding the dispute over the minor saints who have been inserted into the Gregorian Calendar, this is something you should later discuss further. As if the same names, the same saints were not found in both the Julian and the Gregorian Calendar, if they have been printed together; or as if the prince could not remove inappropriate names at his pleasure; or as if the issue of the reception of the Gregorian Calendar had ever been about these saints. Here too Luther's words are relevant, who wrote on the reform of the Calendar in his Jena volumes:[141] *One does not ask whether it is right or wrong that the Calendar is reformed and changed, but who should do it: that is, the majesties, emperors, or kings, etc.* Therefore Luther also conceded this right concerning these indifferent matters to princes who held the rights of majesty. The Protestant princes have shown sufficiently that the pope does not have the authority to impose this Calendar on them, and they can without suspicion of papalism direct their attention to the political reasons in the edict of Rudolph II, *dated September 15, 1583, addressed to the Augsburg Senate,* which Mr. Linker—who supplies sev-

---

140. These are the comic dramatist Publius Terentius Afer (ca. 195–159 B.C.), the poet and epigrammatist Marcus Valerius Martialis (ca. A.D. 40–140 and the satirical writer Petronius Arbiter (first century A.D.).

141. Martin Luther, *Omnia opera Reverendi Patris D. M. L. quae vir Dei ab Anno XVII. usque ad Anni vicesimi aliquam partem, scripsit & edidit, quorum Catalogum in fine Tomi invenies* (Complete works of the reverend father Martin Luther, which this man of God wrote and edited from the year 1517 to part of the year 1520, and of which you will find a catalogue at the end of the volume), 4 vols. (Jena, 1556–58).

eral points which are relevant here—reviews *in his disputation on the Calendar held in Altdorf in 1674, chapter 4.*[142]

16. The assertion in *§8, chapter 2* will seem too paradoxical to many, namely that *the vestments of ecclesiastical persons are not sacred objects.* Therefore it will have to be shown that *the division by Justinian of law into sacred, religious, and holy things smacks of paganism* and the theology of pagans, who devoted sacred things to the upper Gods, religious things to the lower Gods, and holy things to demi-Gods. It will have to be shown that just as among Protestants religious and holy things are not matters of divine law, but of public law, or even private law, so sacred matters cannot among us be counted as matters of divine law without reflecting pagan or certainly papist superstition. And so in the New Testament there are among true Christians no properly sacred matters, for God desires the dedication of our heart: the dedication of other things is superstition. Likewise, certain comments should be made on the origins of Christian churches at the time of Constantine, that is, at the time at which Anti-Christ already occupied the hearts of Christians, which already tended toward paganism.

17. The chapter *on the abrogation of images* also merits further discussion. Friedrich Spanheim's *History of Images and the Restored History of Images*[143] will supply more material on this matter and deserves to be read by all theology students of our sect. We cannot deny that our populace is not far removed from papalist superstition in that respect, and very rarely is the genuine and innocent use of images inculcated by teachers. It is possible to provide an apt example which is well known in this duchy and in this city, where some years ago, because of a superstitious cult of an image representing the little Jesus, the prince was, for prudential reasons, compelled to abolish these superstitious ceremonies. It is evident that the papalists have omitted the precept on images in their catechism on purpose, because of their slavish veneration

142. Heinrich Linck (*praeses*) and Christian Bock (*respondens*), *De Calendario* (On the calendar) (Altdorf, 1674).

143. Friedrich Spanheim, *Historia imaginum restituta* (The restored history of religious images) (Leiden, 1686).

of them. Luther did not sense this as he was focused on other matters, for he could not take note of all defects simultaneously. Superstition grows gradually, and it must also be eradicated gradually. One man does not see everything nor does he purge everything. The disciples of Luther should follow his example, not defend his deeds and his sayings and confuse consciences.

18. On the occasion of the *Latin hymns,* which you discuss in *§10, chapter 2,* there followed a meditation by someone who interpreted the *language of the dragon,* which is mentioned in the Apocalypse,[144] as *Latin,* which seems probable to me. It is a political axiom that princes must command their subjects to use the dominant language. The pope applied the same axiom to signal subjection, when he commanded all clergymen, wherever they are, to use Latin in divine services. Already at the time of Charlemagne this superstition had been introduced into Germany in order to detach universities from the jurisdiction of the prince, and all professors and students were incorporated into the clergy. For this reason as well *Latin became the language of the learned,* because it was the language of the clergy. Oh what miserably blind people therefore we were, who were persuaded that the prince, for example, could not accept the Gregorian Calendar because it was a thing of Anti-Christ, and did not notice that the Latin chants in our churches and the use of Latin in our schools are the true signs of Anti-Christ, which breed unrest, superstition, idolatry, and pedantry.

19. I would prefer it if you had omitted the narration of the *unrest over exorcism in Saxony.* I almost foresee your opponents accusing *you of a crime of lèse-majesté* [violation of majesty], as if you censured deeds which had been approved by the princes of the empire, or performed in their name. I know the councils of men and write this having had similar experiences. It is not necessary that I elaborate on my experiences, this

---

144. "And the beast [the dragon] was given a mouth uttering haughty and blasphemous words, and it was allowed to exercise authority for forty-two months; it opened its mouth to utter blasphemies against God, blaspheming his name and his dwelling, that is, those who dwell in heaven. Also it was allowed to make war on the saints and to conquer them. And authority was given it over every tribe and people and tongue and nation . . ." (Apocalypse 13:5–7).

is to be left to another occasion. Peucer[145] experienced a similar accusation in a comparable case. Peucer had written that the Saxon elector did not know that in the Athanasian creed it was held that Christ according to his human nature was inferior to the Father, and that he turned very pale when this was shown from Athanasius. As Hutter had nothing with which to counter this quite plausible assertion, he launched an impotent attack on Peucer and accused him of the most atrocious crime of *lèse-majesté*. Therefore prepare yourself to provide a just explication *on the abuse of the crime of lèse-majesté*. Tacitus[146] and Ammianus Marcellinus[147] will provide you with several examples from Roman history, and Hutter in his *Harmonious Concord* will provide quite a few in our own modern history (examples not only of the abuse of this crime, but of the crime of lying, perjury, etc., which were imputed without reason to Hospinianus, Peucer, and others). Therefore those who cannot bear the fact that jurists speak of ecclesiastical matters will have to be told that if they do not want to leave juristic doctrines to us [lawyers] altogether, especially those concerning criminal law, they should apply them more soberly than has been done hitherto against dissenters in controversies.

20. Finally, there are also *other examples* relevant to the right in indifferent matters, which have been removed from the jurisdiction of the prince by the clergy, such as the oblates, as they are called, which are used in communion, the sign of the cross in consecration, the distribution of the bread, the formulae used in its distribution, and similar. See Lynker,[148] *in the disputation quoted above On what is just concerning Communion, chapters 3 and 4*. The volumes of theological *consilia* will pro-

---

145. This is probably Kaspar Peucer (1525–1602), a leading Philippist humanist and theologian, who became personal physician of the Saxon elector in 1570. He was imprisoned by his Gnesio-Lutheran opponents but was released in 1586 and entered the services of the Prince of Anhalt in Dessau.

146. Publius (or Gaius) Cornelius Tacitus (ca. A.D. 55–120) was known for his negative portrayals of several of the Roman emperors.

147. Ammianus Marcellinus (ca. A.D. 330–90) wrote a history of the Roman Empire from the death of Domitian (A.D. 98).

148. See note 135 in this chapter.

vide other examples of indifferent matters which, when measured by the same norm, will allow us to reveal many similar fantasies of our opponents. In the meantime, farewell, may the Lord be with you. Reflect on this admonition of what is just and good. I wrote this on the last day of August 1695.

Corollaries

I

It is unjust to impute the crime of blasphemy to those who put forward doctrines in good faith that conflict with the doctrines of our theologians on God and Christ; for there is no crime without evil intent. So Caspar Francus and Hospinianus are unjustly accused of blasphemy by Hutter in *chapter 22 at the end, page 718.* What would Hutter say if someone accused him of blasphemy, because he wrote, with Selnecker,[149] that the Elector Augustus [of Saxony] undertook the plan for a work of Concord not at the behest of men, or out of a human motive, but *from an inspiration of the divine spirit (chapter 9, page 270)?*

2. Those matters in legal procedure that are based on natural law are also to be observed by the church. But it is an injunction of natural law not to condemn an absent person without hearing him, nor to condemn men, who are not subject to our jurisdiction. By contrast, Hutter, *chapter 14, pages 453 and 456,* says that this would be a most inequitable situation if this injunction were included in the government of the church etc.

3. A virgin is a woman who has not admitted a man, not a woman who has a closed uterus. So it is not necessary for proving the perpetual virginity of Mary to claim that she gave birth miraculously without damaging her uterus. But since Hutter together with others believes something different, an appeal is made to the entire ancient tradition of *orthodoxy, page 700, chapter 22.* But our condition is miserable if we are forced to establish articles of faith as well as orthodoxy and heterodoxy in matters of natural science.

---

149. Nikolaus Selnecker and Leonhard Hutter, *Acta Formulae Concordiae* (Acts of the Formula of Concord) (Frankfurt am Main, 1707).

4. The crime of dishonesty is totally different from false reasoning or interpretation in argument. It is thus contrary to the principles of law that Hutter imputes the crime of dishonesty to the jurist Helphantus,[150] *chapter 24, page 760,* and to Hospinianus *chapter 11, page 352 & chapter 33, page 929.*

5. The crime of *lèse-majesté* and of the most atrocious perfidy cannot be extended without violating the principles of sound law. But Hutter does this when he accuses Peucer of these things, *chapter 40, page 967,* for writing that the Elector Augustus did not know some doctrine of the Athanasian symbol; and *in the same chapter, page 975,* [for writing] that this same elector complained about his priests, because they entangled him in perpetual doubts. But if such matters pertain to the crime of *lèse-majesté,* what will happen to Hutter, who accuses John the Prince Palatine of not accepting sensible admonishments *chapter 33, page 930* but allowing himself to be led astray by the censures of certain Calvinist princes and theologians? Likewise he writes about Christian I, the elector of Saxony, that he was badly deceived by some of his councilors and theologians. *Chapter 48, page 1233.*

6. It is repugnant to the principles of natural law that the *Urfehde*[151] forbids the accused to lay claim to a right which belongs to him in law. If therefore a prisoner were to be compelled to renounce the remedies of law in an *Urfehde,* I believe that such an *Urfehde* is void because of the fear which was inflicted on the person swearing the oath. However, the reader may judge whether Hutter justly accuses Peucer of perjury *chapter 9, page 266* because of a violated *Urfehde,* the formula of which he provides *ibid. p. 265.*

7. Let us pretend that some Catholic prince had been persuaded by his clergy to take away from Lutherans their honors, dignities, and benefits because of their religion; and that when they questioned this they received this reply from some clergymen: that *the adversaries suffer what-*

---

150. This possibly refers to the late-fifteenth-century humanist jurist Valentin Helfant, who came from Alsace and trained in Heidelberg.

151. An *Urfehde* (*Urpheda* in Latin) was an oath by a prisoner about to be released, in which he swore not to take revenge for his imprisonment.

ever they suffer because of their false religion. It is therefore a matter of duty not of persecution, of right not of tyranny, what has been decided for this kind of people. But what is it that these people have lost of their possessions? Those who persisted obstinately in a heretical error have been removed from ecclesiastic and academic positions. They are thrust out from public offices; they are deprived of public stipends and benefits, they, who have not done good to the magistrate, the commonwealth, and the church, either as subjects or as clergymen. But have they thereby lost anything which belongs to them? Not at all, the magistrate reclaimed public goods, that is, offices, dignities, honors, benefices, which are his property and not theirs, and does not take away anything that is the private property of anyone. What would Hutter—or the person who has most recently praised him—say to this philosophy, especially as this clergyman ended his discourse with the subject: *What is to be understood by the duty of the political magistrate in reforming the church?* They should apply the same comments to the philosophy of Hutter, when he defends the actions of the Lutheran clergy against the Reformed *chapter 49, page 1257.*

There is no space to add anything more. These matters which we have listed, however, are such that they pertain to juristic or philosophical argument. They are not part of theological questions, even if these questions have been formulated regarding the text of a theologian, as has been explained in the comments on the dissertation.

END

On the Power of Secular Government to Command Its Subjects to Attend Church Diligently

§I. The current dispute presupposes the following situation.[1] Nearly thirty years ago a princely widow in one of the Anhaltine territories (where, as the guardian of her underage princes, she was acting as regent) had publicized an edict, in which her subjects were ordered in general terms to attend church and public worship diligently.[2] Now, as the Lutheran and Reformed communities existed side by side in the Anhaltine territories, it could easily happen that a Calvinist nobleman might own a village with a Lutheran congregation, and that a Lutheran nobleman

---

1. This treatise was printed in a collection of Thomasius's writings with the title *Vernünfftige und Christliche aber nicht Scheinheilige Thomasische Gedancken und Erinnerungen über allerhand Gemischte Philosophische und Juristische Händel. Dritter Theil* (Reasonable and Christian, but not hypocritical Thomasian thoughts and comments, on various philosophical and juristic debates) (Halle, 1725). The piece consists of an introduction by Thomasius, the letter of a nobleman requesting the legal advice of the law faculty at the University of Halle, Thomasius's formal response to this, and finally an account by Thomasius of the way in which his advice was altered by the Halle law faculty.

2. The principality in question appears to be Anhalt-Dessau, which enjoyed close ties with Brandenburg, as several members of the Calvinist ruling family entered the service of the Elector of Brandenburg from the late seventeenth century onward. After the death of Johann Georg II of Anhalt-Dessau in 1693 the principality passed to the regency of his widow, Henrietta Catharina, who was originally from the House of Orange. In 1698 her son Leopold I, who later also served as a Prussian general, succeeded to the government of the principality.

might own a village in which the congregation had a Reformed clergyman. Thus various questions could arise in connection with this edict,
which have to be carefully distinguished from each other. For example,
(1) whether an Evangelical or Protestant magistrate [*Obrigkeit*] has the
right to command its subjects, be they Lutheran or Reformed, to attend
public services diligently (especially on a Sunday) and not to stay away
from them, unless they have an important reason? (2) Whether a Lutheran prince could likewise force his Calvinist subjects to visit Lutheran
churches and, vice versa, a Calvinist prince force his Lutheran subjects
to go to Calvinist churches? (3) Whether a Lutheran or Calvinist nobleman in particular could be ordered to attend the church of his village
community (which might be Calvinist or Lutheran), whatever the circumstances (that is, no matter whether he is resident in the village, or
in a town where there is a church of his confession)? (4) Whether a
nobleman, who normally lives in his village, can be commanded to attend the congregation in his community or whether he could excuse
himself by saying that his peasants were Reformed, but he was Lutheran,
or that his peasants were Lutheran, but he was Reformed? And whatever
other questions of this sort might come up. For there is no doubt that
generally with such questions and the responses to them, quite different
and sometimes contradictory reasons or decisions can arise, which I do
not think it is necessary to examine in detail at the moment. Instead, I
will turn to the dispute submitted to our faculty and the questions directed to us at that time.[3]

§II. A Lutheran nobleman, in fact, had for some time regularly gone to
the church of his Reformed congregation, in the village where he usually
lived. But then he ceased to visit the church and began to hold his Lutheran devotions at home, together with his children's teacher, and to

*The noble-
man's letter of
appeal to his
ruler*

3. Like most other law faculties in the Holy Roman Empire, that of the University
of Halle routinely provided legal advice (*consilia*) to individuals and governments
outside its own territory. The advice was based on the documentation submitted to
the faculty by the party seeking the faculty's advice.

withdraw completely from the Calvinist services. When the Consistory[4] reprimanded him for this, and he was admonished to attend the public service as before with his dependents, he sent the following letter to the most gracious princess.

(Following the usual titles) Your most princely Highness, I am compelled to address you most humbly, as your most princely highness's Consistory recently summoned me and some members of my household and accused us, that we had, contrary not only to the most princely highness's territorial statutes [*Landes-Ordnung*], but also to your most princely highness's recently publicized edict, withdrawn from the public congregation in the church for a time. It [the Consistory] ordered us to attend these congregations in future or else to expect a strict admonishment. Now I can, your highness, most gracious lady, testify before God, that this previous absence from church did not reflect the slightest disobedience or rebellious disposition toward governmental decrees, but arose from a doubt in my conscience, which I entertain in this particular case. It is indeed true, your highness and most gracious lady, and I confess this publicly, that I do not completely reject church attendance in general and without qualification. Rather, I approve it in a certain regard, and especially where it aims at order and discipline among the brutish, disorderly children of the world; and I consider this to be praiseworthy to a certain extent, as I myself have also attended these congregations. I am not convinced in my conscience, however, that I should regard this attendance at church as an absolute necessity and certain sign of a true Christian, such that one can be compelled to it. I am rather convinced of the contrary. For that attendance at church is not an absolute necessity is evident from the lives of the first humans and the patriarchs, the first Christians and the hermits, who, because they lacked temples could not attend them, or hold large assemblies, but who are never doubted by anyone to have possessed true piety. Further, attending public church services is simply not a sign of a true Christian, because even before the construction of the temples, and during the lives of the hermits and the dispersal of the first Christians

4. The Consistory was the supreme disciplinary body within the Protestant church of a particular territory. It was composed of both clerics and laymen.

throughout the world, there were true Christians. And, later, many
hypocrites joined in the public religious worship, so that jurists have
come to consider the all-too-frequent attendance at church not only as
a sign of hypocrisy, but as an indication of witchcraft, as witches usually
claimed to have attended public services most frequently (cf. Crusius,
On the Specific Proofs of Crimes, chapter 32, 10ff.).[5] I therefore believe
that nobody can be compelled to public attendance at church, as long
as he otherwise does not cause offense, but lives piously to the extent
that God's grace permits. For the service that has to be rendered to God
concerns God alone and does not require an assembly of many people.
This service can be rendered to God in silence, outside the churches
and congregations, as was done by the first men, the first Christians,
and the hermits. But if divine service does not absolutely require a public congregation in the temples, then this belongs to the external matters and ceremonies, just as many jurists now even consider the command "thou shalt honor the Sabbath" to be a matter concerning
ceremony and do not want to regard it as absolutely binding morally.
Yet, if this is the case, then one cannot use coercion in such external
and indifferent matters [*adiaphoris*]. For they are not such an essential
part of the veneration of God that a spiritual effect must be attributed
to them, or that they cannot be omitted without sin, as Ziegler has
demonstrated very well against the papalists, who argue that some ceremonies are meritorious (see *Lancelotti's Institutes of Canon Law,* book
2, title 3, §15, at the end and book 2, title 6, §6, and book 2, title 18, §1).[6]
We also find nothing of this in God's word, that one should be com-

---

5. Christoph Crusius, *Tractatus de Indiciis Delictorum Specialibus, cum praemissa
maleficiorum eorumque poenae compendiosa relatione* (Treatise on the specific proofs
of crimes, with a full account of evil-doers and their punishment) (Frankfurt, 1635).

6. Caspar Ziegler, *Jus Canonicum, Notis & Animadversionibus Academicis ad Joh.
Pauli Lancelotti . . . Institutiones enucleatum* (Canon law, explained with academic
notes and comments on the institutes of John Paul Lancelotti) (Wittenberg, 1669).
Christian Thomasius later also published his own edition of Lancelotti's work (*Jo-
hannis Pauli Lancelotti Institutiones Juris Canonici: Cum Notis Variorum, Praecipue
Arcana Dominationis Papalis, Episcopalis, et Clericalis In Ecclesia Romana Detegentibus;
In Usum Auditorii Thomasiani. Partes IV* (John Paul Lancelotti's Institutes of Canon
Law: with various authors' notes, which reveal above all the secrets of papal, episcopal,
and clerical domination in the Roman church; for the use of Thomasius's lecture
audience, in four parts) (Halle, 1715–17).

pelled to the external worship of God. Instead, Christ and his disciples regarded the external church and ceremonial order as a shadow of the true inner worship of God (Luke XVII, verses 20 and 21; John IV, verses 11, 21, 22, etc.; Acts VII, verse 48). Moreover, the apostles have always argued against all such ceremonies and arbitrarily established divine worship on holidays, Sabbaths, feast days, and such like, insofar as they do even the slightest harm to the inner free divine worship; and they explained that the true worship of God is spiritual, inward, and thus free, not tied to a particular place, time, or other circumstances (Galatians IV, verses 10 and 11, Colossians II, verse 16; cf. Romans XII, verse 12, James I, verse 27, Romans I, verse 9, Philippians III, verse 3, 1 Thessalonians I, verse 9; Arnold's *Image of the first Christians,* book 2, chapter 1, 1, p. 145, his *Church History,* book 1, chapter 2, §5, and book 2, chapter 3, §4, chapter 14, 17).[7] And so the first Christians for several hundred years did not perform such an external, ceremonial divine worship, until wealth and splendor as well as superstition entered the church together with the Jews or pagans. As long as the church remained with the early simplicity and manner of the old divine worship, it was pleasing to God. But as soon as it introduced the external religious worship, which was considered a meritorious ceremony, it departed from true Christianity and clung to external worship and drew God's wrath and punishment on itself. And thus it is not an unrestricted duty of a secular government to force someone to perform this external divine worship as something absolutely necessary. Theologians and jurists have always argued this against the papalists, because otherwise this would end in the coercion of consciences, in spite of the fact that the power over consciences belongs to God alone. (See Biedenbach in his *Decade of Theological Consilia, Decas* III, pp. 196ff.; Dürr in *Moral Theology,* p. 374; Lincke *On the Law Concerning Tem-*

---

7. Gottfried Arnold, *Die erste Liebe der Gemeinen Jesu Christi, das ist, Wahre Abbildung der ersten Christen, nach ihren lebendigen Glauben und heiligen Leben* (The first love of the congregations of Jesus Christ, that is, a true account of the first Christians, based on their living faith and holiness) (Frankfurt am Main, 1696); Arnold, *Unparteyische Kirchen- und Ketzer-Historie vom Anfang des Neuen Testaments biß auff das Jahr Christi 1688* (Impartial history of the church and its heresies, from the beginning of the New Testament to the year 1688) (Frankfurt am Main, 1699–1700).

ples, p. 65.)[8] I know well that it might be objected that this causes offense to our fellow Christians, since civil society requires that a person shows his piety to another. But piety does not consist in the uniformity of external rites, for this uniformity in external ceremony is an indifferent matter, especially according to natural religion, and partly unnecessary. For God, who divines hearts, has no need of external signs as a testimony of inner devotion. And these [external signs] have little relevance to civil society, because otherwise even an atheist, who offends his fellow man every day with his godless conduct, could brush off this offense and edify his neighbor by attending church. Yet a righteous, virtuous Christian, who leads a pious life without attending external church services, would have to offend his fellow Christians by his omission of these external actions. But this is false, and thus it is true that external attendance at church is an unreliable sign of piety and a dubious bond of society, and that a Christian, virtuous, inoffensive life, led according to God's will with sincere love, serves this end much better. And therefore neither is my fellow Christian offended nor is the bond of society cut if I withdraw from external public worship. (See Pufendorf, *On the Relationship of Christian Religion to Civil Life* §§3 & 7; Thomasius, *On the Right of the Prince in Indifferent Things,* §1, and his *Ethics,* chapter 3, §31).[9] This is particularly the case as nobody tends to be attacked for a particular opinion in religious matters, since the public peace is not disturbed by such an opinion. Even more applicable in the case of rulers is Bodin's proposal in his *Six Books on the*

---

8. Not Biedenbach, but Felix Bidembach, *Consiliorum Theologicorum Decas III & IV* (Decades III and IV of theological *consilia*) (Laugingen, 1608). J. C. Dürr, *Compendium Theologiae Moralis* (Handbook of moral theology). The edition used here is probably the third, which was published in Altdorf in 1698. Heinrich Lincken, *Tractatus de Juribus Templorum cum discursu praeliminari de Juris Canonici Origine & Auctoritate* (Treatise on the laws concerning temples, with a preliminary discourse on the origin and authority of canon law) (Jena, 1674).

9. Samuel Pufendorf, *De Habitu Religionis Christianae ad Vitam Civilem* (Bremen, 1687). For a modern edition of the 1698 translation of this work, see *Of the Nature and Qualification of Religion in Reference to Civil Society,* trans. Jodocus Crull, ed. Simone Zurbuchen (Indianapolis, Ind.: Liberty Fund, 2002). Christian Thomasius, *De Jure Principis circa Adiaphora* (The right of Protestant princes regarding indifferent matters or *adiaphora*) (Halle, 1695). Translated as chapter 2 in this volume. Christian Thomasius, *Einleitung zur Sittenlehre* (Introduction to ethics) (Halle, 1692; repr. Hildesheim, 1995).

Commonwealth, book 4, chapter 7, that one does not punish anyone because of religion, but allows everybody to perform at least their rituals for themselves, as long as this can be done without public unrest. Otherwise, such people lose all fear of God, because their conscience does not allow them to attend the ceremonies of others, and they are not allowed to have their own. Freedom of conscience is thus granted with the greatest care by the most eminent commonwealths, and almost everybody is permitted to believe according to his opinion, as the famous commonwealth of Holland shows in particular. Conversely, when such people are not tolerated in a territory, there eventuates what the Protestants themselves call a bloodless persecution. (See Kesler *On Persecution,* pp. 143 & 159; Wigand, *On Persecution,* p. 21.)[10] And under these circumstances, those who on grounds of conscience consider the physical attendance in church to be among the matters left to the free decision of a Christian, and to which one quite simply should not be coerced, will not be considered by anyone to be in willful contempt of God and his word. These, however, are the people your most princely territorial statute clearly is directed at, and without doubt your most princely highness's most recent gracious edict, which I revere with most humble respect and submission, as it refers to the territorial statutes, applies to these as well. Therefore I also live trusting humbly in the supreme grace of your most princely highness, that this same grace will permit those people to make use of their Christian freedom, whose conscience suffers as a result of the compulsion to attend these external churches, and who have in part, concerning these and similar doubts, undergone severe struggles with reason and human fear, and who have also experienced opposition from others, before they submitted to the impulses of their conscience, and resolved to resign themselves to the obloquy and judgments of the world. Moreover, as they lead a pious life and do not disturb the common peace, I also trust that they will in that respect be graciously distinguished from other, impious and ma-

10. Andreas Kesler, *Patientia Christiana. Außführlicher Tractat von der Kirchen Christi Persecution* (Christian Patience. A comprehensive treatise on the persecution of the church of Christ) (Coburg, 1630); Johann Wigand, *De Persecutione Piorum* (On the persecution of the pious) (Frankfurt am Main, 1580). Kesler distinguishes between bloody and bloodless persecution, the latter of which results in exile and loss of property but not in loss of life.

licious despisers of God and his word. And in this most humble hope
I remain forever.

§III. Now the above document shows quite clearly that the Lutheran
nobleman did not want to raise or answer the fourth question in the first
paragraph,[11] but that he wanted to reflect mainly on the abovementioned
first question,[12] although he also added other questions and assertions,
which have nothing to do with the matter. But as her highness sent the
nobleman's letter to the Consistory and he was concerned—because of
certain circumstances that will be reported soon—that the matter would
not end well, he sent the following three questions to our faculty:[13]

Three ques-
tions sent
to us

> In the Anhalt principality of N. there is a village N., in which the
> church and pastor are Reformed, but the person exercising jurisdic-
> tional authority, N.N., is a Lutheran. Some time ago a princely general
> mandate was issued that everyone should diligently attend church, but
> the abovementioned nobleman had his reasons for withdrawing for a
> time from the public congregation. When the princely consistory
> found out as a result of a denunciation by the pastor in N. that the
> nobleman of N., together with his children's teacher, had not attended
> church for some time, while otherwise leading a virtuous and pious life,
> the nobleman was summoned and questioned on this. He was then
> ordered to attend church according to the mandate of the prince.
> Thereupon, the nobleman of N. turned to the most gracious princess,
> and appealed against this summons (see the attached document under
> A) [i.e., the letter in §II above]; but this was sent back to the princely
> consistory, which asked the advocate, who had written this letter, *ex
> officio,* whether he had formulated it. He replied that the nobleman of
> N. sent him the documentation and he only brought this into the req-

11. That is, the question of whether a nobleman can be commanded to attend a
village church not of his choosing.

12. That is, the question of whether a Protestant magistrate has the authority to
compel his subjects to attend public church services as such.

13. The following paragraph thus contains the brief that the nobleman sent to
Thomasius's law faculty upon failing to receive the reply he desired from the princess.
In it the nobleman refers to the letter he sent to the princess (see §II in this chapter)
as appendix A attached to his brief.

uisite form, and so did not deal with the material, but [only with] the formal aspect of the question. And as this leads to another claim against the nobleman of N., the following questions are raised: (1) Whether the document under A is such that the nobleman of N. or the advocate, who formalized it, can be summoned or punished for it? (2) What procedure the high princely consistory at N. could adopt and what punishment it could decide on? (3) Whether the nobleman of N., being a Lutheran, can be forced to attend church in N.?

My response to the above questions

§IV. One could conclude from these three questions, that the appellant might have begun to recognize that the reasons listed in his document (see above §II) would hardly release him from the obligation to attend church in his village. Therefore a well-known jurist[14] may have given him the advice that he should set aside the general question, raised previously—on the right of the supreme civil power to force subjects to attend church (see above §I, number 1)—and should rather claim that as a Lutheran he could not be forced to go into a Reformed church. This jurist advising him may have led him to expect that when he sent the case to our faculty he would receive a favorable response. However, the matter turned out otherwise, for the then *Ordinarius* [head of the faculty] sent the case to me in order to present it before the faculty. When I had presented the matter and had clearly pointed out that concerning Lutherans and Reformed the three questions specified above (§I, numbers 2, 3, & 4) should certainly not be confused with each other, the decision of the third question proposed to us was unanimously decided such that the appellant, although he was Lutheran, was nevertheless obliged under these circumstances to attend the Reformed church in his village. And therefore I began work and wrote the reply as follows:[15]

> As the same has [submitted] the account of the case to us, together with the attached material under A and three questions etc., therefore etc. and concerning the first two questions we consider the following

14. Not clear whether this refers to a particular person.
15. What follows is Thomasius's formal response to the nobleman's brief, written as representative of the Halle law faculty.

to be right: it is being asked by him: (1) Whether the document under A is such that he or the advocate, who formalized it, can be summoned or punished because of it? (2) What procedure the supreme princely consistory at N. intends to adopt and to what punishment this could lead?

It could be said against the nobleman and his advocate that the content of the document referred to can indeed be considered punishable, for in it the right of supreme civil power in ecclesiastical affairs is almost continuously attacked and censured, the earlier opposition against the high princely edicts is defended contrary to the rules of sound reason, and various matters, which tend toward fanaticism, or which are at least inappropriate in this case, are being mixed in here. In the present case, however, the question is not what a Christian magistrate is obliged to do. Nor does it concern the advice that duly appointed councillors should give to the magistrate—in accordance with the rules of Christian and reasonable prudence—concerning the administration of justice in the churches. The question is rather what the duty of a subject requires, when the magistrate commands him to attend congregations diligently. Therefore everything listed in the document A [i.e., the nobleman's original letter to the princess] on these points: *That the external attendance at church was no absolute necessity for, or sign of a true Christian; that the external ecclesiastical ceremonies were not to be considered meritorious and were no essential part of the divine worship—which had a spiritual effect—such that they could not be omitted without sin; that Christ and the apostles had agitated against such external ceremonies insofar as they harmed the inner veneration of God etc.*—all this has no bearing on the present questions; for, in its command and ordinance, the high princely consistory did not advance contrary propositions, and nor should such conclusions be drawn from them. This is setting aside the fact that it is not evident how external divine worship can harm internal. For Christ and the apostles did not attack the external divine worship, but those people who clung to the external rituals alone, and who, while they should do one without ceasing to do the other, neglected the inner veneration of God out of the foolishness of their heart. Therefore the princely consistory will be delighted if the nobleman and his children's teacher, in addition to attending services, lead their lives in such a way that everyone is aware of their pious and virtuous conduct (of which they boast in their document A). When they have the testimony of others, they will no longer need to testify for themselves, as this testimony is not valid on the basis of either sound reason or Holy Scripture. Furthermore, the lack of justification for this rebelliousness is evident from the fact that the same nobleman admits in his document that he does not completely reject attendance at church, but approves of it insofar as it aims at order and discipline among the brutish children of the world. Thus, he considers church attendance praiseworthy in a certain sense, or at least concedes that the external ceremonies of divine worship are not morally binding in an absolute sense, but are middle-things [*adiaphora*] and hence indifferent. Nevertheless he does not want to obey the command of the secular magistrate in such indifferent matters, even though the magistrate can command something only in matters that are not morally binding in an absolute sense. Yet if one refuses obedience to the civil power in indifferent matters one tears the levers of government from the magistrate's hands. This was one of the most frequent tactics of the papacy, as it avoided obedience to the civil magistrate by appealing to Christian freedom and used this principle as a cover for its malice. Hereafter signs of fanaticism appear in the words of the document, since the same nobleman says at the end of it that because of these doubts he had undergone many severe battles with reason and with human fear, which is the first step toward lapsing into fantasizing, when one rejects reason and the senses. For we Christians and especially we Lutherans should, according to the interpretation of the first article, thank God every day that he gave us reason and all the senses and preserves them, and that God's holy word does not require an unreasonable, but a reasonable form of worship from us. And the pretext of combating human fear, whenever the civil power commands something in indifferent matters, is also an effect of fanaticism. For those minds which are imbued with this conviction, from an excessive imagined holiness, believe the inner impulses of their disobedient heart to be divine inspirations, and want to convince themselves and others that the civil power has to submit to them, or should at least take second place to them. Moreover, in this case the same nobleman has no cause to battle with reason, since Holy Scripture itself admonishes *that one should not fail to attend public congregations.* Further, although they were neither necessary for salvation nor meritorious, Christ our Savior performed the Mosaic ceremonies and commanded that one should obey the civil power in matters that are not improper (to this belong all matters that are considered to promote good order and discipline in a praiseworthy manner), and that one should obey also for the sake of one's conscience. Furthermore, in this instance of disobedience, the nobleman cannot plead violation of his conscience, since he considers attending church in itself to be praiseworthy and does not reject it completely. And conscience should also urge virtuous and pious spirits to set an example to the brutish children of this world in those matters which are commanded for keeping order among them. For this reason, if the nobleman continues to be disobedient, it is not unfair for the high princely consistory to proceed by commanding him and his children's teacher to leave the territory, while keeping the children behind, and to do as the hermits and first Christians did, who had no temples; or else to send them to the Dutch, especially as he refers to them so often in the document A, and wants to use their example to support his disobedience. One cannot justify the refusal of those who live in human societies to attend church by using the example of those who do not attend public congregations as a result of their living in a desert or having no temples. And neither Holland nor any other state can prescribe to a prince how he should act in the exercise of his regalian right in religious matters. Moreover, even though the same nobleman wanted to argue in his document that such exile is a bloodless persecution, nevertheless the high princely consistory would reply with better justification that exile and removal from a territory are entirely different from [arbitrary] expulsion, and, unlike the latter, are not to be considered a punishment, but a reasonable measure, derived from the nature of all human associations. For nothing is more innocent (and this was practiced by the faithful Abraham and Lot themselves),[16] than the principle that where there are two contrary

16. See Genesis 13:7–11: "[T]here was strife between the herdsmen of Abram's cattle and the herdsmen of Lot's cattle. . . . Then Abram said to Lot, 'Let there be no strife between you and me, and between your herdsmen and my herdsmen; for we are kinsmen. Is not the whole land before you? Separate yourself from me. If you take the left hand, then I will go to the right; or if you take the right hand, then I will go to the left.' . . . [T]hus they separated from each other."

factions in one society and no side (under the pretext that it is in the right and cannot be forced to do anything by the other) wants to make concessions to the other, one side—and this should in all reason be the smaller of the two—gives way to the other and moves to another place. Thus, if the society in which he lives expects no more from the nobleman than this, he must not complain that he is suffering an injustice.

Yet, the question meanwhile is not whether the nobleman produced such reasons, based on his letter, which could free him from worrying impositions if he continues to be disobedient; but whether there is anything improper in this letter, which in itself merits a punishment. Then the nobleman protests early on that he did not intend to be rebellious or disobedient, and repeats this at the end, that he humbly and submissively respected the high princely edicts. He declares at the same time, that with this piece of writing he mainly wanted to preclude the high princely consistory from considering him to be guided by willful contempt of God and his word. In fact, there are indeed no injurious words in the document A. Furthermore, the nobleman appeals repeatedly to his conscience, now to its doubts, now to its conviction, while, moreover, the entire context proves that his document is the *bona fide* outcome of an erring or confused conscience, rather than malicious intent. Such errors are not to be reckoned punishable actions, especially as such erroneous opinions have been fashionable here and there, and since the same nobleman, as a cavalier who has never turned his studies into a profession, could easily be led astray by others; and as his advocate declares, that he [the advocate] did not supply the materials of the document, but only brought it into the form of the usual official style.

So, altogether it is evident from this that neither the same nobleman nor his advocate can be punished because of this document.

As far as the third question is concerned we consider the following to be right. The same nobleman wants to be informed *whether he as a Lutheran can be compelled to attend the church in N. where the preacher is a Calvinist.* He further asks whether this is possible even though many teachers are of the opinion that the Reformed religion differs from the Lutheran in the fundamentals of faith, and teaches things such that a Lutheran cannot with a clear conscience listen to the sermons of the Reformed. He also considers the fact that in many places where the members of a parish are mixed, and some belong to the Lutheran religion, the Lutherans are usually allowed to participate in the services in neighboring places where there are Lutheran preachers. And yet, according to the account of events, the preacher in N. denounced the nobleman's absence to the high princely consistory, and seemed to have given occasion to some enmity.

Nevertheless, anyone can easily determine through a reasonable comparison of both religions, that the different opinions of these related confessions are not such that any of them affects the foundation of faith. Both the Reformed and Lutherans agree that salvation is achieved through belief in Christ and the Holy Trinity, not through good works. Further, the same nobleman does not refer to any reason in his document or in the account of the circumstances, why he as a Lutheran should be justified in complaining about the preacher in N. in doctrinal matters. Rather, he admits quite openly in his document A that he had until then made use of the church in N., and ceased doing so for reasons that are contrary to the principles of both Lutheran and Reformed religion, and cannot be based on the *Augsburg Confession* as the common creed of both Protestant confessions. In this case, however, it might be that the nobleman, once he had been ordered again by the high princely consistory to attend public church services, wanted to refrain from using these reasons, but resorted to the pretext of the Lutheran religion in order to present his further refusals in a more favorable light. If so, then it would indeed seem to be the case and to create a strong suspicion against him, that he was no longer resisting the high princely commands in good faith and out of an erroneous conscience, but rather that he was trying to elude them through his cunning, and tried to cover up deliberate disobedience with the pretext of some scruples of conscience concerning the Reformed religion. For human nature is not such, that someone could switch so quickly from the opinion that all visits to temples and churches (and so also of Lutheran congregations) are indifferent, unnecessary, or even detrimental to the inner service to God (contrary to the opinion of both Lutherans as well as Reformed), to a belief in Lutheran religion as the only path to salvation. For his own benefit, the nobleman should thus examine the minds of those who actually want to harm him with such poorly reasoned advice. Where someone is trying to convince him through such advice, he should consider that it makes no sense that he should ignore the rules of sound reason and the orders of his territorial prince, or that he must combat reason and the fear of men. Then, however, when it was sensed, that this audacious struggle over a long period of time did no good, [these same people] came up with artificial and sophistic arguments and the hatred of others, and thereby wanted to distract him from the observance of the duties he owes to God and the magistrate to whom he is subject. Similarly, the fact that the preacher in N. denounced the matter to the high princely consistory cannot be considered a sufficient and reasonable ground for the nobleman to detest him. This is especially so as, according to his own report, a general edict that one should not miss the public congregations was published shortly before this. Thus the preacher in N. could not act otherwise in accordance with this duty than he did in following the edict. Neither was the gracious command given to him as an unrestricted compulsion, but is to be understood from the nature of the matter as saying that the nobleman and his dependents cannot miss the public congregations without weighty reasons, such as illness and the like; *since all affirmative laws allow the tacit exceptions of place, time, and unsuitableness, and exclude what is far-fetched, etc.* Moreover, there would undoubtedly be no better way for him to refute the suspicion of a willful refusal to attend services—which has not come up without reason—than if he attends church services in N. with his dependents as before. If illness or other similarly urgent circumstances occasionally prevent him from attending the church services, he should nevertheless constantly urge his dependents not to withdraw from the congregations. This is the case all the more as nobody will prevent him from holding his private devotions as before with his children and servants. We also cannot see how attendance at the public congregations, at which a Reformed clergyman preaches, can do any harm to inner worship (which is also part of the beliefs of the Lutheran church).

Thus it seems that under these circumstances the high princely consistory indeed has the right to urge him emphatically to attend services in the church in N. with his dependents. Everything *V. R. W.*[17]

17. "V. R. W." presumably stands for "Von Rechts Wegen" ("in accordance with law"). This concludes Thomasius's original formal advice, provided in his capacity as professor of law at Halle.

§V. On this occasion I want to recount another example, which does not directly prove the decision of the third question, but clarifies it to some extent. The most blessed *Landes-Hauptman* of Fr. (to whom I dedicated my German version of the notable matters in the life of Socrates in 1693),[18] was a sincere Calvinist and, when he was in Dessau, also attended the Reformed church. But while he lived for the sake of convenience on one of his estates at Mehlau (which was not far away from Dessau), he, together with his family, regularly attended the Lutheran church of the congregation at Mehlau, even though this was not just a Lutheran but a Gnesio-Lutheran church,[19] and the pulpit was inscribed in large golden letters with the words:

My clarification of the third question

> *God's word and Luther's teachings*
> *Will not pass away, now or ever.*

Indeed, he was so far from feeling hatred and suspicion toward even the more zealous Lutherans that, whenever the regular Lutheran clergyman could not preach in Mehlau, he usually substituted a Lutheran *Magister* [of theology] from nearby Wittenberg, and afterward invited him for lunch, and treated him very kindly. I also remember, that on this occasion I met for the first time the *Magister* Stoltz, (who subsequently displayed his Wittenberg zealotry against Brenneisen's treatise on the *Right of Protestant Princes in Theological Disputes* in two orthodox publications in 1697).[20] In fact I learned from his sermon and from the con-

18. This is Thomasius's translation of Charpentier's life of Socrates, published as *Das Ebenbild eines wahren und ohnpedantischen Philosophi, Oder: Das Leben Socrates, aus dem Französischen des Herrn Charpentier ins Teutsche übersetzt* (The portrayal of a true and unpedantic philosopher, or: the life of Socrates, translated from the French of Mr. Charpentier into German) (Halle, 1693). The dedicatee is Dodo, Freiherr of Inn and Knyphausen, privy councillor to the Elector of Brandenburg.

19. The Gnesio-Lutherans were a group of Lutheran theologians who were active mainly in the third quarter of the sixteenth century, though Thomasius also uses the term to describe his orthodox opponents. The sixteenth-century Gnesio-Lutherans criticized what they perceived as the corruption of Luther's teachings by the followers of Philipp Melanchthon.

20. Thomasius and Brenneisen published *Das Recht Evangelischer Fürsten in theologischen Streitigkeiten* (The right of Protestant princes in theological disputes) in 1696, as a counterattack to the criticisms that had been launched against the *De jure*

versation with him over lunch that he was more than anybody worthy to be incorporated into the holy order of heretic-mongers [*Ketzermacher*]. Now (to return to the topic) since a Calvinist nobleman and state minister in Anhalt does not scruple to attend services in the Lutheran church of his village, so it also seems to me that the Lutheran nobleman seeking our opinion would have done well, if he had not allowed himself to be incited by others, to cover up his obstinacy with the feeble pretext that he, as a Lutheran, could not be urged to go to church in his village N.

The unusual fate of my reply

§VI. My above response however had a slightly unusual fate. For after I had sent this to the head of our faculty for examination, he returned it to me and let me know, partly orally through the short-hand writer, partly in writing in his own hand, that he would like to see the counterarguments left out altogether in the first and second questions and replaced with the following few words: *Although there are all manner of things in the submitted document which we cannot approve at all . . .* Yet, in the meantime he said "In the third question (these were his own words) I would prefer to see a negative reply,[21] in accordance with the text in the Westphalian peace treaty, article 5, §31,[22] which refers to Catholics and Protestants, but can be used here as it is the same problem,

---

principis circa adiaphora (The right of Protestant princes regarding indifferent matters or *adiaphora*) of the preceding year. Once again, Brenneisen played the role of Thomasius's spear-carrier, presenting his teacher's ideas in a public disputation under Thomasius's supervision. Johann Gottlob Stoltze, church superintendent in Waldenburg, then countered with two further replies to Thomasius, the *Anmerkungen über einige Lehrsätze Christiani Thomasii, vom Recht evangelischer Fürsten in theologischen Streitigkeiten* (Comments on some doctrines of Christian Thomasius, concerning the right of Protestant princes in theological disputes) (Leipzig, 1697), and the *Evangelischer Fürsten Recht in Vertheidigung der wahren evangelischen Lehre* (Protestant princes' right concerning the defense of the true doctrine of the gospel) (Altenburg, 1697).

21. That is, Thomasius's head of faculty wishes him to advise that the nobleman should not be forced to attend church in his village.

22. This is the Peace of Westphalia of 1648. The paragraph referred to allowed private, domestic worship to those subjects whose confession differed from that of the ruling house. The text is cited below in §VII.

although the decision would not be pleasing to the princess, since she had this same controversy with the consistory at an earlier point about the Lutherans. Or one could leave this question out." I found this suggestion rather surprising, especially as the head of the faculty, when I presented the case, did not object anything to my opinion that the question should be answered in the affirmative, and none of my other colleagues commented on this. I also thought about what must have impelled the head of the faculty to this extraordinary resolution: Whether it seemed to him that in the first two questions the principles of the Quakers and Pseudomystics were refuted a little too clearly, though mildly, and that in the third question I moved away from the common Lutheran opinion that there is a fundamental disagreement between Lutherans and Reformed? Or whether perhaps he advised the nobleman seeking our opinion to add the third question and promised him an affirmative decision in advance? Why then (because this last seems very probable to me) did he not present the case himself, but selected me to present it? And so on. Nevertheless, I soon replied to the head of faculty in writing that, as far as the abbreviation of the counterarguments in the first two questions was concerned, he as the head was free to revise the argument and change it at his pleasure. As far as the third question was concerned, I could not understand how, contrary to the conclusion of the faculty, the negative conclusion could be now defended in the place of the affirmative. I also do not understand, how article 5, paragraph 31 of the Westphalian peace treaty can be applied to the present case, even though it otherwise could be applied to both Protestant religions. This is not to mention the fact that article 5 cannot be applied to the controversies between the two Protestant religions, since this is dealt with elsewhere, in particular it is dealt with manifestly in article 7 and, moreover, toward the end of this article the princes of Anhalt are expressly excepted from the general provision. Given this, I nevertheless left it to the head of faculty whether he wanted to leave out this third question and the response to it, or whether he wanted to produce a special response to this under his name (as the matter would probably have been entrusted to him). And so he let me know soon afterward that he had resolved to leave out the third question and the response to it.

§VII. I would consider it unnecessary to recount the circumstances so
far in such detail, if I had not found afterward, that this last promise was
not kept, but that in the minutes of the faculty my above response was
completely changed, under my own name, in the following way:

> As the same sent us a report, in addition to a document under A with
> the seal of our faculty, as well as two questions etc., the same person
> was asked: *whether the document under A was such, that the nobleman or*
> *his advocate, who had put it in the requisite form, could be summoned or*
> *punished for it?* Although in the document he handed over there were
> various irresponsible matters, which undoubtedly had to displease the
> princely consistory and which we too cannot approve at all, yet since
> the same nobleman protested at the beginning, that he had no inten-
> tion of being rebellious etc. (for the rest see above §IV in the counter-
> arguments for questions 1 and 2).
>
> Concerning the other question: *whether the nobleman, being a Lu-*
> *theran, could be compelled to go to the church in N. where the preacher is*
> *a Calvinist?* we believe it is true that it is the duty of a territorial ruler
> to look to it that the regular divine service is upheld, and everyone is
> assigned to the church in his own parish, and that, since both parties
> are Protestant, the difference in religion also cannot be taken into con-
> sideration, as far as attendance at sermons is concerned, since the no-
> bleman is free to take communion in a neighboring Lutheran parish.
> However, the question is precisely whether a person can be compelled
> to attend the service of another religion. This sort of coercion is not
> approved in the Peace Treaty of Westphalia, article 5, §31, but on the
> contrary in these cases permission is granted to hold devotion with
> one's dependents freely and without impediment at home. The word-
> ing is as follows: *If they (the subjects) will profess a different religion from*
> *that of the lord of the territory, and embrace it, they should be tolerated*
> *with patience, and they should not be prevented from privately taking part*
> *in devotions at home, with a free conscience, without inquisition or dis-*
> *turbance, and also, where and as often as they want, to participate in neigh-*
> *boring territories in the public practice of religion, to send their children*
> *to external schools of their religion, or to have them instructed at home by*
> *private teachers.* Although this text refers to Catholics and Protestants,
> nevertheless it must also apply to Calvinists and Lutherans because the

rationale is the same, just as there is no example to be found of a Calvinist government that forces its Lutheran subjects to attend Calvinist services, but so far has left this to everyone's own decision. This is also the best means to encourage Christian tolerance, and so we believe, that the nobleman under these circumstances cannot be compelled to visit the church at N. *V. R. W.*[23]

§VIII. I did not add this change to my reply for the purpose of supposing   Conclusion or obstinately arguing that my own affirmative response is to be preferred to the negative. I thus rather leave it to the judgment of the impartial reader, which of us is in the right. Should he decide in favor of this last change, I would have a bad conscience if the praise that belongs to the true author were accorded to me and I allowed him to be deprived of it.

23. See note 17 in this chapter.

Is Heresy a Punishable Crime?

JULY 14, 1697[1]

Conversation between a (so-called) Orthodox
Believer and a Christian

I

Orthodox My dear Christian, I find you always over the books.[2] What are
you studying, since I see the works of jurists and theologians
spread all around you?

Christian My dear Orthodox, your arrival is timely, as you can help me with
my work. You know what kind of strife rages among the theologians of our church, today worse than ever. You know how in
these controversies it is typical that both parties declare each other
heretics, or at least one party declares the other to be such. You

---

1. This date records the presentation of the Latin disputation *An haeresis sit crimen?*
(Is heresy a crime?). The disputation was delivered by one of Thomasius's doctoral
students, Johannes Christoph Rube, under Thomasius's direction, forming part of
a series of such disputations in which Thomasius campaigned to make religiously
based offenses immune from judicial and political punishment. It provoked immediate and hostile responses from representatives of Lutheran orthodoxy, including
the Rostock theologian, J. Fecht, and, even more problematically, two members of
the theological faculty at Thomasius's own university: the professor of theology, Justus Joachim Breithaupt, and his junior colleague Gustav Philipp Mörl, later a
preacher in Nürnberg. But it was not only the orthodox who were opposed. G. W.
Leibniz, usually regarded as one of the founders of the *Aufklärung*, wrote a hostile
review in 1698. Leibniz rejected Thomasius's arguments for relegating theological

148

know that more than once on such occasions those who seem suspect to others have been dragged before the courts, where they were dealt with according to inquisitorial process. Nonetheless, since occasionally judgments and opinions are handed down by our colleges or by individual jurists, the matter seemed to deserve the effort of a somewhat more exact consideration. For I do not know how it has transpired that certain opinions concerning the crime of heresy, commonly accepted even among Protestant jurists, have already appeared suspect to me for some time. Furthermore, (as others have already remarked), just as in matrimonial cases before Protestant courts many things occur that are redolent of papalism, stemming from the doctrine that marriage is a sacrament, so it seems to me that the doctrines we observe in cases concerning heresy, and which form the basis of our decisions and advice, deviate utterly from the sound teaching of the Gospels. And I must say that the more I peruse the books our [Lutheran] jurisconsults have written about heresy, and compare them with those written on the subject by our theologians, the more I am confirmed in my opinion. But, Orthodox, you will be best able to dispel this worry; for you have dedicated yourself longer than I to the study of law and, before commencing this, had studied theology for several years. So, then, tell me what you think about this.

Orthodox   Gladly! Neither will this be too difficult for me, for our [Lutherans] have already been reproached by the papalists several times, as if our teaching regarding the punishment of heresy

---

doctrine in favor of inner piety, arguing instead that such doctrine was itself necessary to purify the will and that in negligently adopting false doctrine heretics were responsible for their own corruption, therefore deserving of punishment. (See Gottfried Wilhelm Leibniz, "Sur Thomasius, *Utrum haeresis sit crimen,*" in *G. W. Leibniz: Textes Inédits,* ed. Gaston Grua [Paris, 1948], 210–12.) The German version of Thomasius's disputation appeared in his *Auserlesene deutsche Schriften* in 1705, under the title *Ob Ketzerey ein strafbares Verbrechen sey?* (Whether heresy be a punishable crime?), which is the version principally used for this first English translation.

2. The stilted third-person address between the two dialogue partners ("I find him always over the books") has been rendered in the standard second-person form ("I find you always over the books").

agreed with theirs. Our theologians and jurists have responded
to this accusation splendidly, however, showing that there is a
great difference between our standpoint and the papalists'.

Christian   What kind of difference then?

Orthodox   So far as I recall, the papalists generally declare that heretics may
be compelled to believe and, as people who have committed a
dreadful crime, punished with death. Our people, though, wish
to compel no one to believe, nor to pronounce capital punishment on anyone for heresy. In fact, they seldom go further than
excommunication or banishment, unless the crime of heresy is
accompanied by sedition or blasphemy. Now I cannot see what
is wrong with this teaching, but think to the contrary that it is
quite clear, and in good accord with the principles of jurisprudence.

Christian   Yes, it is just as you have said. And I myself have read in many
authors about just such a difference between the papalist and
Protestant teaching. Only, this difference does not satisfy me. *For
it seems to me that the Protestants also papalize in this, in that they
cannot clearly say what kind of thing heresy is; that they regard heresy
as a punishable crime; that they reject religious coercion with one
hand while defending it with the other, in that they think heretics
should be punished with excommunication or exile; that they cloud
the doctrine regarding sedition and blasphemy in such a way that
they can wreak their animus against all heretics with the sword, just
as dreadfully as the papalists; and that they have thus quite carelessly
introduced evidently papalist doctrines regarding heresy into their
juristic commentaries or theological systems.* And so that you do not
think I am just prattling, I could show you all of these things
solely from Benedict Carpzov's text of criminal law, which I have
in front of me.[3] But I would rather discuss each and every matter
with you in an orderly way.

---

3. Benedict Carpzov (1595–1666) was the most famous Saxon jurist of the seventeenth century. A tireless glossator, Carpzov worked on systematizing customary
Saxon law, organizing the reception of civil and canon law, and commenting on
public law. He was an orthodox Lutheran strongly opposed to heresy and witchcraft

Orthodox   I am happy with this. Only mind that you prove everything that you claim.

II

Christian   There is no need for you to worry about that. It is much more important that we reach agreement regarding the sources from which we will prove our opinions.

Orthodox   In juristic matters, from where else would we draw our sources than received laws, namely, from the law of Justinian, canon law, imperial resolutions, and from the common consensus of the church fathers, the theologians, and jurists?

Christian   I think you must be joking. For since I have said that the jurists papalize in this matter—that is, that their doctrines are contrary to divine law and Christ's teachings—anyone could see that no *human laws* would be suitable, least of all *the law of Justinian and canon law.* For the latter papalizes not just a little, but is wholly and solely papalist. The former is stuck so full of anti-Christian doctrine, however, that in a special treatise called the *Roman-Catholic Jurist,* a papalist jurist, Cornelius à Rynthelen used the Law of Justinian to decide in favor of the papalists, each and every controversial question over which Protestants and papalists disagree.[4] Further, considering I have said that the common doctrines papalize, it would be ridiculous if someone wanted to use the common consensus of the scholars against me; for here the question is not whether the scholars agree in common, but whether their agreement is right.

---

and contributed to Lutheran church law through his membership of the Dresden Superior Consistory. Here Thomasius is probably referring to Carpzov's codification of Saxon criminal law, the *Practica nova imperialis saxonica rerum criminalium* (New imperial Saxon practice of criminal law) (Wittenberg, 1635).

4. Cornelius à Rynthelen, *Iurista romano-catholicus: id est, iuridica romanae catholicae fidei confessio* (The Roman-Catholic jurist: that is, the juridical confession of Roman Catholic faith) (Hemmerden, 1618).

Orthodox   Nevertheless, you should not reject the testimony of the church fathers out of hand, especially the testimony of Augustine, who (it seems to me) deals with this doctrine in a very reasonable way, and is everywhere highly esteemed in all three religions of the Holy Roman Empire.[5]

Christian   In fact I honor the fathers of the early church, yet their authority will never be so great with me that it can turn wrong into right or vice versa. I am happy to allow, though, that their texts should be introduced insofar as they are based on weighty reasons. Against those who stand on the authority of the church fathers, however, one may introduce other texts of other church fathers (if one wants to).

Orthodox   But what do you think *about Augustine?*

Christian   Even if I had no other reason, his authority is suspect for me on account of the fact that, as you say, he is regarded so highly by all the religions recognized in the Empire.

Orthodox   I do not understand what you mean. Speak more clearly.

Christian   If I recall correctly, a teacher of the church, Hieronymous, once said: The whole world has surely become Arian. I will not be wrong if I say, the whole world has surely become Augustinian, and has long ceased to be Christian. One can see from the history of Jansenism how much the papalists have squabbled among themselves on account of the authority of Augustine.[6] Even Lu-

---

5. Lutheranism, Calvinism, and Catholicism, which were recognized as legitimate public bodies in imperial law under the terms of the Treaty of Westphalia in 1648.

6. Jansenism was a dissenting movement within the French Catholic church, inspired by the writings of Cornelius Jansen (1585–1638), bishop of Ypres, but during the seventeenth century the movement was centered in the famous abbey of Port-Royal, where it was protected by the powerful Arnauld family. Jansen wrote commentaries on Augustine, developing "rigorist" doctrines stressing the absolute difference between sinners and those in a state of grace, and viewing grace in a semi-Calvinist way as something reserved for an elect chosen by God. These doctrines were declared heretical by Pope Innocent X in 1653, but the independence of the Gallican church, together with the movement's support among the French nobility,

ther, as he had been an Augustinian, occasionally makes too much of Augustine, giving him excessive praise, and taking much from Augustine's Platonizing or paganizing theology which he should rather have taken from the purer springs of Israel. It is no wonder then that today our [Lutheran] theologians and jurists esteem his authority and his books more highly than is proper. I do not know exactly how much the Reformed [Calvinists] commonly hold with him. Yet I think that what I have said could easily be applied to them too, particularly as Augustine teaches at length about particular grace [predestination] in his disputation against Pelagius.

Orthodox   That is as may be, but one must not on this account speak contemptuously of the great Augustine, or flatly reject his authority.

Christian   But I do not speak contemptuously of him. I say myself that Augustine was a great man. He was a great disputant, a great orator, a great philosopher, a great statesman, and—adding these elements together in the way of the world—a great theologian. I say further that he possessed kingly and heroic virtues. I am concerned, though, that in his writings he has not conducted himself as a great Christian. For on every page he reveals his passions of love or hate. One finds no trace of apostolic humility or fortitude, but everything smacks of proud words that excite and please the flesh. Yet perhaps we can speak of this another time, especially as we have another reason why we cannot accept Augustine as a judge or witness in this controversy.

Orthodox   Why then?

Christian   Augustine is heir to the common flaw of the human race, namely: when another wrongs us we easily see what is right and remind them of fairness. As soon as we have the opportunity for revenge, though, we allow ourselves to be blinded, doing wrong under the appearance of right and, forgetting fairness, seek to hide such

---

meant that it remained a significant force throughout the seventeenth century and into the eighteenth.

wicked things from others under the guise of fairness. When the Donatists raged against the orthodox, Augustine splendidly opposed this, teaching them how poorly it sat with Christianity if someone were coerced into religion.[7] But once the orthodox found an emperor who agreed with them, Augustine changed his tune, defending the doctrine that one may compel heretics to believe, even if he did so under a great show of compassion and fairness. And because Augustine contradicts himself so often in this matter, he has given the scholars reason enough to disagree over his exact views regarding the doctrine of the persecution of heretics. So the parties on both sides call on Augustine. To defend the coercion of heretics, for example, he is invoked by Bellarmine,[a] Franciscus Burchard,[b] Hierotheus Boranowsky,[c] and several others.[8] Conversely, their opponents, Antonius Benbel-

a. Bellarmine, *de Laicis,* bk. 3, ch. 21ff. [Robert Bellarmine, *De laicis sive secularibus* (Of the laity or secular members). This is part of a larger work by Bellarmine *De ecclesiae militantis membris* (On the members of the church militant) published in various editions, one of which appeared in Jena in 1629, edited and with a commentary by the Lutheran theologian Johann Gerhard.]

b. Franc. Burchardt, *Von der Freystellung,* pt. 2, chap. 16, pp. 181ff.; chap. 17, p. 188; further, chap. 20, p. 203, and elsewhere. [Francis Burchard (Andreas Erstenberger), *De autonomia. Das ist, von Freystellung mehrerley Religion und Glauben* (On autonomy. That is, on allowing several religions and faiths) (Munich, 1586).]

c. At several places in his *Gerechtfertiger Gewissens-Zwang.* [Hierothei Boranowsky, *Gerechtfertiger Gewissens-Zwang oder Erweiß daß man die Ketzer zum wahren Glauben zwingen könne und solle* (Justified compulsion of conscience, or, proof that heretics can and should be compelled to true faith) (Neyss, 1673).]

7. The Donatists, named after their leader, Bishop Donatus of Carthage, were a fiercely independent faction of African Christendom during the fourth century. Augustine fought a long pamphlet war to subordinate them to the emerging Catholic Church.

8. Robert Bellarmine (1542–1621), a Jesuit and cardinal, was a leading Catholic controversialist and tireless defender of papal authority. Francis Burchard (d. 1592) was the pseudonym adopted by Andreas Erstenberger, Catholic privy secretary to the imperial court, for the publication of his most famous work, *De autonomia. Das ist, von Freystellung mehrerley Religion und Glauben* (On autonomy. That is, on allowing several religions and faiths) (Munich, 1586). In this work, Erstenberger argued against the toleration of Protestantism in the German Empire, insisting that the Peace of

Iona,[a] Samuel Pomarius,[b] and our people have occasionally used his testimony to defend freedom of conscience against the papalists, and to moderate and reconcile contrary opinions, even if often more sophistically than from reason.[9] Jean le Clerc[c] and Philipp van Limborch[d] have complained about Augustine's hard judgment against heretics, which yet Pierre Poiret[e] has endeavored to defend and to explain in a different way—although I

Augsburg (1555) was a plot by "satanic" Lutherans and proponents of state reason against the Catholic church. Hierotheus Boranowsky (1624–77) was a pseudonym of Johannes Scheffler, a Polish-born Catholic convert, who also published works under the names of Angelus Silesius, Bonamicus, and Christianus Conscientiosus. He was a prolific and vehement anti-Protestant polemicist, arguing that rulers could make legitimate use of coercion in seeking to re-Catholicize their territories.

a. In *Suscitabulo pro Principibus,* pt. 1, chap. 4, p. 48; pt. 2, chap. 14, p. 137. [Anthony Benbellona (Bartholomew Gericke), *Ung resveille Matin Sive Tempestivum suscitabulum pro principibus* (An alarum or timely rousing on behalf of princes) (Servestae, 1602).]

b. At various places in his *ungerechten Gewissens-Zwang.* [Samuel Pomarius, *Be wiesener ungerechter Gewissens-Zwang entgegen gesetzet Hierothei Boranowsky Gerechtfertigtem Gewissens-Zwange* (Demonstrably unjustified compulsion of conscience: against Hierotheus Boranowsky's *Justified Compulsion of Conscience*) (Wittenberg, 1674).]

c. *Defense des Sentimens sur l'Histoire Critique,* lett. 14, pp. 366ff. [Jean le Clerc, *Défense des Sentimens de quelques Théologiens de Hollande sur L'Histoire Critique du Vieux Testament. Contre La Reponse Du Prieur de Bolleville* (Defense of the sentiments of some Dutch theologians regarding the *Critical History of the Old Testament.* Against the response of the Prior of Bolleville) (Amsterdam, 1686).]

d. *Hist. Inquis.,* bk. 1, chap. 6. [Philipp van Limborch, *Historia inquisitionis hispanicae cum libro Sententiarum Inquisitionis Tholosanae ab A.C. 1307 ad 1323* (History of the Spanish Inquisition together with the book of sentences of the Toulouse Inquisition 1307–1323) (Amsterdam, 1692).]

e. *Apol. ad. Libros de erudit. solida &c.,* append. 5, pp. 457ff. [Pierre Poiret, *De eruditione solida, superficiaria, et falsa* (On solid, superficial and false erudition) (Amsterdam, 1692).]

9. Antonius Benbellona was one of the pseudonyms used by the Lutheran controversialist Bartholomew Gericke (b. 1557). Samuel Pomarius (1628–83), also known as Samuel Baumgarten, was a Lutheran theologian and church superintendent in Salzwedel whose anti-Calvinist polemics drew the ire of Frederick William I of Brandenburg.

have said elsewhere[a] that I regard their interpretation as the
more plausible.[10]

Orthodox I hear nothing but the names of heterodox authors and, as I have
often said, it does not please me that you read these people. You
should read the writings of our orthodox teachers more closely,
and not set these aside out of idle curiosity and read people of
other sects.

Christian I have learned to test everything and keep what is good.[11] I have
learned that a Christian must live among sects, just as he must
live in the world, but need not form a sect. I live in the sect to
which I was born, and follow its ceremonies to the degree that I
can with a good conscience. For this reason, though, I do not
dislike people who adhere to a different sect. Neither do I dislike
the people of my own sect. But I seek the truth from all or, rather,
examine them all in accordance with the rule of wisdom which
I find in Holy Scripture, allowing no one to confound me as to
my own faith. So, in the matter we are speaking of, I have also

a. In the dissertation *de scriptis Poireti*. [Christian Thomasius, *Christiani Thomasii,
JCTI Dissertatio Ad Petri Poiret Libros De Eruditione Solida, &c.* (The jurist Christian
Thomasius's dissertation on Pierre Poiret's book *On Solid Erudition,* etc.) (Frankfurt,
1694).]

10. Jean le Clerc (1657–1736) was a Swiss Arminian theologian and biblical scholar.
Le Clerc had preached in France and England before finally settling in the Netherlands, where he identified with the cause of the Remonstrants, or moderate Calvinists. Philipp van Limborch (1633–1712), too, was a Remonstrant pastor and Arminian
theologian in the Netherlands. He was a friend of John Locke's and the author of
numerous books on theological controversies and the history of religion. His *Historia
Inquisitionis* (History of the Inquisition) was published in 1692 and translated into
English by Samuel Chandler in 1731. Pierre Poiret (1646–1719) was a French-born
mystical theologian who had initially followed Descartes but then developed his mystical doctrines under the influence of Antoinette Bourignon, whose lifelong disciple
he became. Despite this, his scholarship and his moderate teachings were widely ad-
mired by Thomasius, Bayle, and Le Clerc, among others. Poiret's *De eruditione solida,
superficiara et falsa* (On solid, superficial, and false erudition) (1692) drew a critical
but respectful response from Thomasius.

11. This was the catchcry of the eclectic philosophers with whom Thomasius identified. Eclecticism had an antischolastic intellectual ethos, and its objective was to
obviate sectarian commitment to a particular philosophical or theological tradition
by encouraging selective use of different schools of thought.

turned to writers belonging to the sect in which I live. A theologian in Ulm, Elias Veielius—in fact a Lutheran theologian whom you regard as orthodox—has written a *Theological Disquisition on Augustine's Opinion regarding Whether Heretics may be Compelled to Believe.*[12] This author agrees that Augustine's initial opinion that one should tolerate heretics—in accord with Holy Scripture too—has altered in his last writings. Although, like others, he offers as an excuse that Augustine nonetheless did not defend the killing of heretics, and that the Donatists had no reason to complain about Augustine's somewhat harsh position. But in my view this scarcely touches the issue. Meanwhile this author admits that: *Augustine occasionally fashions ineffective weapons from the texts of the Bible, and the scholars find in fact that Augustine is an orator but not an acute disputant. And that in this example, according to Grotius, it appears that we judge in one way when we look into something dispassionately, but in another way when the question of action cuts this short, which is why second thoughts are not always the wiser ones.*[a] With this explanation, I have shown why in the present matter I must exercise caution with Augustine's authority in particular.

Orthodox Now, because you can abide neither human laws nor the testimony of the scholars, I must ask, what kind of grounds will you accept as a basis for proof?

Christian None other than the eternal and universal grounds, namely, divine revelation and sound reason.

---

a. See [Veiel], *Dissertation,* pp. 44–45 [Elias Veiel, *Disquisitio Theologica de Sententia S. Augustini* (Theological discourse on the opinion of Saint Augustine) (Ulm, 1680)]; see Dommaireinus à Dissingau, *von der Autonomia,* c. ii, pp. 216ff. [Dommarein von Dissingau, *Kurtze Information und Anleitung, von der Autonomia, zu Erleuterung des Hochberümbten Tractats* (Brief information and instruction on the *Autonomia,* for the explanation of this most famous tract) (Christligen, 1610).]

12. Elias Veiel, *Disquisitio Theologica de Sententia S. Augustini* (Theological disquistion on Saint Augustine's opinion) (Ulm, 1689). Veiel (1635–1706) was an orthodox Lutheran theologian who taught at the Ulm higher gymnasium.

Orthodox   But this would be to commit a metabasis.[13] We are jurists and
              you want to discuss a juristic question. Something proved from
              divine revelation or Holy Scripture belongs to theology; some-
              thing proved via reason belongs to philosophy.

Christian   I don't know what kind of jurisprudence you have studied. My
              jurisprudence is grounded in divine laws, likewise in human laws
              that are in agreement with reason.[14] If you have a jurisprudence
              that is removed from divine revelation and reason, then you
              should take care that all reasonable people do not regard it as
              godless and unreasonable.

                                     III

Orthodox   Enough of this! I think that the common doctrine on the crime
              of heresy has sufficient basis in Scripture and reason. If you think
              otherwise, then tell us what has made you dubious.

Christian   All right, I want to proceed neither as a sophist nor as an orator,
              but shall set out my key doubts in clear questions, as a good
              friend. In my view, where it is not false, the opinion that heresy
              is a punishable crime is surely uncertain. You say it is agreed that
              heresy is a punishable crime. Do you think, though, that we can
              dispute properly if we do not know what kind of thing heresy
              is, or if we do not agree in our conception of a heretic?

Orthodox   Certainly not. For heresy is not a thing that can be grasped with
              the senses, but must be conceived and understood in thought.

    13. Metabasis: to prove or assert something in one discipline by improperly using
another.
    14. This is something about which Thomasius changed his mind. The view alluded
to here, according to which jurisprudence could incorporate "divine positive law" or
biblical commandments so far as these were interpreted by jurists, was the one outlined in his *Institutiones jurisprudentiae divinae* (Institutes of divine jurisprudence)
of 1688. But he had abandoned this view by the time he published his *Fundamenta
juris naturae et gentium* (Foundations of the law of nature and nations) in 1705, arguing instead that all laws could be derived from a rational reflection on the rules
required to maintain inner and outer peace.

Christian   If you think heresy is a punishable crime then say what kind of thing heresy is. For I have doubts about this and am sure that I do not rightly understand what a heretic and heresy might be, and that you and those like you, who regard heresy as a punishable crime, know just as little as I do.

Orthodox   You are confusing things which are clearly difficult with those that are impossible. For although Augustine had already said in his day that it is a difficult thing to define a heretic, yet it is not impossible even if it is difficult, but, according to the proverb, beautiful once the difficulty is overcome.

Christian   All right then, so offer a definition. Is someone a heretic *who it is decided deviates even in the slightest thing from the judgment and path of the universal (or Catholic) religion?*

Orthodox   No. For Wissenbach[a] has already observed that this definition is uncertain and false.[15] Following the opinion of Augustine, not all errors are heresy, in that for an error to be heresy it must be accompanied above all by obstinacy.[b]

Christian   But this definition is from the laws of Justinian,[c] and you can see even from this example that one may depart from Justinian Law in this matter. Ultimately, things can be as they may for Augustine, for, regardless of what he might have said, this definition would be obscure and uncertain, as the nature of the universal religion or universal way is likewise obscure and uncertain. And you know full well that the papalists always like to insult us with this definition,[d] in that they claim for themselves the pseudotitle

a. Ad Cod. tit. de haeret. init. [*Code of Justinian,* "On Heretics," beginning.]

b. C. dixit 29, qu. 3. [*Canon Law,* canon 29, question 3.]

c. l. 2, C, de haeret. [*Code of Justinian,* lex 2, "On Heretics."]

d. See Cornelius à Rynthelen, *Jurist. Rom. Cathol.,* §70, p. 154. [Cornelius à Rynthelen, *Iurista romano-catholicus: id est, iuridica romanae catholicae fidei confessio* (The Roman-Catholic jurist: that is, the juridical confession of Roman Catholic faith) (Hemmerden, 1618).]

15. Johann Jakcob Wissenbach (1607–65) was the author of numerous works intended to expose errors and contradictions in Justinian and canon law.

of Catholic on the basis of long-lasting possession. What do you think then of the definition given in canon law, where *someone is a heretic*[a] *who introduces or accepts false and novel opinions, for the sake of temporal benefit, principally from ambition and the desire for glory?*

Orthodox   This is even more vague and false, because philosophical, medical, or juristic errors do not make a heretic, only errors in faith; although, perhaps this can be understood from the *cited canon.*

Christian   I will not press you on this at the moment, otherwise I could easily show that ultimately all heresy arises from nothing other than the pretext of an error in philosophy.[16]

Orthodox   I could in fact grant you this with regard to the papalists, for they make scholastic philosophy into the foundation of their theology. But we can let this go for the moment.

Christian   Yet this is even true according to the views of the Protestants. But enough of this. I now ask: Is heresy thus an error in faith?

Orthodox   One must add a little more to that: *Heresy is an obstinate error in the foundations of faith by a person who is or was a member of the church.*[17] For in this, papalist, Lutheran, and Reformed teachers, theologians as well as jurists, for the most part agree with each

a. C. Haereticus, 28. c. 24, q. 3. [*Canon Law,* "Heretic," canon 28, causa 24, qu. 3. The footnote marker, missing from the German text, has been restored following the Latin.]

16. This is an allusion to Thomasius's standard argument that faith as such cannot be erroneous, as it is a matter of the will and heart, making no claims to falsifiable knowledge. Only faith contaminated by philosophical explication can be a matter of correct knowledge, leading to charges of error and thence to persecution.

17. This was the cardinal early modern juristic definition of heresy, introduced into the legal codes of Protestant states from canon law, much to Thomasius's displeasure.

other.[a] Here, everything is quite clear. For when I say that heresy is an *intellectual error,* then I have distinguished it from punishable crimes which arise from the will, such as murder, adultery, and so on. Through the word *obstinacy,* flagrant heretics are distinguished from the weaker and more innocent ones, who are not so bad, and who are not so much the seducers as the seduced. Through the words *error in faith,* a heretic will be distinguished from those who err in philosophy and other sciences. Through the words *error in the foundations of faith* one can distinguish a heretic from those who err in articles which do not belong to the foundations of faith, who should be regarded as schismatics rather than heretics. Finally, through the fact that a heretic is a *member of the church,* heresy is distinguished from paganism, the Mohammedan faith, and Judaism. Now that all the words in the definition of heresy have been distinguished from those related to them, I do not see how you could object to anything in this definition.

IV

Christian   We will soon see. For if one wants to present a thing clearly, it is not enough to dress it up in so many words just as obscure, or even more obscure, than the thing one wants to explain. Rather, it is necessary that one has in mind clear and certain notions of each and every word in the definition. It seems to me, though,

---

a. Farin. p. 8, qu. crim. 178, §1 [Prospero Farinacci; possibly a reference to vol. 8 of his *Opera omina,* the *Tractatus de haeresi* (Treatise on heresy) (Frankfurt, 1686)]; Carpzov, qu. crim. 44, n. 4 [Benedict Carpzov, *Practica nova imperialis saxonica rerum criminalium* (New imperial Saxon practice of criminal law) (Frankfurt, 1635), question 44, §4]; Ziegler on Lancellotti p. 939 [Caspar Ziegler, *Jus Canonicum, Notis & Animadversionibus Academicis ad Joh. Pauli Lancelotti . . . Institutiones enucleatum* (Canon law, explained with academic notes and comments on the institutes of John Paul Lancelotti) (Wittenberg, 1669)]; Voet, *Dissertationes selectae,* disp. 4, de error. & haeres., p. 723 [Gisbert Voetius, (possibly his) *Selectarum Disputationum Theologicarum,* part 4 (Select theological disputations, part 4) (Utrecht, 1667)]; Limborch, *Historia inquisitionis,* bk. 3, chap. 1, p. 175.

that for all of the words you have presented, just as many obscure or dubious or false things lie beneath them. I do not want to insist on anything concerning the word *church,* since this term, if any, is subject to a multifarious obscurity, and you will perhaps argue to Judgment Day about the signs of the true church. Not to mention that here your orthodoxy departs from the rule of Holy Scripture in several regards. This is partly because, instead of interpreting the word *church* as a society of the faithful, orthodoxy—together with anti-Christian doctors and the papalizing laws of Justinian[a]—applies this term to bricks and mortar or church buildings. But it is also because orthodoxy joins the papalists in seeking the unity of the true church—invisible and scattered across the whole world—in a visible assembly.[18] Finally, it is because orthodoxy has imported into your theological systems the following doctrine taken from the papalists: the whole assembly of the true church is visible, the individual persons of the faithful, however, are invisible—which is self-contradictory and conflicts with the doctrine of the relation of the universal and the particular. But enough about this, because at least the word *church* in this definition provides me with some sense of the difference between a heretic and a Jew etc. Now tell me what you mean, though, by the *foundations* of faith? Because by using this phrase you say that a heretic will be distinguished from a schismatic; although here again doubts arise as to whether this is a correct distinction, in that some scholars interpret the phrase in one way, others quite differently.[b]

a. t. t. C. de SS. Eccles. [*Code of Justinian,* "On the Most Sacred Churches."]

b. Lancellotti in Ziegler, pp. 938ff.; Limborch, bk. 3, chap. 7, p. 199; Pomarius, in *Ungerechten Gewissens-Zwang,* pt. I, p. 199.

18. Although the separation of the invisible from the visible church was standard in Protestant theology, Thomasius uses the distinction to attack Lutheran orthodoxy. In treating true Christians as permanently scattered and unknowable by any outward signs, Thomasius separates Christianity as an inner moral condition from the church as a public institution. This not only strikes a theological blow against the notion of heresy—by undermining the notion of a visible religious community from which heretics deviate—but also permits the political secularization of the public church by separating it from the invisible community of the faithful and treating it as an assembly of citizens rather than of Christians.

Orthodox   The clarification of this matter belongs to the theologians, who dispute much over the fundamental articles of faith.

Christian   You are certainly right that they dispute over this; in fact they will dispute about it forever. And that is just as I have said: you would not know what heresy is because you do not know what the foundations of faith are, about which there is no end of different opinions among the orthodox. For when one of them deems an article of faith to be a basic article, then others will not agree with him about this. No fixed number of articles of faith has been settled, and in their systems the doctors themselves lay down sometimes this, sometimes that, now more, now fewer. Neither would it help were one to say that the articles belonging to the foundations of faith are all those included in the creeds, in that our [Lutheran] theologians deem that several of the basic articles are given expressly in the *Augsburg Confession*,[19] while others are there only implicitly.[a] This depends on time and place. Further, often the basic articles alter between different persons. For a long time Flacius was held to be a heretic; that is, as someone erring in a basic article.[20] He was publicly denounced as a Manichaean; that is, as the worst heresiarch. Today, after his death, when his disciples have quite died out, and after the hate and self-interest of his opponents have changed a little, most speak of him more mildly, and count him only among the schismatics; that is, they

a. See Grübel's appendix to Dedeken's *Consilia theologica,* p. 8. [Georg Dedeken, *Thesauri consiliorum et decisionum, volumen primum, ecclesiastica continens* (Treasury of opinions and decisions, volume 1, containing ecclesiastical matters) (Hamburg, 1623). Republished with an appendix by Christian Grübel in 1671.]

19. The Augsburg Confession, intended to state and distinguish the Protestant articles of faith, was presented to Emperor Charles V on behalf of the Protestant princes and cities in January 1530. By the end of the sixteenth century it had been somewhat superseded by the stricter formulations of the Formula of Concord (1577), at least in the eyes of orthodox Lutherans, who thus began to reinterpret the Augsburg Confession, giving rise to the kind of disputes mentioned here by Thomasius.

20. Matthias Flacius Illyricus (1520–75) was a noted Lutheran theologian who had been associated with Luther and Melanchthon at Wittenberg. Flacius participated in several controversies surrounding the demarcation of Lutheran orthodoxy and became notorious for holding the doctrine that original sin inheres in man's being or substance.

declare that his doctrine of original sin does not overturn the foundations of faith. In defending Christ's thousand-year empire, the ancient teachers of the church were certainly not deemed heretics. In fact they were counted among the holy martyrs, as they still are today, which is a sign that this opinion of the fathers is not held to be erroneous, let alone contrary to the foundations of faith; for it would be senseless and mutually contradictory for someone to be a heretic and yet also a martyr. Those who teach Chiliasm[21] today though—and in fact to the shame of their adversaries—will be proclaimed heretics by many of our people. We deem the papalists and they deem us to be heretics. And yet many people hold such papalists as Tauler, Thomas à Kempis, Saint Theresa, and others to be holy, and not in fact without reason (although doubtless, if not in all their statements then certainly in many, they held the errors of papalist teaching to be true, contrary to the *Augsburg Confession*).[22] How can it make sense, though, for someone to be holy and yet a heretic? There are many among our Lutherans who have held that the conflict between us and the papalists and Reformed is such that an accommodation could easily be reached between the parties— or at least that they could tolerate each other—because this division does not upset the foundations of faith. Yet others are so vehemently opposed to them that they have branded them with the hateful name of syncretists, and have produced many harsh texts against them, as heretics who have committed dreadful errors against the foundations of faith.[23] But these last [the syn-

21. The doctrine that Christ will return in bodily form and rule over the earth for a thousand years; hence, too, millenialism.

22. Johann Tauler (1300–1361), a member of the Dominican order at Strasburg, was a leading mystical theologian and preacher. The author of the famous *Imitation of Christ*, Thomas à Kempis (1379/80–1471), was a monk among the Canons Regular of Windesheim, where he cultivated an ascetic and mystical style of Christian life modeled on the imagined simplicity of life of the early Christians. Theresa of Ávila (1515–82), a Spanish nun in the Carmelite order, was also an ascetic mystic. Her works on the contemplative life played an important role in spreading the devotional fervor associated with the Counter-Reformation.

23. The foremost Lutheran exponent of (so-called) syncretism was Georg Calixt (1586–1656), professor of theology at the University of Helmstedt. Calixt argued for

cretists] are now once more acknowledged as brothers in Christ, and no longer as heretics, even though they have not changed their earlier opinion regarding the reconciliation of faiths one iota, but simply because they have united with their former opponents in a new act of damnation against a third party. Further, regardless of the difference between fundamental and nonfundamental articles, anyone who is not wholly subject to the prejudice of authority can easily see nonetheless that there is a great difference between our conflicts with the papalists, and the conflicts we have with the Reformed. Yet it is known that a great many of our [Lutherans] who wish to appear supremely orthodox have a different view, and currently argue the case that it is *better to be papalist than Calvinist* in entire books. From this vague and uncertain standpoint regarding the fundamental articles of faith there has arisen an absurd state of affairs, whereby several controversies have arisen among the theologians, such that tradesmen or laypersons possessing a little wit could easily understand that the conflict does not concern the Christian faith, much less matters pertaining to the foundations of faith. Regardless of this, one of the warring parties, keener than the others to persecute other people under the guise of godly zeal, makes use of innocent talk or talk pertaining only to philosophical matters in order to fabricate heresy, by appealing to the consequences of consequences. This [fabricated heresy] is repugnant to the articles of faith agreed on as fundamental by the majority, even though the other party vainly protests that an injustice has been done to them and that such consequences do not follow. So much has this wicked habit gained the upper hand, that it could scarcely have been controlled through severe edicts from the prince.

Orthodox　The things you have spoken of are so evident that they arouse some doubt in me, since I have not thought about them until now. Yet, in order not be hasty, I will consider these things some-

---

reconciliation between Lutheranism and Calvinism by downplaying the significance of doctrine and stressing the importance of living a shared Christian life. He was opposed by orthodox Lutherans, especially by Abraham Calov (1612–86) of Wittenberg, who sought to have Calixt's teachings proscribed as heresy.

what more exactly on another occasion. The theologians with whom I will consult will know how to answer your scruples.

Christian   There will never be a shortage of answers. But if you should hear an answer that is to the point, impartial, and free of passion and bitterness, then all to the good, and do let me know of it. For until now the circumstances of the thing have not allowed me to think other than that the passions of the clergy have caused if not all, then the majority of heresies. And that the most courteous of the clergy called their adversaries schismatics, a name less hated today. The rest, however, being oafishly proud and having little intercourse with civilized people, decry it as a heresy if someone disagrees with them, their teachers, or their good friends in the slightest thing.

Orthodox   Do you hold then that there is simply no foundation of faith, but that everything touching faith is uncertain?

Christian   Far be it that you should think this of me. The doctors may well lack certainty, but that does not mean we do. There is indeed a foundation of faith, there are fundamental articles that will be easily found if we do not bind ourselves to the prejudice of authority, but look for this in the teacher of all teachers, the Holy Scriptures.

Orthodox   I would very much like to hear your opinion about this.

Christian   That would not be well suited to our plan. For I have begun a discourse with you so that I could learn something from you. But if you want to hear about my creed, then I say: The foundation of faith is love of God and one's neighbor, and disdain of oneself.[24] Now all errors that contradict this attack the foundation of my faith, but the other errors—especially those regarding the mysteries of the divine being—do not concern the foundation

24. In reducing the Christian religion to these three elementary principles, Thomasius sought to consign the mass of theological doctrine to the domain of *adiaphora,* or matters of indifference, thereby removing the basis for doctrinal conflict and heresy allegations, and giving the prince the right to resolve doctrinal conflicts, to the extent that these might affect civil peace.

of my faith and that of other Christian and Protestant people. If on the basis of my view one were to say what a heretic is, then I fear that many of the most orthodox—by which I mean all those who tie saving faith to formulas and creeds—would have to be inscribed in the list of heretics.

Orthodox   And I fear that your opinion would not find much applause among our Lutherans, since what you regard as the foundation and origin of faith, they count as the fruits of faith, or would otherwise oppose something similar to it.

Christian   They can say what they like. I am always ready to offer a justification for my faith. For the moment I will only ask you, where does the chicken come from?

Orthodox   What have we to do with the chicken? This question does not touch our issue. Doubtless the chicken comes from the egg.

Christian   You say this, strangely and implausibly: the egg is really a fruit of the chicken.

Orthodox   Now I see where you are going with this, but listen to me: It does not work if one attempts to prove something by deriving it from a quite different thing.

Christian   Yet I prove nothing from that, except for showing that your proof and faulty distinction are false. But let that be sufficient, for, as I said, my plan is not to dispute about the foundations of faith with you. I am much more concerned to proceed with my objections against your definition of heresy.

Orthodox   It seems to me that what you have already put forward is not to be made light of. Have you then still more to object against this?

V

Christian   In fact I still have much to say against it. You have said heresy is an error in the foundations of faith. Now tell me, what is *faith*? For I do not know this either.

Orthodox   It grieves me that you do not understand the principles and rudiments of Christianity or the Catechism. Did you not learn the definition of faith in school, from *Hutter's Compendium?*[25]

Christian   Naturally I learned it, if by this you mean learning by rote something that I do not comprehend, and believing to be true something I do not understand because great and famous people deem it to be true. I can say by heart what our people teach in their creeds regarding the things required for faith, occasionally in opposition to the papalist definition of faith. I can easily understand that the papalist conception of faith is an error. Yet I still do not understand clearly and sufficiently the conception of faith taught by our Lutherans, because it seems to me that this conception is not always coherent, and our Lutherans are not constant and unanimous in this conception. As someone who takes his salvation seriously (as any Christian properly should), it annoys me when reading our Lutheran texts to find that *Hutter's Compendium*—which is supposed to set out the basics for tender minds—contradicts itself in innumerable places. In other words, Hutter's own German translation—which he claims to have prepared with great diligence and at princely command—often completely alters the meaning of the Latin compendium. Not only this, but in the confessional books [*Libris symbolicis*] the Latin text agrees poorly with the German text. For example, in the *Apology of the Augsburg Confession*[26] when justifying faith is spoken of in the chapter on justification, following the Latin text the words run thus:[a] *The faith that makes one righteous is not a*

---

a. *Formula of Concord,* p. 68. [In fact this refers to the Apology of the Augsburg Confession (1531) in the *Book of Concord,* which also contains the Formula of Concord (1577).]

25. Leonhard Hutter (1563–1616) was a leading orthodox Lutheran theologian at the University of Wittenberg who specialized in anti-Calvinist polemics. In 1610 he published the *Compendium locorum theologicorum* (Compendium of theological topics), which became a basic text for teaching the Lutheran articles of faith, being frequently republished during the seventeenth and eighteenth centuries.

26. After a series of Catholic attacks on the publication of the *Augsburg Confession* in 1530, a defense or *Apology* was prepared the following year, under the direction of Luther's lieutenant, Philipp Melanchthon.

mere historical knowledge, but is an acceptance of the divine prom-
ise, in which forgiveness of sins and justification are offered gratui-
tously, for Christ's sake.[27] The German version though runs somewhat more fully, as follows: *The faith that makes one pious and*
righteous before God is not only that I know the history of how Christ
was born, suffered, and so on, but is the certainty, or the certain strong
trust in the heart, where I hold God's promise for certain and true
with my whole heart, through which is offered to me, by means of
Christ and without any merit on my part, forgiveness of sin, grace,
and all holiness.[a]

Orthodox   But it seems to me that as far as the meaning is concerned there
             is no difference here, or it is a slight difference indeed.

Christian   But there is a great difference between them. The expressions "to
             have faith in someone" and "to believe someone" have two
             wholly different meanings. On the one hand, faith and belief are
             taken to be an *intellectual* act, which assumes an inward certainty
             or acceptance of our thoughts in the *brain.* This is the kind of
             faith parties in a lawsuit are looking for from the judge, as we see
             in the whole title of the Pandects, *on the faithfulness (or certitude)*
             of the instruments [de fide instrumentorum].[28] On the other hand,
             the word *faith* signifies a *trust* in the *will,* which is an affect of
             the *heart* arising only from love; for it is impossible for me to
             trust a man or his promise unless I love him. Intellectual faith
             differs little from historical faith, and is in no way a saving faith
             because even devils could have it. It is necessary, therefore, that

a. Ibid., under the heading "What Is Justifying Faith?" the verse "thus regarding
proper Christian faith."

27. A standard modern English translation of this passage runs thus: "The faith
that justifies, however, is no mere historical knowledge, but the firm acceptance of
God's offer promising forgiveness of sins and justification." Theodore G. Tappert,
ed. and trans., *The Book of Concord: The Confessions of the Evangelical Lutheran*
Church (Philadelphia, 1959), 114. Note that the emphasis on the gratuitousness of
God's gift of grace is missing from this modern version.

28. Thomasius is referring to section 22.4 of the first part of *Justinian's Digest* (also
known as the *Pandects*), *De fide instrumentorum et amissione eorum* (On the certitude
of the instruments and their loss), stipulating the trustworthiness of legal and ecclesiastical documents as instruments giving effect to testimony, covenants, and similar.

saving faith be a trust or confidence of the will, and not a mere intellectual assent. Now one can see that the German text of the [*Apology of*] *the Augsburg Confession* speaks of the *trust of the will in the heart,* for there we find these words: *the strong trust in the heart, where I with my whole heart,* and so on. The Latin text, though, speaks of the intellect, of *assenting* to God's promise. Not a word is said regarding the heart.

Orthodox   For this reason, following the rule of a generous interpretation, one must emend the Latin text from the German exemplar, understanding the meaning of assent as if it signifies a trust, even though this meaning reads somewhat harshly and strange. For it is well known that if something absurd follows from the exact understanding of a word, then one must understand it in an inexact or foreign sense.

Christian   I would gladly agree with you, if only *Hutter's Compendium* allowed this explanation; if only the *Apology* did not make it dubious; if only the common erroneous principles of pagan philosophy, still generally accepted by our orthodoxy, were not opposed to this explanation; if, finally, the whole religious system of our orthodoxy were not so strongly opposed to it.

Orthodox   Describe this a little more clearly.

Christian   At locus 12, question 15 of the *Compendium,* in the Latin text (for again the German translation does not agree here), Hutter explains the trust of faith in terms of the conviction in conscience [*conscientia, Gewissen*] of a thing's certainty. According to the common doctrine of our universities, however, conscience pertains to the *intellect* and not to the will. Yet, trust of the will is either a kind of love or, as mentioned, arises from love and does not precede it. In the *Apology,* however, faith is set apart from love, and it is said that love follows from faith.[a] But this can be true only of intellectual faith, when one accepts the common doctrine according to which the intellect is supposed to rectify the will. This pestilential error—that the intellect can rectify the

a. See, *Formula of Concord,* p. 74. [That is, Apology of the Augsburg Confession.]

will—common to all of the pagan philosophers, arises from the fact they sought the essence of God in speculative thought, rather than in love. As a result, they also looked for the essence of man in his mind rather than his heart. Thus they said that their philosophy, which taught that men became like God, consisted in the doctrine of the purification of the intellect, in the discovery of truths, and in the mind's ideal contemplation of the essences of things. Further, they awarded the office of councillor to the intellect, and the office of king to the will, fabricating other similarly absurd fables which, so far as I know, rule everywhere and in all three religions of the Holy Roman Empire, and from which arose, amongst other things, the false precept that intellectual faith awakes love in the heart. Yet anyone who carefully considers the nature of man sees without doubt that all corruption and all improvement of the intellect arise from the will and its affects, so that the concept of truth in the intellect of itself never produces anything good in the will. I have often had to wonder how we could be so stupid. The verse from the poets is preached in front of us everyday: *Video meliora proboque,* that is, I see the good and approve it (in the intellect); *deteriora sequor,* that is, yet I follow the bad (in the will).[29] Nevertheless, they want to persuade us that thinking and intellectual assent to the truth rectify the will. Further, we can see that for our [Lutheran] orthodoxy, saving faith ultimately resolves into intellectual faith, when we consider, amongst other things, the following: Theologians hardly ever quarrel with each other regarding the things one should do, or the things of the will, but over concepts in the intellect, which they call things one must believe, as opposed to things that one should do. And the Greek words *orthodoxia* and *heterodoxia*—which one calls *Rechtgläubigkeit* [orthodoxy] and *Falschgläubigkeit* [heterodoxy] in German, even if this does not properly express the Greek words—are derived from the word for opinion. An opinion, though, is not a thing of the will, but of the intellect. And yet they present these opinions, this intellectual faith, and this creed as if they were damning or saving. According to the

29. Ovid, *The Metamorphoses,* bk. vii, 20–21.

Athanasian Creed: *any man who wants to be saved must above all things hold to* [*teneat*] *the universal faith, and whoever does not preserve* [*servaverit*] *this faith entire and inviolate must without doubt be eternally lost.* Even here it looks as if the words *tenere* and *servare* (to hold) were words pertaining to the will. Under these words, though, the whole Creed teaches nothing about matters of the will, but only about mysteries pertaining to the intellect, which are not in the heart but in the mind. And then, in the sentence *Who wants to become blessed must therefore believe in the Trinity etc.,* the Creed explains the words *tenere* and *servare* (to hold) through the words *to know* [*sentire, wissen*], *to believe* [*credere, glauben*], and *acknowledge* [*confiteri, bekennen*]. Further, our [Lutherans] often use saving faith and saving doctrine synonymously. But doctrine is a thing of the intellect and doctrine cannot save. Judas did not change doctrine, remaining orthodox, and was damned nonetheless. So we have a saving work that damns, making it something of a wooden poker. Additionally, in accordance with the usual expressions and practice, repentance and conversion, which are both works of the will, have become intellectual objects for our orthodoxy. In fact, they are often not even intellectual objects but mere sounds without meaning. When someone from the papalist, Judaic, or Turkish religion comes across to us, he is called a convert. Yet he changes his life not in the least, altering only the formulas and creed on his lips. Often such people do not even understand the grammatical meaning of the words they learn by heart (and here I speak from personal experience). Yet some are not ashamed to thank God from the public pulpit that they have converted an infidel or heretic to the saving faith. I could introduce much more of this if I did not have to move on. I take it, though, that I have already said enough to show that those who claim that heresy is a punishable crime do not know what faith is, which yet remains a part of their definition of heresy. Nor is it possible to derive a genuine concept of faith, consistent with the Holy Scriptures, from their writings, or from common doctrine and practice.

Orthodox   The more I reflect on the things you have spoken of, the more confused I become, and I will not rest until my doubts have been resolved by a learned theologian.

VI

Christian   That is your choice. Now we want to discuss the word *obstinacy*, which you have likewise included in your definition of *heresy*. This obstinacy is otherwise called a malice impervious to all admonition.[a] But here again it is very difficult to comprehend exactly what is to be understood by obstinacy. In fact, it is well known that our Lutherans distinguish between formal and material heretics, or, between the seducers and the seduced, describing the former but not the latter as obstinate people, and regarding them as heretics properly so called.[b] It is well known that papalist law first paved the way for this distinction.[c] But it is also well known that some among the papalists were not happy with this distinction, wishing to declare all heretics to be obstinate people—the seduced as well as the seducers.[d] Our theologians themselves admit that it is difficult to judge the obstinacy of heretics, and that one can not always tell with certainty whether a heretic defends an error from willful obstinacy or from human weakness, as a result of persuasion by others or from ancient custom.[e] It is easy to see, however, that whether someone is seducer or seduced has little to do with obstinacy. For an erring and seducing teacher need not be obstinate, just as a seduced learner can be obstinate enough. Moreover, obstinacy need not always contain malice. Setting aside that here we are not talking about an obstinacy of the will, or a deliberate opposition to things one should do, but about an obstinacy in matters of the intellect, so this obstinacy regarding intellectual matters can be explained in

a. Ziegler on Lancelottus, p. 939.
b. Pomarius, in the foreword to *Unrechten Gewissens-Zwang*, p. 6.
c. C. dixit Apost. 29. C. 24. qu. 3. [*Canon Law*, canon 29, causa. 24, question 3.]
d. Boranowsky in Pomarius, as above, p. 499.
e. Wittenberg Theological Faculty, *Gründlichen Beweiß wieder der Rinteler Syncretistische Neuerung*, pp. 60, 61 [Wittenberg Theological Faculty, *Gründtlicher Beweiß daß die Calvinische Irthumb den Grund des Glaubens betreffen und der Seligkeit nachtheilig seyn: Dabey auch angeführet welcher Gestalt Christliche Einigkeit zu stifften, und der Rinteler Syncretistischer Neuerung zugleich begegnet wird* (Thorough proof that Calvinistic errors concern the foundation of faith and are harmful to salvation. With this it is also shown in which form Christian unity should be grounded and, at the same time, the Rinteln syncretistic innovation is countered) (Wittenberg, 1664)]; Pomarius, as above, p. 155.

two ways. On the one hand, it signifies a shortcoming of the intellect if someone can put forward nothing against the truth, yet will not change his opinion, refusing intellectual assent to the truth because of the prejudice of authority. On the other hand, obstinacy signifies a maliciousness of the will if someone is convinced of the truth of a thing in his intellect, yet refuses to acknowledge this recognized truth, instead teaching falsely and contrary to his conscience. We are not concerned here with the first meaning—as just illuminated through that which we have introduced from our theologians—which thus cannot be properly called obstinacy. As for the second meaning, such obstinacy is rarely to be found, for in human nature it is quite impossible that someone should speak about matters of the intellect other than he intends, unless he acts from fear of torment. It is well known that among a thousand heretics, most of them—even doctors—err in good faith. It is thus a slander when the papalists say that our theologians teach contrary to their conscience. Likewise, we must ascribe it to lack of contact with our adversaries, or to lack of travel, when our people want to persuade us, as perhaps they have persuaded themselves, that the papalists, together with the Reformed theologians or teachers of other sects, are ordinarily obstinate and convinced in their conscience of the falseness of their doctrines. Further, the judicial way of convincing heretics, which presupposes their obstinacy, is typically very uncertain, if not to be wholly repudiated. To convince does not mean to arouse fear in a man through a legal action, or to force him to acknowledge the truth of something through judicial authority. Rather, it means to show him his error in a friendly way, with proper proofs, or through a spiritual power and virtue, mediated by a discourse or clear questions. This is how Christ and his apostles refuted their adversaries. But the Anti-Christ[30] raged against dissenters with imprisonment, murder, and banishment; with judicial authority; with majority votes; and with confiscation of their books. And this is called convincing or enlightening the erring! Heretics are exiled, or banned

30. The pope.

from the halls of disputation, or, if they are allowed in, are prevented from opposing and disputing. Thus one disputes against the absent, or against those who may not speak. And this is called convincing! One might wish that this papalist way of convincing did not also reign among the Protestants. I would gladly keep quiet about this if the very stones did not cry out, and if common public practice did not testify to this.

VII

Orthodox I would not have thought that the definition of heresy could be subject to so many doubts. Yet now we will be finished with it.

Christian No, there is still something to consider regarding the word *error.* I know full well what an error is, but I do not know what an error regarding the divine mysteries might be. An error is a deviation from the truth. Truth is an agreement of the understanding with a thing. God is an infinite being. That which is infinite cannot be comprehended by a finite intellect (neither wholly nor in part, or if comprehended in part gives rise not to knowledge but only to an opinion or mere negative concepts). One cannot conceive of an infinite being other than through analogies drawn from finite things; indeed, not even through such analogies properly speaking, in that these possess nothing that is similar to it. A conception through analogy is not a conception properly speaking. And a conception in an improper sense is not a true conception. On account of this, one cannot say precisely what an infinite being is; nor, therefore, can one show that a particular positive concept of an infinite being is erroneous. Now, most disputes with heretics are over the question: What is the infinite being? I say again: there is no judge who could decide the error here, because a man cannot be a judge in this matter, as our Lutherans prove long windedly against the papalists. I know full well that our [theologians] call on Scripture, but I wish that they could clarify this doctrine such that we laypeople could understand it. The book of Holy Scripture is caught in the middle. There are conflicts, for example, between the doctors of our sect and the Calvinists, likewise the Socinians, Quakers, Anabaptists, and so on. Each party calls on Scripture, using it to prove their opinion about this. One party explains Scripture in this way, another in that. Both parties claim that their interpretation is the meaning of the Holy Ghost. Now, who is the judge in this matter?

Orthodox   Other texts—that is, parallel *loci*—explicate Scripture with Scripture, and show that the adversary's explication contradicts the true meaning provided by the analogies of faith [*analogiae fidei*].[31]

Christian   But the adversary says the same thing about us; and just like us they have parallel Scriptural texts and the so-called analogy of faith. Now, who is judge?

Orthodox   But their explication is not right, while ours is.

Christian   So I am told that the explication of the Scripture should be the judge. But the explication is human. And so you see how much papalizing occurs among the Protestants. The Bible is only a pretext, while the commentary or gloss is turned into the norm or judge of Scripture itself. Calling on the analogies of faith is typically a cloak for ignorance. It contradicts the duty of a good disputant to deny the conclusion [to a sound argument]. Invoking the analogies of faith, however, often amounts to denial of the conclusion, even if this is hidden under another name. The adversary presents a proof, compelling a response. The respondent concedes the major premise and the minor premise is correct. Then the respondent claims that the adversary's conclusion is contrary to the analogies of faith; that is, even if his conclusion were true, it cannot be reconciled with principles to which the respondent already adheres. For this reason, he begins to preach about his principles and the analogies of faith, and the respondent becomes an opponent. I will leave it for others to judge whether this agrees with the rules of good disputation and of proper inquiry into the truth.

31. This refers to a hermeneutic doctrine and practice in which disputed biblical passages were interpreted via their analogy or agreement with other passages whose meaning was not contested.

Orthodox   I had not imagined that you would say such things to me, which, even if they do not persuade me, at least influence me and give rise to doubt. I am concerned, though, that those who defend the common doctrine will denounce you as a wicked heretic.

Christian   By the grace of God I am already hardened to such honorifics and, on the other hand, wish these people well. Yet to please you I will read something from Salvian, who was a pious religious teacher and lover of heretics, but no heretic-monger.[32] He writes thus: *With the barbarian peoples, the statutes of their magistrates and their ancient doctrines were regarded as law; they are people who know what is being taught to them. They are heretics, but they do not know it. In fact, they are heretics for us, but not for themselves. For they consider themselves so orthodox that they apply the name heretic to us. What we now regard them as, they regard us as. We are certain that they dishonor the Son of God because they say that the Son is not as great as God the Father. They, however, think that we dishonor God the Father, because we believe the Father and Son are equal to each other. The truth is with us, but they imagine it is with them. The honor of God is with us, but they think that God's honor is what they believe. They are undutiful, but for them this is the highest religious duty. They are impious, but hold just this to be the true piety. They err on this account, but they err in good faith, not from hate but from love of God, in that they believe that they honor and love God. Although they do not have proper faith, yet they hold this to be the perfect love of God. What they will suffer on Judgment Day on account of the errors of their false doctrines, no one can know except the judge. In the meantime, I think God will be patient with them, because he sees that although they do not believe correctly, they err with pious intentions; especially because he is aware that they do what they do not know, whereas we do not do what we believe. And thus they sin through the fault of their magistrates, while our people sin through their own fault; they unwittingly, we knowingly; they do what they take to be right, we, on the other hand, do that which we*

32. Salvian was a fifth-century Gallo-Roman writer who contrasted the decayed virtues of Christian Rome with the sturdy virtue of such barbarian peoples as the Saxons, Franks, Goths, and Vandals.

know to be wrong. And for this reason, from his just judgment God bears them his divine patience, but chastises us with punishments. For ignorance can be forgiven to some degree, while contempt has no hope of grace.[a]

Orthodox   It seems to me that Salvian's words beautifully explain the things you have briefly advanced regarding *obstinacy* and the *judgment of error.* After this, though, hopefully your criticism of the definition of heresy is concluded, so that we can turn to other things you have mentioned above: namely, that our Lutherans papalize when they deem heresy to be a punishable crime.

VIII

Christian   If there were no other way, then I could still use the proof that it appears to be a cruel tyranny to treat as the wickedest criminals people whose crime cannot be proved, in fact because you have no clear and certain conception of this crime. And certainly, if the truth be told, I do not know what the patrons of the common doctrine could properly bring against this proof. I will not dwell on this, however, but will show from other nearer reasons that heresy is not a punishable crime.

Orthodox   I cannot wait to hear, mainly because you yourself said that you would use no other foundations than Scripture and reason. But do you not know that Holy Scripture itself regards heresy as a work of the flesh, including it with such other gross vices as adultery, whoring, idolatry, sorcery, murder, drunkenness, and the like?[b]

Christian   It is good that you have reminded me. For I would have forgotten the most needful remarks against the definition of heresy, with-

---

a. Salvianus, *de Gubern. Dei,* bk. 5, pp. 162ff. See also similar texts of Arnobius and Lactantius in the notes of Rittershusio on Salvianus. [Salvianus of Massilia, *De Gubernatione Dei,* (On the providence of God) (Geneva, 1600). Thomasius is referring to the notes in Konrad Ritterhausen's edition of Salvianus's *Opera,* published in Altdorf in 1611.]

b. Galatians IV, 19. [In fact, Galatians 5:19–20.]

out which we could expect little that is solid or clear from the discussion of this question. Those who defend the common doctrine are in the habit of continually calling on texts from the Bible, as is the wont of all those who err. Even if, as we shall soon see, the texts of Scripture are of absolutely no use to dissenters, and even assuming that the word *heresy* in the Holy Scriptures has the same sense as today, and which you have given in your definition. Nonetheless, it will do much to clarify discussion of the present controversial question if we exactly investigate *whether the word* heresy *is used with the same sense in the Scriptures as it is usually given in orthodoxy.*

Orthodox But who would have any doubt about this? For, so far as I remember, all writers on the doctrine of heresy draw their arguments from Holy Scripture.

Christian I doubt that very much, and neither am I perturbed by your proof from common usage. For I have found that *common usage has twisted the most important words of Holy Scripture to the profane usage of pagan philosophy.* I will give just one example. You know that in the common usage, *wisdom, understanding, knowledge,* and the like occur among the *intellectual virtues.* And certainly someone would be laughed at—as if he did not understand the rudiments of philosophy—if he looked for these virtues in the will, or suggested that they were tightly bound to moral virtues. Meanwhile, I will be able to show you clearly on another occasion that Holy Scripture distinguishes its wisdom, its understanding, and its knowledge from the knowledge of this world—which it regards as false knowledge [*gnosis pseudonymos*][a]—in this way: Scripture thinks of the virtues as arising from the heart, and as flowing from love and leading to love; *gnosis,* though, which is in the intellect and arises from its activity, puffs man up, so that he is led to a knowledge which is a false knowledge and thus should not be called knowledge at all.[b]

a. I Timothy VI, 20.
b. I Corinthians VIII, 1–2.

Orthodox   We can speak about that another time. In order to return to our path, do you want to say that the word *heresy* in the Holy Scriptures is occasionally understood in a positive sense?

Christian   I would not be so foolish, for it is commonly said and no one can deny that the word *heresy* is often included among the vices in the Scriptures. Hence, although there are things which could be added concerning this indifferent meaning, I will dwell on it no longer.

Orthodox   On what basis do you think, then, that the meaning introduced in the churches deviates from that of Scripture?

Christian   I will tell you; but you answer me yourself: Today, following the common usage, is there not a difference between heresy and schism?

Orthodox   Of course, and in fact we have already spoken of this difference.

Christian   *But in Scripture the words* schism *and* heresy *were used with the same meaning.* For when Paul the apostle admonished the Corinthians that there were disagreements in their holy assemblies, he named these disagreements from the Greek sometimes *schismata,* sometimes *haereses.*[a] And Luther himself used such words in German as mostly agree with the Greek, in that he rendered the word *schismata* as *Spaltungen* [divisions], *haereses* though as *Rotten* [factions]. For those who create schisms normally seek adherents who hold with them or with the others. Further, where the apostle Jude[b] according to your interpretation speaks of heresy—although he does not use this word and calls heretics by another synonymous term *tous apodiorizontas*[33]—Luther has nicely conveyed the meaning with the same clear words: *those who form factions.* Erasmus has rendered it, *those who segregate themselves (qui segregant).*[34] In the Scriptures, therefore, the words

a. I Corinthians XI, 18–19.
b. Jude I, 19.
33. Those who set themselves apart.
34. The King James translation renders Jude 19 thus: "These be they who separate themselves, sensual, having not the Spirit."

schismatics, heretics, and *those who segregate themselves* are used synonymously.

Orthodox   But even if I accept this, I still cannot see how the Scriptures differ from the meaning of heresy used by the churches because, according to the common meaning, heretics create schisms, stir up unrest, and separate themselves from others. I don't see how your remarks are supposed to help upset my opinion that even in accordance with Scriptural tradition heresy is counted as a punishable crime.

Christian   Be patient a little. We must first clarify the synonyms of *heresy,* so that we can the more clearly show that Scripture does not speak of heresy such as you define it. For the heresy that you speak of as a punishable crime is an error in the intellect. But when Scripture speaks of heresy, it never speaks of an error in the intellect, but always of a vice of the will. And the text of the apostle [Paul] that you introduced earlier, I can thus use against you. All *works of the flesh* about which Paul warns the Galatians are vices of the will, some punishable crimes, others frailties damaging to the reputation among good men. Now, in the middle of these he also places heresies. It would be quite absurd, though, if someone wanted to place an intellectual error in the middle of punishable crimes, even if one wanted to claim that errors concern works of the flesh, which is very difficult to sustain. Further, when in the above-cited passage Paul admonishes the Corinthians that there were *schisms* among them *and heresies in their holy assemblies,* the whole text shows that he is not speaking about controversies over the articles of faith—as we would say today—but that the schisms and heresies arise from bad morals, which led to segregation in the practice of the Eucharist. Jude, though, explains particularly clearly who are the *apodiorizontas,* those who segregate themselves, namely: *poreuómenoi tàs heauton epithymías ton asebeion,*[a] or, in Luther's German, *those who turn to godless ways following their own lusts.* Given that, to the best of my recollection, apart from the cited texts the word *heresy* (or *haeresis*)

a. Jude I, 19. [In fact, Jude 1:18.]

does not appear in the New Testament, it is clear that Scripture does not use the word *heresy* for intellectual error. With regard to your definition of heresy, this means that the heresy of which Scripture speaks, and heresy as the church understands it, are, to speak precisely, wholly and completely different from each other.

Orthodox   No doubt what you have said has its point. Yet perhaps one could object against it that one is asking not how the term *heresy* is used (in the abstract), but how the word *heretic* is used (concretely); for it is quite usual that words deriving from other words often change the meaning of these words that they derive from.

Christian   I will let this go, even if the text from the Epistle of Jude speaks of a heretic in the concrete.

Orthodox   But not with such express words as Paul when he admonishes Titus to avoid heretical men,[a] a text which our people have been wont to use many times in the doctrine of the punishable crime of heresy.

Christian   Fine. But this text too is apparently on my side. For Paul himself describes a heretical man as someone who is wicked and sins, *kai hamartánei*. Yet a sin, *hamarteía*, is not an intellectual error but an act of the will.

Orthodox   But one must also take note here of what precedes this in the text. Now, prior to this he was speaking of legal questions and of the trouble and strife over genealogy. This shows that Paul speaks of someone who errs in intellectual controversies over religion.

Christian   What is this supposed to prove? First, it is doubtful whether the admonition to avoid a heretical man continues the preceding admonition that one should renounce foolish questions, or whether it begins a new point. Second, regarding the things that you call religious controversies, how can the apostle refer to these as foolish, useless, and vain questions? Which yet he does. Why does he not immediately characterize the [heretical] man as one who errs, rather than as fractious and a disturber of the peace? Which yet

a. Titus III, 10.

he does. I fear, therefore, that if the apostle speaks of heretics in the preceding verses, your orthodoxy profits little by it.

Orthodox   Why, truly?

Christian   Because then someone who errs in debates and controversies, while remaining peaceable, would not be a heretic. Yet someone would be a heretic who starts controversies, who cavils, rails, and quarrels over them, who damns dissenters, and who pretends that certain questions—mostly useless and vain but often also foolish and impious—are controversial questions pertaining to saving faith.

Orthodox   I see clearly where you are going with this. But in this way the names would be dreadfully confused. For those we call orthodox would be heretics, and a heretic-monger would himself be a heretic.

Christian   What is that to me? There could be no greater confusion than that which I have spoken of above, where you have converted the faith of the heart into a thing of the intellect. Common orthodoxy not the Holy Scripture is the cause of this confusion. Not to mention that someone can well be a heretic and a heretic-monger at the same time. For just as love and toleration of dissenters is an unmistakable characteristic of a true Christian, so in my theology the heretic is a heretic-monger and a man full of hatred for dissenters; just as in my system, it is not the heresy of which you speak, but heretic-mongering that is a crime worthy of punishment. It is wholly agreeable to this position that the heretics whom the apostle Jude calls *tous apodiorízontas* should be referred to by Luther as *those who form factions;* which is the same as if he had said, *who make heretics.* But more about this another time perhaps. Now, without further digression, I will proceed to show that heresy is not a punishable crime.

IX

Orthodox   I have already waited a long time. So present the argument for your view, because I cannot guess it.

Christian   No guesses are required. Rather, one must be amazed at our blindness that through prejudice of authority we have allowed ourselves to be persuaded of things which are contrary to the basic principles of jurisprudence and moral philosophy. I will say it in a few words: Heresy is not a punishable crime because it is an error. You laugh at me. You will soon stop smiling though. Answer me if you will: What is a punishable crime?

Orthodox   It is a shameful deed against the criminal laws.

Christian   Then can something be a punishable crime if no evil intent accompanies it?

Orthodox   Normally evil intent is required, yet sometimes blame itself is enough; that is, if the deed is manifest. For we have negligent homicide [*homicidium culposum*].

Christian   Perhaps we can leave this exception, in that all culpable offenses [*delicto culposo*] appear to be accompanied by a *dolus* (or maliciousness), or at least to be preceded by it. But I will also let this pass. So, an evil intent or at least blame will nonetheless be required.

Orthodox   Of course.

Christian   You have laughed at my proof, so now answer me these questions. Given that error is a shortcoming of the intellect, and heresy is an intellectual error, so I ask: Is then a shameful deed (i.e., crime) the predicate of a deliberate act? Is it thus possible to give a law to the intellect? Is evil intent a quality of the intellect or of the will? Are not error and evil intent forever opposed to each other? Is guilt not from negligence? Is negligence not a shortcoming in the will? Now you see, for each question asked you must provide me with an answer, and each answer will show that heresy is not a punishable crime.

Orthodox   You overwhelm me with questions, and I have heard that it is dangerous to dispute by posing questions. But because it pleases you thus, first answer me this. Did you not say earlier, against the common viewpoint, that it is the will which either corrupts or improves the intellect?

Christian   It is dangerous (as you say) to argue by posing questions, but only to the erring and the sophists. The lover of truth answers gladly, so I will honestly answer your question. I have said, and continue to say this, mainly because, apart from other texts of the Bible, my opinion is wonderfully confirmed by Paul's saying in which he warns the Corinthians that the *intellect of the pagans is darkened through the blindness of their hearts.*[a] But what follows from this?

Orthodox   We will soon see. First answer me this. Does not the error of heresy also arise from the corruption of the will? Why are you reflecting so long on your answer? Now I have captured you.

Christian   I do not hesitate inwardly—as if I doubted my opinion and the proof of its truth—but because your question contains the fallacy of [combining] several different questions.

Orthodox   How so? It is a simple question that speaks of a single thing and says this unambiguously. You reproach me with this in vain. I say again that you should answer.

Christian   We will soon see that I am not blaming you in vain. And what if I answered the question in the affirmative? What would follow from that?

Orthodox   Answer me categorically, yes or no, and we will see soon enough.

Christian   But I cannot answer categorically so long as your question hides a fallacy of several different questions. In the meantime, you can take my response as if I had answered categorically. But what if anything follows from this?

Orthodox   I will soon show you what this anything is. For I have caught you so that you cannot give me the slip. If all errors, and thus also the error of heresy arise from corruption of the will, yet punishable crimes are works of the corrupted will, then heresy will also be such a work and, consequently, a punishable crime. And this is what was to be shown.

a. Ephesians IV, 18.

Christian   You have trapped me so well that there are several ways out of your snare. For you have made as many false moves as there are words you have uttered.

Orthodox   How can that be possible when everything I have said is clearly demonstrated?

Christian   You will soon see. First, when I said that your question contained a fallacy drawn from several questions, this is what I meant: You asked whether the error of heresy arises from the corrupted will. Then, just as in the well-known example, a false conclusion follows from several questions when it is asked: Has Titius returned the horns? Has he stopped stealing? Here it will be understood that Titius has had the horns and that he must have stolen them, even if these questions contain only one subject and one predicate. So too in your question certain things are implied, namely: that heresy is an error, or that it is certain that heresy is an error. Now, I have shown above not only that heresy proper, as spoken of in Scripture, is not an error, but also that with regard to heresy as it is described by the clergy, one cannot know with clarity and certainty whether it includes an error or not. For there is nowhere to be found a judge who could show the error in it, manifestly and to the full satisfaction of the adversaries. Further, it is well known that this deceptive way of arguing that you use is very common. It happens when, through questions or otherwise, something is elicited from the adversary, such that through consequences or the consequence of consequences that are usually sophistical, the adversary is imputed something which he has never thought, and the battle is won without being fought. Christ and the apostles did not do this when refuting their adversaries, for they persevered with questions until the adversaries fell silent. Why did you not continue with your questions? For you would have seen that this conclusion would never have followed from my answer.

Orthodox   Why not? I will attempt it. You have declared that the error of heresy arises from the corrupted will. Do you deny then that a punishable crime is a work of the corrupted will?

Christian   Who would deny that?

Orthodox	Now, then, is heresy not also a work of the corrupted will?
Christian	It is and is not.
Orthodox	What does that mean?
Christian	When you push someone and he falls, fracturing a limb, is this fracture your work or that of the one who has fallen?
Orthodox	It is my work indirectly and, in an immediate way, it is also the work of the one who falls. It is primarily my work and secondarily a work of the fallen one. It is morally my work and physically that of the one who has fallen.
Christian	Similarly, as something whose primary and moral cause is the will, common heresy is an indirect work of the will. Immediately, though, in a secondary and physical sense, the working of the intellect is the cause of heresy. Now, go on!
Orthodox	This distinction will not help you, but is in fact against you. For one should punish heresy as a punishable crime all the more severely if, as you hold, the will is its primary and moral cause.
Christian	But your phrase *all the more severely* sits badly here.
Orthodox	You are being a sophist. You have acknowledged that heresy is a work of the will and that all punishable crimes belong to works of the will. Yet you will not acknowledge that heresy is a punishable crime?
Christian	I refuse to acknowledge it because not all works of the will are crimes. Your fallacy consists in the fact that, while you wanted to convince me, you confused two different things with each other; firstly, that crimes are works of the will, which is true; secondly, that works of the will are crimes, which is evidently false if one understands by this immoral workings of the will. For naturally there is a great difference between vice and crime. Crime is inseparable from punishment. But, as you know yourself, there are also many vices of the will that are subject to no human punishment (which is what we are speaking of here). For this reason, no one will be punished for thinking. Further, even if they are expressed in external actions, to the degree that these do no great harm to the commonwealth, we do not punish the flaws which

are shared by the whole human race and could never be eliminated, such as envy, ambition, greed, and licentiousness. Now, if no one is to be punished for thinking of crime, so it will be even less the case that someone can be punished for thinking erroneously.

Orthodox But I can turn this around and say: Because there are crimes of such enormity that even thinking them is punishable—for example, in the crime of violation of majesty [*crimen laesae Maiestatis*]—so someone can be justly punished on account of his erroneous thoughts in the case of heresy; for by this divine majesty is violated, which is a much worse crime than the violation of human majesty.

Christian The proof will not work, because it draws on completely different things. The jurists have already shown in several places that the division of the crime of violation of majesty into the violation of divine and human majesty is an ambiguous distinction, and the crime of violating divine majesty is actually not a punishable crime. For something will only be called a punishable crime in relation to human laws and punishments. God has not commanded worldly kings to protect his divine majesty. And just as this is spiritually violated, so the violator will be spiritually punished. But the authorities punish nobody spiritually.

Orthodox So do you seriously mean that heresy is not a punishable crime?

Christian Why should I not mean this when there are so many reasons for seriously intending it? Neither is this viewpoint so novel that others have not remarked on it, even if such remarks have not been purged of the prejudice of the common error with proper care. From among all the Lutheran theologians I will introduce only Samuel Pomarius who opposed the disguised papalist Hierotheus Boranowsky.[35] Boranowsky alleges that heresy is a crime of the greatest enormity. It belongs with thievery, murder, sacrilege, whoring, and adultery. It is a worse crime than counterfeiting. It joins blasphemy, sedition, violation of majesty, is worse than

35. See note 8 in this chapter.

apostasy and idolatry, and so on.[a] Pomarius has shown extensively that this teaching, which presumes that heresy is actually a punishable crime, is against the light of Scripture and the light of nature,[36] and also against the theologians and jurists.[b] There he also prudently responded to the slanderers who would perhaps wish to accuse him of being a lover and defender of heresy, which is a defense I will put to use for myself.

X

Orthodox These and similar authors will be of little help to your position. For they teach that heresy may also be subject to human punishment, even if not by death. In denying that heresy is a punishable crime though, you, as I understand it, claim heresy should be exempt from all human punishment.

Christian Yes, that is my view. But I do not rely on these authors, and I introduce them only in order to show that there is nothing new in saying that heresy is not a punishable crime. At the same time, I have warned that these same authors do not proceed carefully enough in this matter, but import falsities. They accept, for example, that heretics can well be subject to human punishments— namely, *removal from public office, monetary fines, exile, and imprisonment*—which unfortunately is the common viewpoint of our [Lutheran] teachers.[c] For what could be more improper and inconsistent than to teach that heresy is not a punishable crime, yet that it must be punished by human coercion? Could an author be more self-contradictory than when he argues at length against the papalists, adducing many proofs, that nobody should be coerced into religion; that conscience must be free; that the faith and conversion of heretics is a gift of God; that coercion

a. Hierotheus Boranowsky, *Gerechtfertigen Gewissens-Zwang,* chap. 2, pp. 156ff.

b. Pomarius, *Unrechtigen Gewissens-Zwang,* chap. 2, pp. 177ff.

c. Carpzov, *Practica nova imperialis saxonica rerum criminalium,* qu. 44, n. 30, 31; Tarnovius, in Dedeken's *Consiliorum,* pt. 2, fol. 93; Pomarius, as above, pp. 185, 311, 326, and pt. 2, pp. 417ff.

36. That is, reason.

of conscience results in nothing but making hypocrites and always occasioning disturbances of civil peace; and similar things (as is normally argued by our Lutherans, Pomarius in particular)? Yet such an author concludes nothing more from this than that heretics should not be killed, but can otherwise be punished as one sees fit. But these reasons apply to every sort of punishment, because all punishment is a form of coercion.

Orthodox   If I am right, however, Pomarius denies this, in these words: *Such things (the excommunication and exiling of heretics) are not means of religious coercion. Neither does Carpzov, who is highly opposed to the coercion of faith and conscience, treat them as such. Rather, they are a necessary Christian protection, ecclesiastic discipline, and political duty.*[a]

Christian   I know it and regret it. It is as if something advanced against the papacy by such zealots were infallible, and as if there could not be zealotry accompanied by stupidity. To deny that exile and such like are means of coercion is to deny that they are punishments. It would be no more impudent were the papalists to claim that the execution of heretics is not a coercive measure. Pomarius himself elsewhere calls these things a *severe external means of coercion,*[b] thereby contradicting himself.

Orthodox   But through such mild punishments our people do not intend to compel heretics to the *faith,* only to the *means of faith.*[c]

Christian   They themselves do not know what they intend. For, on the other hand, they also say that compelling the means of faith should not be used against heretics, but only against the people of their own religion.[d] They can understand this any way they please, for it is purely papalist[e] and quite pitiful. Even in a dream, could they imagine a compulsion to the means of a thing that is not at the

a. Pomarius, pt. 2, p. 418.
b. Pomarius, pt. 1, p. 519.
c. Pomarius, pt. 1, p. 264, and pt. 2, p. 443.
d. Pomarius.
e. See ibid., p. 443; Boranowsky, chap. 10, p. 495; Pomarius, pt. 1, p. 269.

same time also a compulsion to the end of the thing, or to the thing itself? They themselves say that the means are present on account of the end, and are subservient to the end. A compulsion to the means is therefore also a compulsion to the end. What would they say if the papalists excused themselves by saying that they used the fear of death not to force heretics to change their religion or to believe, but only to the means [of faith], such as hearing the mass and similar? Has not this same cloak for heretic-mongering been used to mask the cruel religious coercion of the Calvinists in France, or could it not be so used?

Orthodox   Yet surely you will at least accept the *excommunication of heretics* as a spiritual punishment.

Christian   I do not accept it as such.

Orthodox   But I see no reason. You yourself acknowledge that heresy is still a spiritual vice. Therefore you will not oppose spiritual punishment.

Christian   I well recall commendation of the Christian's spiritual shield, but never of spiritual punishment, which God has reserved to himself. Moreover, how can excommunication be a spiritual punishment when, for all that, it is used to execute secular sanctions? For example, loss of office, public infamy, continual fear of death at the hands of the rabid mob whipped up by unceasing imprecations and public curses, and so on. Like all other associations, a Christian association is permitted to forbid membership to someone who will not conform his conduct to its mores. This is no punishment, however, because all associations may do this, and it does not give rise to infamy. But, as it is commonly practiced, excommunication is, if not wholly, then at least three-quarters papalist and anti-Christian.

Orthodox   Beware that you do not blaspheme. For how can that be anti-Christian which Christ himself commands or at least permits? And how can that be papalist which Paul has made use of?

Christian   But, my dear friend, please tell me where Christ has permitted this excommunication to his church.

Orthodox   Everybody knows this. Do you not know that Christ says if your brother trespasses against you, and will not heed the church, then *he should be regarded as a heathen and a publican?*[a]

Christian   I know this well. But what follows from it?

Orthodox   Namely, that one should regard him as excommunicated, or as someone to be excommunicated.

Christian   I do not believe my ears! At the time when Christ spoke this, was there a society of Christians? Did the Christians excommunicate the heathens then? Did Christ approve of blind and godless Jewish excommunication?

Orthodox   You are piling up a heap of scruples, which is giving me pause. Nonetheless, this is still the common explanation.

Christian   But I have warned you from the beginning and throughout, there are also common errors.

Orthodox   How do you understand the words of Christ then? What does he mean by talking about regarding a brother as heathen or publican?

Christian   I believe that Christ would want it to be possible, if the matter were sufficiently grave, for such a person to be brought before a pagan magistrate like a heathen and publican, without having to fear scandal and the violation of Christian patience. Neither does this explanation seem too difficult or far-fetched if one juxtaposes Christ's teaching with Paul's admonition to the Corinthians, that they should not arraign a brother before a pagan judge.[b,37]

---

a. Matthew XVIII, 17.
b. I Corinthians VI, 1ff.
37. This paragraph is not immediately clear. Thomasius's argument is that someone whose conduct leads to their exclusion from the Christian community is no longer a "brother," may be treated as a "heathen," and can thus be dealt with by the civil magistrate in cases subject to secular law. This enables him to reconcile Christ's admonition with Paul's insistence that a "brother" should not be brought before the civil authorities. Lying behind this somewhat forced exegesis is Thomasius's attempt to separate religious admonition from civil punishment.

Orthodox   Yet you cannot deny to me that Paul wished to excommunicate a person guilty of incest.[a] For he scolded the Corinthians that they had not done this themselves.

Christian   I see nothing more here than that Paul wanted the Corinthians to declare that this person should remain outside their holy assembly. If it goes no further than the right which attaches to all associations in common, this declaration is neither an excommunication nor a punishment.

Orthodox   Yes, but something a little different lies behind this, because Paul also consigns him to Satan, which is a formula still used in excommunication by the churches.

Christian   How pitiful to be consigned through a formula! Do you mean then that Paul, or someone acting for him, has pronounced in a public assembly the horrendous damning incantation of excommunication, in which the excommunicant is consigned body and soul to the devil? This is very far removed from the piety and charity of the apostle. Further, the text itself is against this, for it speaks of the corruption of the flesh and the salvation of the spirit. Even though he was absent, I think that through the power of Christ, Paul caused the body of the incestuous person to be afflicted with a severe illness by Satan, similar to the way in which Job's body was thus consigned to Satan. And perhaps the papalists or papalizing clerical excommunicators imitate Paul in this consignment, if they have that power of Christ. If they do not have this power, though, they should not be surprised if the laity begin to despise their brutish incantations and fulminations.

Orthodox   Nonetheless, there are to hand other texts from the Holy Scriptures which appear to confirm ecclesiastical excommunication.

Christian   I am also fully aware of these,[b] for here someone is always copying them from someone else. But these [texts] are not important enough for us to lose time over, in that they are even more dis-

---

a. I Corinthians V, 2ff.

b. Galatians V, 12; I Timothy I, 20; Romans XVI, 17; II John X, 11. See Pomarius, pt. 1, p. 420, from Gerhard.

torted than those which we have already discussed, and can be readily answered using that which I have already briefly laid out.

XI

Orthodox   There is still another answer that occurs to me, which might save the common position. Heretics will not be punished on account of intellectual shortcomings or error. Neither can the authorities compel their subjects to change religion through threat of punishment. They can prohibit heretics from spreading discordant beliefs among the people, and scandalizing the church, by attaching a punishment if heretics act against this, which is in accordance not only with canon law but also with civil.[a] The prince can properly do this, because the deed that he forbids is a work of the will, at the disposal of human judgment, and is thus subject to human governance. As a result, this position is grounded in the laws, in reason, and in the writings of the scholars, for Ziegler has written about this in exactly these terms.[b]

Christian   It is to be regretted that this pious and highly learned jurisconsult let these words slip, which he without doubt borrowed from the standard Lutheran doctrine, failing to note their inadequacy because he was intent on other things. As for matters concerning canon and civil law, I have begged from the beginning to be spared this. Nor can refuge be found in the cited texts of civil and canon law, where it is certain that heresy is regarded as a punishable crime according to both kinds of law. Only this reason [i.e., the spreading of discordant beliefs] remains, therefore, which at first glance seems so attractive that I also shared this opinion for a long time. After more exactly considering the issue, however, I have decided that there is no substance to it, and that beneath this mask lies only a tyrannical coercion of conscience.

a. c. resecandae, 16, C. 24, qu. 3 [*Canon Law,* canon "resecandae" 16, chap. 24, qu. 3]; L. 1. C. De SS. Eccles. [*Code of Justinian,* On the Most Sacred Churches, law 1].

b. See Lancellottus, bk. 4, tit. 4, §2, p. 941. [Ziegler, *Notis et animadversionibus academicis ad Joh. Pauli Lancelotti.*]

My reasons are as follows. First, we have already noted in the preceding that a requirement of a punishable crime is that it be an act of the will. Not all acts of the will are punishable crimes, though, or become crimes through their restraint, or are subject to authority of the legislator. This is to say nothing of the widely noted view that such virtues as gentleness, generosity, gratitude, and the like—which are closer to love than to strict right—are by nature so composed that they lose this character and forfeit all grace, as soon as they are touched by the command of human law or the compulsion of punishments. Acts compelled by law thus lose their esteem as gentle, liberal, gracious, and so on. Already in his time, in his book *De beneficiis,* Seneca had shown comprehensively that nobody could be sued on account of ingratitude.[38]

Orthodox   I see where you are going with this. But to teach and propagate error has nothing in common with the examples you have introduced, for it appears to concern the regulation of actions subject to human law, to which your examples have little relevance.

Christian   I was still not ready with my discourse, but only wanted to show through an example that even if something is an act of the will, it does not follow from this that it may be legally prohibited by man. For there are also other acts of will which are subject to no law, which appear at first glance to be matters of free human choice, but on closer examination are things that happen necessarily. [These are] things regarding which a man has no free will, and are thus so composed that a contrary action will be regarded as morally impossible. Among these I place someone expressing the religion which he himself holds to be true; that is, someone spreading his religion. For, if we carefully consider human nature, we discover that it is possible for someone to keep quiet in a certain place, for a certain time, about a known truth, especially one that has been trusted to him in confidence. It is impossible, however, for him to keep quiet about this perpetually, especially

38. For an English translation, see Seneca, "On Favours," in *Moral and Political Essays,* ed. and trans. J. M. Cooper and J. F. Procopé (Cambridge: Cambridge University Press, 1995), 181–308.

when he imagines that this is a truth beneficial to the human race, and as such commanded by God, so that one should tell other people about it. It is even more impossible that a person would conceal such truth from those asking after it and who appear to ask in good faith. However, most impossible of all is when someone asks after this and a person speaks otherwise than what he means in his heart, and that he should pretend that this opinion is his own which he yet regards as false in his heart.

Orthodox   I already understand what you intend by this. Yet the principles of moral philosophy lead me to entertain a great doubt against your doctrine. For, given that you accept that one can conceal or hide the truth for a certain time or in a certain place, this is not a physical impossibility but would be a so-called moral impossibility. But the blessed Pufendorf has already taught that a moral impossibility does not prevent an action being subject to the laws, as long as no physical impossibility is involved.[a] And he explains this with a splendid example: It is impossible that all men should agree to hand down a lie to the following generation, although it is not impossible that a single man might do this. Similarly, it is impossible that a republic should be so happy that all the people would refrain from lying; it is not impossible though that someone or other should refrain from lying. For this reason, one can properly frame laws against lying, and liars can be punished. So, even if it is morally impossible that all men could keep quiet about what they regard as the truth, yet this is not impossible for an individual person. On this account, individual persons can be prohibited from testifying and commanded to stay silent.

Christian   That does not follow. For I have said that it is also impossible for individual persons to be quiet all the time, which means that your conclusion should be: it would be unjust if a continual silence were imposed on them. For moral and physical impossibility converge here, as I have already proved from the common nature of the human race. So I can invert that which you have put for-

---

a. Samuel Pufendorf, *De jure naturae et gentium* (On the law of nature and nations), bk. I, chap. 5, §8.

ward by saying: Just as it is not possible to make a law that the truth should be spoken at all times by all men, so it can much less be commanded by law that one should conceal the truth. Various authors have already observed, and I have already remarked above, that those weaknesses common to the whole human race, and which do no great harm in the commonwealth, are not subject to punitive laws. For this reason, it is not feasible—at least not without bringing ruin to the whole human race—to wish to impose severe, even capital punishments on greed, ambition, envy, and similar vices, even if they break out in minor deeds. Neither will minor lies that bring no harm to the commonwealth ever be punished. If for this reason some vices themselves cannot be punished, how then can truthfulness be coerced by law, or one be prevented from speaking about that which one regards as true, when this is to be esteemed more as a virtue than a vice?

Orthodox   But here you are forgetting your own limiting condition: that those things cannot be punished which do no particular harm to the commonwealth and its general peace and calm. The propagation of an erroneous and false religion causes grave harm to the commonwealth, however; for through this the citizens are deprived of their eternal salvation.

Christian   This common objection assumes that guardianship of his subjects' eternal salvation is a matter for the prince; yet I have shown elsewhere that the prince finds himself in a quite different situation.[39] It is the prince's business to oversee external security, which is not harmed even if a false doctrine is published.

Orthodox   But this is always harmed by that which occasions disorder.

---

39. Here, Thomasius is probably referring to his treatises on *Das Recht evangelischer Fürsten in theologischen Streitigkeiten* (The right of Protestant princes in theological conflicts) of 1696, and *Vom Recht evangelischer Fürsten in Mitteldingen oder Kirchenzeremonien* (The right of Protestant princes regarding indifferent matters or *adiaphora*) of 1695 (see chapter 2 of this volume). In these works, Thomasius argues that the prince's rights and powers extend to all matters capable of threatening social peace, while denying that they have anything to do with his subjects' inner morality or salvation.

Christian Yet various writers have shown that it is not those who profess their faith that cause disorder, but those who wish to repress such profession with force—in a word, the heretic-mongers not the heretics.

Orthodox How can this be, though, when the heretics themselves also become heretic-mongers and will not tolerate the true religion?

Christian That is not relevant to the present question. For I do not intend that the dissenters should be permitted to spread their doctrines with violence or injury to others. Nor would I concede them a public exercise of their religion equal to that of the country's primary religion. Neither do I wish them to be permitted to stage public disputations and challenges. I only wish them to be left free to follow their confession and to worship in private, such that their friendly gatherings and ordinary conversations about religion should not be denounced as conventicles and as a design against the laws. I see that this is also the opinion of the celebrated Johann Christoph Becmann,[40] who argues in his disputation *On the Right of Subjects in Religious Matters* that subjects professing a different religion to that of the country's prince should be permitted not only to believe what they take to be right and true, but also that they should be able to discuss their religion.[a] I mention these words of agreement to show that my viewpoint is not new, even if it is against the common opinion.

Orthodox Shortly before you said that the common opinion prohibiting the spreading of errors is nothing more than a mask for tyranny of conscience. I want you to explain this more clearly.

---

a. See Becmann, *Dissertatio de jure subditorum circa sacra* (Dissertation on the right of subjects in religious matters), chap. 3, §§11ff.

40. Johann Christoph Becmann (1641–1717) was a Calvinist political theologian at the university of Frankfurt an der Oder. His *Dissertatio de jure subditorum circa sacra* (Dissertation on the right of subjects in religious matters) of 1689 argues for toleration in terms of the subjects' basic rights in relation to the power of the state. In this regard Becmann differed from Thomasius, who relied on theological arguments regarding the inward and noncredal character of faith, and politico-juridical arguments regarding the incapacity of such faith to disturb social peace. Subjective rights play no significant role in Thomasius's arguments for toleration.

Christian   Gladly. Consider the consequences when, in accordance with this opinion, dissenters would be permitted to believe what they profess but would be prohibited from propagating this doctrine. Then, one such supposed heretic speaks to one of his co-believers about religion while just one subject of the country's ruling religion is standing by. Or, consider the case where in an ordinary conversation with subjects of the other religion he talks modestly about his religion, which is naturally wont to occur—perhaps from a common human impulse to persuade others of that which we believe to be true, or from the desire to defend his religion from the objections and consequences attributed to it by others. [In such cases], he will be immediately denounced as a lawbreaker and, on the pretext that only an external act of the will and not his faith is to be prohibited, he will be punished all the more severely at the instigation of the heretic-mongering clerics. Those who know the world will doubtless have already observed that such heretics—even if they are taciturn by nature—are set up by papalist or papalizing clerics in such a way that they can instruct a cunning fellow from the country's ruling religion, who approaches the heretic and, insinuating himself as a friend, confidentially presents some dubious questions, pretending to vacillate in his own religion and to be interested in hearing the truth of the other's confession. Who here could restrain himself from opening his heart to such a spy in trust, rejoicing in his recognition of the truth, encouraging him to continue with his plan, and even loaning him books for his better instruction? After he has achieved this the spy will report to his cleric, and this cleric to the prince. Now the decent pious heretic, who is probably a more loyal subject than both his accusers, will be condemned to severe punishment, accused of a great crime, namely, obdurate disobedience.

Orthodox   Yes, this happens just as you say. But because the crux of the opposed viewpoints lies in this, I would like you to prove your view not only from reason but also from the Holy Scriptures.

Christian   I am put in mind of the trial of the apostles at the hands of the Pharisees, which is described in the Acts of the Apostles.[a] The religion of the Pharisees was dominant in the country, at least with regard to the Christian religion, so that the Christian religion taught by the apostles was deemed heretical. It annoyed the priests that the apostles taught the people, not that they believed this religion personally. So they put them in prison, taking from them in fact not their freedom to believe what they liked, but prohibiting them only from propagating their doctrines. Because the apostles would not obey, the priests put them in prison again, and when the angel had freed them and they were arraigned again, the priests accused them not on account of an intellectual act, but for an act of the will: namely, that they had taught the people in the name of Jesus in contravention of the senate's prohibition. Under this pretext they would have been killed as rebels, if the priests had not been moved by Gamaliel's admonishment to substitute the milder judgment of birching for the harsher one. Now, consider whether one egg is more like another than the proceedings of the Pharisees are to the proceedings flowing from [today's] common doctrine that heretics are to be punished not for their heretical belief, but for spreading it.

Orthodox   I hold though that there is a very great difference between the two. For the apostle's religion was the true religion, but the other case concerns heretics.

Christian   But I have said above that there is no civil judge on this earth who can decide which of the parties is right or not. And as the above-cited words of Salvian confirm, even heretics believe in good faith, and all sects claim for their own side the saying of the apostle: *One must obey God* (in professing faith) *rather than man* [b] (in concealing it).

XII

Orthodox   There is still one opinion of our [Lutherans] remaining with regard to the crime of heresy: namely, that heretics who are also

a. Acts IV & V.
b. Acts V, 29.

blasphemers or rebels may still be executed, not in fact as heretics, but as blasphemers and rebels.[a] I believe that there is no reason to reject this opinion, for it is established law that the seditious and blasphemous must be executed, or [at least] can be executed without injustice.

Christian   I have nothing to say regarding the punishment of sedition. But with regard to the punishment of blasphemy there is much to be said, in that there is just as much doubt surrounding the common definition of blasphemy as surrounds the definition of heresy. For holy people once might well have cursed God in their travails, and it is against all reason that one should extend the crime of blasphemy to those who had no intention of cursing God, but thought they were acting rightly, even if they were in grave error. If that is accepted then, following the common doctrine, but against the common principles of jurisprudence, many kinds of blasphemy would be found which, without exception, occur in good faith and without malice. But the doctrine of blasphemy needs its own investigation. For the moment, though, I will refrain from that discussion, and will just say this as a word to the wise, that these limitations[41] in accordance with the common doctrine and practice [of heresy prosecutions] are nothing more than a new cloak for the tyranny over conscience. The point of the exercise is to provide a pretext, even for our [Lutheran] papacy, to rage against all heretics as blasphemers and rebels. [Indeed, the less astute of the papalists clearly assert that all heretics are blasphemers and rebels[b]],[42] even though it is well known that under the pretext that they were tainted with dreadful vices, preeminently blasphemy and sedition, the first Christians were cruelly martyred, about which the blessed Kortholt has written a

a. Ziegler on Lancellottus, pp. 791 & 941; Carpzov, *Practica nova imperialis saxonica rerum criminalium,* qu. 44, n. 41ff.; Chemnitz, *Exam. Concil. Trident,* pt. 2, p. 93 [Martin Chemnitz, *Examinis Concilii Tridentini* (Examination of the Council of Trent) (Frankfurt am Main, 1615)]; Pomarius, *Ungerechten Gewissens-Zwang,* pt. 1, pp. 8, 24, 162, 165.

b. Pomarius, pt. 1, pp. 8, 24, 162, 165.

41. That is, limiting the punishment of heresy to cases also involving blasphemy and sedition.

42. The section in square brackets is missing from the German version.

scholarly treatise.[43] Who can tell the whole story of how often our [Lutherans] were accused of blasphemy by the papalists, or the Calvinists by our [Lutheran] heretic-mongers?[a] In fact, a moment ago you yourself accused me of blasphemy. In the papalists' legal proceedings against our people, the crime of violation of majesty is often alleged against them, as if they suspected the country's prince of bidding them do something unjust and contrary to conscience.[b] I must ask you just one question: Which of the two do you think is the rebel or disturber of public peace? The one who tyrannizes over another's conscience, or the one who modestly defends himself against this?

Orthodox   The first, without doubt.

Christian   But you are mistaken, my friend. The second is a disturber of the peace.

Orthodox   Sure! Like the lamb in the fable who disturbed the water for the wolf waiting above. Perhaps you are joking.

Christian   Unfortunately I am not joking, for this was taught in all seriousness by our leading doctors. Do you know the book?

Orthodox   Why would I not know it? It is the *Formula of Concord.*

Christian   How does it read then, here in the preface?

Orthodox   Thus: *they can be called turbulent and quarrelsome people who will adhere to no form of pure doctrine.*[c] I had not considered this nor remarked on it before.

Christian   Now one sees what effect the prejudice of human authority has. But now I have other business, and I must close and thank you for a friendly conversation. Should something occur to you, or

a. See, amongst others, Council of Wittenberg, pt. 1, fol. 246.
b. Pomarius, pt. 1, p. 81.
c. *Formula of Concord,* preface, halfway to the end.
43. Probably a reference to Christian Kortholt, *De persecutionibus ecclesiae primaevae sub imperatoribus ethnicis* (On the persecution of the early church under the pagan emperors) (Kiel, 1689).

should another present you with something that might answer my objections, would you be so good as to communicate this to me. Were this to prove my errors, then I would be the first to publicly recant and condemn them.

Orthodox   I will gladly do that. Take care.

Summary of This Dissertation

I. Occasion of this disputation and status of the controversy.

II. For this controversy, no human laws, least of all the Law of Justinian and canon law, can be taken as sources or bases of proof. Why Augustine's authority is not valid here. The only suitable sources here are reason and revelation.

III. The definitions of heresy given in civil and canon law are rejected. The common definition of heresy, in which Catholics, Lutherans, and Calvinists agree: that heresy is *an obstinate error in the foundations of faith by someone who is or was a member of the church.* Explanation of this.

IV. That in the definition of heresy, the word *church* is obscure, allowing many papalizing things into our schools. That the phrase *foundations of faith* is equally obscure and incomprehensible. Uncertainty of our [Lutherans] in this matter. Time, place, and diversity of persons have often altered the fundamental articles of faith. This is explained with the example of Flacius, the chiliastic church fathers, and others. The fabrication of consequences from consequences. Today's distinction between schismatics and heretics arises from the politeness or coarseness of the clergy. Confession of the true foundations of faith. The fruits of faith must not be opposed to the origin or cause of faith.

V. The word *faith* is obscure. Vacillation of our teachers regarding the requisites of faith. Variations between the Latin and German texts of *Hutter's Compendium* and the confessional books. Example of this from the *Apology of the Augsburg Confession.* The faith of the intellect in the mind and the faith of the will in the heart are two different things. It is uncertain whether our Lutherans seek saving faith in the mind or in the heart. The former is more likely. This is proved from *Hutter's Compendium* and from the *Apology.* Faith and love have become opposed to each other. The notion that love arises from intellectual faith originates from pagan philosophy's false doctrine that the intellect rectifies the will. Conflict among the theologians is with regard to intellectual faith. The words *orthodox* and *heterodox* pertain to the intellect. The saving faith in the Athanasian Creed is a mere intellectual faith. The words *saving doctrine* and *saving faith* have become synonymous. Theoretical doctrine saves no one. The orthodoxy of Jude. For us [Lutherans], repentance and conversion are a work of the intellect, and often not even that. Our new converts do not change their way of living.

VI. Which heretics are *obstinate* is obscure. Several hold that all those who err, including the listeners, are obstinate. Our teachers state that it is difficult to say whether a heretic is obstinate or not. The distinction between material and formal heretics—or between seducers and seduced—does not clarify the matter. Obstinacy is either in matters of the intellect or in matters of the will. The former is either a shortcoming in the intellect or a maliciousness in the will. The first is not obstinacy and is not relevant here. The second occurs very rarely. It betokens either slander or ignorance when it is alleged that the erring doctors teach against their own conscience. Christian or apostolic refutation of heretics. Papalist refutation of the same. This last kind also reigns among us Lutherans.

VII. What an *error in faith* might be is obscure. There is no judge. Those who present the Holy Scriptures as the judge of religious controversies in fact substitute commentaries on Scripture for Scripture itself. When the *analogies of faith* are invoked, this amounts to denying the conclusion of the adversary's proof. Fine text from Salvian that clarifies the preceding.

VIII. So long as man cannot say what kind of thing heresy is, one cannot declare heresy to be a punishable crime. In common usage, the principal words of Holy Scripture are harnessed to profane meanings. The example of intellectual virtue. False knowledge [*gnosis pseudonymous*]. The Bible uses the word *heresy* in a different sense from today's common usage. In the Bible, *schisms* and *heresies* are synonyms. So are *hoi apodiorízontes*, divisions, factions. In the Bible, the word *heresy* always signifies a vice of the will. Explication of the texts Galatians V, 19, 1;

Corinthians XI, 16; Jude I, 19. Even when used concretely in Scripture, *heretic* does not refer to an intellectual error. Titus III, 10. When the apostle (Titus III, 9) speaks of heretics, the heretic-monger is the heretic. Interchangeability of the names. It is no contradiction to be a heretic-monger and a heretic at the same time. Luther had translated *apodioŕizontes* as *those who make factions*. The synonym is *those who make heretics*.

IX. Heresy cannot be a punishable crime because it is an error. The will corrupts the intellect. Ephesians IV, 18. It does not follow from this, though, that heresy is a punishable crime. False conclusion from plural questions. Fallacious drawing of inappropriate consequences from the disputation through questions. A heretical error is partly a work of the intellect, partly of the will. Fallacy of an inept inversion. Vice is one thing, punishable crime another. Not all vice can be punished. Heresy is not the crime of violation of divine majesty. God has not commanded princes to punish the violation of divine majesty. Other authors who deny that heresy is a punishable crime.

X. The papalizing opinion of our [Lutherans theologians] that heretics can be punished with infamy, exile, imprisonment, and similar. Pomarius shamelessly denies that exile and the like are means of coercion. Pomarius's papalist distinction between compulsory faith, and compulsory means of faith. Can one excommunicate heretics? Excommunication is a secular rather than a spiritual punishment. It is common to all associations that someone who does not conform to the customs of the association can be excluded from it. But this is not a punishment and excommunication does not stay within these limits. In the majority of cases, excommunication smells of papalism. Christ speaks not of excommunication (Matthew XIIX, 17) but of the arraignment of a brother before a pagan judge. Other texts which are falsely adduced in favor of excommunication.

XI. Whether a prince can command that a false doctrine cannot be taught and propagated on the basis that teaching and propagation are acts of the will? One cannot give laws for all acts of the will; for example, for generosity, mercifulness, gratitude, and so on. It is morally impossible for a man not to speak of the things that he takes to be true and right, or that he should speak otherwise than he believes. Several things which are morally impossible can be subject to laws, but this cannot be extended to the propagation of religion. No harm comes to the commonwealth through such propagation, only through the tyranny over conscience. How to temper the permission given to heretics to talk about their religion. The prohibition of religious discussion is shown to be an aid to the tyranny over conscience. This is clarified through the example of the Pharisees' prosecution of the apostles.

XII. Finally, it is briefly shown that the common doctrine, that seditious and blaspheming heretics may be executed, is typically extended so far that the heretic-mongers can do what they like with all who disagree with them. And the doctrine of blasphemy contains many common errors. In the preface to the *Formula of Concord,* those who would not bind themselves to a certain religious formula are held to be seditious.

On the Crime of Sorcery

1. I have recently been thinking whether it is possible to return to the Introduction question of the so-called crime of sorcery and subject it to renewed examination, even though the matter has already been discussed extensively by so many papalist and Protestant theologians and jurists.[1] I therefore consulted many works on magic and was quite surprised to find nothing in them but meaningless claptrap and fairy tales. I never found anything substantial, only on occasion a shadow of the truth! Given the significance of the matter, the threat to so many innocent people, and the benefit of liberating all of humanity from stupid, superstitious notions, it is past time to open not only the eyes of scholars,

---

1. "On the Crime of Sorcery" was first published as the Latin dissertation *De crimine magiae* in November 1701, when it was defended by Thomasius's doctoral student Johannes Reiche. It was translated into German in 1702 and again in 1704 under the title "Kurtze Lehr-Sätze von dem Laster der Zauberey." The second German translation, probably by Reiche, provides the text that we have used here in conjunction with the Latin exemplar. Thomasius had first encountered witchcraft prosecutions in 1694 when the Halle law faculty had been asked to provide advice on an actual case. During the later 1690s he was able to place such prosecutions in the larger account of the relations between church and state developed in such works as his *adiaphora* disputation (chapter 2, this volume). For Thomasius, witchcraft cases—like heresy prosecutions—were symptomatic of the clerical capture of the state, as they represented an attempt to apply legal categories and political coercion to matters of the spirit lying outside the proper concern of civil authority with "external" social peace. But, again like heresy, witch-mongering was also a product of the superstitious beliefs that flourished when men sought to extend their limited understanding to the divine being, thereby falling into useless and dangerous speculations rather than seeking inward individual grace.

but also those of simple-minded people, and to eradicate these all-too-papalist errors, which have until now taken hold of people's minds and, so to speak, bewitched them. When, however, I consider the reasons (which I will discuss below) why false notions of the crime of sorcery and of pacts between witches and sorcerers and the devil are daily inculcated in the people, and when I see that those who are able to tear off the mask of false wisdom and bring truth to light are regarded as impious or as atheists or even as sorcerers by almost everyone, even by pious and peaceable men, then I realize that I must now proceed with caution. I fear, though, that it will be difficult to put forward an argument that will win either broad public support or approval from the minority of sincere truth-seekers. The former is scarcely to be hoped for, owing to the prejudice of authority in which most people are immersed. But I cannot expect the latter—in part because of my shortcomings and the errors arising thereby, and in part because of the limited time that I could dedicate to the present treatise—and will have to apologize to truth-loving people if my doctrines on this difficult subject do not completely meet their expectations. To anyone who can prove the contrary [to my argument], either from Holy Scripture (as long as the interpretation is not contrived) or from true and sound reason, I sincerely promise that I will happily applaud them.

The writings   2. As for the papalist writers, especially Torreblanca, Bodin, Remigius, of the most   Delrio,[2] and others, one should not be surprised that they lied, or, to be

2. Francisco Torreblanca y Villalpando (d. 1645) was a jurist in Granada who wrote two books on the subject of sorcery: *Epitomes delictorum, in quibus aperta vel occulta invocatio daemonium intervenit* (Epitome of crimes, in which demons are openly or secretly invoked) (Sevilla, 1618); and *Daemonologia sive de magia naturali daemoniaca, licita & illicita* (Demonology or on permitted and prohibited natural magic) (Mainz, 1623). Jean Bodin (1529–96) was a jurist who taught Roman law at the University of Toulouse before he became an adviser to King Henri III and later to the king's brother, the Duke of Alençon and Anjou. He is well known as the author of the famous book *Six livres de la République* (Six books of the republic) (1576) and for representing the position of the moderates (*politiques*) in the French wars of religion, but he was also interested in sorcery and the persecution of witches. His influential book *De la Démonomanie des Sorciers* (On the demonomania of the sorcerers) (Paris,

more polite, misled the learned and judicious world by telling the most tasteless and ridiculous fables, although this often seems to have been unintentional. Nowadays, though, nobody will doubt that the entire papacy is anything more than a fable concocted from paganism and Judaism. This will be especially clear when we explain below that everything that was firmly believed concerning the crime of sorcery must be ascribed to pagan deceptions and to the naive superstitions of the Jews. Naudé confirmed this in his *Apology for Great Men Falsely Accused of Sorcery.*[3] In the last chapter he stated that it was *indeed rather strange that Delrio, Loyer, Bodin, de Lancre,* and *Goedelmann—who used to enjoy a considerable reputation and remain meritorious individuals—could write so passionately about evil spirits, sorcerers, and wizards.*[4] *They never dis-*

famous Catholic and Protestant writers are filled with many tales of sorcerers and witches.

1580) was reprinted several times. Nicolas Rémy (Remigius) (ca. 1525–1612) was a French witch-hunting jurist in the duchy of Lorraine who claimed to have executed nine hundred witches. His reflections on this and on witchcraft more broadly are contained in his *Daemonolatreia libri tres* (Lyon, 1595), in English as *Demonolatry,* trans. E. A. Ashwin (London: J. Rodker, 1930). Martin Anton Delrio (1551–1608) was born in Antwerp. His early career as a politician in the Spanish Netherlands was cut short by the victory of the Dutch Protestants. In Spain he joined the Jesuit order and later studied theology in Mainz and in Leuven, subsequently becoming a professor of theology. His *Disquisitionum magicarum libri sex* (Six books of magical investigations) was first published in 1599 in Leuven and reprinted twenty-six times up until 1755.

3. Gabriel Naudé, *Apologie pour tous les grands personage qui ont esté faussement soupçonnez de magie* (Defense of all the great men who have been falsely acccused of sorcery) (Paris, 1625). In the Latin version of Thomasius's disputation, the italicized citation from Naudé is in French. The German translation of Naudé's work, *Gabriel Naudaei Schutz-Schrifft, worin alle vornehmen Leute, die der Zauberey fälschlich beschuldiget sind, vertheidiget werden,* was published as an appendix to the 1704 German edition of Thomasius's *On the Crime of Sorcery.* Naudé (1600–1653), polymath and state-theorist, was librarian for Cardinal Mazarin and later for the Swedish queen.

4. Pierre le Loyer (1550–1634) was a French philosopher and jurist. He is the author of *Discours, et histoires des spectres, visions et apparitions des esprits, anges, demons, et ames, se monstrans visibles aux hommes* (Paris, 1605), in English *A Treatise of Specters or Straunge Sights, Visions and Apparitions Appearing Sensibly vnto Men. Wherein is delivered, the nature of spirtes, angels, and divels: their power and properties: as also of witches, sorcerers, enchanters, and such like* (London, 1605). Pierre de Lancre (1553–1631) was magistrate of the parliament of Bordeaux and presided over witch trials in the southwest of France. He described his experiences in his *Tableau de l'inconstance des mauvais anges et démons, où il est amplement traicté des sorciers & de la sorcelerie*

missed a single tale among so many foolish stories, however fictitious and ridiculous it was. Everything was jotted down haphazardly and indifferently and without setting apart the real and true occurrences. One wishes that one could speak differently about Protestant writers. Since the above-mentioned Naudé attributes the same errors to Goedelmann (who denies that witches make pacts with Satan while accepting that sorcerers do), then one can easily anticipate what to expect from other writers who condemn both Goedelmann and Wier[5] by saying that they dared to defend magic or witchcraft or to deny its existence. The most important among them is Carpzov, who is (so to speak) regarded as the king of today's Protestant criminal jurists, mainly since in question 48 of the first part of his *Praxis Criminalis* he earnestly attempts to refute Wier's proofs against the existence of sorcery, and to defend the common errors.[6] Even though he presents these issues in the thirty-six judgments

---

(Tableau of the inconstancy of bad angels and demons, where sorcerers and sorcery are treated in detail) (Paris, 1612). Parts of this book were translated into German in 1630. See also his *L'incrédulité et mescréance du sortilège pleinment convaincue* (Complete evidence of the disbelief and infidelity of sorcery) (Paris, 1622). An extract of this book was translated into German in 1683, under the title *Kurtzer aber jedoch außbündiger Außzug der Zauberey, gezogen auß Peter de L'ancre, Rathsherrn des Königs im Parlement zu Bordeaux* (s.l., 1683). Johann Georg Goedelmann (1559–1611) taught jurisprudence at the University of Rostock and was later a jurist in Dresden. He was well known as the author of the *Tractatus de Magis, Veneficis et Lamiis recte cognoscendis et puniendis* (Treatise on the right way to discern and punish sorcerers, poisoners, and witches) (Nürnberg, 1676).

5. Johann Weyer (Wier) (1515/16–1588) studied medicine in Orléans and was later physician in the entourage of the Duke of Jülich-Cleve-Berg. He was one of the most famous and influential opponents of witch trials and witch-hunting in Germany. His book *De praestigiis daemonum, et incantationibus, ac veneficiis, libri V* was first published in Basel in 1563, with at least ten further editions appearing during Weyer's lifetime. In English: *Witches, Devils, and Doctors in the Renaissance: Johann Weyer, De praestigiis daemonum*, ed. G. Mora and B. Kohl, trans. J. Shea (Binghamton, N.Y.: Medieval and Renaissance Texts and Studies, 1991). The book ended the witch trials in the dukedom Jülich-Cleve-Berg, but its influence was limited by the negative reaction of Jean Bodin.

6. Benedict Carpzov (1595–1666) presided at several Saxon courts and was professor of law at the University of Leipzig. He is regarded as a founder of German criminal jurisprudence because of his systematization of customary Saxon law, especially in his *Practica nova imperialis saxonica rerum criminalium* (New practice of

that he attached to the fiftieth question and which were taken from various court documents, they are such obvious and bizarre fictions that one should feel ashamed even to have read them.

3. As early as the beginning of the sixteenth century the jurist Johannes Franciscus de Ponzinibus doubted the existence of pacts with the devil (see the second part of the *Malleus Maleficarum,* near the end).[7] At the end of that century, the physician Johannes Wier published the rather lengthy treatise *De Praestigiis Daemonum,* or *Of the Devil's Arts* where he tries to prove that the crime of sorcery indeed does not exist as was usually believed.[8] And he attempts to defend this opinion against many critics and opponents in an appendix with several apologias. Carpzov (op. cit.) associates him with Petrus de Apono, but I do not know when the latter wrote because so far I have not seen anything by him.[9] Perhaps Carpzov meant Petrus de Abano, whose *Elementa magica* is quite well known. However, all who discover a truth usually only break the ice for

Those authors are listed who denied the vice of sorcery, especially Johannes Wier, Anthony van Dale, and Balthasar Becker.

---

imperial Saxon criminal law) (Wittenburg, 1635). Carpzov was an orthodox Lutheran strongly opposed to heresy and witchcraft and contributed to Lutheran church law through his membership in the Dresden Superior Consistory. Here Thomasius is referring to part 1, question 48 of the *Practica nova,* De Crimine Sortilegii (On the crime of soothsaying), at pp. 307–25. Our references are to the 1670 edition published in Wittenberg.

7. Giovanni Francesco Ponzinibus was a jurist in Florence and attacked the *Malleus Maleficarum* (The hammer of witchcraft) in his *Tractatus subtilis & elegans de lamiis* (Subtle and elegant treatise on witches) (Pavia, 1511). Ponzinibus accepted the existence of sorcery but attacked legal proceedings against witches by denying the elements of the crime—witches' sabbaths, pacts with the devil, child murder, and so on—as delusions. For the key doctrines of the *Malleus Maleficarum,* see note 80 in this chapter.

8. See note 5 in this chapter.

9. Petrus de Apono (also Petrus Abanus or Petrus Aponensis, 1246–1320?), philosopher and first professor of medicine at the University of Padua. The *Heptameron, seu elementa magica* appeared as an appendix to Heinrich Cornelius Agrippa von Nettesheim's (posthumous) *Liber quartus de occulta philosophia* (1565); its ascription to Abano (as to Agrippa) may be spurious. In English: *Henry Cornelius Agrippa's Fourth Book of Occult Philosophy, and Geomancy. Magical Elements of Peter de Abano. Astronomical Geomancy [by Gerardus Cremonensis]. The Nature of Spirits [by Georgius Pictorius]. And Arbatel of Magick,* trans. Robert Turner (London, 1655).

others. Thus, while the above-mentioned authors saw much they also overlooked much, so that they were not able to prove these obvious errors to the world, bewitched for centuries by crass lies. I have not seen the book that Petrus Pomponatius wrote on witchcraft, nor the one by the Englishman Reginald Scotus that deals with the same topic and was burned by public order.[10] The former ascribes everything that was told and believed about witchcraft in former times to secret forces of nature. The latter ascribes it to melancholy, certain illnesses, and the tricks of charlatans, as can be seen in Voetius's *Disputationes Selectae,* in the third part on p. 564.[11] In our own time the abovementioned Gabriel Naudé wrote an *Apology for Great Men Falsely Accused of Sorcery,* in which he provides many learned arguments against the common dogmas.[12] Among contemporary papist authors Malebranche, in the last chapter of his second book on *The Search after Truth,* inclines to the view that all tales of sorcery and witchcraft are a product of the imagination.[13] Most of all, the Dutch physician Anthony van Dale deserves to be praised. His learned works on pagan oracles, the origin and development of idolatry and superstition, true and false prophesies, as well as on idolatrous prophesies by the Jews, are very much esteemed by the learned

10. Pietro Pomponazzi (1462–1526?) taught philosophy at the University of Padua. His book *De naturalium effectuum causis, sive de incantationibus* (On the causes of natural effects, or on sorcery) was published posthumously in Basel in 1556. Reginald Scott (1538?–99) was a member of the English gentry who offered a purely social account of the emergence of witchcraft. Scott's *The Discoverie of Witchcraft* (London, 1548) was designed as a refutation of Bodin's *Démonologie* (1580) and considerably sharpened Johann Weyer's arguments, which Scott knew. There is no contemporary evidence for the later story that Scott's work was burned.

11. Gisbertus Voetius (1589–1676) was a professor of theology in Utrecht where he opposed Descartes' teachings on the basis of Calvinist doctrine. His *Disputationes Theologiae Selectae* (Select theological disputations) appeared in five volumes between 1648 and 1669.

12. See note 3 in this chapter.

13. Nicolas Malebranche (1638–1715), French philosopher and Oratorian priest who argued that miracles are the outcome of divine laws of nature. This was part of a fervent defense of the unison between reason and faith, an argument that made his works influential in the French Enlightenment. See his *De la Recherche de la Vérité* (Paris, 1674–78), and for a modern English translation, *The Search after Truth,* trans. T. M. Lennon and P. J. Olscamp (Cambridge: Cambridge University Press, 1997).

world.[14] In those books he uncovers in detail many common errors about the devil and his deeds. Unfortunately he has found few adherents, especially among the theologians, apart from the Dutch theologian Balthasar Becker who took most of what is contained in his *The World Bewitched* from Dale.[15] But it is widely known how unfortunate Becker was when it came to the public reception of his work, since he questioned all external effects of the devil on man and almost brought the existence of the devil himself into doubt. (Dale too had done this in his writings, but very surreptitiously.) In Becker's case this meant that he could not help but strengthen the hand of his enemies, enabling them to reject the truths he had discovered and to defend all the common errors.

4. More caution was exercised by an anonymous jurist who, seven years ago, published the *Cautio criminalis seu de Processibus contra sagas (Caution on Criminal Cases, or a Book on Witch Trials)*, dedicating it to all the magistrates of Germany.[16] This author does not deny the existence of the devil or of witches, and responds affirmatively to the initial question

The author of *Cautio criminalis seu de processibus contra sagas* is recommended.

14. Antonius van Dale (1638–1708) was a Dutch physician working at a hospital in Haarlem. Thomasius refers here to *De oraculis ethnicorum* (On the oracles of the pagans) (Amsterdam, 1683) and *Dissertationes de origine ac progressu Idolatriae et Superstitionum, de vera ac falsa Prophetia, uti et de Divinationibus Idolatricis Judaeorum* (Dissertations on the origin and progress of idolatry and superstition, on true and false prophecy, and on the idolatrous divinations of the Jews) (Amsterdam, 1696).

15. Balthasar Bekker (1634–98) was a Protestant preacher in Amsterdam. His famous book *De betoverde Wereld* (Leuwaarden, 1691), which was translated into German (1693), French (1694), and English (*The World Bewitch'd*, 1695), caused great theological controversy, and he was banned from preaching in 1692.

16. The author of the *Cautio criminalis* was the Jesuit priest Friedrich Spee von Langenfeld. He published his book anonymously in 1631, the first attributed edition appearing in 1721 in Augsburg. The full title is *Cautio criminalis seu de Processibus contra sagas Liber. Ad Magistratus Germaniae hoc tempore necessarius, tum autem Consiliariis & Confessariis Principum, Inquisitoribus, Judicibus, Advocatis, Confessariis reorum, Concionatoribus, caeterisque lectu utilissimus. Auctore incerto theologo orthodoxo* (Rinteln, 1631); in English as *Cautio criminalis, or, A Book on Witch Trials*, trans. M. Hellyer (Charlottesville, Va.: University of Virginia Press, 2003). Friedrich Spee was one of the most famous and influential opponents of witch trials in Germany. He argued for their immediate cessation and was convinced that the idea of the crime of witchcraft was caused only by the use of torture and by the persecutor's obsessive belief in witches.

of whether sorcerers and witches exist. *Even if I know that many doubt it,* as he writes in Latin, *even Catholics and scholars, whose names are not relevant here; even if some men seem to suspect, not without reason, that there were times in the Church when people did not believe that there were physical witches' sabbaths; even if, when I myself frequently and attentively, not to mention curiously, ministered to various women accused of this crime in prison, my own mind was often so overwhelmed that I hardly knew what to believe in this matter. Nevertheless, when I finally gathered together the essence of my perplexed thoughts, I concluded that one must believe completely that there really are some sorcerers in the world. This cannot be denied without rashness and all the marks of a preposterous opinion. You may read the authors who argue that they do exist: Rémy, Delrio, Bodin, and others. It is not our intention to dally here. However, neither I nor many pious men along with me believe that there are so many witches, nor that all those who have flown away in ashes until now were witches. Indeed, anyone who wishes to examine the matter with judgment and reason, and not pressure me with his passion and shouting or with his authority, will not easily convince me to believe it either.*[17] No matter who the author of this little treatise is, he was certainly prudent enough to prevent his opponents from seizing the opportunity to regard him as an atheist, in accordance with the common prejudices. At the same time, he provided clear and strong arguments for all friends of the truth, and especially for political officials. And this little treatise seems to be of such importance that nobody has tried to contradict it, allowing us to conclude that no reasonable jurist or prudent politician could be found who would have any doubts about the injustice of witch trials after reading this booklet, let alone attempt to refute it. If someone dared to refute it, I am certain that this would contribute to his disgrace rather than his honor, because this unnamed author executed everything so brilliantly.

17. Here we have used Marcus Hellyer's translation of the passage. See Spee von Langenfeld, *Cautio Criminalis, or, A Book on Witch Trials*, 15–16.

5. Here it is fair to ask whether our disputation is still necessary? I freely admit that I could have refrained from writing it and been content with the above author, yet I do not consider it completely superfluous. The author, whoever he may be, pretends to be a Catholic. Perhaps he does so in order to astonish Protestant jurists all the more if they see that, in the midst of papalism, jurists recognized the darkness through which the works of the papalist clergy have until now obscured the light of our Protestant jurisprudence. But if one takes a closer look at the matter one will easily see that the author's approach is simply a healthy deception, and that hidden behind this mask is none other than one of the Protestant jurists. Without doubt it was for the reasons mentioned above that he avoided the public defense of his views in front of those among us [Protestants] who are still sunk in papalist errors. I also believe, for many reasons that it is all just a masquerade and legend when he pretends in the passage quoted in the previous paragraph that there are indeed witches (that is, those who make certain pacts with Satan, according to Remigius, Delrio, Bodin). I am persuaded of this when I contrast the learning and diligence of his answers to the remaining questions with poor and trivial reasons evident in the entire answer to the first question. In fact, he posed as a Catholic in order to suit himself to the times. If he had denied the fact that witches really exist, then he would have had to contradict those who defended this illusion and show why it had been maintained and defended in every possible way. But in this case no one would have believed that his writings were produced by a Catholic jurist. Just as the questions that the author of the *Cautio criminalis* left aside will supply plenty of theses for our present disputation, so there may well be reason to have a second look at some things concerning trials that this author has omitted or passed over, although I do not intend to simply complete his work.

But the author, who pretended to be a Catholic, still left much work for others.

6. Even though Goedelmann accepted there were pacts between sorcerers and the devil, he denied they existed between witches and Satan. Becker, on the other hand, doubted, if not the devil himself, then certainly his power and influence. The author of the *Cautio criminalis* only pretends to believe in the existence of witches and their pacts with Satan. The common people and the half-educated are under the illusion not

We concede that there is a devil who works in the wicked, but we deny that there is a crime of sorcery.

only that the devil exists but also that there are many witches, and that the witch trials against them are most laudable and just, striving not only to fool themselves into believing this, but others also. I disagree with all these opinions and say that there is a devil outside man and that, from without, he nonetheless works inwardly and invisibly in the wicked. I deny, however, that witches and sorcerers form particular pacts with Satan. I am sure, rather, that everything believed about this is nothing more than a fairy tale, compiled from Judaism, paganism, and the papacy, and confirmed by most unjust witch trials which were for a time also common among the Protestants.

The difference between our view, Becker's, and the common dogma. A description of the devil.

7. If I wanted to adopt Becker's opinion [that the devil is nonexistent or ineffective], which also seems to be van Dale's, then I would not need to collect arguments to prove that pacts with Satan cannot exist, because one cannot attribute properties and activities to something that is nothing in itself. Since I am departing from Becker in this respect, I have to proceed in a different fashion. No one should think I am only pretending to disagree with Becker. I am doing this in all seriousness, and I hope to be spared all hostile accusations. But I will thoroughly refute all suspicions below by putting forward a description of the devil. I cannot see how those who adhere to Aristotelian philosophy—which still rules in the higher disciplines and has nourished and sustained the common errors regarding sorcery—might refute Becker's teachings.[18] Similarly— if they understood their own pronouncements and could make others understand them without using self-contradictory concepts—then I cannot imagine how it would be possible for those who profess the cor-

18. Aristotelian philosophy (physics, cosmology, metaphysics, and ethics) remained dominant in Lutheran universities until the latter part of the seventeenth century and in Catholic (Jesuit) universities until long after this, not least because of its scholastic merging with Christian doctrine. In Protestant universities Aristotelianism was challenged by new conceptions of scientific method associated with Bacon, Descartes, and Galileo, and by new conceptions of philosophy and politics associated with Hobbes, Pufendorf, and the eclectic philosophers, including Thomasius himself. Aristotelian physics and metaphysics were used to support belief in witches as these doctrines showed how (nonspatial) spiritual substances such as angels and demons could exist inside corporeal beings like man, taking over his faculties.

puscular and mechanistic philosophies to seriously contradict Becker's principles and his conclusions.[19] In adhering to the ancient philosophy of spirits (*Philosophia spiritualis*),[20] however, I not only believe but to some extent even grasp with my understanding that the devil is the lord of darkness and the prince of the air, that is, a spiritual or invisible being which affects godless people in spiritual and invisible ways with the help of the air, or particles of water and earth.

8. Here I cannot understand why pious men regarded those who, like Becker, denied the devil, to be atheists. On the contrary, one should consider them ademonists, that is, people who do not believe in a devil. For when I believe in God it does not follow that I must believe in the devil; and neither does it follow that if I do not believe in the devil then I do not believe in God. Moreover, it amazes me that most of those who have persuaded themselves of the most absurd tales about the devil and his power will tolerate no tales of the good angels and their influence, but describe those who invent or believe in these tales as enthusiasts among other things.[21] In other words, why are they so eager to build up and strengthen the empire of darkness, rather than the empire of light? I easily foresee that my sincere declaration about the existence and in-

Our view and Becker's are defended against the suspicion of atheism.

19. Corpuscular philosophy, as elaborated by the French philosophers Pierre Gassendi and René Descartes, explains natural phenomena in terms of the qualities and movements of atoms (*corpuscula*). It is thus somewhat similar to mechanistic philosophy, which explains phenomena in terms of quantifiable force, motion, and resistance, but it also supports Epicurean ethics by freeing the world from divine control.

20. Thomasius is referring to his own *Vom Wesen des Geistes* (On the nature of spirit) (Halle, 1699). Here he tries to forge a link between physics and metaphysics by constructing a theory of spirit in which spirit is the moving power of passive matter, in this regard paralleling his Aristotelian opponents. Thomasius's theory derives from mystical sources and was developed as an alternative to Cartesian mechanics, which Thomasius regarded as leading to atheism through its emphasis on matter.

21. Before Shaftesbury's positive interpretation of enthusiasm in his *Letter concerning Enthusiasm* (1708), the term was used as a synonym for antirational fanaticism and a pathological form of fantasy and imagination. In the eighteenth century, it was of ambiguous connotation.

fluence of evil spirits will not free me from slander, perhaps only because I do not want to recognize the so-called crime of sorcery, or the pact between witches and the devil. The falsehoods told by Bodin in his book on devils and ghosts also include the following: in the year 1453 someone named Wilhelmus Luranus who was punished with death in France for witchcraft, had confessed explicitly that he had not only forsworn all religions in his pact with the devil, but had also had to promise Satan to teach and preach publicly that everything that had been said about sorcery and black magic was mere lies and fairy tales, and that it would indeed be the greatest cruelty to punish someone for this crime. Any person endowed with powers of understanding will easily be able to guess why the papalist clerics coerced Luranus through torture and torment to confess such things. I only regret that this and other tales misled and deceived many pious men among our theologians such that they consider all those who deny the crime of witchcraft to be atheists. In lieu of many others I will here point only to Theophilus Spizelius.[22] Spizelius seems to have written his German treatise, entitled *The Power of Darkness Broken,* only to urge the authorities in Germany to forcefully maintain the existing criminal prosecutions of witches, and to cast suspicion of atheism and impiety on those who repudiate such trials and who doubt the diabolical pact. Generally I do not repay slander with slander, but I want to oppose the good Spizelius with the gentleness of Virgil's words, when he says: *Fallit te incautum pietas tua.* In other words, your piety leads you astray. Thus I claim nothing else but the right to ask every reasonable person's conscience, why anyone denying the crime of sorcery or witchcraft should be suspected of godlessness. Those who have alleged this or will do so, perhaps on the basis of their status and authority, I wish to implore that they examine their own piety, no matter how evident it appears, to see whether there might not be hypocrisy hidden beneath it. After they have closely examined their own conscience,

---

22. Theophilus Spizelius (1639–91), a Lutheran theologian and pastor in Augsburg, *Die gebrochene Macht der Finsternüß oder Zerstörte teuflische Bunds- und Buhls-Freundschafft mit den Menschen* (The broken power of darkness or destruction of the devil's friendship-pact with men) (Augsburg, 1687).

and if they still believe that the rules of true Christianity demand it, then they may nevertheless slander and harshly judge others.

9. Even though I deny that sorcery is a crime, I do not want to repeat those who have shown in detail that the Latin word *magia* was formerly used in a positive sense, and was ascribed in particular to priests. One can look it up in Bodin's *Daemonomanie,* in the first chapter of the second book, in Osiander's book *on Magic,* Thes. I, §4, in Caelius Rhodiginus's fifth book, chap. 42, in the Peucerus of the *divinat.,* p. 287, and in Goedelmann's work on sorcery, in the first book in the second chapter, §2.[23] I note from these authors that it appears that the word *magia* has long been used to refer to any occult science and wisdom; that is, to the understanding of things whose causes were not only unknown to the common people, but were kept concealed from them, so that they could be ascribed to a higher power than that of humans. This observation confirms the common division of magic into natural, artificial, and diabolical magic.[24] For each of these kinds of magic represents a science of things, not of things in general, but of hidden things, or at least of things that have been hidden.

Magic previously signified any occult science.

10. Since one generally divides magic into the permitted and prohibited, everyone will concur (and I do not exclude myself) that natural and artificial magic should be considered permissible, but that demonic magic is a punishable crime. Thus it is unnecessary that I discuss the first

Here our concern is not with natural or artificial magic, but with demonic.

23. Johann Adam Osiander (1622–97) was professor of theology in Tübingen. See his *Tractatus theologicus de magia* (Theological treatise on sorcery) (Tübingen, 1687). Ludovicus Caelius Rhodiginus (1469–1525) taught Greek and Latin at the University of Milan and later at the University of Padua. See his *Lectionum Antiquarum Libri XVI* (Lectures on antiquity in sixteen books) (Venice, 1516). Caspar Peucer (1525–1602) had a chair in mathematics and later in medicine at the University of Wittenberg. Thomasius refers here to the *Commentarius de praecipuis divinationum generibus* (Commentary on the main kinds of divination) (Wittenberg, 1553).

24. Natural and artificial magic were products of Renaissance Neoplatonism. They were taught as esoteric arts for acquiring knowledge and control of things through the discovery and manipulation of hidden correspondences, signs, and influences, particularly those linking man as microcosm with the heavens as macrocosm. "Artificial" here means technical or based on the rules of an art.

two kinds in detail, because we are concerned only with the question of the existence of the latter. In German the latter is also called sorcery. As far as I know, except for Spizelius, in the first part of his book, chapter 1, §9, nobody has identified natural and artificial magic—that is, permitted magic—with witchcraft. But this negligence should be forgiven because of this dear man's simplicity and piety, which shines forth from the entire treatise and from every page.

Whose defini-
tion is conven-
iently left out
by most writers.
11. The question remains: does satanic magic or sorcery exist? First, there should be a definition of it, which most authors have conveniently omitted. As it is futile to talk about things that the senses cannot perceive, it is also futile to examine anything before one is certain that it really exists. Thus it would be absurd in moral and legal matters, and indeed in all other things arising as complex aggregates, if one wished to deal with the question about their existence before clearly defining them.

Added by us.
12. Drawing on the writings and consensus of those who believe in it, we can define the crime of sorcery as a delict in which people enter into a pact with Satan—who appears to them in bestial, human, or monstrous form—that obliges them, when the devil wishes to satisfy his lust, greed, and pride, to have intercourse with him; and obliges them further to gather in a certain place, to which the devil may conduct them through the air, where they will worship, dance, and carouse with the devil and his consorts and, indeed, with the devil's assistance, do harm to men, animals, and crops by raising tempests or by other supernatural means; and finally, after a certain time has passed, to belong to the devil in body and soul, remaining thus for eternity.

The burden of
proof lies not
with us but
with those
who claim that
the crime of
sorcery exists.
13. Since the question is whether there is such a crime as sorcery, we have to proceed as follows. Any crime is an act, and one that is not just presumed or surmised. The person who affirms there is a crime of sorcery must therefore prove this, and may not demand a proof from someone who denies it. For even if I offer no reasons for my denial, even the most ignorant judge would have to rule in my favor. Carpzov should thus have

to appear first and argue against the famous Wier and others that there is indeed a crime of sorcery.

14. *First,* Carpzov argues that this judgment concurs with divine law, which demands that all witches and sorcerers be burned, since God sentenced diviners, soothsayers, sorcerers, and witches to death, Exodus XII, 18; Numbers XX, 27. (See Carpzov, op. cit., qu. 48, no. 40.)[25] But how can this be possible? The malefactors dealt with in divine law are not sorcerers in the sense I have defined them. They did not make a pact with the devil, and what they did was without such pacts, whether through clever deceit or through occult powers of nature, that is, either through artificial or natural magic—it makes no difference—but not through diabolical magic. It does not matter that I have already declared natural and artificial magic to be permissible while, according to the above-mentioned passages and other texts from Scripture, God still wanted them punished. For that which is lawful by virtue of its method can become unlawful by virtue of its intention and aim. God wanted them to be punished not because of certain pacts made with the devil or harm done to people, but because they were the source and propagators of idolatry.

> Carpzov's arguments for the existence of sorcery together with our responses. First, his claim that sorcerers should be executed according to divine law. We reply that sorcerers are not punished for their pact with the devil but for idolatry.

15. He also says that this divine law should be understood not only with reference to those who mix potions to poison others, as Wier believes, but encompasses all who do harm to others with all kinds of deception, as did the sorcerers of Pharaoh, Exodus VII.[27] Now Wier himself may decide how he will respond to Carpzov's argument. I am not concerned with this, since I pursued a different path in the preceding paragraph. No matter what arts were used by Pharaoh's sorcerers, they nonetheless performed nothing with the help of the devil or diabolical pacts. God

> Carpzov responds that the divine law does not only refer to poisoners,[26] yet he is refuted.

---

25. See Carpzov, *Practica nova,* pr. I, qu. 48, §40, pp. 312–13.

26. The Latin word is *veneficus* (m.) or *venefica* (f.), which signifies a sorcerer or witch in the sense of a mixer of potions and poisons.

27. Carpzov, *Practica nova,* §40, p. 312.

thus ordered their execution not on account of their arts but because of their idolatrous superstition.

Reply to the new objection concerning Pharaoh's sorcerers, that they made a pact with the devil.

16. Here someone could object in favor of Carpzov that the illusions performed by the Egyptian wizards could not have been achieved through either natural or artificial magic. Not through the former, because then Moses's deeds would not have been miracles but natural phenomena. And also not through the latter, because it is unimaginable and incomprehensible how it would be possible thereby to change sticks into serpents by throwing them on the ground. Thus it must have happened through diabolical magic. But I reply to this, first, that the difference between miracles and natural operations itself remains indeterminate. Everything commonly taught in scholastic metaphysics and in the higher faculties about the difference between natural, artificial, and supernatural works—as well as about the difference between the power of God and that of the devil—is all vain chatter and still requires proof. Secondly, it cannot be argued that Moses's deeds were also acts of natural magic simply because the Egyptian sorcerers produced such effects from occult natural powers—that is, from powers unknown to and hidden from Aristotelian and Cartesian philosophy (since neither of them and least of all the latter can demonstrate anything substantial concerning natural causes). The deeds that Moses and Aaron performed and that Pharaoh's sorcerers could not imitate were sufficient evidence of a power far superior to theirs. Thus one cannot draw conclusions about Pharaoh's sorcerers from Moses's deeds. Thirdly, who does not know that if two people perform the same action, it does not mean that they are identical. Fourthly, it is often the case that something that we could not imagine to be possible through mere skill turns out to be very simple and trivial, once it has been explained to us. There are certainly many tricks that people commonly ascribe to supernatural powers and that yet are nothing but mere deception. The card tricks of Abraham Columni are undoubtedly an example. Spizelius discusses them in the above-mentioned book, p. 62, but they are also ascribed to the devil without a shred of reasonable evidence. The fifth and last point is that if Pharaoh's wizards performed these actions with the help of the devil, then

the devil would have done so either through natural powers or by using skill and deceit. However, neither is possible: not the former, because then even Moses's miracles would have been only effects of nature; but not the latter, because I cannot imagine how the devil at that time could have been able to deceive the senses of the people. I put forward this argument only to show how easily I can turn the objection directed at me against my opponents, since I do not intend to shift from the persona of respondent to that of opponent.

17. Now, to return to Carpzov, he continues by saying that it is also commanded in Leviticus XX, v. 26 that all sorcerers must be punished with death.[28] He argues that this law was always applied by the Israelites, as is clearly proven by the example of the soothsayer of Endor who was afraid of Saul because he had forbidden all sorcery on pain of death.[29] In addition, both the Jewish king Manasseh and the entire people of Israel were very severely punished by God because of sorcery.[30] But we might respond to this as follows: First, Carpzov confuses idolatrous magic with diabolical magic, which consists of a pact with the devil. Secondly, he is not concerned to prove that sorcery exists—as he should have done in arguing against Wier—but to show that it must be punished with death. Thirdly, moreover, this is not sufficiently proven by the divine laws, since they bound the Jewish commonwealth but do not concern Christians today. One can satisfy oneself about this by observing that the divine law orders that the high priest's daughter should be burned if she whores. If this is a general law, why does one not likewise burn the daughters of our church superintendents when they commit the same sin? For there is certainly a closer relation and similarity between the former Jewish high priests and our current superintendents than between the sorcerers mentioned in the Mosaic Laws and those we are arguing about now. Fourthly, there is no mention of the diabolical

Concerning the witch of Endor, who conjured [an apparition of] Samuel, and Manasseh.

28. Carpzov, *Practica nova*, §§41–42, p. 313.

29. See 1 Samuel 28:9.

30. King of Judah (690–640 B.C.) whom the Bible portrays as promoting idolatry and sorcery and incurring God's wrath. See 2 Kings 21:1–18.

magic we are concerned with in Deuteronomy XVIII, 10, which lists the many kinds of magic forbidden by God to the people of Israel. But all those who are mentioned in Deuteronomy were idolaters, tricksters, and mountebanks, whom van Dale has already examined extensively in the above books on pagan oracles and the idolatrous soothsaying of the Jews.

The witch of Endor deceived Saul, since she saw neither Samuel nor his shadow, but nothing at all.

18. I myself want to help Carpzov a little: one might say that the witch of Endor had conjured up either the devil in the shape of Samuel or the soul of Samuel himself, which could not have happened without the support of the devil. I will reply to this that, first of all, no devil, or even a pact with the devil, is mentioned in the passage in Scripture where this story is told. Secondly, the devil did not appear and neither did the soul of Samuel or his image, as this was sheer deception. This woman was a ventriloquist and thus deceived the fearful Saul, an interpretation that is fully supported by the text, 1 Samuel XXVIII. Saul did not see anything, hearing merely a voice, and only the woman said that she saw something, which was just an untruth.

Regarding Carpzov's second argument in which he invokes natural law, I respond that he did not prove this assertion.

19. So Carpzov's first argument proves nothing. Now I want to look at the *second* one, which I will describe very briefly. Not only, he says, does natural law agree with divine law—as can be seen both in pagan decrees stating that all sorcerers should be punished by death and also in book II of Plato's *Laws,* which prescribes the death penalty for sorcerers[31]— but legal judgments always followed divine law, never imposing anything other than the death penalty on sorcerers and witches, as we can see even in the laudable practice of the Romans and Persians.[32] Yet here I must note again, as I have done several times before, that Carpzov begins by confusing the question of whether there are sorcerers who pact with the devil, with the question of the punishment imposed for natural and artificial magic. He then confuses natural law with the mores and customs

31. In his *Laws,* Plato (427–347 B.C.) sketches a comprehensive legal code, including penal law. The death penalty for sorcerers is suggested in book XI (933c–a).
32. Carpzov, *Practica nova,* §§43–45, p. 313.

of a few nations. And finally he mixes the fantasy of the Platonic republic with the mores and customs of the nations in an absurd fashion.

20. *Thirdly,* Carpzov continues, *it is indubitable that the civil law punishes both sorcerers and poisoners (Magos seu Veneficos) with the death sentence.*[34] Here I begin by praising Carpzov, in that he does not distinguish between sorcerers and poisoners and thus deviates radically from the question that concerns us, because the Latin word *venefica* does not refer to a witch—as is often assumed due to this common error—but to a mixer of poisons. This art, however, does not require the assistance of the devil or a pact with him. Here we should note that the civil law never mentions pacts with the devil, referring only to soothsayers, diviners, mathematicians, or astrologers, etc. We are going to set aside other replies that could be repeated here, but which have already been made. In addition, we can state that the civil law can just as little be used to prove the existence of the crime of sorcery as it can to confirm the existence of other things.

Regarding his third argument, taken from the civil law,[33] one can reply that it is invalid to draw inferences from poisoners to sorcerers.

21. Now I will address the main argument that Carpzov provides to support his view. *Fourthly,* he writes, *it cannot be denied that sorcerers make a pact with the devil in which they completely renounce the covenant they formed with God during baptism. Bodin, Remigius, Chirlandus,[35] and others explicitly attest to this.*[36] In a matter so central to the whole question, however, Carpzov should have been ashamed to offer nothing more than the testimony of papalist writers. Their books are filled in part with old wives' and monks' tales, in part with the depositions of melancholics, and in part with statements obtained through torture and torment,

The fourth argument, from the testimony of papalist writers, is completely absurd.

33. Here civil law is the Roman *Corpus Juris Civilis,* codified by the Roman emperor Justinian in 534.

34. Carpzov, *Practica nova,* §46, p. 313.

35. An author with the name Chirlandus could not be verified. It is possible that here Carpzov is referring to Paulus Grillandus, a famous papal judge in the witch trials in the district of Rome, whose writings include the *Tractatus de hereticis et sortilegiis* (Treatise on heretics and witches) (Lyon, 1536).

36. Carpzov, *Practica nova,* §47, p. 313.

where people were forced to confess to everything they were questioned about. Certainly, if our jurists had not slavishly imitated others, particularly the papalists, but had instead followed their own reason in properly investigating both the natural and moral issues with which the laws are concerned, then our jurisprudence could have been regarded by scholars as a discipline leading to true erudition. Until now, however, one author has copied from another without reflection, and has amazed himself by discovering that this case or that question is *in terminis terminantibus*.[37] Thus one should not hold it against those scholars if on hearing the name jurisconsult they can form no other concept of this *in terminis terminantibus* than that of a sophist and pettifogging lawyer. But we should now go back to our friend Carpzov.

Where we show the absurdity of the doctrine of a tacit pact between witches and the devil.

22. *Although,* he continues, *not all sorcerers always make an express pact with the devil and pledge perpetual obedience, they nonetheless abjure God, since they have commerce with the devil, which in truth is nothing other than a tacit or implicit pact.*[38] To this I reply: (1) If there is no express pact—and this has so far not been proven—then the implicit pact is null. For if someone cannot openly make a contract or a pact, then no contract is concluded by him or with him, tacit or otherwise. (2) There is still the question of whether sorcerers, who deceive people with all kinds of illusions, engage in corporeal intercourse [*commercium corporale*] with the devil, thus tacitly abjuring God. (3) But if all those who have only spiritual intercourse [*commercium spirituale*] with the devil were supposed to have a tacit pact with him and were thence burned as sorcerers, then there would be a complete confusion of malefactors. For adulterers, liars, and all those who perform works of the flesh engage in spiritual intercourse with the devil.

37. Legalese meaning a case or precedent that is exactly on point, or falls within exact and determinative boundaries. In the following sentence Thomasius uses the phrase to mock the pedantry of his fellow jurists by suggesting that when other scholars form an idea of lawyers that is *in terminis terminantibus*—or exactly on point—then it is not at all flattering.

38. Carpzov, *Practica nova,* §47, p. 313.

23. Carpzov further adds: *The punishment for homicide and adultery is death, yet sorcery is a worse crime than homicide or adultery because in sacrificing their own children to the devil witches are murderers, and in lying down with the devil they are also adulteresses.*[39] This statement does not deserve a real response. I will simply point out again that Carpzov continues to confuse the question of the punishment of sorcery with the question of whether it exists, thereby assuming that which he has still to prove true.

> It is wrong to infer the punishment for witches from the punishments for murderers and adulterers.

24. There remains one final argument, which I must not ignore. *Fifthly,* he says, *it is in the witches' and sorcerers' own interest to be dispatched in a timely fashion and removed from the scene. For, so firmly are they held in the devil's grip that nothing will release them more speedily than death. Remigius, who was councillor to the Duke of Lorraine and who had more than nine hundred sorcerers sentenced and executed, is a credible witness; and he assures us that among the many thousands that the devil had ensnared, he never heard of any way by which they could be freed from the devil's bonds other than by confessing their crimes voluntarily or through coercion—or by suffering the death penalty.*[40] But I respond: (1) Who could imagine that Lutheran jurists would fall for such absurdities and could believe that the executioner is a proper instrument of conversion? (2) Why does the imprudent Carpzov believe Remigius, a superstitious person who was, so to speak, a slave of the clergy as well? Carpzov's reason for believing him—that is, that Remigius attended so many executions in Lorraine—sits badly with me. (3) In addition, he did not even understand Remigius correctly, who did not say at all what Carpzov infers from his words. Remigius says only that witches could not free themselves from their pacts with the devil until they had confessed their crime, after which

> The fifth argument, that it is in the witches' own interest to be put to death, will be responded to, and many inconsistencies will be demonstrated.

39. Ibid. Despite purporting to quote Carpzov, on this occasion Thomasius is paraphrasing him, albeit accurately.

40. Carpzov, *Practica nova,* §48, p. 313. In this quotation from Carpzov, Thomasius also silently includes a paraphrase of Carpzov's quotation from Nicolas Remy's *Daemonolatreia* (bk. 3, chap. 12). See note 4 in this chapter.

death inevitably followed as a result of the priests' laws. (4) But if Carpzov felt it necessary to base his jurisprudence on fables and the authority of others, why did he not have more faith in our [Lutheran] theologians? For they teach that many witches and sorcerers could have been returned to the right path without the death penalty; and moreover they turn the devil into such a powerless spirit that he can be driven away by a fart, lacking even the power to remove the signature of the person who made a pact with him from the Bible, something even the smallest puppy could do. See Luther's *Table-talk*[41] and Spizelius's *Power of Darkness Broken,* first part, pp. 211ff., and the entire third part. (5) Carpzov's argument would provide an excellent defense of murder. If one killed a useless person or someone suffering from the French disease[42] or some other painful ailment, then one could use the pretext that it was in the person's best interests to be given a timely death. (6) Others may judge whether a person who seeks to defend capital punishment on such baseless pretexts, which one would not even accept from students, understands the true purpose of capital punishment.

Carpzov's conclusion is rebuffed. 25. Carpzov concludes his arguments in the following way: *Now,* he writes, *I will leave it to anyone who possesses even a little piety and a sound mind to judge whether the authorities' actions are just and commendable when they punish witches and sorcerers.*[43] My conclusion, however, is the following: Anyone who possesses even a little common sense and prudence—we refuse to say anything about Carpzov's imprudent piety which consists only of faith in old wives' tales—should judge whether it is not highly disgraceful for such an eminent jurist to try to deceive and cheat others about such a serious and important matter in such a slovenly fashion.

---

41. The *Tisch-Reden* (Table-talk) of the reformer Martin Luther (1483–1546) was first published in Eisleben twenty years after his death in 1566. The book contains a collection of Luther's conversations, held in his house in Wittenberg.

42. That is, syphilis.

43. Carpzov, *Practica nova,* §49, p. 314.

26. Since Carpzov did not make any progress with his argument, Spizelius came to his aid—a theologian helping a jurist! I do not want to reveal the disgrace of this pious man here, nor point out all the mistakes in his book on the *Power of Darkness Broken,* which has been mentioned several times. But I do want to explore briefly his major arguments with which he seeks to prove in the second chapter of the second part that there are cases of an actual pact between humans and the devil. *Firstly,* he says on p. 112, that *the opposite opinion is a malicious and gross error which Thomas Aquinas, Bonaventura, and Johannes à Turrecremata opposed many years ago as mean and damnable heresy.*[44] *Indeed, it is a very dangerous and harmful error because it paves the way to atheism.* I answer: (1) This is not a proof of the argument and amounts only to a slandering of opponents out of unreasonable zealotry. (2) Thomas Aquinas, Bonaventura, and Johannes de Turrecremata would doubtless reject Lutheran doctrine as a damnable heresy, and yet Spizelius would not be moved by their authority to believe them. (3) Here I do not see how the opinion of those who do not believe in the vice of sorcery could pave the way to atheism. On the contrary, in my view, by preaching superstitious dogmas instead of the biblical doctrine of salvation, it is the theologians and clergy who are to blame when so many people, still in possession of their reason and common sense and seeking to free themselves from the extreme of superstition, fall into the other extreme of atheism. (4) The established opinion, which is defended by Spizelius, leads people to adopt the most crude and more than childish superstitious beliefs. In his *Various Thoughts on the Comet,* the learned Bayle has shown extensively that superstition is not only a more foolish, but also a more dangerous vice than atheism, and he has not been decisively refuted by anyone.[45]

> Contrary to Spizelius it is shown that our opinion does not lead to atheism.

44. Thomas Aquinas (1224–74) and Bonaventura (1217–74) were famous philosophers and theologians of High Scholasticism. Johannes de Turrecremata (Juan de Torquemada) (1388–1468) was an influential theologian who argued for the absolute power of the pope within the church.

45. See Pierre Bayle, *Pensées diverses, écrites à un docteur de Sorbonne, à l'occasion de la comète qui parût au mois décembre 1680* (1st ed. under different title, 1682; 2nd definitive ed., Rotterdam, 1683; English trans. 1708). For a modern English edition,

Spizelius
argues badly
from those
called sorcerers
in Scripture to
those that we
are concerned
with.

27. *However,* Spizelius continues on p. 214, *if there were no real and true pacts between sorcerers and the devil, then God would not have given us specific laws against such sorcerers and everything in the Bible concerning that matter would also be false.* My answer is that this conclusion is completely wrong, because, as could be seen above, no plausible reasons have been provided to show that those sorcerers mentioned in the Scriptures ever formed a pact with the devil.

He appeals to
the reputation
of the Fathers
of the Church
in vain.

28. Spizelius objects that *if there were no pact between witches and Satan then one would be impudently contradicting all the ancient and meritorious doctors of the Christian church, such as Augustine, Tertullian, Epiphanius, and Chrysostomus,*[46] *who not only believed that such pacts between the devil and humans were true and real, but also fiercely resisted any contrary suggestion.* I reply that first of all, it is insolent to abuse the honorable reputation of the ancient fathers to lend authority to old wives' tales. It is also known that because of their piety and simplicity these men of great merit in the Christian church were often completely credulous, and even today we see that such people are often deceived by swindlers and hypocrites. As a result, nothing is so absurd that it cannot be defended with a quotation from one of the church fathers. And if one can safely contradict the ancient fathers' opinion that there were no antipodes, then why should it be impossible to contradict them in this case? We will show below why the church's teachers were so sure about the devil's pact with humans.

And, even more
vainly, Spizel-
ius appeals to
the authority
of others and
to daily
experience.

29. *Indeed,* Spizelius continues, *it would be the greatest presumption to contradict so many, almost innumerable, sound, and credible writers, and even daily experience.* My answer is that it is a far greater presumption to spread ridiculous tales that captivate credulous people and to pass off superstitious writers as credible historians. His other proofs of the devil's

---

see Pierre Bayle, *Various Thoughts on the Occasion of a Comet,* trans. R. C. Bartlett (New York: SUNY Press, 2000). Thomasius is thinking of the Seventh Letter, especially, perhaps, sections 114–22 and 129–32 (pp. 144–51, 159–65).

46. Fathers of the Church, who lived between 155 and 430.

pact in the second and third chapters are unimportant and do not deserve to be repeated here.

30. Such are the reasons that lead people to believe that sorcerers make a pact with Satan, together with the rest mentioned in paragraph 12 above. It is for these worthless reasons that many thousands of people who were either innocent or at least not really tarnished with this crime were cruelly executed under the pretext of exceptional piety, laudable justice, and holy zeal. One might well be content with the arguments presented thus far, but to supplement these I present some further reasons for my viewpoint. However, first of all, I assume that no one will demand mathematical proofs from me. For even though jurists frequently consider sorcerers, witches, and mathematicians to be the same thing, philosophers regard the devil as something that cannot be a subject of mathematics and demonstrative proof. In the meantime I will strive to present such reasons whose probability will equal the certainty of mathematical proofs.

Now we will prove the contrary, namely, that there is no crime of sorcery.

31. The devil has never assumed bodily form, nor is he able to assume one. Thus he cannot physically enter into a pact,[47] and he never did this, much less satisfy his lust with witches and sorcerers, or, in the shape of a goat, lead them to the famous Blocksberg,[48] etc. The example of Satan trying to tempt Christ presents no difficulty. I reply that first of all the exegetes need to agree among themselves about the meaning of this

1. The first reason is that the devil cannot assume bodily form. Satan, who tempted Christ, was

47. This is a central plank of Thomasius's argument. Without denying the devil's (moral) existence, as Bekker does, he argues that as a spirit the devil lacks the body required to do such things as enter into contracts and fornicate with witches, which were key elements of the crime of witchcraft (see paragraphs 32 and 33). In arguing thus, Thomasius was not only rejecting popular beliefs about the devil but also turning his back on that entire dimension of Christian metaphysics that is concerned with the way in which spiritual substance can occupy corporeal things. This was a set of speculations that had been applied to the phenomenon of diabolical possession but, far more centrally, to the crucial and divisive question of Christ's presence in the Eucharistic host.

48. Popular name of several German mountains where, according to folk belief, witches celebrated their Sabbath on the night of April 30.

not a corpo-
real devil.
Many preju-
dices are
listed, which
originated
from little pic-
tures in the
catechism.

story: whether it was something Christ imagined while he was awake,
or something in his dreams, or whether the name Satan in fact refers to
a human being, which it quite commonly does in the Bible and seems
to me the most plausible explanation. None of these three interpretations contradicts my argument. Secondly, one should set aside all childish prejudices when explaining this story, even though they are still defended by so many people who should finally stop behaving like
children. Among these prejudices is the belief that Christ was conducted
through the air to the pinnacle of the Temple. This belief arises from
ignorance of ancient Jewish history, as does our imagining that the devil
comes to Christ in a visible form; because even assuming that the devil
himself tempted Christ, it is still an untruth, or at least it cannot be
claimed with any plausible reason that he did this in the shape of a man
or a monster. In fact the entire error seems to have its origin in the little
pictures in the Bible, or the Gospels, in which the papalists depict the
Tempter in all kinds of monstrous forms, whereas we Lutherans depict
him in the guise of a monk in his habit. Certainly, one could write an
entire treatise about this and similar matters; that is, about the way in
which papalist superstition is taught to children in Lutheran churches
using pictures from the Catechism and the Gospels, and will remain with
these children for the rest of their lives. If one wants to learn about such
illustrations, I refer, for example, to images used for the third commandment, the sixth supplication, the chapter about the household and
marriage, and in the Gospel for Sunday *Oculi*,[49] and in other places.

2. Because
Christ himself
says that a spirit
has neither
flesh nor bone.

32. If the devil could assume a physical shape, then Christ's statement[50]
that a spirit has neither flesh nor bone would be wrong, and the argument
by which Christ sought to convince his disciples would be inept. But
one could not entertain either thought without blasphemy.

49. Sunday *Oculi* refers to the observances carried out on the third Sunday in
Lent.
50. See Luke 24:39.

33. If the devil cannot disturb or suspend the power and order of invisible nature, then neither can he assume a body, cause tempests, transport a person through the air, etc.

3. Because the devil cannot disturb the power of invisible nature.

34. There is no coherence between what these good people claim about the devil's great power over invisible nature, and the common fables that he can be chased away with nothing more than a fart, for which no evidence can be found in the Bible. Neither is it necessary to refer to a man's faith in this regard. For if Satan is driven away through faith what need is there of a fart unless, that is, you draw a distinction between these farts,[51] which would be an even more absurd and blasphemous undertaking.

4. Because the devil is such a powerless spirit, according to our opponents, that he can be chased away with a fart.

35. The pact with the devil benefits neither man nor the devil in the slightest. Man does not benefit, for if it is said that sorcerers entered into these pacts solely in order to satisfy their lust and to obtain wealth, and honor, then it must also be said that most of the sorcerers are being cheated. But if it is assumed that they are not being cheated, is it not possible to achieve all of this without the help of the devil, quite easily and through cunning, or even in a permitted manner? What need, then, for a pact with the devil?

5. The devil's pact with man has no effect and no benefit, not on the part of man.

36. Since, however, there is no animal more foolish than man, let us assume that he is foolish enough to make a pact with the devil, as I have known many people stupid enough to try this. Yet why should we think the devil so foolish as to enter such pacts with humans without receiving the slightest benefit? The person who indulges in lust, avarice, and pride is already the devil's slave. What would be the benefit of a pact for the devil? Maybe he could harm other men with the help of his allies? But whom? Not the faithful. As for the unbelievers, who are already his slaves, the devil either can or cannot harm them. If the former is true, what is the need for sorcerers? If the latter is the case then he would not be able to do so with the help of sorcerers either. Perhaps the devil makes

Nor on the part of the devil.

51. That is, presumably, between those rendered effective by faith and those not.

a pact because a twofold obligation binds more firmly than a single one, so that the sorcerer cannot escape as easily as if he were only a slave of his sinful desires? But this agrees neither with the nature of mankind nor with that which our people themselves say about witches and sorcerers (see Spizelius, 3rd part), because [they say] sorcerers can retrieve their signature from the devil without too much effort. In addition, one should consider the nature of mankind, that is, how difficult it is for a person, even a Christian, to master his desires. I will pass over some other reasons, which I will save for another occasion.

The origin of the fable of the crime of sorcery is explained, and it is shown why one ought to begin with the doctrines of the Greeks.

37. Now I must also investigate the source of the fable of witches and sorcerers. Becker has already commented extensively on this in the first book of his *Enchanted World,* as has van Dale in his writings which have been mentioned several times. Yet they did this in such a way that others might still augment and perhaps improve their opinions. I consider it advisable to examine this question briefly in the following way. If one divides them according to their religion, all nations in the entire world are either pagans, Jews, Christians, or Turks. There is no need for an extensive investigation of the Turks, in part because their religion is composed of the first three, in part because it was the last to emerge. Thus an examination of their ideas on sorcery will not contribute much to showing the origin of the error among Christians. But paganism and Judaism are more ancient than Christianity, and the first Christians, especially after the death of Christ, had been either pagans or Jews. Thus it is reasonable that I deal with these two first. If it were true that sorcery did indeed exist, then the Jewish doctrine in Scripture should be presented first. Since this is not the case and I am now investigating the origin of this error, and since the Jewish fables are taken from the books of the Rabbis[52] who lived long after the pagan writers whose writings we still possess, it would be better to consider first the opinions of the pagans. As for pagan philosophy, we can divide it into two kinds, the

52. Here Thomasius is referring to the Talmud, completed in the fifth century and the most important collection of doctrines and traditions for postbiblical Judaism.

Barbarian and the Greek. The former is older than the latter. Since we know very little about the former, and what we do know is uncertain, and since the books of the Greeks are widely available and the first Christians were mostly Greeks—and, moreover, since in the New Testament the Greeks frequently stand for all pagans and are contrasted with the Jews—I should begin with the Greeks.

38. I will leave aside skeptical philosophy, because it contributes less than nothing to my endeavor.[53] The skeptics questioned the existence of all visible things and, more than all other sects, were disposed toward atheism rather than superstition. I will also postpone consideration of the mythical or poetic philosophy of the Greeks,[54] and now will deal only with dogmatic philosophy. But since even this is subdivided into several sects, I will leave it for another time to show from the works of Laertius and Plutarch the views of Thales and other Ionian philosophers on devils and sorcery and, from Scheffer's *Italian Philosophy*, the views of the Pythagoreans.[55] My present concern is with the four main sects that were

Their views on devils in corporeal form and on their commerce with men.

53. According to tradition, the school of skeptical philosophy was founded by the Greek Pyrrho (ca. 360–270 B.C.). It opposed all "dogmatic" schools by arguing that nothing can be known with certainty. In his *Introductio ad philosophiam aulicam* (Introduction to court-philosophy) (1688) Thomasius calls the skeptics the "enemies of the philosophy."

54. The "poetic philosophy" of the Greeks is represented by the poetry of Homer (lived at the end of the eighth century) and Hesiod (lived around 700 B.C.). Early modern thinkers found philosophical themes in mythological and poetic form in the *Iliad* and the *Odyssey* of Homer and the *Theogonia* of Hesiod.

55. Diogenes Laertius's biographical history of ancient Greek philosophy, *Lives and Opinions of Eminent Philosophers* (first half of the third century A.D.), had been rediscovered and republished in 1533. It had a lasting influence on the conception of the history of ancient philosophy. Plutarch (ca. 50–125), a Greek philosopher and historian, was a prominent representative of Middle Platonism. Thomasius refers here to his *Lives* of famous Greeks and Romans. The Ionian Philosophers were a group of early Greek philosophers who were interested in the basic principles of nature and the originating substances of matter. Thales of Miletus (ca. 624–ca. 547 B.C.) is traditionally considered the first one of them and as such the first Greek philosopher in a strict sense. Johann Scheffer (1621–79) was professor of rhetoric and politics at the University of Uppsala and librarian to the Swedish queen. Here Thomasius is referring to Scheffer's *De naturae & constitutione philosophiae italicae seu Pythagoricae librum* (Of the nature and the constitution of Italian philosophy, or a

flourishing in the old Roman Empire when Christianity first emerged: namely, the Epicurean, Stoic, Platonic, and Aristotelian.[56] The Epicureans, as well as all past and present followers of corpuscularian philosophy,[57] provide no opportunity for superstitious belief in witches and sorcerers, since most of those in the past denied the existence of any spirits, while those in the present do believe in a devil, but are indeed far removed from a superstitious belief in magic. Nor do I believe that any Epicurean philosopher has ever converted to Christianity. The Stoic and Platonic philosophers, however, flourished especially during the early period of Christianity, and the church fathers of the first centuries adhered to these two sects in particular, although Aristotelian philosophy cannot be wholly excluded. In a future work on this subject I will show what is characteristic of each of these three. In the meantime, we should note that it was a common superstition of the pagans, especially among the Platonists and Stoics, to believe in the existence of higher, lower, and intermediate gods; and further to believe that between divine and human nature there were many other intermediate substances, which they usually called spirits (*Daemonia*) and divided into good and evil ones. In order to establish their special authority among the people, these philosophers also ascribed to the spirits various effects in soothsaying and magic. However, they did not acknowledge the existence of a third and distinct satanic form of soothsaying and magic. Instead they subdivided both soothsaying and magic into two categories, that is, natural and artificial. In order to deceive the common people, they made use of all kinds of superstitious ceremonies for both types and pretended to be in communion with the gods and the intermediate substances, the spirits. The Stoics also attributed some form of corporeal being to these spirits.

---

book on the Pythagorians) (Uppsala, 1664). A second edition appeared in Wittenberg in 1701. The followers of Pythagoras (ca. 580–ca. 500 B.C.) founded a society in southern Italy that was both a religious community and a scientific school.

56. Thomasius followed tradition by dividing ancient philosophy into four main "sects," or schools, founded by Epicurus (341–271 B.C.), Zeno (ca. 336–ca. 264 B.C.), Plato (427–347 B.C.), and Aristotle (384–322 B.C.). See Thomasius, *Introductio ad philosophiam aulicam,* chap. I, §17.

57. See note 24 in this chapter.

39. Among the various Jewish sects flourishing at the time of Christ (I will also discuss these more extensively in a future work) the Pharisees, who enjoyed a great popular reputation, were the most superstitious.[58] As we can see from the writings of Philo[59] and of the rabbis, the Pharisees deceived the Jewish people by telling them innumerable tales of evil spirits, or of the devils and their powers, of the arch-devil Sammael and his mother Lilis, of the efficacy of letters, names, and numbers against devils—ideas they presented in their Kabbalah[60] or esoteric doctrine—and also of the divinity of Batkol[61] and many other similar fables. Like many pagans, they attributed bodies to devils, or the power to assume such, and the capacity to harm humans physically, to have sexual intercourse with them, and hence to form certain pacts and unions with them.

This particular doctrine was also fashionable among the Pharisees.

40. Although, for many reasons and over many doctrines, the Jews and Greeks among the new Christians came into conflict soon after the death of Christ, and all later heresies have their origin in these disagreements, nevertheless, neither the Greek nor the Latin fathers (even after they had suppressed the Jews in the fourth century) dismissed the Jewish doctrines, as long as these conformed to the superstitions of Greek philosophy, in particular to those of Platonic and Stoic philosophy. Most of the fathers were addicted to one of the two sects, and it is well known from Augustine's *City of God* what esteem and respect Platonic philos-

The blending of the Pharisaic, Platonic, and Stoic teachings by the early church fathers.

58. A Jewish party that emerged in the second century B.C., the Pharisees were scribes influential in the time of Jesus. They tried to harmonize the tradition of oral exegesis of revelation with revelation itself.

59. Philo was a Jewish philosopher who lived in Alexandria between ca. 20 or 15 B.C. and A.D. 42. He combined Platonic philosophy with the Jewish religion.

60. Jewish esoteric mysticism, which appeared in the thirteenth century in the north of Spain and the south of France. The aims of the Kabbalah are unity with God, spiritual knowledge of the last and hidden things, and an earthly messianism. By interpreting individual letters in biblical passages and by using mystical numerology, the Kabbalists claimed to discern the esoteric meaning of any sentence in the Bible.

61. According to the Talmud, Bat Kol is a heavenly voice coming from God and leading men to decisions and insights that are authorized by God.

ophy enjoyed at that time.[62] Among these fathers there were many, especially Lactantius in book 2, *Divin. Inst.*,[63] who found little regarding
devils and their powers in the Bible and yet still wished to teach much
about these things (on the others, such as Athenagoras, Tertullianus, Hieronymus,[64] etc., see Lipsius *Physiol. Stoic.*[65] lib. I). As a result, they
twisted various passages of Scripture toward the devil, even though he
is not mentioned in them, teaching, for example, that the tempting ser-
pent [in the Garden of Eden] was the devil, and that Isaiah's prophecy
regarding the fall of the king of Babylon[66] and references to him as Lu-
cifer should be understood as references to the devil and his apostasy
from God. In part, they silently substituted Jewish, Platonic, and Stoic
fables for the Holy Scriptures. This time also saw the emergence of the
well-known interpretation of Moses's words on the marriage of the children of God with the daughters of man, an interpretation that implied
that the children of God were the angels.[67] And from this intercourse
of angels with women, some have attempted to derive if not the origin
of devils then at least the increase in their numbers. As most reasonable
exegetes of the Holy Scriptures among the Protestants have now dis-

62. Augustine of Hippo (354–430), who began his intellectual life as a Neoplatonist, was converted to Christianity but then used Neoplatonic philosophy to elaborate Christian doctrine, particularly in his seminal *City of God.*

63. Lucius Caelius Lactantius lived from ca. 250 to ca. 335. His *Divinae Institutiones*
(Divine institutes), written between 304 and 313, marks the first attempt to develop
a system of the Christian doctrine.

64. Athenagoras (ca. 133–ca. 190) was a Platonic philosopher who converted to
Christianity and wrote important defenses of Christian belief. Tertullian (ca. 155–
ca. 225) was one of the most innovative theologians prior to Augustine and dealt with
such practical questions as marriage, prayer, and penance. Eusebius Sophronius Hieronymus (a.k.a. St. Jerome, ca. 347–419) was a church father who wrote commentaries on all the books of the Bible, which he also translated into Latin.

65. Justus Lipsius (1547–1606), an influential Dutch humanist and philologist,
taught at the universities of Jena, Cologne, Leiden, and Leuven. Thomasius refers to
Lipsius's *Physiologiae Stoicorum libri tres* (Three books on the physiology of the Stoics) (Antwerpen, 1604).

66. See Isaiah 13–14. The reference to Isaiah's prophecy regarding the king of
Babylon is not in the Latin dissertation, appearing first in the 1704 German translation.

67. See 1 Genesis 6:4.

carded this false interpretation of Moses's statement about the marriage of angels with humans, so they should have dismissed also the erroneous conclusions that were drawn later from this cardinal error. For it seems to me that all false beliefs about witchcraft and about pacts and relations between the devil and humans, about *incubi* and *succubi*,[68] can be ascribed to this false doctrine about the intercourse of angels with humans. I purposely ignore the many fables about the apparition of the devil in a physical form that are included in the lives of Paul and Anthony.[69] Many Lutherans regard these as true stories, although Erasmus[70] has already noted that the entire book is nothing but fiction which emerged from Hieronymus's brain.

41. As Protestants must admit, when schools and academies were rebuilt after the age of barbarism, superstition reached its highest point in papalism. Even though at that time the scholastic teachers followed Aristotle, who had not followed the Platonic and Stoic philosophers in retailing fables about demons and their bodily efficacy, yet, for many reasons the Scholastics, and especially the so-called Scotists,[71] stupidly accepted everything concerning pacts between devils and sorcerers. Since they wanted to claim that their teachings were Catholic, it was necessary for them to obtain the consensus of the church fathers of the first centuries. These, however, mostly belonged to the Platonic and Stoic schools, and thus the Scholastics had to try to reconcile Platonic and Stoic philosophy with Aristotelianism (although this necessarily involved the greatest foolishness). They also used false miracles to strengthen belief in their papalist superstitions. The old tales about the pacts between sorcerers and the devil were best suited for this. Sometimes

Why, during the restoration of the universities by the papalist theologians, they canonized these Platonic and Stoic fables about commerce between demons and men, even though they adhered to Aristotelian philosophy. Various reasons are canvassed.

68. *Incubi* and *succubi* are, respectively, male and female demons, with whom witches were supposed to have sexual intercourse.

69. Hieronymus (St. Jerome) wrote imaginary lives of St. Anthony and St. Paul of Thebes, probably as illustrations of the monastic life.

70. Erasmus of Rotterdam (1469–1536), theologian and leading humanist in Europe, edited St. Jerome's *Opera omnia*, 9 vols. (Basel, 1516–20).

71. Followers of John Duns Scotus (1265–1308), a scholastic metaphysician who taught in Oxford, Paris, and Cologne.

the papalist clerics themselves invented such sorcerers, whom they then converted. At other times they invented various diseases and fooled people into believing that these were caused by witches and sorcerers, and then by curing them, went on to produce even more miracles, through which they gained authority among the common people. Indeed, the tale of pacts with the devil served another purpose: when a pious and honest man who was a thorn in the side of the clerics for whatever reasons (for who can number all the reasons for which one could cause the displeasure of the clerics), but who behaved cautiously so that they could not touch him under the pretext of an error in doctrine, or of heresy, then there was no better means of bringing him to the stake than to cast the suspicion of the crime of sorcery on him. Then, through cruel torture and torment, he was compelled to make a forced confession and confirm innumerable lies invented by the papalist clerics, including the pacts between the devil and sorcerers.

The civil laws do not mention pacts between the devil and man. The L. 4. C. de Malef. & Mathem. is freed of iniquity.

42. When Justinian's civil law[72] began to flourish at its universities, Italy was full of superstitions. In it are a number of laws about the punishment of poisoners and astrologers, particularly in the title of the Code *de Malef. & Mathem.*[73] Astrology was hated so much because many superstitious people consulted astrologers about the death of emperors. This was probably the main reason why philosophers, and among them particularly the Platonists and Stoics, were expelled from the entire Roman Empire during the time of Emperor Augustus.[74] It is also why Constantine the Great,[75] despite consulting astrologers, was afraid of them and enacted special laws for their punishment. As far as the rest of superstitious magic was concerned, Constantine in L. 4 Cod. wanted sorcerers to be punished if they harmed someone or incited forbidden lust. But he never regarded as punishable the superstition that cured various

72. See note 34 in this chapter.

73. See *Corpus juris civilis,* title 18 in bk. 9 of the *Codex Justiniani: De Maleficiis et Mathematicis et ceteris similibus* (On sorcerers, astrologers, and others similar).

74. Augustus (63 B.C.E.–14 C.E.) was the first Roman emperor, ruling from 31 B.C.E. to 14 C.E.

75. Constantine the Great (b. between 274 and 288), Roman emperor 306–37.

diseases and performed other feats. Even though (just to mention it in passing) he is generally not much praised for this law—and I myself do not approve of either the superstition or the rationale of the law—I do see that Constantine did nothing wrong in refusing to sanction the civil punishment of those who had not harmed others, because it is preferable that such vices be remedied through teaching and instruction rather than judicial punishments. Meanwhile, it is clear that the Christian bishops of that time did not believe that sorcerers formed pacts with the devil, for otherwise they would not have allowed the emperor—who did almost nothing without the approval of the clerics—to draw this distinction between good and bad sorcery in the above-mentioned law.

43. From tender youth, the civil law glossators had been contaminated by priestly teachings that were advanced with greatest urgency by the canon lawyers,[77] and among which the doctrine of pacts between the devil and witches was not the least important. Thus, despite disagreeing with the canonists over certain doctrines, the civil glossators propagated the usual errors through forced interpretations of civil law. The standard doctrine on the crime of sorcery thus did not derive from Justinian law but arose from the common prejudices of the glossators. They propagated the prejudice that because sorcery was a species of the crime of *lèse-majesté* it was an extraordinary offense, heinous and occult, the slightest signs of which were enough to justify torture; for example, if someone accused of this crime named another person. It was further

The reasons why the Italian commentators on the civil law[76] included so many erroneous doctrines regarding the crime of witchcraft in their glosses.

76. The school of the glossators was founded by Irnerius (ca. 1055–ca. 1130), a jurist and philologist who founded the Bologna School of Law. Through their commentaries on the Roman legal texts the glossators expanded and adapted them to deal with contemporary problems. The *Glossa ordinaria* of Accursius (ca. 1185–1263) was a particularly influential example of this practice.

77. The canons (from the Greek *canon*, or rule) were the laws of the church. The monk Gratian collected all the church laws enacted since the councils of the fourth century and published them in 1140 in his *Concordantia discordantium canonum* (The concord of discordant canons). Gratian created with his so-called *Decretum Gratiani* the basis for the latter *Corpus juris canonici,* which contains not only the collection of Gratian but also the *Decretals* and the *Extravagantes.* The *Corpus juris canonici* was promulgated by Pope Gregory XIII in 1592.

argued that because this and similar crimes justified even worse torments, those who had been found guilty could be sentenced after their
death, and that it was no injustice to confiscate the property of such a
person, regardless of the fact that the most recent constitution of Justinian does not agree with it; see among others Anton, Matth. *de Crimin.*
lib. 48, tit. 2, cap. 1 n. 2, & tit. 5, cap. 7. n. 13.[78]

Origin and
progress, in
Germany prior
to the Refor-
mation, of the
view regarding
the crime of
sorcery that
sorcerers
should be
punished by
burning even
if they are
innocent.

44. What the Germans from the times of Tacitus[79] thought of the crime
of sorcery will be discussed more extensively on a different occasion. For
now it will be enough if we learn from the strength of today's superstition—which is not confined to the German nations given to Catholicism but still remains among the Protestants—just how firmly the papalist clerics prior to the Reformation sought to persuade so many people
of their fables regarding the crime of sorcery. There is thus no doubt
that prior to the foundation of the universities, the Germans believed
that sorcerers entered into pacts with the devil, so that even after their
foundation the glossators' view of this found easy acceptance. Anyone
who wants to know more about this should open the book entitled *Malleus Malleficarum* or the *Witches' Hammer.* In it, a papal bull on sorcerers
precedes the first part and deals with the question of how this depraved
heresy should be punished by the Inquisition in Germany.[80] This view-

78. Antonius Matthaeus (1601–54) taught Roman law in the Netherlands; see his
De criminibus, ad lib. XLVII et XLVIII dig. commentarius (Utrecht, 1644). For a recent English translation, see M. L. Hewett and B. C. Stoop, *On Crimes, a Commentary on Books XLVII and XLVIII of the Digest by Antonius Matthaeus* (Cape Town:
Juta, 1987–96).

79. Cornelius Tacitus (ca. 55–120) was a Roman historian who wrote an ethno-
graphical study of Germany that played an important role in political discussion in
early modern Europe.

80. See Heinrich Kramer and James Sprenger, *Malleus Maleficarum* (ca. 1486/87).
In English, *Malleus Maleficarum: The Hammer of Witchcraft,* trans. M. Summers
(1928; repr. New York: Dover, 1971). Kramer (1430?–1505), a Dominican, was the
zealous inquisitor for Tyrol, Salzburg, Bohemia, and Moravia. Sprenger (1436/38–
1494), likewise a Dominican, was the inquisitor extraordinary for Mainz, Trèves, and
Cologne. Their activities were authorized by Pope Innocent VIII, whose bull *Summis
desiderantes affectibus* of December 1484 prefaced the book. *Malleus Malleficarum*
defines the four elements of the crime of sorcery: the contract with the devil (*pactum*

point, however, is not expressly stated in the laws, and should rather be considered part of general opinion and of unwritten law. Thus it is written in the second book, Artic. 13, *Land-Recht* [territorial law]: *Any Christian man or woman who is an unbeliever, or who engages in sorcery or in poisoning and who is captured, should be burned at the stake.* Although these words refer only to harmful sorcerers they were interpreted more broadly by the Leipzig lay assessors to be applicable whether sorcerers have done harm or not, as Carpzov explains in his forty-ninth question on criminal law, n. 8.[81] Indeed, the author of Charles V's penal code, who must obviously have been either a German or Italian jurist,[82] did not include anything explicit in the statutes regarding those sorcerers who were supposed to have made pacts with the devil. On the contrary, he apparently repeated the short pronouncement of the Justinian Code, with its distinction between harmful and nonharmful sorcery, but ascribed an arbitrary punishment to the latter. In the 109th article he says that if someone causes harm or some disadvantage to others through sorcery, then they should be punished with death and the punishment should be executed by fire. However, when someone engages in witchcraft but does not harm anybody, he should be punished as befits the occasion, and the judges should seek council, as is explained later in a passage concerning seeking advice. If we examine it according to the rules of good interpretation, then this author's view is that those who have not caused any harm through their sorcery should be punished more leniently, not with burning at the stake or some other capital punishment. Although the author of the code did not say anything about

---

cum daemone), harm caused by sorcery (*maleficium*), sexual intercourse with the devil (*coitus cum diabolo*), and the participation at the witches' Sabbath.

81. Here Thomasius is outlining a crucial expansion of the scope of the crime, from causing actual harm—for example, by poisoning or causing illness—to worship of the devil. This change brought sorcery and witchcraft closer to heresy.

82. The penal code of Emperor Charles V, the *Constitutio Criminalis Carolina*, was law for the whole of the German Empire. It was promulgated in 1532 in Regensburg and based on the progressive *Constitutio Criminalis Bambergensis* (1507). The latter was written by Johann von Schwarzenberg, the president of the Episcopal court of justice in Bamberg, and by his collaborators who were—in contrast to Schwarzenberg—learned jurists educated in Italy.

pacts with the devil, and it is likely that he did not consider such pacts to be true, nevertheless, according to their custom of squeezing something from anything [*quidlibet ex quodlibet*], the exegetes have declared the other case in the penal code to be harmful sorcery too. According to them, one should consider not only the question of whether anybody was harmed but other circumstances as well; that is, whether the witches made a pact with the devil, or whether they had sexual intercourse with him. These are all circumstances that require punishment by fire. See also Carpzov, op. cit. n. 7.[83]

This was continued after the Reformation by jurists of both Protestant confessions.

45. One might think that Luther's Reformation, which had liberated people from so much papalist superstition, would also have freed them from this monks' and priests' babble about the pact of sorcerers with the devil. But nothing like this happened. On the contrary, this charming opinion, which had previously been considered an unwritten law, was incorporated into the *Constitutiones Electorale* P. IV. Constit. 2 under the government of the Elector August [of Saxony][84] in the following express words: *If someone, forgetful of his Christian faith, forms pacts with the devil, or has anything to do with him, then this person should be punished and executed by being burned at the stake, even if they have not harmed anyone through sorcery.* Since the Elector of Saxony was also one of the most prominent Lutheran princes, it is no wonder that this common fantasy was later spread to other Lutheran and even Calvinist territories. The reason for this may be either that Luther himself still believed many prejudices about the might and power of Satan, as has been illustrated both in his writings and, occasionally, from his *Table-talk*. Or it may be because Philipp Melanchthon[85] firmly reestablished scholastic theology and philosophy in Protestant universities after Luther's death, for when

83. Carpzov, *Practica nova,* pt. I, qu. 48, §7, p. 308.
84. August was Elector of Saxony from 1553 to 1586.
85. Philipp Melanchthon (1497–1560) was a philologist and theologian who taught at the University of Wittenberg. He was a friend of Martin Luther but nevertheless an independent reformer who tried to harmonize humanism with the aims of Protestant Reformation. Because of his engagement in the reorganization of schools and universities he was called the "teacher of Germany."

it came to philosophy the Lutherans considered him to be Germany's teacher [*praeceptor Germaniae*], while the Calvinists were favorably disposed toward him, because in their theological quarrels with other Lutherans his views seemed quite similar to their own. Or perhaps the cause was that several Protestant theologians had developed a taste for the benefits that they could derive from this falsehood, just as we saw above had occurred with the papalist theologians. Or perhaps it was just that Lutheran jurists had grown used to copying their treatises on criminal law from the judgments of papalist doctors.

46. These are the reasons why so many trials against witches took place after the Reformation, not only under papal authority, but also among Protestants in Europe. The Lutherans in particular staged many strange and gruesome spectacles, above all because those who should have better informed the judges' consciences instead used to whip the magistrate and judges into a frenzy, partly for reasons of state, partly from good intentions, and partly out of simple-minded piety. In the preface to his frequently mentioned treatise, Spizelius himself praises and commends the judges who diligently conduct witch trials. Writing about himself, he says that he has for many years considered himself to be under a strong obligation to further such beneficial work to the best of his ability. If one heard inhabitants of Lower Saxony and Sweden talk about this, one would learn what great havoc these witch trials and the intemperate zeal for the honor of God had caused there. I remember a credible man who happened to be traveling through Germany and who had himself been an assessor at the courts which the king of Sweden had established against witches. He told me how he and other assessors quickly noticed that there was no basis to initiate an inquisition[86] against the accused,

The multitude of witch trials in Lutheran regions. Spizelius's zeal and the inappropriateness and outcome of a trial in Sweden.

86. The inquisition was the main part of a witch trial, which started with a denunciation. Everybody was obliged to denounce people who were suspected of witchcraft. After the denunciation the judge initiated the judicial proceedings with an inquisition designed to obtain a confession from the accused person. As the interrogators were able to use unrestricted torture, those accused of witchcraft had little choice but to confess to the crime and to denounce others for participating in the witches' Sabbath. As a result, each witch trial produced a chain of other trials. Tho-

since there was no other sign or indication than the fantastic statements of some immature adolescent boys. Nonetheless the clerics kept the upper hand by pretending that the Holy Ghost, who was always eager to preserve the honor of God against the kingdom of the devil, would never have allowed these boys to lie. To this end, the priests quoted the words from the psalm: *Out of the mouth of babes and sucklings hast thou ordained strength because of thine enemies, that thou mightest still the enemy and the avenger.*[87] Finally, after many innocent people had been burned at the stake and one of the boys had accused an honorable man of participating in the debauchery, one of the secular assessors at last tried to tempt the boy with the knowledge of the other assessors. He offered the boy half a taler to admit he had erred and to denounce someone other than the accused. When that was easily achieved and the theologians clearly saw that the Holy Ghost did not speak through the child, the court usher chastised the accusing boys with rods, and the trial was closed, even though this was all too late, since so many innocent people had already been burned alive. That the Swedish inquisition was also based on nothing but pernicious fairy tales can be recognized easily by anyone who reads without prejudice the published description, which Spizelius includes in the first part of his treatise, chapter 17, pp. 172ff. And this is so, even though the author wrote this description in order to support the common viewpoint and Spizelius included it in his treatise for the same reason. If anything is remarkable here, though, it is that which Spizelius quotes from the said author on p. 187 and following, where it is clearly shown that the most innocent persons were denounced by these boys.

Reasons why the multitude of trials is

47. Such has been the situation with witch trials in Germany until today. In the Netherlands, however, some of the Reformed theologians went over to Cartesian philosophy, which is opposed to the doctrine of spirits

---

masius attacked the use of inquisition in witch trials in a special disputation, *De Origine ac Progressu Processus Inquisitorii contra Sagas* (On the origin and progress of inquisitorial proceedings against witches) (Halle, 1712).

87. See Psalms 8:2.

taught in Platonic and scholastic philosophy. Thus, just as among the Reformed in the Netherlands—especially the non-Voetians[88]—so too among Germans with whom they had frequent contact, a gentler attitude began to appear, and a view in much closer agreement with sound reason, so that now we do not hear so much of witch trials. As many German theologians and jurists have already discarded most old prejudices, there is thus hope that this one will soon be rejected as well. And even if we do not adhere to Cartesian philosophy—because his views on spirit incline to the other extreme, as is clear to many—it is enough to say that through this philosophy the fantasies of the Scholastics, including the imaginary crime of sorcery, were eliminated from many universities. Nor is it to be feared that they will regain their former reputation in the territories of the Protestant princes.

now coming to an end and why one should hope for better times.

48. Since a true *corpus delicti* was never found for this crime,[89] it follows automatically that a probable proof cannot exist. A matter that does not exist cannot have a proof. And even assuming that a thousand witches had confessed to everything that Carpzov had listed in the sentences included in his fiftieth question on criminal law,[90] it is obvious to everyone that they did not confess voluntarily. On the contrary, everything was either supplied by the judges or was extracted from them through cruel and horrible torture. Assuming, too, that a thousand witches had confessed this voluntarily and freely (though I worry whether ten who were guilty could be found among the myriads who were consigned to the flames), I ask, which judge could be so absurd and foolish as to believe a thousand women were they to declare unanimously, for example, that they had been to heaven, had danced with St. Peter, or slept with his hunting dogs. For the depositions collected regarding witches are stupider than these claims—but I will not say that they are more laughable,

There has never been a corpus delicti in a witch trial. Therefore it is superfluous to deal with the proofs for this crime.

88. Followers of Gisbertus Voetius; see note 11 in this chapter.

89. In a strict sense the *corpus delicti* is the body or the thing that is injured by a criminal act. In a broader sense the *corpus delicti* is any perceptible element of a criminal offense. Thomasius argues that as concrete evidence of harm cannot be adduced for charges of sorcery, the crime is impossible to prove.

90. Carpzov, *Practica nova*, pt. I, qu. 50, pp. 326–43.

as the cruelty of witch trials occasions only sadness. This makes it easy
to answer the common excuse of our jurists who say that in such hidden
and transitory crimes as adultery, whoring, sodomy, heresy, poisoning,
and divination it is not possible to provide a *corpus delicti* otherwise than
through conjectures and signs, so that presumptions and speculations
must replace full proof; see Carpzov's 119th question, number 61.[91] In
these other crimes one occasionally has a *corpus delicti* whose existence
no reasonable person could doubt. But since a *corpus delicti* has never
existed in any case of sorcery, this crime cannot be compared with the
others.

The unlawful,
false signs
of sorcery.

49. In this way everything the jurists used to teach about signs of sorcery
is also automatically invalid. There are two kinds of signs. Some are
based on imperial public law—that is, the criminal code—while others
have been added by jurists. With regard to the latter, I do not think them
worthy to be mentioned here because they are solely based on the authority of papalist inquisitors and for the above reasons have no validity.
Nonetheless, Protestant jurists consider them to be true and unthink-
ingly incorporated them into their commentaries. I will now cite only
Christoph Crusius as an example that demonstrates how obsessively he
compiled such absurdities in his treatise, *De Indiciis Delictorum Specialibus,* chap. 32, and how zealously he tried to defend them.[92] To refute
everything now would be a vain task, because such trivial and uncertain
signs were recently snubbed in an inaugural dissertation at this university. In addition, the author of the *Cautio Criminalis*[93] explicitly refuted
these signs.

It is com-
pletely absurd
that external

50. I cannot refrain, though, from touching on the fact that it is also
considered to be a particular indication of sorcery if the accused person displays conspicuous signs of piety, as can be seen in the above-

91. Carpzov, *Practica nova,* pt. III, qu. 119, §60, p. 174.
92. Christoph Crusius, *Tractatus de indiciis delictorum specialibus* (Treatise on the
specific proofs of crimes) (Frankfurt, 1635).
93. That is, Friedrich Spee; see note 16 in this chapter.

mentioned book by Crusius, 102ff. The apostle [Paul] says that piety is beneficial for everything. Nonetheless, such individuals [as Crusius] declare it to be an indication of the most abominable and serious crime. Could a reasonable person dream of or imagine such an argument? Indeed, they say, this is a hypocritical, not true piety. First, assuming this were true, would it be an indication of witchcraft? Hypocrisy is a vice, to which all people are prone, and primarily those who are devoted to an honorable lifestyle, either by habit or by nature. If all of those leading a wicked life considered all honest people to be sorcerers because of a slight or even serious suspicion of false piety, who could tolerate this without just anger? But it is simply not true that the outward demonstration of great piety is a sign of hypocrisy. Such a profession of piety cannot thus be a sufficient indication of sorcery, so that another sign must be found to strengthen these pseudo-indications. Meanwhile, those suspected of sorcery on these grounds need only appeal to this popular verse for their defense: *Omnia dum liceant, non licet esse pium.* This means: everything is permitted except for piety. This ridiculous proof of sorcery instead confirms what we have already observed in paragraph 41: namely, that papal clerics invented the vice of sorcery so that under the pretext of justice and divine zeal they could eliminate those pious people they despised. If someone desires to see a specific example of the malevolence of papalist clerics, he can read about it in the entire French treatise called the *Histoire des diables de Loudun*[94] and in Becker's *Enchanted World,* chapter II of book IV. He will certainly not be able to do so without being horrified. If someone reads with similar care the fable of the terrible sorcery of Ludovicus Godofredus—included by Franciscus Rossetus in the *Sad Events of His Time,* and by Martin Zeiler,

demonstrations of piety should be a sign of sorcery.

---

94. See Nicolas Aubin (b. 1655), *Histoire des Diables de Loudun ou de la possession des Réligieuses Ursulines et de la condemnation et du Supplice d'Urbain Grandier* (Amsterdam, 1693). A Dutch translation appeared in 1694 in Utrecht and an English one in 1703: *The Cheats and Illusions of Romish Priests and Exorcists. Discover'd in the history of the devils of Loudon, being an account of the pretended possession of the Ursuline nuns, and of the Condemnation and punishment of Urban Grandier a parson of the same town* (London).

having translated it from French, in his *Sad Murder Stories*[95]—he will quickly realize that Spizelius had no reason to refer to this story so many times in his often-mentioned book. For in Rossetus's description itself there are many circumstances which suggest that Ludovicus Godofredus was an honest and pious man whom the clerics condemned as a sorcerer out of pure hatred and jealousy, and that they had earlier arranged everything in such a way that a woman had to make a false accusation against him. I will save everything else that could be said here for a future work.

The signs of sorcery listed in the penal code of the emperor Charles V are also inadequate.

51. Now I must also look at the signs of sorcery that are included in the penal code of Charles V. The words from article 44 are: *If someone offers to teach sorcery to other people, or threatens to perform magic, and the person, who has been threatened suffers accordingly, or keeps close company with sorcerers and witches, or has to do with suspicious things, gestures, words, and beings, which seem related to sorcery, and is known for sorcery, then this is a serious sign of witchcraft and offers sufficient cause for a criminal investigation.*

1. If someone offers to instruct others in sorcery.

52. These signs would be of some importance and not to be easily dismissed, if it had been proven that the crime of sorcery does actually exist. However, since this has not been done so far, these proofs must therefore be considered futile and improbable. Let us assume a case where someone has, with sufficient evidence, been proven guilty of offering to teach sorcery to others (even the satanic variety). Should this automatically be a sign that he had made a pact with the devil? I do not think so at all. I have already said above in paragraph 36 that there are many foolish peo-

---

95. François de Rosset (ca. 1570–ca. 1630) was a French man of letters well known as one of the first translators of Cervantes's *Don Quixote*. His book *Les Histoires tragiques de nostre temps* (Tragic stories of our times) was a best-seller, appearing first in 1614 with a further forty editions being published before 1758. Thomasius refers here to the German translation of Martin Zeiler (1589–1661): *Theatrum tragicum, Das ist: Newe Wahrhafftige traurig, kläglich und wunderliche Geschichten die wegen Zauberey, Diebstal, unnd Rauberey . . . sich vor wenig Iaren mehrertheils in Franckreich zugetragen haben* (Tübingen, 1628).

ple who long to make a pact with the devil and I have no doubt that there will be malicious individuals who will try to cheat such fools and take their money. They might offer to act as middlemen in making a pact and in order to fulfill their promise, and they might persuade others to represent the devil. Although these and similar events may occur quite frequently, it does not follow that they who do this are sorcerers and that sorcery actually exists. I do not praise these people and I do not excuse them either. I freely admit that both the trickster and his victim should be severely punished. But I am also saying that one cannot punish them for sorcery, and that this kind of deed is not a sufficient sign of sorcery.

53. I myself do not understand this second sign. Who would be so foolish and threaten another person with sorcery? And if someone did threaten to do harm to another person's life, health, or belongings, then these threats do not signify a harm coming about through actual sorcery and a pact with the devil. Even if someone explicitly threatened to harm another person through sorcery, how can one be so certain that the harm actually was the result of sorcery, since no such thing exists? If it is known and obvious that the person who uttered these threats did harm to another through mere natural or mortal means, then to this extent he cannot be considered a sorcerer. If there is only a suspicion that the harm he caused others was through secret means, then one still cannot accuse him of sorcery, in part because it remains doubtful whether he was responsible, in part because these secret means are not necessarily acts of the devil. For there is much hidden in nature with which one can harm another person without the help of the devil. These miraculous effects are undoubtedly based on the magnetic power of nature, but neither the Aristotelians, nor the Cartesians can explain them. But we encounter the ancient refuge of academic ignorance when it is argued that whatever effects have not been proved by university physics, and cannot be properly ascribed to God, must necessarily be attributed to the devil.

2. The threat to cause injury through sorcery.

54. Concerning the third sign, that is, the consorting with witches and sorcerers, the question remains unresolved. Where there are no witches and sorcerers, no one can consort with them. Even if I admitted the

3. Consorting with sorcerers and witches.

existence of witches, consorting would be no proof of anything, because there could be many reasons for it; for example, friendship, neighborliness, a common upbringing, a desire for profit, a similar social status, and countless other reasons why someone would associate with a sorcerer. Would one consider all those to be adulterers, tricksters, gluttons who keep company with these kinds of people? Indeed, there is a well-known proverb: *Noscitur ex socio, qui non cognoscitur ex se,* that is, if there is someone you cannot get to know, you can get to know him through the company he keeps. But it is common knowledge that proverbs such as these are insufficient evidence to have someone tortured. Otherwise one would also have to follow the proverb: *Solus cum sola non praesumitur orare Pater noster,* that is, it is hard to believe that when a man and a woman are alone together they are reciting the Lord's prayer, with the consequence that any man found alone with a woman should be tortured as well. It is true that these proverbs arise because of what usually happens, but they commonly hide a multitude of other circumstances not expressed in the proverb. Primarily, however, the proverb quoted above fails concerning the conclusions to be drawn from the company a person keeps. If, for example, I did not know, among other things, that Titius was suspected of a vice and I still associated with him until this became apparent, why should this be held against me? Yet sorcery is regarded as a hidden vice. If someone associates with a person at a time when he passed as an honest man, and if this person is later accused of sorcery and convicted in a general trial, then would it not be a great absurdity to suspect someone of the same crime just because of this association? And it seems that the verse can hardly be referring to someone who has been accused of witchcraft. For either he has already been sentenced to death or else acquitted due to insufficient signs. If he has been sentenced, then it is unlikely that anyone would associate with such a person, because it is difficult to find an example of a sorcerer condemned to death who was pardoned. But if he is acquitted, even if this happened due to lack of evidence, why should a person who associated with him be suspected of sorcery when even the judges did not consider him to be a sorcerer? There are many other things I am not going to address here.

55. The fourth proof—that is, if someone uses things, words, and facial expressions that lead to the suspicion of sorcery—is so general, confused, and obscure that the author of the penal code of Charles V should have been ashamed to admit such an uncertain sign in such an important matter, thereby giving inquisitors the opportunity to include everything, even the most absurd matters, under this category. For, in elaborating the general and specific indications of crimes, it is rare for those who comment on the indications of other crimes to depart too far from the prescriptions of the penal code and multiply the indications. Since, however, they generally do this with regard to witchcraft, it seems likely that these commentators were seduced into this error because they were led to believe that through this or that sign a new case had been uncovered through which a fourth sign could be declared, and so on; for example, if someone under inquisition were found to have a pot filled with toads, human limbs, a book of magic spells, and suchlike, or if such were found under the entrance of a house or barn where it might infect people, and so on; see Crusius chapter 32, number 4. From these and similar matters it is often concluded that there is a case of sorcery and that these signs are sufficient proof that someone is a sorcerer, even though neither is true.

4. If someone uses suspect magical objects.

56. How cautious does a judge have to be in trials against witches so that the innocent will not be punished? The author of the *Cautio Criminalis* or *Precaution in Criminal Cases*[96] listed and recommended many different precautions (in qu. 16ff.), pretending to believe in the crime of sorcery. However, since these are still subject to numerous abuses, they must be examined elsewhere. As for me, because I hold the crime of sorcery to be a fable, I offer only a single caution. The prince should never permit judicial inquisition into the crime of magic, that is, into pacts with the devil—the harm someone might do through occult magic, either natural or artificial, is not the issue here—and the lower court judges should never execute such an inquisition. And although I am not unaware of

The sole caution regarding witch trials: the prince should not permit trials and lower court judges should not conduct inquiries into the crime of sorcery.

96. That is, Friedrich Spee; see note 16 in this chapter.

the fact that the intermediate authorities must execute the authority of the commonwealth's sovereign power, and that they cannot improve or abrogate received laws and mores, I am convinced that there will never be sufficient indications for an inquisition. Further, when the lower court judge allows persons accused of witchcraft to defend themselves in order to avert inquisition, I believe that he should be able to protect himself and his procedure adequately through the law itself and through that which it prescribes regarding the indications of crime.

THE END

On the Right of a Christian Prince
in Religious Matters

In the appendix to the *Historia contentionis inter Imperium & Sacerdo-*   **Foreword**[1]
tium (chap. I, §55, p. 453),[2] I mentioned, amongst other things, that in
my public lectures of 1695[3] I had already dictated certain propositions
on the right of a prince in religious affairs, and that I had developed
these in a discourse in which I took on the task of here and there improving and completing Pufendorf's propositions [on this matter].[4]
Now, although I have said that this discourse was in need of riper re-

---

1. Thomasius's "Vom Recht eines Christlichen Fürsten in Religions-Sachen" was
first published in 1724, in the second of three yearbooks of *Gemischte Philosophische
und Juristische Händel* (Miscellaneous philosophical and juristic essays) (Halle, 1723–
25). This was only four years prior to Thomasius's death, yet he records in the foreword that the tract originates in lectures given in 1695, when Thomasius was writing
his other major works on the prince's right in relation to the church, including his
"Right of Protestant Princes Regarding Indifferent Matters or *Adiaphora*" (chapter
2 of this volume).

2. Christian Thomasius, *Historia contentionis inter imperium et sacerdotium* (History of the contention between state and church) (Halle, 1722).

3. Correcting 1595 in the 1724 edition.

4. Samuel Pufendorf (1632–94)—political philosopher and historian, adviser to
the Swedish and Brandenburg courts—was Thomasius's greatest intellectual influence. Thomasius's lectures on church-state relations relied heavily on Pufendorf, and
the central section of the *Right in Religious Matters* (paragraphs 19–51) consists of a
paraphrase of and commentary on the central arguments of Pufendorf's major work
on this theme, *De habitu religionis christianae ad vitam civilem* (On the nature of
religion in relation to civil life) of 1687. Like several other works by Pufendorf, this
was translated into English; see note 13 in chapter 2, above.

flection, until recently I have had no time to undertake many changes to it; but I provide them herein, together with footnotes containing the summary content of the explanations I have advanced on this topic. I have made few changes, among which the most important is the restriction of the title, which now refers to the right of a *Christian* prince. For, although I noted in the *Historia contentionis* (p. 449 and p. 455) that Pufendorf had not distinguished clearly enough between the right of a prince in general and the right of a Christian prince in particular, at that time I had not myself dealt accurately enough with this difference. Some of the propositions to be found herein, however, will lessen this confusion somewhat, especially numbers 63 and following, which deal with the threefold duty of a Christian prince. Further alterations and improvements, which the present propositions might otherwise occasionally require, may be taken in part from the *Historia contentionis* pp. 455–502, and in part from my writings and disputations published from 1699 onward and identified in the *Historia contentionis* on p. 452 and following.

Explanation of the word "prince" 1. By a *prince,* I here understand all persons who exercise supreme power and authority in a commonwealth.

Of "commonwealth" 2. By *commonwealth* I understand a civil society deploying supreme power for the purposes of general peace.

And of "princely rights" 3. The *rights or regalia of the prince* and of the supreme power cannot be conceived in the absence of the right and the power to coerce or to punish[a] the unruly.[b]

Origin of the commonwealth 4. If peace reigned everywhere, then there would be no commonwealth and, consequently, no prince or supreme power.[c]

---

a. Both within the commonwealth and without. From this arises the division of regalia into *immanentia & transeuntia* [internal and transterritorial].

b. For these [regalian rights] are perfect (*perfecta non imperfecta*) and in fact supreme (*summa*) rights, which acknowledge no other man as judge.

c. This follows from number 2. And just as it is said in metaphysics that "if the purpose ceases to exist, so does the action directed to it," so it is also said in political science that "if the purpose [i.e., of society] ceases to exist, so does society itself."

5. Accordingly, there would have been no commonwealth or republic in the state of innocence.

6. For as long as there is discord and unrest in the world as well as lack of piety and mistrust in God, there must also be civil authorities. Once men have ceased to trust in God, the authorities are the divine order, as are the physician and surgeon for as long as men are unhealthy and imperfect.

And how the civil authorities are the divine order

7. Accordingly, who resists the authorities resists God's order.

8. If in this world men were so perfect that everything went peacefully, and there were no need for republics, then this would not be a miserable or disorderly condition.

9. All prerogative rights [*regalien*] of a prince have the preservation of the common peace as their purpose.[a]

10. That conduct of subjects which can neither hinder nor promote the common peace is not subject to the prerogative right of a prince.[b]

Rules determining which conduct of subjects is not subject to the rights of a prince

11. Human conduct that is subject to the will of no man is thus not subject to the will of a prince and, consequently, not subject to his [regalian] rights.

12. Here belongs, for example, that which God has otherwise commanded or forbidden.

13. Also, all conduct of the human understanding, insofar as it has to do with the conception of a thing.[c]

14. The same applies to the evil inclinations that are basic to natural men, not only insofar as they consist in mere thoughts, but also insofar as they

---

a. This follows again from number 2.

b. Becmann provides further instances of subjects' conduct not subject to the rights of the prince, in his *De Jure subditorum circa sacra,* chap. 2. [Johann Christoph Becmann, *Dissertatio de jure subditorum circa sacra* (Dissertation on the right of subjects in religious matters) (Frankfurt an der Oder, 1689).]

c. See Becmann, same dissertation, chap. 2, §2, and chap. 3, §§2 & 4.

are made known through words that do not disturb the common peace; for example, when someone laments or confesses his evil inclinations.

15. In fact this even applies to such inclinations expressed in words and deeds, assuming that this does not jeopardize the external peace of mankind and that no one suffers injustice thereby; for example, when the lustful, ambitious, and avaricious make their desires known through words and deeds, as long as they weaken no one's rights thereby.

16. Further, a man should not tell anyone how he should understand the nature of a thing, or what he should hold to be true; or that he should always speak otherwise than he thinks in matters of knowledge. [a]

17. If a prince wants to extend his right to such matters, then the subjects are not obliged to obey him; yet they are not to oppose him but are bound to tolerate the injustice done to them. [b]

18. There cannot be two supreme powers or authorities in a commonwealth, for this would make it impossible to preserve the common peace. [c]

Rules of religion independent of the republic

19. Before civil society or the commonwealth arose, religion and religious worship already existed. [d]

20. Each person is responsible for his own worship of God, which may not be done through others. [e]

21. For the worship of God, it is not necessary that there be a society. [f]

---

a. See Becmann, *De Jure subditorum circa religion,* chap. 3, §11.

b. Also see below, number 79.

c. The preceding propositions are further clarified in my *Institutiones jurispruden-tiae divinae* (Institutes of divine jurisprudence), bk. I, chap. 1, and bk. 3, chap. 6.

d. Pufendorf, *De habitu religionis ad remp.,* §1. [Samuel Pufendorf, *De habitu religionis christianae ad vitam civilem* (On the relation of the Christian religion to civil life) (Bremen, 1687).]

e. Pufendorf, *De habitu,* §2.

f. Pufendorf, *De habitu,* §3.

22. People who are not subject to civil authority do not have to account for their worship to any man.[a]

23. Parents, however, have always been responsible for raising their children to the worship of God.[b]

24. Yet with teaching, entreaties, and admonition, not with coercion. For religion suffers no coercion.[c]

25. Civil society did not arise from and was not formed for the purpose of religious worship. It does not promote piety, and neither invented religious worship nor requires it as an instrument for ruling subjects.[d]

And after the establishment of the republic

26. Following the establishment of civil society, no people has subordinated its will in religious matters to the civil authorities, nor could it rationally do so.[e]

27. In the preceding propositions, by *worship* and *religion* we have understood the inner fear, reverence, trust, and love of God, so far as each man can recognize his obligation in this regard from the light of nature.[f]

Natural religion

a. Pufendorf, ibid., §3.

b. Pufendorf, ibid., §4.

c. Pufendorf, ibid., §4 & §3. See also Becmann, *De jure subditorum,* chap. 3, §4 and following; special note should be taken though of §13.

d. Pufendorf, *De habitu,* §5.

e. Pufendorf, *De habitu,* §6; even if in this paragraph several things are presented that need explanation or improvement. [Thomasius further explicates Pufendorf's §6 in the commentary on the *De habitu* provided in his *Vollständige Erläuterung der Kirchenrechts-Gelahrtheit* (Complete explanation of ecclesiastical jurisprudence) (Frankfurt and Leipzig: 1740), pt. I, pp. 47–48. Thomasius's main concern is to emphasize that the freedom of citizens in religious matters should not be a pretext for disobedience to the civil authorities. He does this by arguing that obedience to God and to the civil authorities takes place in completely disparate spheres of life, and thus one cannot interfere with the other.]

f. Cf., Pufendorf, §8, and my *Einleitung zur Sitten-Lehre,* chap. 3. [Christian Thomasius, *Einleitung zur Sittenlehre* (Introduction to ethics) (Halle, 1692; repr. Hildesheim, 1995).]

28. This natural religious worship, however, is not adequate for human salvation, and natural reason may not derive it [natural worship] from the external forms of worship displayed in great ceremonies.[a]

Revealed
religion

29. From the beginning, God revealed to man not only what he needed to know in order to attain salvation, but also the kind of external ceremonies by which he wished to be venerated by him.

Various kinds
of true religion

30. According to its origin, true religion[b] is either natural or revealed; according to its operation it is either insufficient[c] or saving; according to its nature, either a matter of belief or of love;[d] and, finally, according to its disposition, it is either internal or external.[e]

God intro-
duced revealed
true religion to
man through
covenants

31. God gave man revealed religion after the Fall, by means of a covenant with him.[f]

a. See my *Institutiones jurisprudentiae divinae,* bk. II, chap. 1.

b. Here I am discussing true religion rather than false. False religion, however, can also be divided up, in a different way. For it is also either natural or revealed; it also consists in matters of belief or of love. Yet in its operation it is not saving but insufficient, in fact damning. Briefly, false religion in fact amounts to blasphemy in matters of faith and idolatry in external worship. This idolatry is of two kinds: either of false gods, or of the true God in a false way. All religions, false and true, are opposed to atheism.

c. That a religion could be true even if insufficient [for salvation], and that one cannot thus declare natural religion false *tout court,* is something I have shown in my *Institutiones jurisprudentiae divinae,* bk. II, chap. 1.

d. By matters of belief, I understand things believed via the intellect; by matters of love, things done through the will.

e. These four divisions of true religion can be compared with each other in the following way. Natural religion is insufficient, revealed is saving. Natural religion is only internal because external religion is always false. (See number 28.) However, natural religion also consists in matters of faith [belief] and matters of love: namely, in the love of other men. Therefore, by external religion, one usually means worship consisting in ceremonies. Further, revealed true religion is either internal or external, and consists of both matters of faith and matters of love.

f. From this comes the division of the Holy Scriptures into the books of the old and new covenant that we [Lutherans] are still wont to call the Old and New Testaments. This is a remnant of papalism. For even though in Greek *Diadeke* can signify a testament as well as a covenant, it is quite unthinking to call the old covenant the Old Testament, in that God the Father did not die.

32. God has either made this covenant directly with man, or through certain intermediaries.

33. He did so directly with Adam, Noah, and Abraham, and indirectly with the Jews through Moses, and with the whole human race through Christ and his apostles.

34. Now, although there is no doubt that during the whole time of the old covenant the true believers were directed toward a future child of man as their messiah, nonetheless, their confession did not consist in particular religious formulas[a] and jargon, but in humble simplicity.[b]

Simple condition of revealed religion until Moses

35. With regard to conduct, the covenant with Adam, Noah, and Abraham thus required very few external ceremonies of divine worship, over and above a properly pious life for God.[c]

---

a. Those who want to persuade people that the religion of Adam, Noah, and Abraham is in agreement with our confessions of today, twist the texts of the Scriptures with a false interpretation. They seek to claim this in long-winded disputations, through scholastic abstractions, or circular arguments; for example, Dr. Wilhelm Leyser, *In trifolio religionis verae Vet. Testam. Adamiticae, Abrahamiticae § Israeliticae iuxta Unifolium religionis Lutheranae;* and to a certain degree, Dr. Balthasar Bebel, *Historia Ecclesiae Antediluvianae, item Noachicae.* Dr. Pfeiffer does this more crassly in his *Pansophia Mosaica,* where he undertakes to derive all of the articles of faith in the *Augsburg Confession* from the first book of Moses. Generally, though, these people agree in understanding the unity of religion in terms of brain-faith in the intellect, and seek it there. [Wilhelm Leyser, *Trifolium verae religionis V. T. Adamiticae, Abrahamiticae et Israeliticae, juxta unifolium religionis Lutheranae* (The trifoliate true religion of the Old Testament: Adamitic, Abrahamic, and Israelitic, compared with the unifoliate Lutheran religion) (Wittenberg, 1664); Balthasar Bebel, *Ecclesiae antediluvianae vera et falsa* (Truths and falsehoods of the antediluvian church) (Strasburg, 1665); August Pfeiffer, *Pansophia Mosaica E Genesi Delineata* (Mosaic pansophy, outlined from Genesis) (Leipzig, 1685).]

b. And, in fact, in such a simplicity that now and again was associated with no small errors in the understanding. Eve, the mother of the living—whose true faith no one doubts, or at least no one would dare declare a heretic—thus believed that Cain was the Messiah (Genesis IV, 1). Lamech, the father of Noah, fell into a similar error (Genesis V, 29).

c. For the commandments that God gave to Adam and Noah are few in number, and Abraham was given no new commandments other than that of circumcision. See Genesis IV, 6–7; IX, 1ff.; XII, 7ff.; XV, 1ff.; and XVII, 1ff. Therefore, those of us [Lutherans] who pretend or imagine that the ceremonies of those days agree with

36. The earliest external religious worship consisted in sacrifices, as a symbol of the true reconciling sacrifice [of Jesus], until in Abraham's time[a] circumcision was required in addition.

37. In the beginning, though, the direction of this kind of worship rested with the father of the household.[b]

The Jewish religion introduced through Moses

38. However, after Moses at God's command had led the Israelite people by signs and miracles, and ruled them as a prince in God's name, and also imposed religious laws at God's command, the Jewish religion was combined with the state[5] and commonwealth of the Jews, in such a way that one could almost not exist without the other. God here perpetually reserved the right in religious matters for himself, never conceding it to the kings of Judea and Israel.[c]

---

ours, are mistaken; for example, when Luther claims with regard to Genesis that Adam would have preached in the state of innocence. Cf. Chemnitz, preface to *Locos Theol. & Observ. Hist. Eccles.* MSC. obs. 18, p. 82. [Probably refers to Martin Chemnitz, *Locorum theologicorum Martini Chemnitii pars 1–3* (Theological topics of Martin Chemnitz, parts 1–3) (Frankfurt, 1604).]

a. Pufendorf, *De habitu,* §8.

b. Pufendorf, ibid., §8, p. 25. It would be worth investigating from whence arose the erroneous opinion that primogeniture gave the firstborn son a governmental and clerical right over his brothers and sisters. Perhaps from the text of Genesis XLIX, 3, which Luther did not translate correctly, however. See Saubert, *Opera posthuma,* pp. 225ff., who nonetheless wants to defend this error at pp. 289ff. Compare this with p. 305. Perhaps this opinion also arose from the fact that one likewise finds different doctrines concerning Christ's prophetic, priestly, and kingly offices. See Pearson, *Symboli Apostolici,* in the section under the heading "Messiah"; and, on prophets, Saubert, *Opera posthuma,* pp. 317ff. [John Pearson, *Expositio symboli apostolici* (Exposition of the apostolic creed) (Frankfurt an der Oder, 1691).]

c. Pufendorf, §§9, 10, 12.

5. This is Thomasius's first use of the political term "state" (*Staat*) in this tract. For the most part, Thomasius uses it as a synonym for "commonwealth" (*gemein Wesen*) and as a means of formalizing the separation of polity from religion. But see also note b to paragraph 85, where he refers to uprisings against the "state of the commonwealth," suggesting a distinction between that state as agent of sovereign political authority and the commonwealth as the territorial community more broadly. This distinction might be implied in the present reference to the "state and commonwealth of the Jews."

39. One cannot derive the Christian religion and the [regalian] rights of a Christian prince from the Jewish religion and the [regalian] rights of the kings of Judea and Israel. For Christian kings have more power than Jewish ones, while Christian teachers have less power than the Levites.[a]

40. For the Christian religion of the new covenant concluded with all men is quite different from the Jewish religion and, insofar as it is not tied to a particular state, the Christian religion is in fact opposed to the Jewish. This explains why Christ neither acted as a prince nor instituted a particular form of government but, before his death, merely occupied the office of a miracle-working teacher.[b]

41. The apostles spread the teachings of Christ as they received them from him, and although they derived their power to teach from God and thus depended on no human dominion, yet, by virtue of the same office and the things pertaining to it, they did not receive from Christ the power to rule over men, or to bring men to the Christian religion through coercive means, or to make use of such means.[c]

42. The office of a teacher requires love and is impossible to practice through compulsion, least of all, though, the office of a teacher of the Christian religion.[d]

43. The office of the Keys—or declaring forgiveness of the repentant and the stain of sin in the unrepentant—entails no civil power or right of coercion.[e]

a. Arising from political papalism, the error against which this proposition is directed still largely rules among many theologians and jurists.

b. Pufendorf, *De habitu,* §§11, 13–17.

c. Pufendorf, §§18–20, 28.

d. Pufendorf, §21. Hovever, if this is juxtaposed with the beginning of §20, what is said there about the punishment of boys needs some restriction. See in any case §33.

e. Pufendorf, §§22–25.

44. From the standpoint of its origin and earliest use, excommunication in itself is not actually a punishment or a deprivation of civil honor, and entails no right of compulsion.ᵃ

45. Christ's kingdom is not of this world, and has nothing in common with civil or human power.ᵇ

46. The Christian church or congregation has nothing in common with the secular state or commonwealth. As a result, no form of government used in the commonwealth may be used in the Christian church; for it is nothing but an association which should consist of teachers and listeners (who in the sight of their only common Father are all brothers to one another).ᶜ

Condition of the Christian religion under the pagan emperors

47. Under the pagan emperors, the Christian church had no secular dominion, administering only such justice as is possessed by other such honorable associations in the commonwealth, which involves no dominion but only good discipline and order, (grounded in the voluntary agreement of all). To this [discipline and order] belongs the fact that the community chooses particular teachers; gathers alms freely and without compulsion; consults its teachers in cases of conscience; appoints Christian arbitrators to decide outbreaks of controversy; refrains from disorderly conduct; endeavors to correct faults through reminders and admonition; retains the repentant in the community; and excludes the obstinate from it.ᵈ

a. Pufendorf, §§27 & 39, p. 137. The text of Matthew XIIX, 15–17 allows for another interpretation than the one advanced by Pufendorf. See also I Corinthians V, 3–5; and II Corinthians II, 5ff.

b. Pufendorf, §29.

c. Pufendorf, §§30–33 &c.

d. Pufendorf, §39, where many other important remarks are to be found; for example, page 134 regarding the freedom of religious associations in the Roman republic; also that Christ prescribed no particular formula for the ordination of priests, or for the laying-on-of-hands undertaken by the bishop or the elders, and so on. I do not agree with him, though, when he treats the counsels of Paul in I Corinthians chap. 7 as statutes. In fact, the Christian church or congregation has no statutes, but follows good rational rules voluntarily and without compulsion. Also, it has no monetary penalties, only admonitions. Statutes are proper laws that effect a compulsion,

48. In being adopted by the emperor and kings, the Christian church was not made more perfect, nor was the prior duty between teachers and listeners changed or transformed. Much less were regents on this account given a special obligation by the Christians.[a]

49. The Christian religion alters the duties of ruler and subjects not in the slightest; in fact it confirms these. But just as blessedness is also beneficial to the secular peace, while reason, deprived of the Holy Scriptures, is easily reduced to ambition and suchlike under the appearance of true virtue, so too there is little doubt that the Christian religion brings many benefits to the commonwealth and must greatly alter it.[b]

50. Even if it is in a commonwealth, the Christian church does not cease to be an [voluntary] association[6] as it was before, and all secular domin-

---

even though they arise from a common promise. For all human power to prescribe laws arises from a binding promise. So one must not confuse advice or counsel with judgment or legal decisions (although this confusion still occurs very often today) much less with laws. One must also not make the mistake of thinking that blessed Luther teaches there is no difference between the gospel commandments (*praeceptis*) and advice. See Seckendorff, *Histor. Lutheranismi*, bk. I, fol. 171, no. 2. [Ludwig von Seckendorff, *Commentarius historicus et apologeticus de Lutheranismo* (Historical and apologetic commentary on Lutheranism) (Frankfurt an der Oder, 1688).]

a. Pufendorf, §40. In fact the condition of the church became much worse. The Christian church grew through tribulation and persecution, and withered in times of ease and abundance. As can easily be seen from the biography of Constantine the Great.

b. Here I again depart from Pufendorf's argument in §40, p. 138, *Nec ad civitatem religione Christiana etc.* Cf. §41; even though there is no doubt that if we were all perfect Christians we would have no need of a commonwealth. I have given a detailed discussion of the transformation of republics by the Christian church in a program-statement accompanying the disputation *De jure principis circa adiaphora,* by Herr Brenneisen, now chancellor of East Frisia. [Here Thomasius is referring to his *Programma super quaestione: annon ecclesia saltem alteret politias* (Declaration on the question: whether the church changes states). This was published as a foreword to the Latin version of the *adiaphora* dissertation and then in a collection of program-statements (*Programmata Thomasiana*) in 1714, but it was omitted from the German version of the dissertation translated in the present volume.]

6. Here Pufendorf uses *collegium,* or college, in the sense of a voluntary association of teachers and learners.

ion and civil offices are suspended when prince and subjects are viewed as members of the Christian church.[a]

51. Princes do not become bishops or teachers by adhering to the Christian church. In fact a prince may not at the same time rightly hold the office of a Christian teacher.[b]

The true Christian religion: end, means, and only foundation

52. The end of Christian, apostolic, and Protestant religion is peace with God.[c]

53. The means to attain this end is faith, which works through love.[d]

54. Here faith is not understood as the mere intellectual knowledge of truths associated with the contemplation of divine things, for the devil also has this;[e] still less is it such knowledge as is grounded in the texts of men not moved by God;[f] but it is the heart's hope and trust in God.[g] Love, so far as it signifies the activity of faith,[h] we understand as good works in relation to men.

a. Pufendorf, §41; although the remark found at the end of p. 140—to the effect that in the commonwealth the church receives greater security—needs correction or a clearer explanation.

b. Pufendorf, §42. See above number 42 [in the present work]. The episcopal right of the prince is a different question; for this takes the word *bishop* in a different sense, in which it does not signify a teacher. In my notes to *Monzambano,* I have already shown that the term *episcopal right* (*Jus episcopale*), when it is spoken of and ascribed to a Protestant prince, does not correspond to the dignity of a true right in ecclesial affairs. [Thomasius is referring to the notes he added to his 1695 student edition of Pufendorf's ("Monzambano's") *De statu imperii Germanici* (On the constitution of the German Empire).]

c. Romans V, 1; Ephesians II, 14f.; VI, 15; also Matthew X, 34.

d. Galatians V, 6; James II, 14–16; Matthew VII, 21; XXV, 34.

e. James II, 19; Mark I, 23; I Corinthians II, 2; XV, 14, 17; I Timothy V, 8.

f. I Corinthians II, 5.

g. Hebrews XI, 1, *hypostasis* &c. Cf. the following verses and the whole chapter except verse 3.

h. In fact it is usually said that love is a fruit and effect of faith. With regard to this, however, we should consider that: (1) Holy Scripture mentions the fruit or fruits of repentance or remorse (Matthew III, 8; Luke III, 8); of the spirit (Galatians V, 22; Ephesians V, 9); of justice (Hebrews XII, 11; James III, 18); and of wisdom (James II, 17); but I find no mention of the fruit of faith therein. (2) Love is first mentioned under the fruits of the spirit, and faith is next (Galatians V, 22), which means that

55. If one hates somebody, then one has no trust in him. If, though, one loves somebody, then one trusts in his promises. In this way, those who do not love God do not have faith.

56. Accordingly, the only true ground of Christian religion is the love of God and of all men.[a]

57. This ground of the Christian religion requires not so much an exact and especially subtle knowledge of the inconceivable essence of God, but, much more, a clear knowledge of his will, which is easily understood and needs no metaphysical subtleties.[b]

58. Inconceivable things cannot be conceived as they are, but only by analogy with conceivable things.

59. In its reflections on the nature of inconceivable things, the human understanding cannot fully hope for truth—which consists in the agreement of our understanding with the thing itself—but may well fall into error if it dwells too long on these things, because it can find no ground in them to serve as a foothold

60. All disputation or quarreling over such things is therefore in vain, in that the most one can hope for is to demonstrate an error to someone,

---

faith is just as much a fruit of the spirit as love. (3) If one wants to say that the fruits of justice and the fruits of faith are the same, because faith makes one just, one must at least understand this fruit of faith as appearing with faith, and not something first appearing after a considerable time (Colossians I, 10; also James III, 14–26). If one wants to claim the example of the thief on the cross (as usually happens)—showing that he was saved through faith alone without good works—then I would be able to deny this claim with better justification. For, by works of love we are to understand not only such things as alms-giving, but all good works which have their source in love. The thief, though, performed one such good work before he professed his faith in Christ (Luke XXIII, 40). For it is one of the greatest works of love when one defends the innocent, and punishes the guilty sinner gently and in friendship.

a. Those who claim that the Mosaic Laws do not apply to Christians—and include in this the Ten Commandments which decree love of God and one's neighbors—deceive themselves mightily, and have looked only superficially at the commandments in the gospel, especially the sayings, I John II, 9–11; & chap. III, 6, 17, 23.

b. Job XXXVIIIff.; Romans XI, 33f.; I Corinthians XIII, 2, 9, 12; Ephesians I, 17ff.; Colossians 2; I John IV, 7f.; II John III, 4.

not, though, to defend an incontestable truth. This is because the unsurpassable excellence of the subject means that all predicates are applied to it improperly, or else analogically.

61. The veneration that we owe to God requires that we speak of the secrets of his nature as he in his Word wants himself spoken of. And because the foundations of Christianity teach us that illumination by the Holy Ghost is required to understand this, it is a great presumption and a sign of paganism if one tries to persuade oneself and others to hold a candle to the sun of wisdom with the jargon of human reason.

62. It thus follows from the preceding (numbers 57 and 60) that we should not regard the expressions and analogies that God applies to his nature via his creatures, as if God by this would have us form a complete idea of his nature, or the secrets of his works. Instead, through them there should be awakened in us a sense of his will, and of the love and benevolence shown to us, and also of our insignificance and misery, and a desire for and trust in him.

63. A Christian prince, as a prince, should observe the office of a prince and, as a Christian prince, the duty of a Christian.

Threefold duty of a Christian prince 64. The office of prince—namely, his sovereignty [*Majestät*] and dominion—must be exercised in a way that does not conflict with the duty of a Christian; that is, the duty of a prince should give way to Christian duty, but not the latter to the former.

65. And because a prince should also observe the common natural duties of a man, the wisdom of a prince consists in knowing how to observe together the duties of a man, a prince, and a Christian.[7]

66. Accordingly, the right of the prince in religious affairs must be derived not only from human laws or associations, or from instituted cus-

---

7. In stressing common observance, this initial formulation of the prince's threefold duty is a little misleading for, as explained in paragraph 68, the prince's duties as man, prince, and Christian are quite different, and his wisdom consists in not confusing them.

toms, or from examples, but from the juxtaposition of these threefold duties.

67. Because all human rights or freedoms are generally bound to duties so, it is most reasonable, when discussing the doctrine of the right of a prince in religious matters, also to represent his duties.

And its relation to his right in religious matters

68. The duty of a Christian prince insofar as he is a man, is to do good for other men in accordance with his capacity. Insofar as he is a prince, his duty is to protect peace-loving men and to punish those who disturb the peace. (See above, number 9.) Finally, insofar as he is a Christian, his duty is to restrain his desires with the prayed-for assistance of divine grace and, by means of this same grace, to do more good to all men (including his enemies) than he is otherwise obliged to do according to natural law (see above, number 56), and in general to place everything in God's will.

69. Since all those who want to hinder him in the exercise of his duty do wrong and anger God, the right of a Christian prince consists in the fact that he is justified in calmly fulfilling his duty, without regard to the obstacles placed in his way, with true trust in God's assistance, and in punishing the unruly if they are his subjects.

In general

70. With regard to other peoples of a different faith, a Christian prince has no power to wage war on them for the sake of religion.[a]

And in particular with regard to other peoples of a different religion

71. But he can defend himself with force if another prince who, having no right over him, refuses to respect his religious freedom. However, he

a. From this one can easily judge whether Charlemagne's wars against the Saxons and Westphalians—like those of the Spaniards against the Moors in more recent times—could be justified from the intended conversion of the heathens. This notwithstanding the fact that Christianus Nifanius strenuously seeks to defend (even if poorly and without judgment) Charlemagne's war and to distinguish it from the Spaniards'. (In his book where he tries to prove that in most of his articles of faith Charlemagne was not *formally* a papalist: in the preface §9, p. 34ff., also §13, p. 50ff.) [Christian Nifanius, *Ostensio historico-theologica: quod gloriosissimi Imperator Carolus M. in quamplurimis fidei articulis formaliter non fuerit Papista* (Historico-theological demonstration: that in regard to many articles of faith the most glorious Emperor Charlemagne was not formally a papalist) (Frankfurt an der Oder, 1670).]

should remain within the limits of defense, and be quite certain that his defense would please God.[a]

72. The prince can certainly offer refuge in his country to the subjects of another prince, when their prince has driven them out because of religion, or subjected them to religious coercion.[b]

73. If they accept subjection to his laws and wish to live peacefully, then the prince can accept as his subjects foreign peoples of a different religion. In fact, he does well in this regard if he endeavors to deliver them from error without compulsion, by teaching the truth and by displaying Christian love. He does not do well if he refuses to accept them as subjects for no other reason than difference of religion.[c]

a. As explained in number 68, at the end. See also my more detailed discussion of toleration in the *Einleitung zur Sitten-Lehre,* chap. 5, §59ff. Further, see my remarks on Duke Johann Friedrich of Saxony in the annals of the *Testament of von Osse,* p. 58. Here also belongs the saying, "War is sweet to those with no experience of it," which Erasmus discusses at length in his *Adagia.* See, *Adagia variorum conjunctim edita* (Adages of various authors, collected and presented), Frankfurt ed. 1646, fols. 295ff. So too from the Holy Scriptures, there is the example of the Israelites, who waged what seemed to be a not unjust war, yet were nevertheless abandoned by God because they had not asked the obligatory question whether they should make war on the Benjaminites (Judges XX, 18ff.; & *ibi Cleric. in notis* [possibly a reference to Jean Le Clerc's notes to his edition of Erasmus's *Adagia,* which was published in 1703]). The Anabaptist error that all wars are contrary to Christianity conflicts not just with sound reason but also with the Holy Scriptures (Luke III, 14). Yet it cannot be denied that most wars amongst Christians are accompanied by a gross misuse of divine worship. For, when they are unlucky in war, both contending parties declare days of repentance; yet when they have been victorious over their opponents, they hold solemn thanksgiving celebrations, and by singing "praise be to thee O Lord God" celebrate with pretty martial music and acts of devotion, and so on.

b. See below, number 74 and following. He can also intercede for them, but not to wage war against the other prince, on account of number 70. This is assuming that the other prince has not bound himself through pacts and peace treaties to allow his subjects the free exercise of religion, and then violated such pacts. Becmann's disputation, *De jure principium recipiendi exules fidei socios* (On the prince's right to accept exiled fellow believers), also pertains here.

c. [This applies] when religious difference consists only in theoretical speculations and assertions, and in the ceremonies of external religious worship. If, however, this religious group teaches a morality according to which all disgrace and vice, such as whoring, adultery, murder, are regarded as permissible or even as praiseworthy—so that one should hold heretics to no faith, and one could secretly murder a regent who

74. As far as his own subjects are concerned, it is agreed and follows from the preceding (numbers 13, 24–26, 41ff., and 50f.) that a Christian prince may not compel them to his religion, not a single one of them, let alone all.

Then with respect to his own subjects

75. As a prince cannot compel his subjects, so he must tolerate them, because for people who live in a society, there is no other means between these two.[a]

76. He is obliged to tolerate their doctrines, even if they are erroneous, and the religious customs they hold sacred, even if these deviate from his.[b]

77. At the same time, a prince also has the freedom to practice his religion, to believe what he holds to be true, and to honor God in the manner he thinks pleasing to him.[c]

---

disagreed with the foreign religion—then I would not advise such a regent to accept such guests, particularly if he were not in a position to decisively repress the eruption of such vice.

a. I am speaking here of the religion to which the subjects adhered at the time the prince assumed his government. See below, number 90. The relevant rule will be as follows: the circumstance that was present at the time of the promise, and did not prevent the parties from making their promise, cannot hereafter be used as a reason not to keep this promise. Thus the following objection—that I had forgotten something or left something out—collapses. For it does not follow that the prince must tolerate subjects of another religion because he cannot coerce them, as there is a third possibility, namely, that he bids them leave or emigrate. Not to mention that through the words "who live in a society" this objection is preempted; and it is also the case that, in certain measure, enforced emigration is also a kind of coercion. (See number 79.) What is the situation, though, when the prince becomes a Christian after taking over the government? In this case too God has never commanded the prince to compel the unbelievers to adopt the Christian religion, but that he should endeavor to bring them to this through good education. The Christian religion is not contrary to warlike courage (see number 71, note a), but nor does it follow the pagan Aristotle and other philosophers by according it [courage] primacy, but rather recommends gentleness and humility, especially the Christian teaching: "But not so with you" [Luke 22, 26].

b. For were he not to tolerate them, then he coerces them, which conflicts with number 74.

c. He must also be allowed to practice his form of worship in his palace, for there at least he must have the right of a household head with no superior.

78. [This remains true] even if he has already promised the subjects to adhere to their religion. For matters of religion are matters of conscience, and conscience is not bound by promising.[a]

79. If the subjects seek to prevent the prince from exercising his freedom and rights, he can punish them. If, however, the prince seeks to compel the subjects to his religion, they must themselves give way,[b] and cannot resist this with force.[c]

80. The prince is not obliged, however, to tolerate those doctrines that, under the pretext of religion, directly disturb the general peace and calm, and overturn common human duties.[d]

81. Even if it seems implausible that a religion should teach such doctrines (which would promote its own misfortune), nonetheless, a prince must keep an eye on those doctrines which grant a particular religion the privilege not to be bound in all matters to the common rules of law and of love. Considering that God has preserved the sparks of natural law in all men and allowed no other commandments to be renewed through Christ than the love of God and of men, for him to wish to be honored through suspension of the law of nature would be contrary not only to Christianity but also to sound reason. As such doctrines neces-

a. Especially when the promisee had no real interest in the matter, and was not justified in requiring this promise. This is true unless, in making the above promise at the assumption of his reign, the prince also promised that he would relinquish his reign if he changed his religion. If so, then he would be obliged to do this, even if in this case still other circumstances would have to be taken into account; for example, whether the reign is by election or succession; further, whether the subjects' desire for this promise was motivated by fear of future persecution, or by a heretic-mongering rooted in themselves; and so on.

b. Cf. Becmann, *Dissertatio de jure principum recipiendi exules fidei socios,* chap. 2.

c. Becmann, *De jure subditorum circa sacra,* chap. 4. And when Luther says: It is a cause from God. He himself will do it. If they drive you from one city, flee to another; and so on—he is right if the prince possesses a truly monarchical power. But he errs when he applies this to the electors and princes of the empire, because the German Empire is not ruled monarchically. (Cf. *Historia contentionis,* p. 570.)

d. For example, when it is taught that theft, plunder, and killing, etc. are permissible or honorable things; that one need not keep promises, and so on.

sarily give rise to rebellion and discord, a Christian prince cannot tolerate them without disturbance to the general peace.

82. Such doctrines are, for example: that it is not necessary to keep promises to heretics. That kings and others excommunicated by the clerisy cease to be kings, or are in a condition in which they may no longer be shown common love. That the orthodox and those standing in God's grace may dispossess the members of other religions. That those belonging to other religions are not to be tolerated or accepted. That the creeds and commentaries produced by men should set guidelines for Holy Scripture, [allowing] other men to be bound by these, and those who refuse to be bound should be banished. That indifferent things [*Mitteldinge, adiaphora*], which can be ignored in accordance with Christian freedom, cease to be indifferent if those adhering to the prince's religion are offended by this— [especially if] the prince was happy about these being ignored, or left the various subjects of his religion free to use these [indifferent things] or not. That controversies in religious matters must be resolved judicially through councils and synods—in a word, coercively, by the clerisy and the princes as their secular arm, and so on.

83. Neither is a Christian prince obliged to tolerate religious groups whose religion requires them to obey above their own prince, another man or association not under their prince's dominion. (See above, number 18.) It does not matter whether this man or this association is in Constantinople, Rome, Wittenberg, or anywhere else.[8]

84. Neither is a Christian prince obliged to tolerate an atheist, or him who denies the creator of the world and his providence.[a] For the prince

a. Here it should no less be observed that the argument of number 80—that a Christian prince is *not obliged to tolerate* certain doctrines and those who defend them—should not be extended such that he is *obliged not to tolerate* such people. [Editors' emphasis.] In such cases it is thus necessary to take heed of the prudent teaching of Paul: "I have power to do everything, but not everything is useful." In other words, that which I am not obliged to tolerate implies only a freedom to act or refrain, and in no way a command.

8. That is, it does not matter whether such groups have their allegiance to the Eastern Orthodox, Roman Catholic, or Lutheran Church.

must always expect that if the atheist dares to give free reign to his desires and their exercise in secret, he will not respect the laws and peace of the commonwealth, but will rather disturb these.[9]

85. Those, however, whom a Christian prince is not obliged to tolerate—for the reasons already advanced—he is not justified in repressing with civil punishments. [He is not justified] either as a Christian or as a man, for these statuses give him no right of punishment. But neither is he [justified] as a prince, because the doctrines advanced by the above-mentioned people, while they are dangerous in the sense that they could easily violate the common peace,[a] yet, as doctrines, they have still not done so, since they remain within the domain of doctrine without actually issuing in external actions[b]—assuming that such doctrine is not itself real action.[c]

a. For if a prince wanted to punish all those who could violate the common peace, then he would have to forbid all or at least most human behavior. If, against my argument, one wished to introduce from Roman law [the notion of] *legal action concerning a corrupt servant,* such action in fact is merely an invented and legalistic thing, especially in that [the notion of] the *action of a corrupt servant* itself has no clear value, but is a figment of Paul's. (Cf. notes to the *Institutes of Justinian, de actione,* p. 261, and at *de servo corrupto.*) ["Paul" may refer to Giovanni Paolo Lancellotti (1522–90), the Italian canonist and Roman law glossator whose commentaries Thomasius criticizes from time to time.]

b. For example, in real uprisings against the prince or the state of the commonwealth, or through incitement of the people to drive out other religious groups. In this regard, Melanchthon's counsel against the Anabaptists, who were beheaded in Jena in 1536, was not made in a rational and Christian manner, as I have argued in more detail in the *Historie der Weißheit und Thorheit,* pt. III, pp. 27–45. [Christian Thomasius, *Historie der Weißheit und Thorheit* (History of wisdom and folly) (Halle, 1693).]

c. See above, number 16. And from this remark it is easy to see what we should think of the papalizing counsel of the clergy: namely, that those subjects who depart from the ruling religion should be forbidden from mentioning their doctrines to others, so that if they did not obey they could be punished as malefactors, not so much on account of their false religion as on account of their disobedience.

9. Paragraphs 83 and 84—characteristic of a standard Protestant view on the non-toleration of Catholics and atheists—do not represent Thomasius's final position on the matter. By 1720 at the latest, Thomasius had signaled a change of viewpoint, arguing that both Catholics and atheists should be tolerated to the degree that they are good citizens and do not bring civil disturbance to the commonwealth. See Tho-

86. In this case, the right of a Christian prince goes no further than that he is not obliged to tolerate such people, but is in fact justified in ordering them to leave the republic. This right, however, does not automatically entail a duty, especially if the command to leave were to place the commonwealth in danger.[a]

87. He must also let them take their wealth and that which belongs to them, apart from that which must be handed over by those who choose to leave voluntarily. For otherwise he punishes them.

88. If he is permitted to impose nothing more than emigration on such people, then a Christian prince can scarcely impose anything greater on those who are subject to the false accusations of the ruling religion, as if they taught things that were dangerous and disturbing to the commonwealth; for example, [the accusations] that they teach that one should tolerate different religions; that one must restrain the lust for power and invective of the so-called religious [*Geistliche*, clergymen]; that one must start to repent and become more pious; and so on. If one does not wish to tolerate such doctrines and their followers,[b] then one should never demand the otherwise customary departure tax [from them], because they do not leave willingly, and nor have they deserved banishment.

89. Accordingly, there is thus a great difference between emigration and expulsion from the territory.[10] The former flows from the natural free-

---

masius, *Vollständige Erläuterung der Kirchenrechts-Gelahrtheit* (Complete explanation of ecclesiastical jurisprudence) (Frankfurt and Leipzig, 1740; repr. Aalen 1981), pt. I, pp. 349–50. We can already see this change taking place in the distinction that Thomasius draws in footnote a to paragraph 84.

a. These are the circumstances under which one must decide the question of whether and how far a Christian prince is justified in expelling the Jesuits from his country.

b. I thus do not say that one should not tolerate such people, but argue only that one should not sin against them any further, in that Christian princes are often persuaded by the heretic-mongers to banish them, under the pretext that they cause unrest.

10. Under the terms of the Treaty of Westphalia (*Instrumentum pacis osnabrugensis*, 1648), the *ius emigrandi*, or right of emigration, operated within narrow limits.

dom of all associations to discharge without insult those who will not accommodate themselves to the purpose of the association.[a] The latter, though, flows from subjection and, being a punishment, in and of itself robs the exile of his good name.[b]

90. If there is a split (or differences of opinion) in the religion of the prince or the subjects—for there is no religion in which divisions do not occur on account of doctrine or practices—the prince should not take this as an opportunity to suppress his subjects' religion with force, or to treat the split as breaching the peace of the commonwealth so as to drive out the dissenters. Instead, he should see if through gentle persuasion peace-loving people on both sides can overcome this division and, if not, he should tolerate them in accordance with the preceding propositions, and prevent both parties from abusing and maligning each other.[c]

91. For the prince has no right in religious matters to decide differences in religious opinion through a legal judgment capable of being executed by force. [He may not claim this right] either as a man or as a Christian (because these statuses give him no right of coercion), or as a prince, because differences in religious opinions and practices do not hinder the common peace.

It applied only to members of religious groups who had not been granted toleration under the provisions of *Normaljahr* (standard year), which required rulers to tolerate those congregations that had enjoyed rights of private or public worship in the year 1624. Members of congregations who had not enjoyed such rights, or those who had changed their religion after the signing of the treaty in 1648, could make use of the *ius emigrandi,* or could be required to make use of it. The right to live in exile might strike the modern reader as a highly ambivalent right. Yet it needs to be seen against the background that subjects were normally prevented from emigrating—due to manpower shortages in the German states and the common assumption that a country's strength consisted in its population—and thus faced the prospect of being subject to religious persecution in homelands where they remained against their will. The *ius emigrandi* thus made its own contribution to freedom of conscience and conflict avoidance, which is the light in which Thomasius views it.

a. As a result, subjects are normally permitted to leave when it suits them. Cf. number 79, above.

b. This observation will often meet resistance (even among the Protestants), in that those who are commanded to emigrate are decried by the clergy as infamous exiles.

c. Becmann, *De jure subditorum circa sacra,* chap. 3, §11.

92. Much less should the prince allow other men to execute such enforceable judgments. It does not matter whether such men are his subjects or not; or whether they are religious or secular; councils, synods, ministries, theological faculties, or whatnot; or whether they use Scripture, councils, or traditions to mask their lust for power and strife. For Scripture and the spirit of Scripture itself judges each man in a spiritual way before God; and this is not a secular judge requiring secular weapons to coerce other men.

93. A Christian prince has to ensure that everything in his religion and that of his subjects proceeds in an orderly way. For, without order, the common peace cannot be preserved.

94. And just as the supreme right to ensure the good order of everything in the commonwealth belongs to the prince, while, for its part, the church exists as an association within the commonwealth, so the ordering of religious affairs is thus also a prerogative right of the prince.

95. In fact, with regard to religious customs commanded by God, or which his subjects believe to be commanded by God, the prince can command or change nothing. Otherwise, he would either be superior to God or else engaging in religious coercion. But when it comes to arrangements viewed by his subjects' confession as commanded by God, or to circumstances and customs which his subjects' confession itself views as a matter of choice, he can dispose over these, making laws and ordinances, and altering them.

96. Now, insofar as such ordinances prescribe aspects of divine worship believed to be commanded by God, and are thus equivalent to the repetition of divine commands, they cannot be brought under the class of human laws properly so called, because they apply no secular punishments and cannot go further than excommunication. See number 44, above.

97. Insofar, though, as such ordinances touch on matters of shame and vice prohibited by natural or secular law, they are real laws, and can sharpen the usual punishments in accordance with the circumstances of time and place.

98. Finally, insofar as they dispose over things which the subjects regard as matters of indifference [*Mitteldinge, adiaphora*], the ordinances bear the character of real laws, justly punishing transgressors, especially those who resist the prince under the pretext that it is not necessary to obey him in indifferent matters.

WORKS CITED BY THOMASIUS

Agrippa von Nettesheim, Heinrich Cornelius. *De incertitudine et vanitate omnium Scientiarum et artium et de excellentia verbi Dei.* Antwerp, 1530.

Anon. [Hermann Conring]. *Glossa ordinaria ad litteras circulares Alexandri Papae septimi. Quas praetextu pacis procurandae inter catholicos principes a patriarchas, archiepiscopos, episcopos, cleros, . . . scripsit.* S.l., 1655.

Anon. [Ulrich von Hutten, Crotus Rubianus]. *Epistolae obscurorum virorum.* Hagenau, 1515/16.

Antwort und warhafftiger Gegenbericht auff die Leichpredigt, welche Nicolaus Blum, Pfarherr zu Dona, bey der Begrebnuß Herrn Doctor Nicolai Crellens . . . am 10. Octob. Anno 1601 zu Dreßden sol gethan haben. S.l., 1605.

Arnold, Gottfried. *Die erste Liebe der Gemeinen Jesu Christi, das ist, Wahre Abbildung der ersten Christen, nach ihren lebendigen Glauben und heiligen Leben.* Frankfurt am Main, 1696.

———. *Unparteyische Kirchen- und Ketzer-Historie vom Anfang des Neuen Testaments biß auff das Jahr Christi 1688.* Frankfurt am Main, 1699–1700.

Aubin, Nicolas. *Histoire des Diables de Loudon ou de la possession des Réligieuses Ursulines et de la condemnation et du Supplice d'Urbain Grandier.* Amsterdam, 1693.

Aventinus, Johannes. *Annalium Boiorum libri VII.* Basle, 1554.

Bayle, Pierre. *Pensées diverses, écrites à un docteur de Sorbonne, à l'occasion de la comète qui parût au mois décembre 1680.* Rotterdam, 1683.

Bebel, Balthasar. *Ecclesiae antediluvianae vera et falsa.* Strasburg, 1665.

Beckmann, Friedrich. *Dissertatio de Exorcismo.* Frankfurt an der Oder, 1689.

Becmann, Johann Christoph. *Dissertatio de jure principum recipiendi exules fidei socios.* Frankurt am Main, 1686.

———. *Dissertatio de jure subditorum circa sacra.* Frankfurt an der Oder, 1689.

Bekker, Balthasar. *De betoverde Wereld.* Leuwaarden, 1691.

Bellarmine, Robert. *De laicis sive secularibus*. In his *De ecclesia militantis membris*. Jena, 1629.

Benbellona, Anthony (Bartholomew Gericke). *Ung resveille Matin Sive Tempestivum suscitabulum pro principibus*. Zerbst, 1602.

Bidembach, Felix. *Consiliorum Theologicorum Decas III & IV.* Laugingen, 1608.

Blancanus, Josephus. *Sphaera mvndi sev Cosmographia demonstratiua, ac facili methodo tradita: in qva totivs mvndi fabrica, vna cvm novis, Tychonis, Kepleri, Galilaei, aliorumque astronomorum adinuentis continetur.* Bologna, 1620.

Blume, Nicolaus. *Leichpredigt uber den Custodierten D. Nicolaum Krell, welcher den 9. Octobris, wegen seiner verbrechung, auff der Römischen Kayserlichen Maiestat Endurtheil, öffentlich zu Dreßden enthauptet worden.* Dresden, 1601.

Bodin, Jean. *De Republica Libri Sex, Latine ab Auctore reddita. Editio quinta prioribus multo emendatior.* Frankfurt am Main, 1609.

Bona, Johannes. *Rerum Liturgicarum Libri Duo.* Rome, 1671.

Boranowsky, Hierotheus. *Gerechtfertiger Gewissens-Zwang oder Erweiß daß man die Ketzer zum wahren Glauben zwingen könne und solle.* Neyss, 1673.

Brunnemann, Johann Jakob. *De Jure Ecclesiastico Tractatus Posthumus.* Frankfurt an der Oder, 1681.

Burchard, Francis (Andreas Erstenberger). *De autonomia. Das ist, von Freystellung mehrerley Religion und Glauben.* Munich, 1586.

Calixt, Georg. *De Baptismo.* Helmstedt, 1611.

Carpzov, Benedict. *Jurisprudentia Ecclesiastica seu Consistorialis.* Leipzig, 1673.

———. *Practica nova imperialis saxonica rerum criminalium.* Wittenberg, 1635.

Chemnitz, Christian. *Praelectiones in locos theologo Huttero cundisianos.* Jena, 1670.

Chemnitz, Martin. *Examen Concilii Tridentini.* Frankfurt am Main, 1615.

———. *Locorum theologicorum Martini Chemnitii.* Frankfurt, 1604.

Compendium Historiae Ecclesiasticae in usum Gymnasii Gothani deductum. Gotha, 1660.

Conring, Hermann. *De Antiquitatibus Academicis Dissertationes.* Helmstedt, 1651.

———. *De Iudiciis Reipublicae Germanicae.* Helmstedt, 1647.

———. *Exercitatio Politica de Maiestatis Civilis Auctoritate et Officia circa Sacra.* Helmstedt, 1645.

[Coquaeus, Leonardus, and Juan Luis Vives.] *S. Aurelii Augustini Hipp. Episcop. de civitate Dei libri XXII . . . cum commentariis novis & perpetuis R.P.F. Leonardi Coquaei . . . et Joanni Ludovici Vivis.* Paris, 1651.

Crusius, Christoph. *Tractatus de Indiciis Delictorum Specialibus.* Frankfurt, 1635.

Dannhauer, Johann Conrad. *Collegium Decalogicum.* Strasbourg, 1638.

Dedeken, Georg. *Thesauri Consiliorum et Decisionum Volumen Primum, Ecclesiastica Continens.* Jena, 1671.

Dietericus, Conrad. *Institutiones Catecheticae, depromptae e B. Lutheri Catechesi & variis, recenter etiam B. Dn. Christiani Chemnitii Notis Illustratae. Editio novissima.* Frankfurt am Main and Leipzig, 1685.

Dissingau, Dommarein von. *Kurtze Information und Anleitung, Von der Autonomia: Zu Erleuterung des Hochgerümbten Tractats, von Fragstellunge mehrerley Religion und Glaubens, welcher zu München . . . unter Weiland . . . Francisci Burchardi . . . nahmen, durch den Druck offt außgelassen, . . . worden ist.* Christligen, 1610.

Duarenus, Franciscus. *De Sacrae Ecclesiae, Ministeriis ac Beneficiis.* Paris, 1551.

Du Pin, Louis Ellies. *Nouvelle Bibliothèque des auteurs ecclésiastiques.* Paris, 1686–1714.

Durandus, Gulielmus (William). *Rationale Divinorum Officiorum.* Lyon, 1592.

Dürr, Johann Conrad. *Compendium Theologiae Moralis.* Altdorf, 1698.

Erasmus of Rotterdam. *Adagiorum chilidades iuxta locos communes digestae.* Basle, 1530.

———. *Familiarum colloquiorum.* Basle, 1518.

———. *Morias Enkomion sive Laus Stultitiae.* Basle, 1511.

Farinacci, Prospero. *Tractatus de haeresi. Opera omnia,* pars 8. Frankfurt, 1686.

Filesac, Jean. *Statutorum sacrae facultatis theologiae parisiensis origo prisca.* Paris, 1620.

Fleury, Claude. *Traité du Choix & de la Methode des Etudes.* Brussels, 1687.

Gallaeus, Servatius. *Lucii Caecilii Lactantii Firmiani opera, quae extant cum selectis variorum commentaries.* Leiden, 1660.

Grotius, Hugo. *De Imperio Summarum Potestatum circa Sacra: Commentarius Posthumus.* Paris, 1647.

Havemann, Michael. *Dissertatio Theologico-Politica De Jure Episcopali.* Hamburg, 1646.

Hospinianus, Rudolf. *Concordia Discors, Hoc est, De Origine et Progressu Formulae Concordiae Bergensis, Liber Unus.* Geneva, 1678.

―――. *De origine et progressu Monachatus ac Ordinum Monasticorum, Equitumque militarium, libri VI.* Tiguri, 1588.

Huber, Ulrich. *Institutiones Historiae Civilis.* Franeker, 1692.

Hutter, Leonhard. *Compendium locorum theologicorum.* Wittenberg, 1610.

―――. *Concordia Concors. De Origine Et Progressu Formulae Concordiae Ecclesiarum Confessionis Augustanae.* Frankfurt and Leipzig, 1690.

Jena, Gottfried von. *Fragmenta de Ratione Status.* S.l., 1667.

Kesler, Andreas. *Patientia Christiana. Außführlicher Tractat von der Kirchen Christi Persecution.* Coburg, 1630.

Kortholt, Christian. *De persecutionibus ecclesiae primaevae sub imperatoribus ethnicis.* Kiel, 1689.

Launois, Jean de. *Academia Parisiensis illustrata.* Paris, 1682.

Le Clerc, Jean. *Défense Des Sentimens De quelques Théologiens de Hollande: Sur L'Histoire Critique du Vieux Testament. Contre La Reponse Du Prieur de Bolleville.* Amsterdam, 1686.

Leyser, Wilhelm. *Trifolium verae religionis V. T. Adamiticae, Abrahamiticae et Israeliticae, juxta unifolium religionis Lutheranae.* Wittenberg, 1664.

Limborch, Philipp van. *Historia inquisitionis hispanicae cum libro Sententiarum Inquisitionis Tholosanae ab* A.C. *1307 ad 1323.* Amsterdam, 1692.

Lincken, Heinrich. *Tractatus de Juribus Templorum cum discursu praeliminari de Juris Canonici Origine & Auctoritate.* Jena, 1674.

Lincken, Heinrich (*praeses*), and Christian Bock (*respondens*). *De Calendario.* Altdorf, 1674.

Luther, Martin. *Eyn deutsch Theologia. Das ist eyn edles Buchleyn von rechtem verstand, was Adam und Christus sey, und wie Adam yn uns sterben, und Christus ersteen sall.* Wittenberg, 1518.

―――. *Omnia opera Reverendi Patris D.M.L. quae vir Dei ab Anno XVII. usque ad Anni vicesimi aliquam partem, scripsit & edidit, quorum Catalogum in fine Tomi invenies.* 4 vols. Jena, 1556–58.

Lynker, Nicolaus Christoph. *De eo quod circa Sacram Coenam justum est.* 2nd ed. Leipzig, 1690.

Major, Johann Tobias. *Disputatio Theologica de Sabbato.* Jena, 1647.

Malebranche, Nicolas. *De la Recherche de la Vérité.* Paris, 1674–78. English trans.: *The Search After Truth,* trans. T. M. Lennon and P. J. Olscamp. Cambridge: Cambridge University Press, 1997.

Matthaeus, Antonius. *De criminibus, ad lib. XLVII. et XLVIII dig. commentarius.* Utrecht, 1644.

Meier, Gebhard Theodor. *Liber Tria Novellorum Nascentis Ecclesiae Christianorum Initiamenta Baptismum, Catechesin et Manuum Impositionem continens.* Helmstedt, 1690.

Meisner, Balthasar. *Collegium Adiaphoristicum, in quo controversiae circa Adiaphora inter nos et Calvinianos agitatae, perspicue tractantur, veritasque orthodoxa defenditur.* Wittenberg, 1663.

Mentzer, Balthasar. *Exegesis Augustanae Confessionis: cujus Articuli XXI breviter & succincte explicantur.* Giessen, 1613.

Mevius, David. *Jurisdictio Summi Tribunalis Regii quod est Vismariae.* Stralsund, 1664.

Naudé, Gabriel. *Apologie pour tous les grands personage qui ont esté faussement soupçonnez de magie.* The Hague, 1603. The German translation, *Gabriel Naudaei Schutz-Schrifft, worin alle vornehmen Leute, die der Zauberey fälschlich beschuldiget sind, vertheidiget werden,* was published as an appendix to the 1704 German edition of Thomasius's *On the Crime of Sorcery.*

Nifanius, Christian. *Ostensio historico-theologica: quod gloriosissimi Imperator Carolus M. in quamplurimis fidei articulis formaliter non fuerit Papista.* Frankfurt an der Oder, 1670.

Osiander, Johann Adam. *Dissertationes de Sabbatho.* Tübingen, 1672.

——— . *Tractatus theologicus de magia.* Tübingen, 1687.

Pearson, John. *Expositio symboli apostolici.* Frankfurt an der Oder, 1691.

Peucer, Caspar. *Commentarius de praecipuis divinationum generibus.* Wittenberg, 1553.

Pfeiffer, August. *Pansophia Mosaica E Genesi Delineata.* Leipzig, 1685.

Poiret, Pierre. *De eruditione solida, superficiaria, et falsa, libri tres.* Amsterdam, 1692. Thomasius's edition, 1694.

Pomarius, Samuel. *Bewiesener ungerechtester Gewissens-Zwang: entgegen gesetzet Hierothei Boranowsky Gerechtfertigtem Gewissens-Zwange.* Wittenberg, 1674.

Pufendorf, Samuel (Severinus de Monzambano). *Basilii Hyperetae Historische und politische Beschreibung der geistlichen Monarchie des Stuhls zu Rom.* Leipzig, Frankfurt, 1679.

——— . *De habitu religionis christianae ad vitam civilem.* Bremen, 1687. English trans.: *Of the Nature and Qualification of Religion in Reference to Civil*

Society, trans. J. Crull (1691), ed. S. Zurbuchen. Indianapolis: Liberty Fund, 2002.

———. *De jure naturae et gentium.* Lund, 1672.

———. *De statu imperii Germanici.* Verona, 1667.

Reinking, Theodor. *De Regimine Seculari et Ecclesiastico.* Giessen, 1619.

Rhez, Johann Friedrich von. *Institutiones Juris Publici Romani-Germanici.* Frankfurt an der Oder, 1687.

Rhodiginus, Ludovicus Caelius. *Lectionum Antiquarum libri XVI.* Venice, 1516.

Rosset, François de. *Les Histoires tragiques de nostre temps.* Paris, 1614.

Rynthelen, Cornelius à. *Iurista romano-catholicus: id est, iuridica romanae catholicae fidei confessio.* Hemmerden, 1618.

Salvianus of Massilia. *De Gubernatione Dei.* Geneva, 1600.

Saubert, Johannes. *Opera posthuma.* Altdorf, 1694.

Schilter, Johann. *Institutiones Juris Canonici Ad Ecclesiae Veteris et Hodiernae Statum Accommodatae.* Jena, 1681.

Scultetus, Abraham. *Medulla Theologiae patrum.* Amberg, 1598.

Seckendorff, Ludwig von. *Commentarius historicus et apologeticus de Lutheranismo.* Frankfurt an der Oder, 1688.

Spanheim, Friedrich. *Historia imaginum restituta.* Leiden, 1686.

Spee (von Langenfeld), Friedrich. *Cautio criminalis seu de Processibus contra sagas.* Rinteln, 1631.

Spizelius, Theophilus. *Die gebrochene Macht der Finsternüß oder Zerstörte teuflische Bunds- und Buhls-Freundschafft mit den Menschen.* Augsburg, 1687.

Thomasius, Christian. *Christiani Thomasii, JCTI Dissertatio Ad Petri Poiret Libros De Eruditione Solida, &c.* Frankfurt an der Oder, 1694.

———, ed. *D. Melchiors von Osse Testament gegen Hertzog Augusto Churfürsten zu Sachsen.* Halle, 1717.

———. *Das Recht Evangelischer Fürsten in theologischen Streitigkeiten.* Halle, 1696.

———. *De Jure Principis circa Adiaphora/Vom Recht evangelischer Fürsten in Mitteldingen oder Kirchenzeremonien.* Halle, 1695. Reprint. Hildesheim: Georg Olms, 1994.

———. *Einleitung zur Sittenlehre.* Halle: Salfeld, 1692. Reprint. Hildesheim: Georg Olms, 1995.

———. *Historia contentionis inter imperium et sacerdotium breviter deli-*

neata usque ad saeculum XVI. Halle, 1722. Reprint. Aalen: Scientia-Verlag, 1994.

———. *Historie der Weiszheit und Thorheit.* Halle, 1693.

———. *Institutiones jurisprudentiae divinae.* Leipzig: Weidmann, 1688. German trans.: *Drey Bücher der Göttlichen Rechtsgelahrteit.* Halle, 1709. Reprint. Hildesheim: Georg Olms, 2001.

———. *Rechtmaeßige Eroerterung Der Ehe- und Gewissens-Frage, Ob zwey Fuerstliche Personen in Roemischen Reich, deren eine der Lutherischen die andere der Reformirten Religion zugethan is,/ einander mit guten Gewissen heyrathen koennen?* Halle, 1689.

———. *Scholia continua in textum Severini de Monzambano de statu Imperii Germanici. Liber unus.* Halle, 1695.

Thomasius, Jacob. *Meditationes de philosopho Artista, also in Observationes Selectae ad rem litterariam spectantes. Tomus VI.* Halle, 1706.

———. *Origines Historiae philosophicae et ecclesiasticae.* Leipzig, 1665.

Tribbechov, Adam. *De doctoribus scholasticis et corrupta per eos divinarum humanarumque rerum scientiae.* Giessen, 1665.

Veiel, Elias. *Disquisitio Theologica de Sententia S. Augustini, an haeretici vi ad fidem sunt cogendi?* Ulm, 1680.

Vives, Juan Luis. *De disciplines Libri XII.* Bruges, 1531.

———. *De initiis, sectis et laudibus philosophiae.* Leuven, 1518.

———. *Introductio ad veram sapientiam.* Bruges, 1524.

Voetius, Gisbert. *Politica Ecclesiastica, Pars Prima, Libri Duo Posteriores.* Amsterdam, 1666.

———. *Selectarum Disputationum Theologicarum.* Utrecht, 1667.

Werenfels, Samuel. *Dissertationes VII. de Logomachiis eruditorum.* Basle, 1688.

Weyer, Johann. *De praestigiis daemonum, et incantationibus, ac veneficiis, libri V.* Basle, 1563.

Wigand, Johann. *De Persecutione Piorum.* Frankfurt am Main, 1580.

Wittenberg Theological Faculty. *Consilia theologica Witebergensia.* Frankfurt am Main, 1664.

———. *Gründtlicher Beweiß daß die Calvinische Irthumb den Grund des Glaubens betreffen und der Seligkeit nachtheilig seyn: Dabey auch angeführet welcher Gestalt Christliche Einigkeit zu stifften, und der Rinteler Syncretistischer Neuerung zugleich begegnet wird.* Wittenberg, 1664.

Ziegler, Caspar. *De Juribus Majestatis: Exercitatio V, quae est De Jure circa Sacra et Religionem.* Wittenberg, 1660.

————. *Jus Canonicum Notis et animadversionibus academicis ad Joh. Pauli Lancelotti jcti Perusini institutiones enculeatum, et quale sit, remoto velamento publicae luci expositum; Praemittitur dissertatio de juris canonici origine et incrementis.* Wittenberg, 1669.

INDEX

Abelard, Peter, 26, 31, 38
abrogation rather than introduction
  of ceremonies, 119
absent persons not to be condemned,
  125
absolute sovereignty. *See* princes;
  sovereignty
Acts of the Apostles, 9n, 37n, 57, 82,
  132, 199–200
adiaphora (indifferent things), most
  theological doctrine consigned by
  Thomasius to, 166n
adiaphora (indifferent things), rights
  of princes regarding, xvi–xvii, xix,
  49–127; abrogation rather than
  introduction of ceremonies, 119;
  Augsburg Confession, 50, 77–78,
  111, 112; Christian liberty and, 53,
  80–82, 88, 96–99, 109; Christian
  teaching and, 51, 52, 55–57, 67–68;
  church attendance, power of
  prince to compel, 133, 138, 143–
  44n; clergy commanded by prince
  to inform people about, 88, 96–99,
  119–20; confession, 89, 108–9, 116–
  17; conscience, arguments from, 53,
  82–83; Constantine, Theodosius,
  and pre-Reformation period, 51,
  57–60, 66–67, 76, 83, 84; corol-
  laries, 125–27; council of other
  regarding, 87, 93–94; *Cuius regio,
  illius est religio,* 52, 67; definition

of *adiaphora,* 51, 63–65; distinction
between internal and external
matters of religion, 52, 67–71, 115;
etymology and use of term, 50–
51n; exorcism, 89, 90, 98, 106–8,
116–17, 123–24; external worship of
God as *adiaphoron,* 50–51, 53–55;
Formula of Concord and (*see*
Formula of Concord); foundations
of right, 50–87; general church
councils, *adiaphora* decided in, 53,
78–79; Gregorian calendar, introduction of, 88, 99–101, 120–22;
heresy, whether a punishable
crime, 197n; images, use of, 88–89,
90, 103–4, 122–23; instrumental
music, 88, 101–2; Israelite kings,
appeals to, 51, 53, 55–57, 66, 80,
86–87; jurists, as proper subject
for, 51, 60 63, 114; Latin hymns,
89, 104–6, 123; Magdeburg, Ecclesiastical Ordinances for Duchy of,
49–50, 96; narrow *vs.* broad sense
of *adiaphora,* 51, 63–65; natural
law, rights of princes solely derived
from, 68; Peace of Westphalia and,
52–53, 73–78, 114–15; political form
of government and, 84–86; practical application of right, 87–109;
prince's understanding of indifferent and non-indifferent matters,
87, 91–93, 116–17; prudent use of

This book is set in Adobe Garamond, a modern adaptation by Robert Slimbach of the typeface originally cut around 1540 by the French typographer and printer Claude Garamond. The Garamond face, with its small lowercase height and restrained contrast between thick and thin strokes, is a classic "old-style" face and has long been one of the most influential and widely used typefaces.

Printed on paper that is acid-free and meets the requirements of the American National Standard for Permanence of Paper for Printed Library Materials, z39.48-1992. ⊚

Book design by Louise OFarrell
Gainesville, Florida
Typography by Apex Publishing, LLC
Madison, Wisconsin
Printed and bound by Worzalla Publishing Company
Stevens Point, Wisconsin